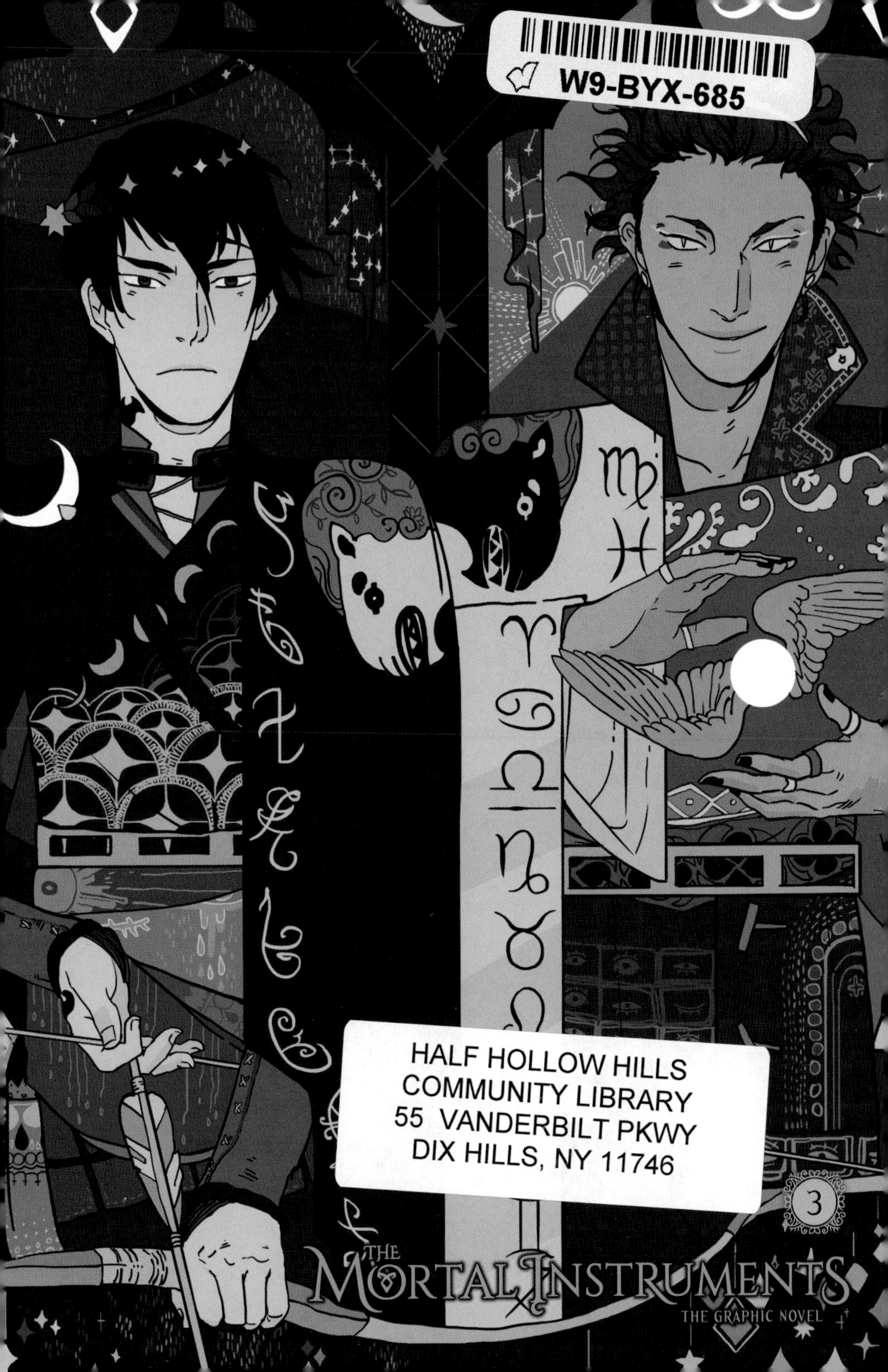
3
THE
MORTAL INSTRUMENTS
THE GRAPHIC NOVEL

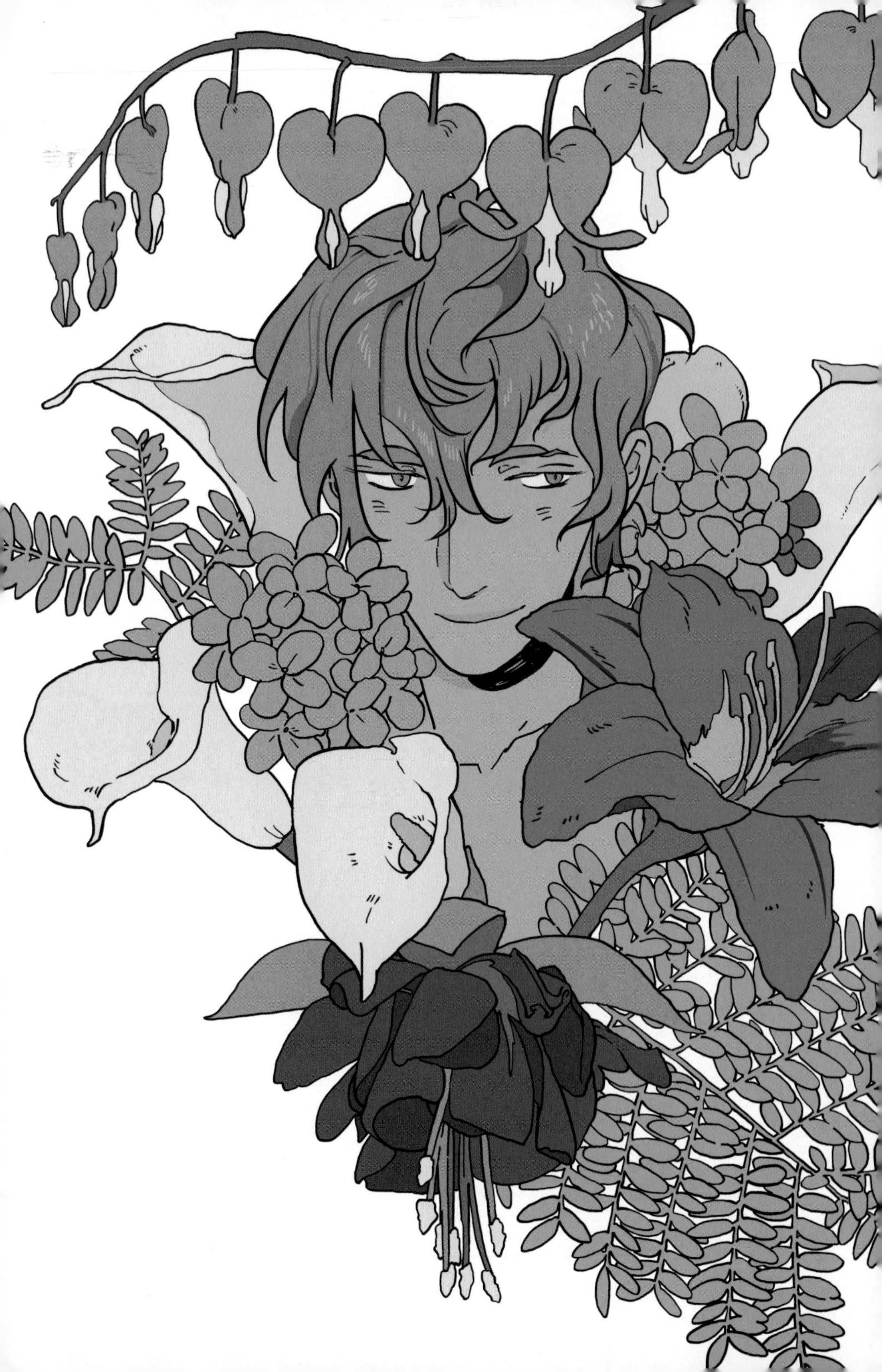

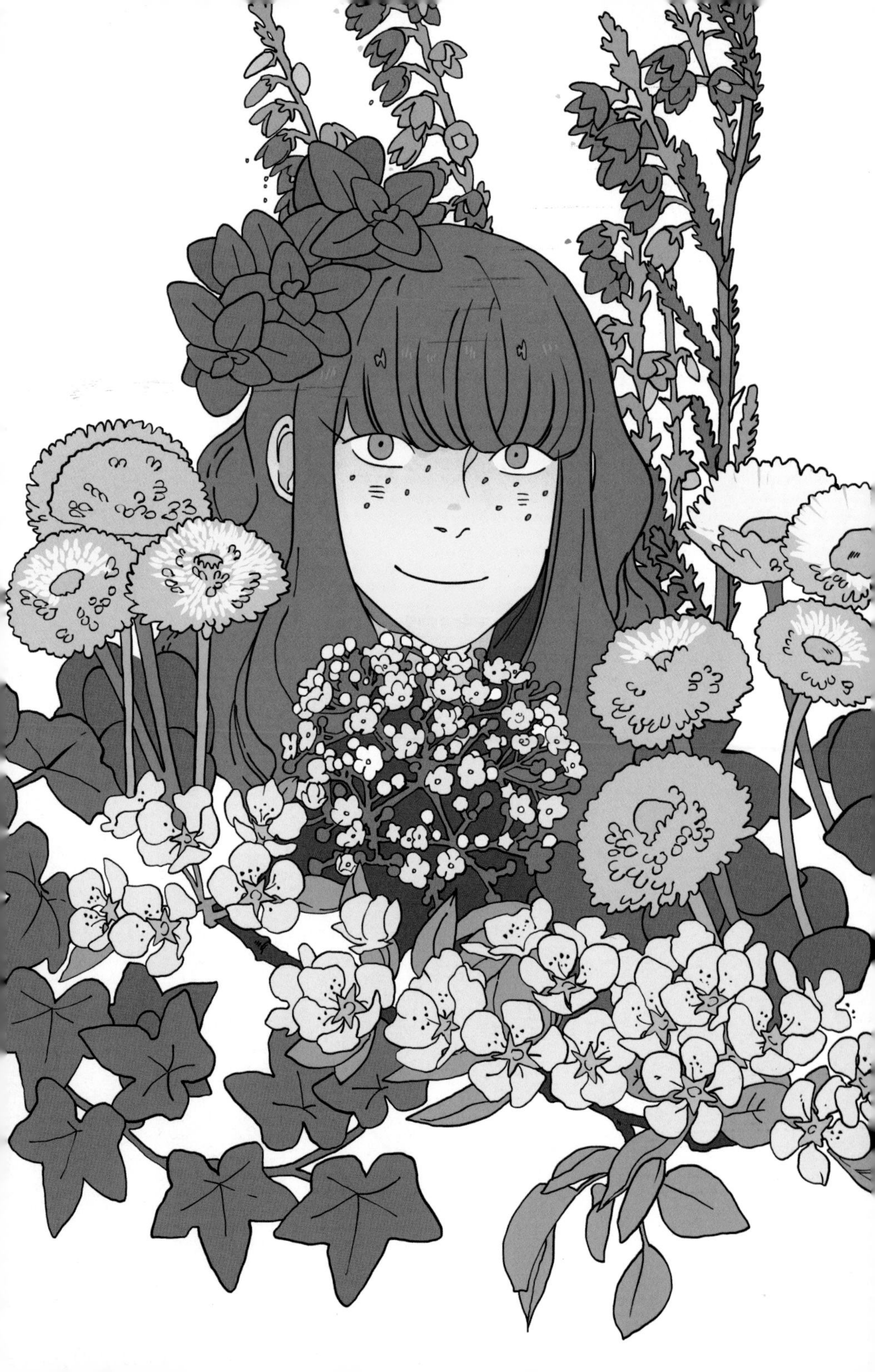

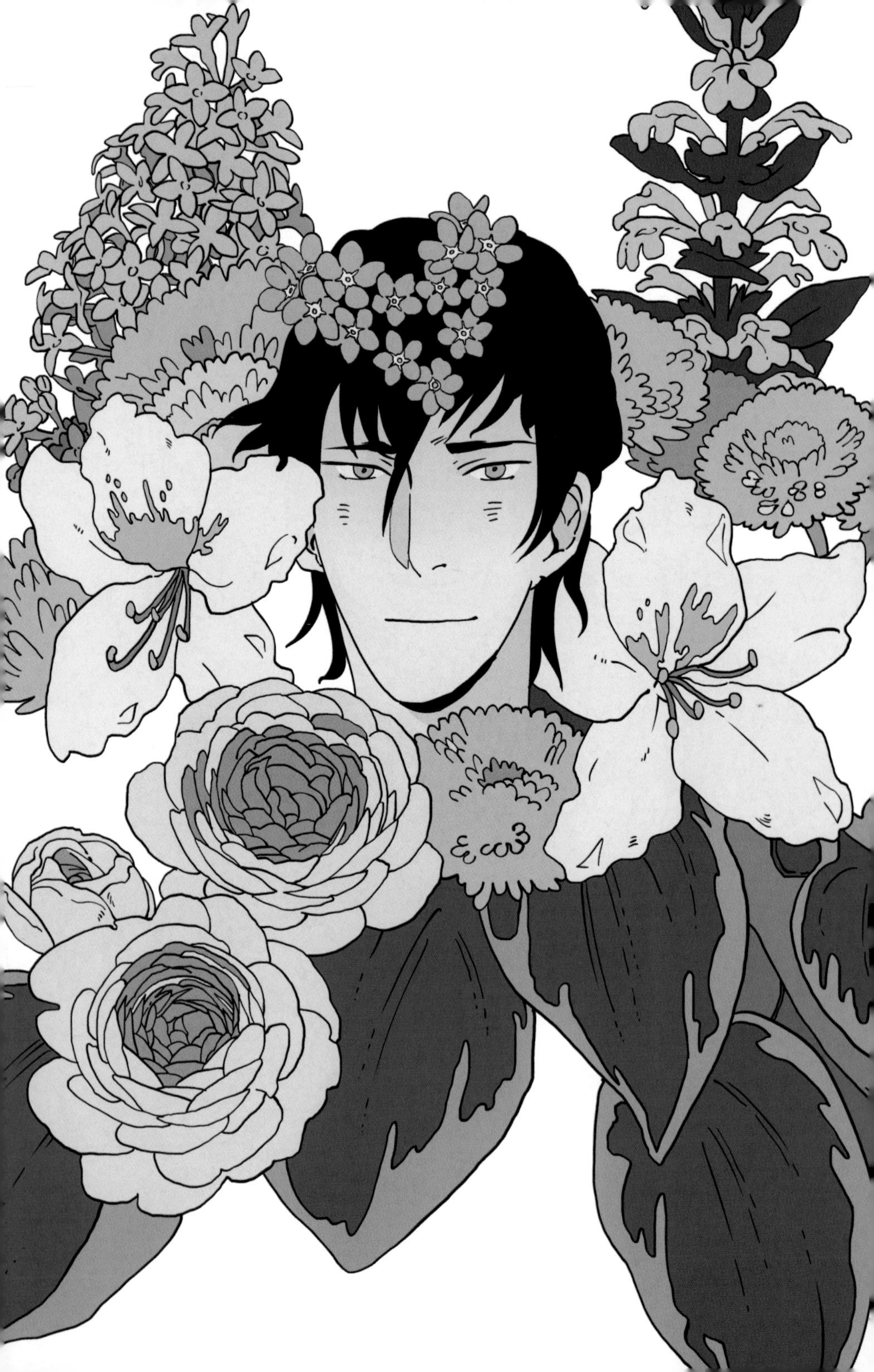

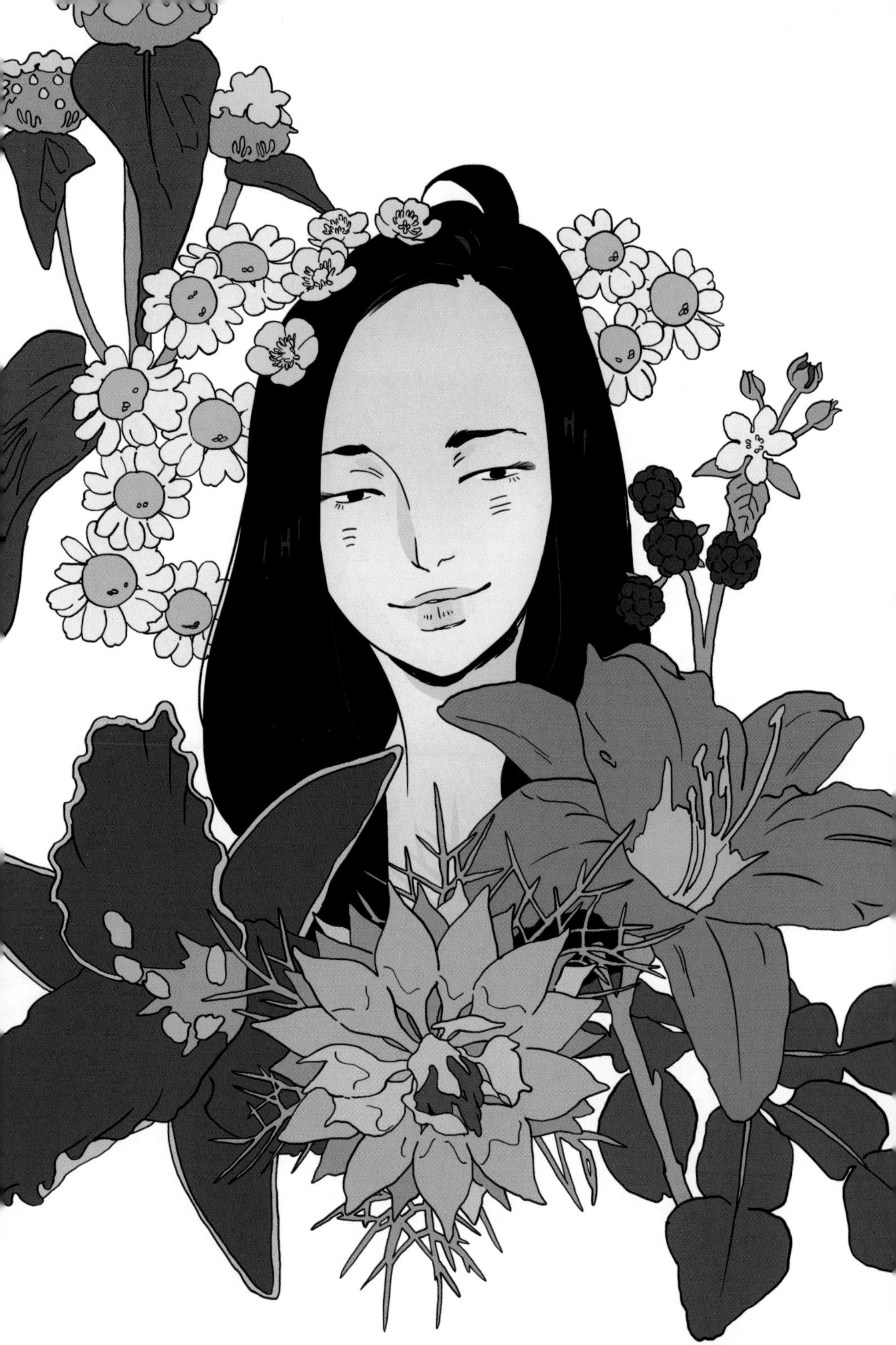

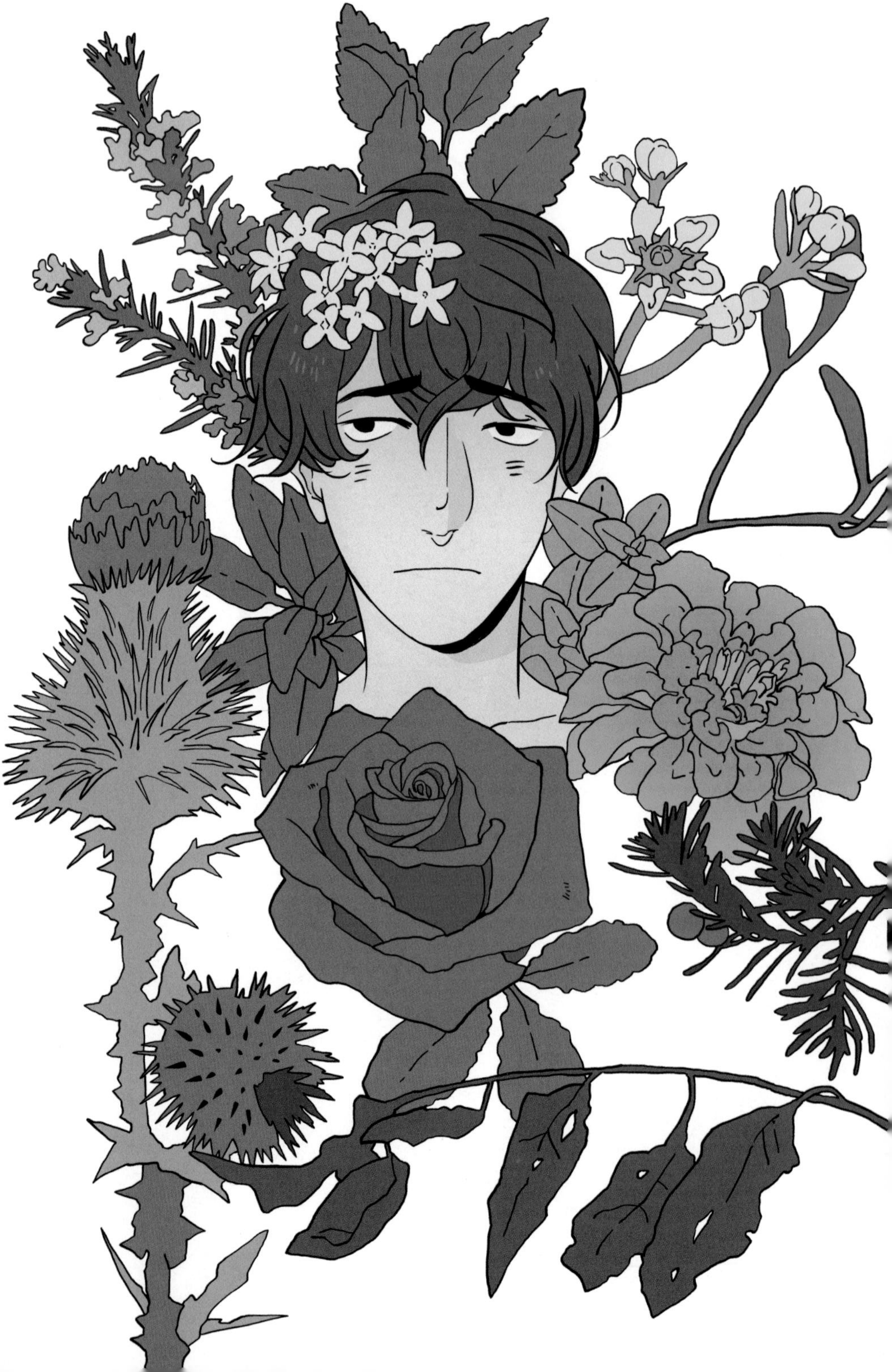

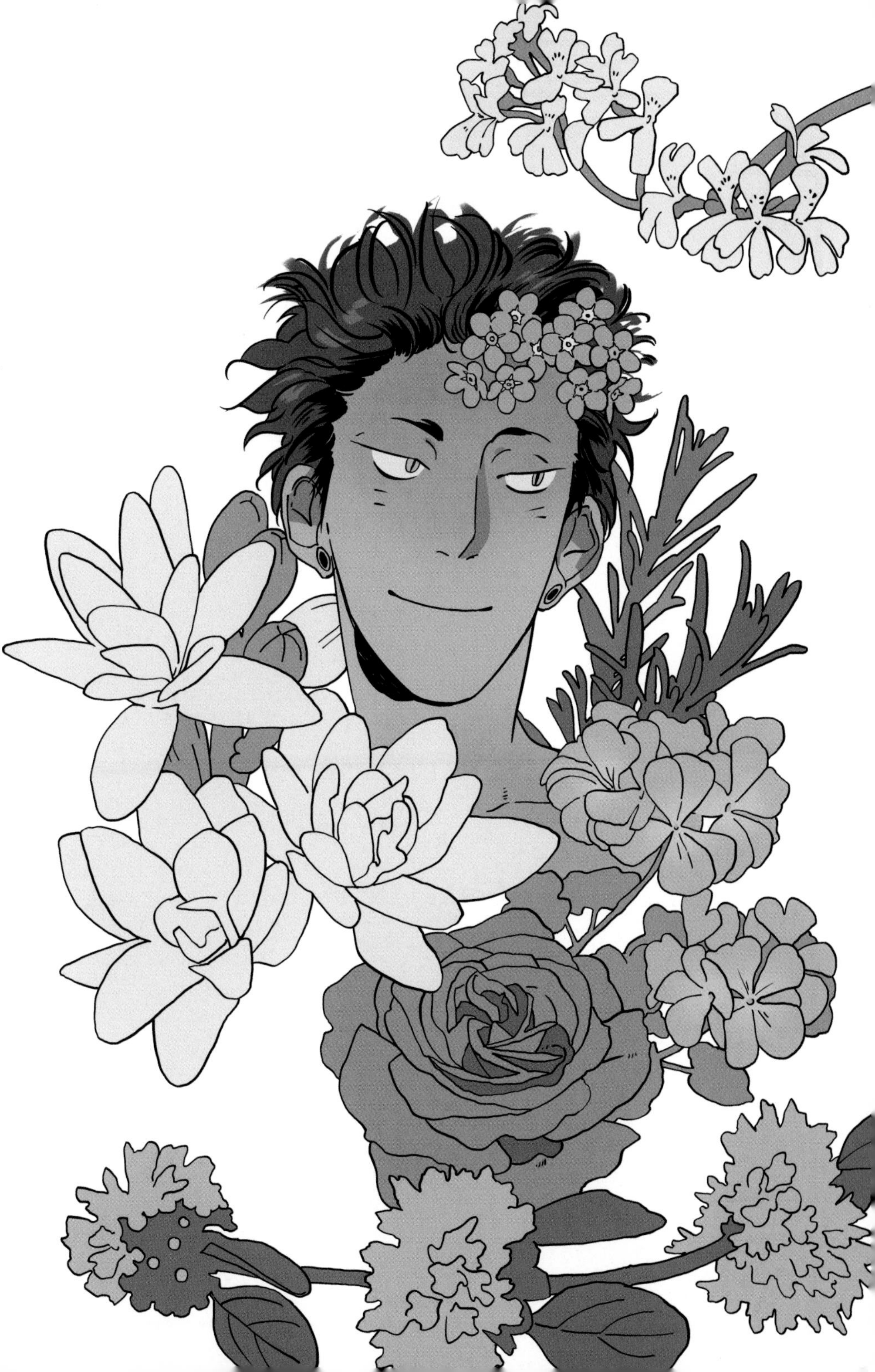

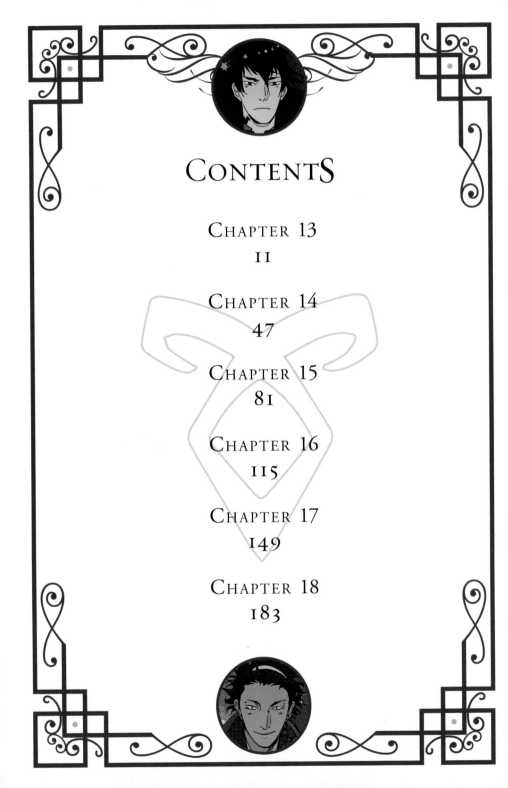

CONTENTS

THE MORTAL INSTRUMENTS

THE GRAPHIC NOVEL

STORY BY
CASSANDRA CLARE

3

ART BY
CASSANDRA JEAN

THE MORTAL INSTRUMENTS
THE GRAPHIC NOVEL — 3

CASSANDRA CLARE
CASSANDRA JEAN

Art and Adaptation: Cassandra Jean
Lettering: Abigail Blackman

Text copyright © 2008 by Cassandra Clare, LLC

Illustrations © 2019 by Yen Press, LLC

Yen Press
150 West 30th Street, 19th Floor
New York, NY 10001

Visit us at yenpress.com
facebook.com/yenpress
twitter.com/yenpress
yenpress.tumblr.com
instagram.com/yenpress

First Yen Press Edition: October 2019

Yen Press is an imprint of Yen Press, LLC.
The Yen Press name and logo are trademarks of Yen Press, LLC.

The publisher is not responsible for websites (or their content) that are not owned by the publisher.

Library of Congress Control Number: 2017945496

ISBNs: 978-0-316-46583-0 (paperback)
978-1-9753-5874-7 (ebook)

10 9 8 7 6 5 4 3 2 1

WOR

Printed in the United States of America

Chapter 13

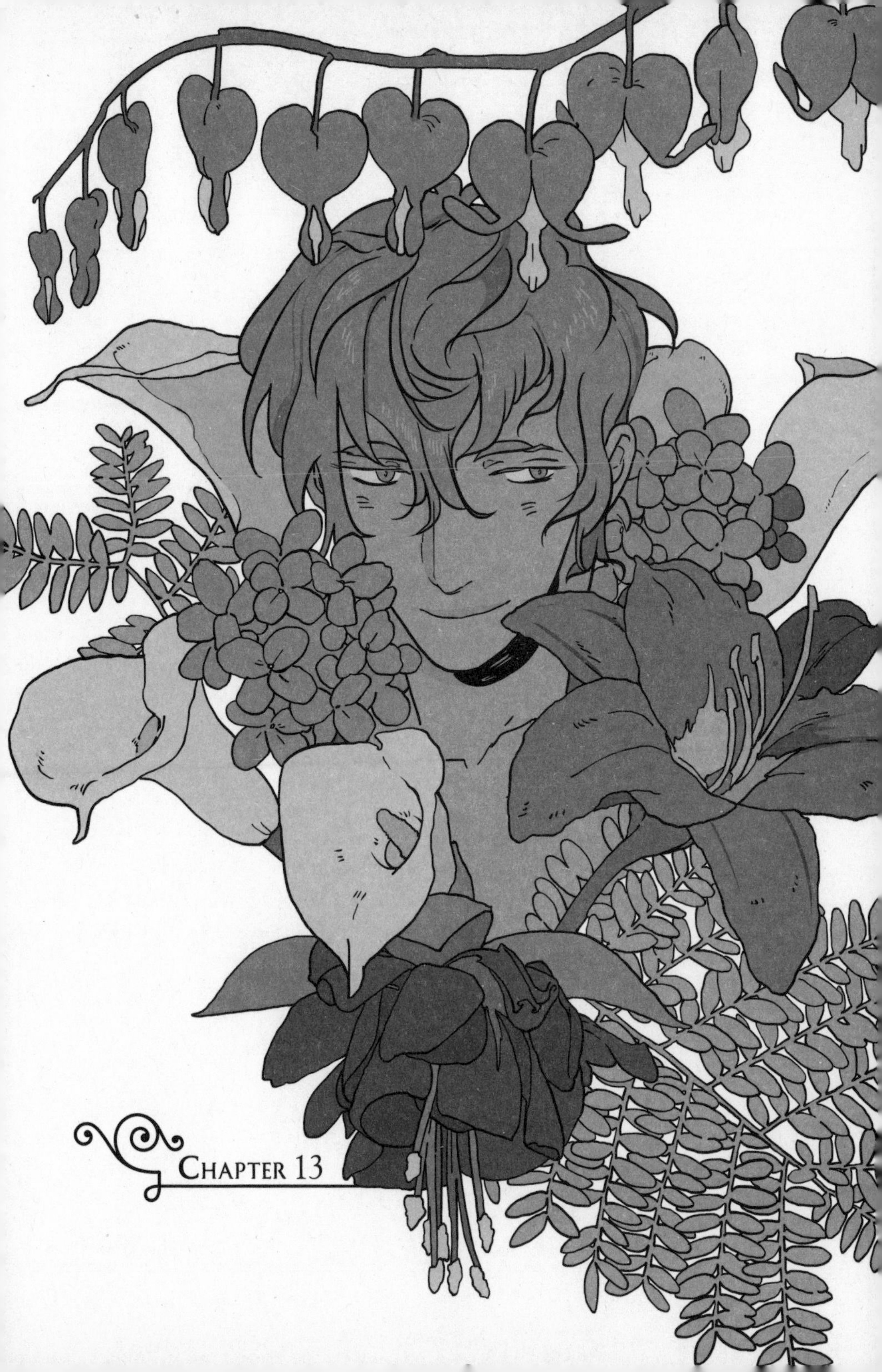

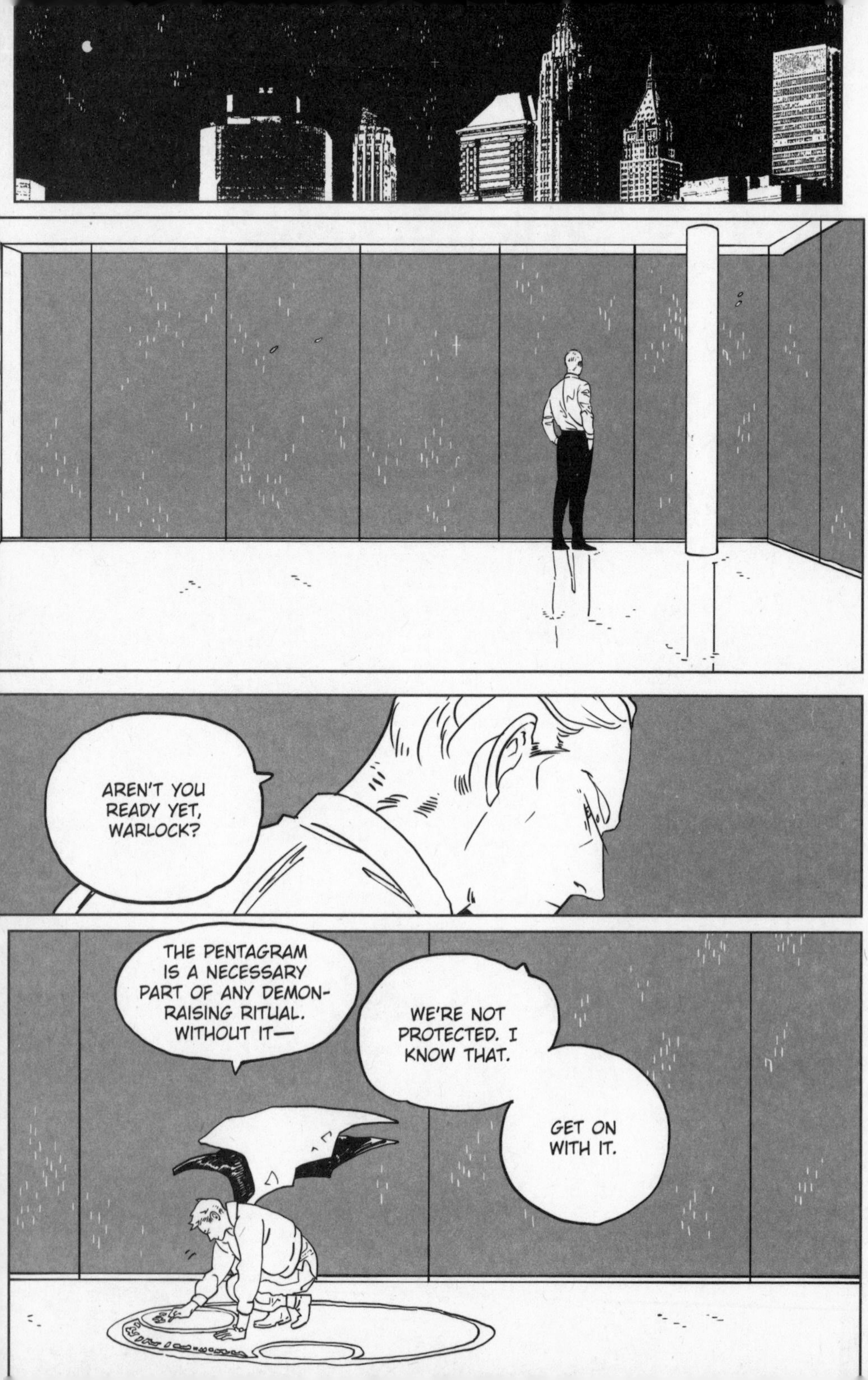
AREN'T YOU READY YET, WARLOCK?
THE PENTAGRAM IS A NECESSARY PART OF ANY DEMON-RAISING RITUAL. WITHOUT IT—
WE'RE NOT PROTECTED. I KNOW THAT.
GET ON WITH IT.

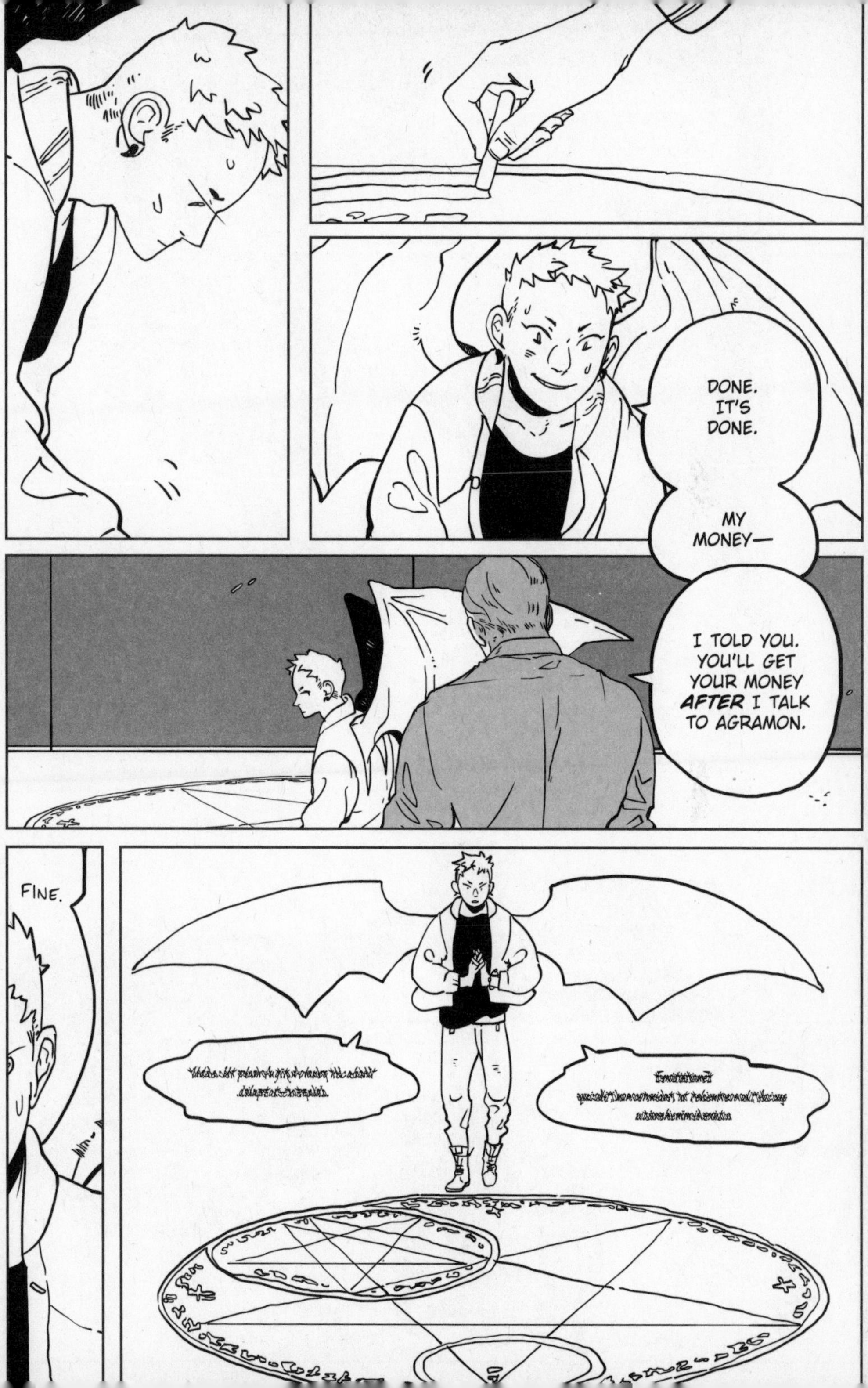
DONE. IT'S DONE.
MY MONEY—
I TOLD YOU. YOU'LL GET YOUR MONEY **AFTER** I TALK TO AGRAMON.
FINE.

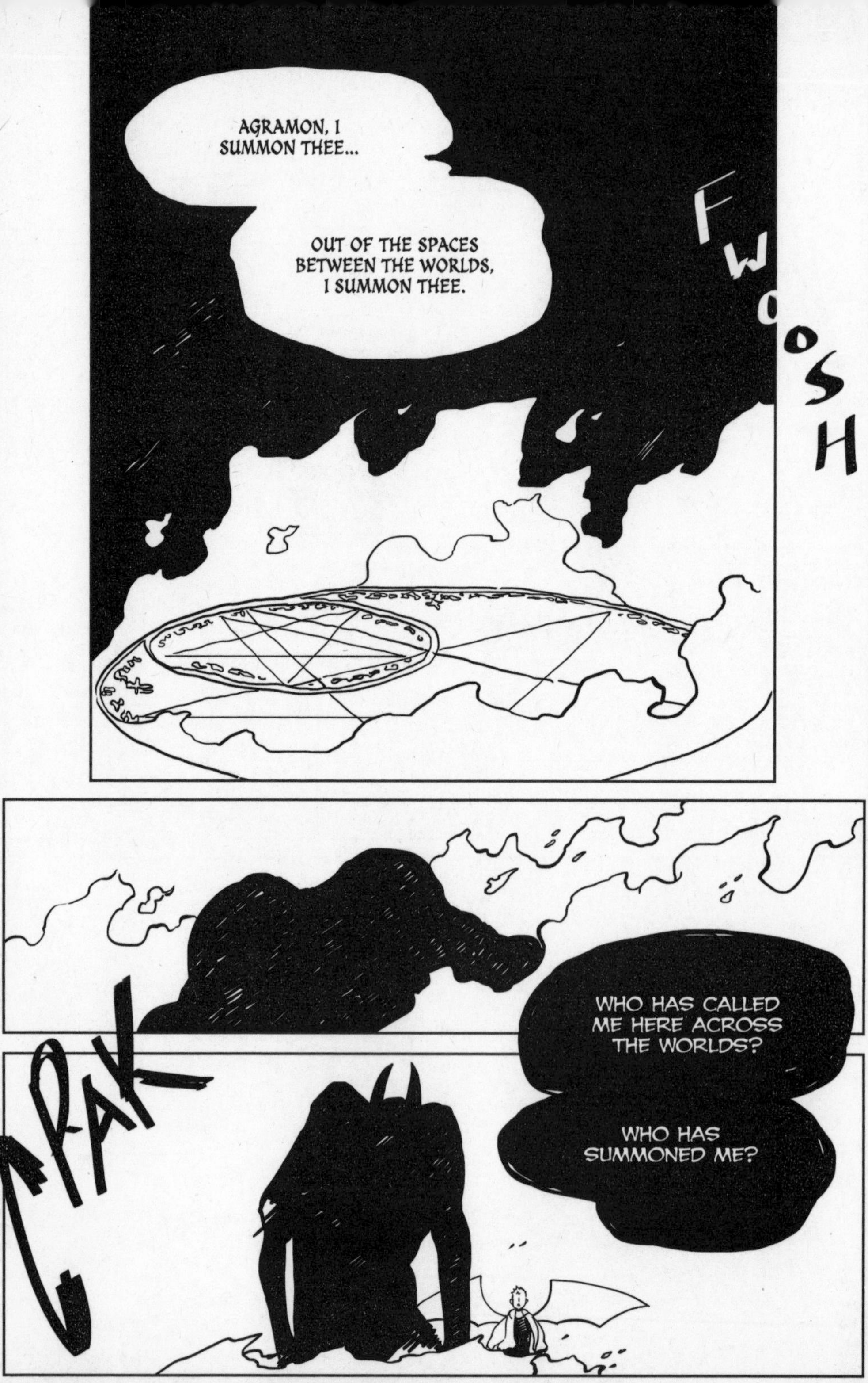
AGRAMON, I SUMMON THEE...
OUT OF THE SPACES BETWEEN THE WORLDS, I SUMMON THEE.
FWOOSH
WHO HAS CALLED ME HERE ACROSS THE WORLDS?
CRAK
WHO HAS SUMMONED ME?

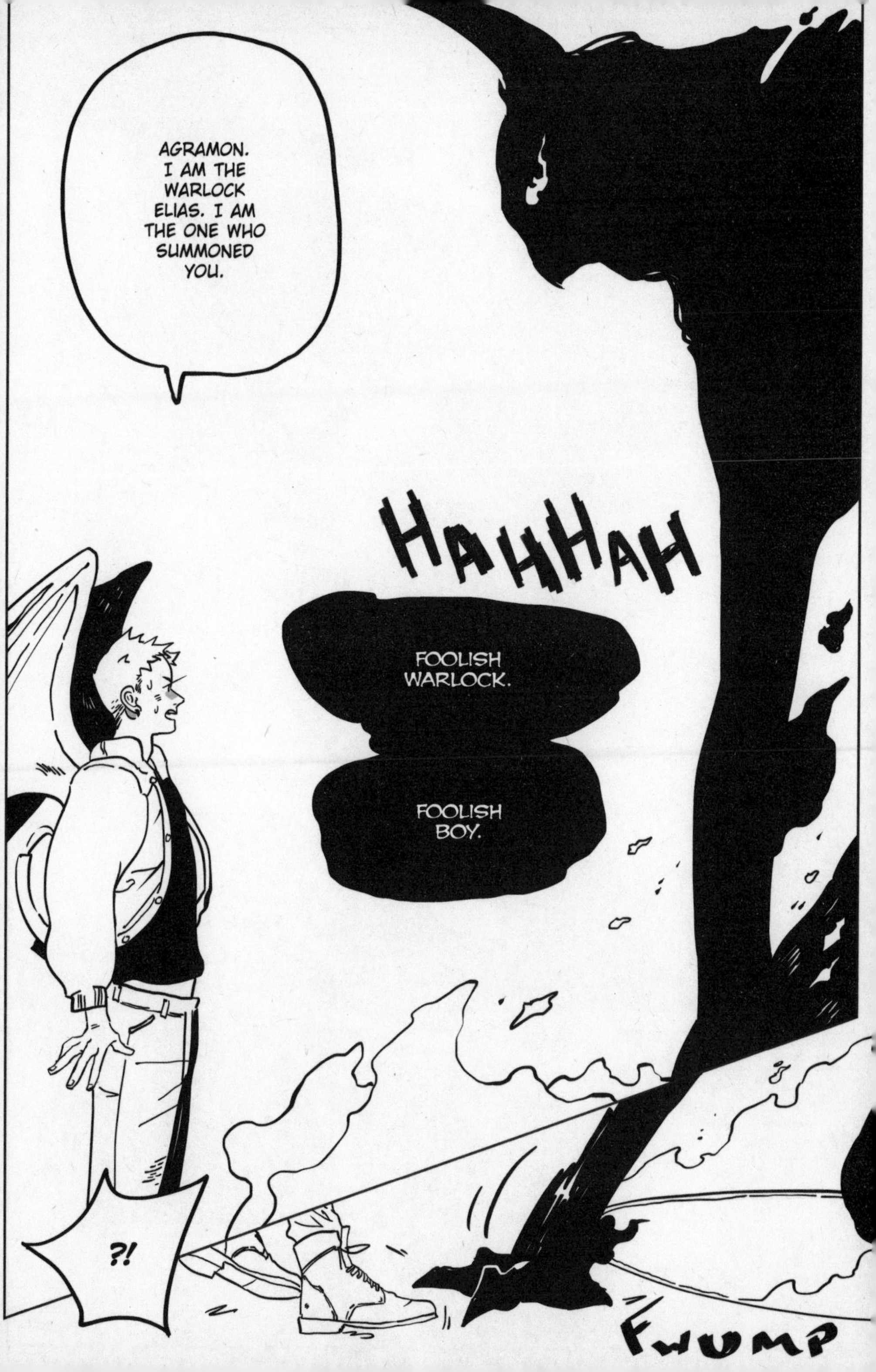
AGRAMON. I AM THE WARLOCK ELIAS. I AM THE ONE WHO SUMMONED YOU.
HAHHAH
FOOLISH WARLOCK.
FOOLISH BOY.
?!
FWUMP

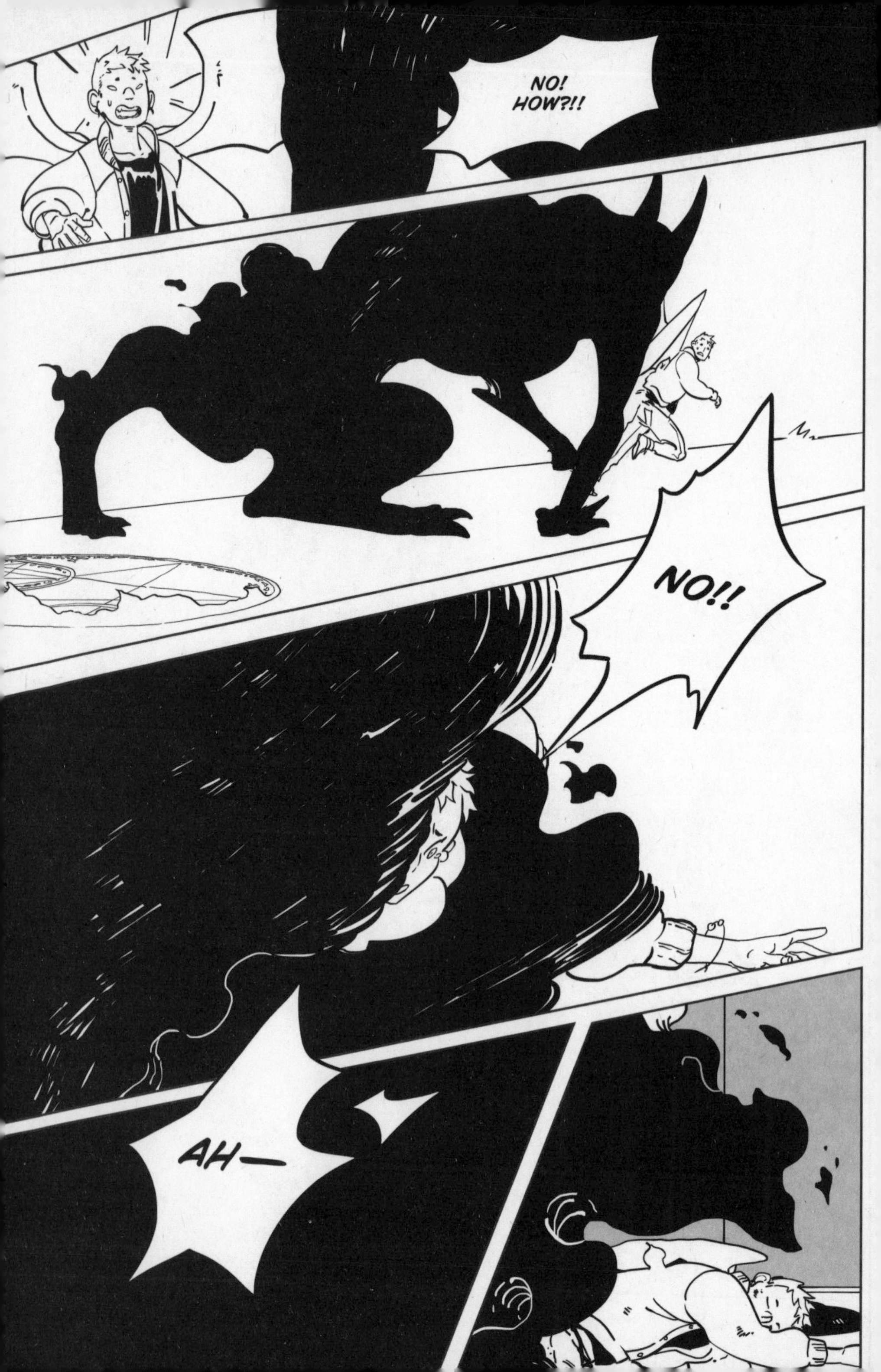
NO!
HOW?!!
NO!!
AH—

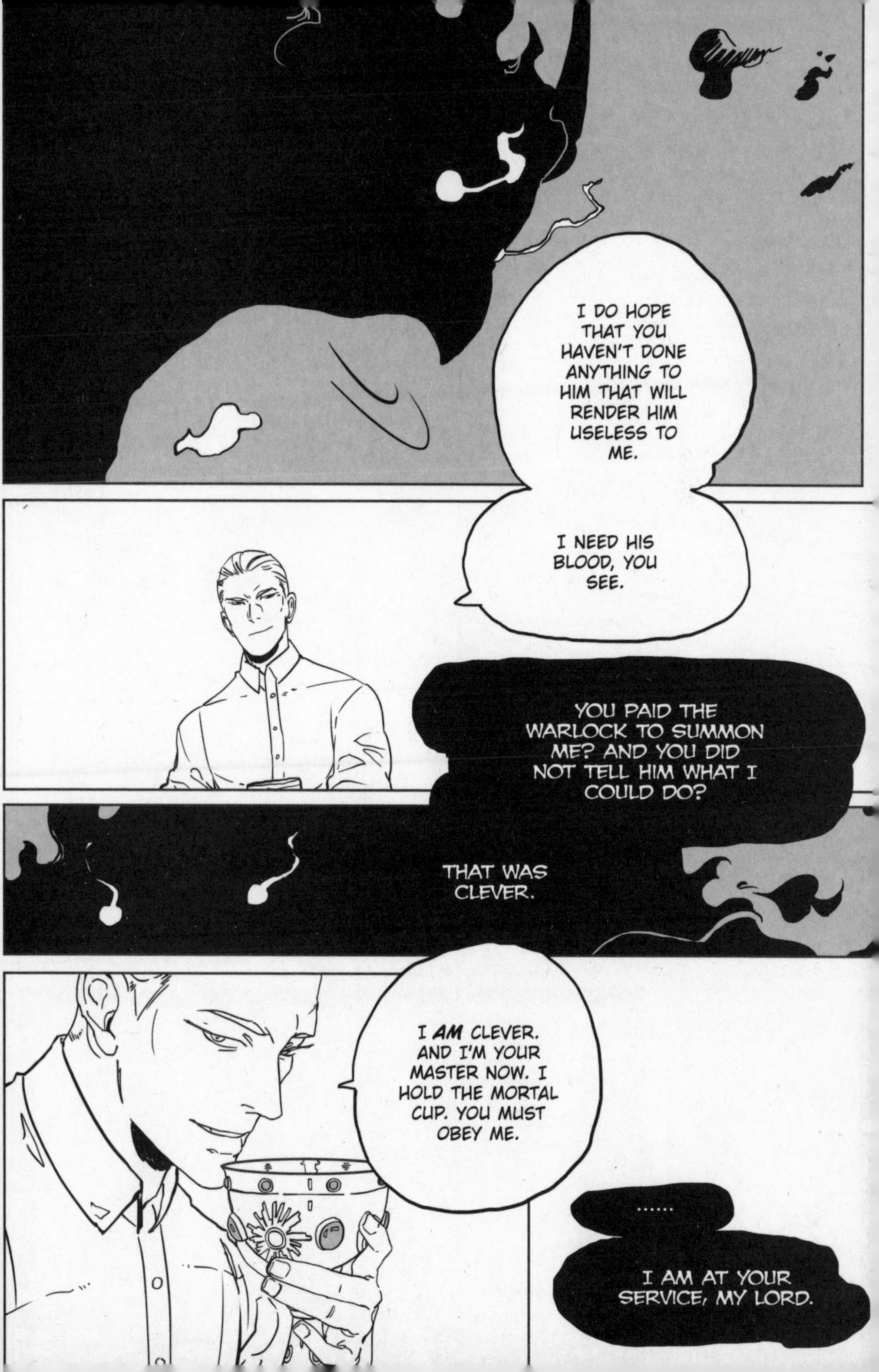

I DO HOPE THAT YOU HAVEN'T DONE ANYTHING TO HIM THAT WILL RENDER HIM USELESS TO ME.
I NEED HIS BLOOD, YOU SEE.
YOU PAID THE WARLOCK TO SUMMON ME? AND YOU DID NOT TELL HIM WHAT I COULD DO?
THAT WAS CLEVER.
I *AM* CLEVER. AND I'M YOUR MASTER NOW. I HOLD THE MORTAL CUP. YOU MUST OBEY ME.
......
I AM AT YOUR SERVICE, MY LORD.

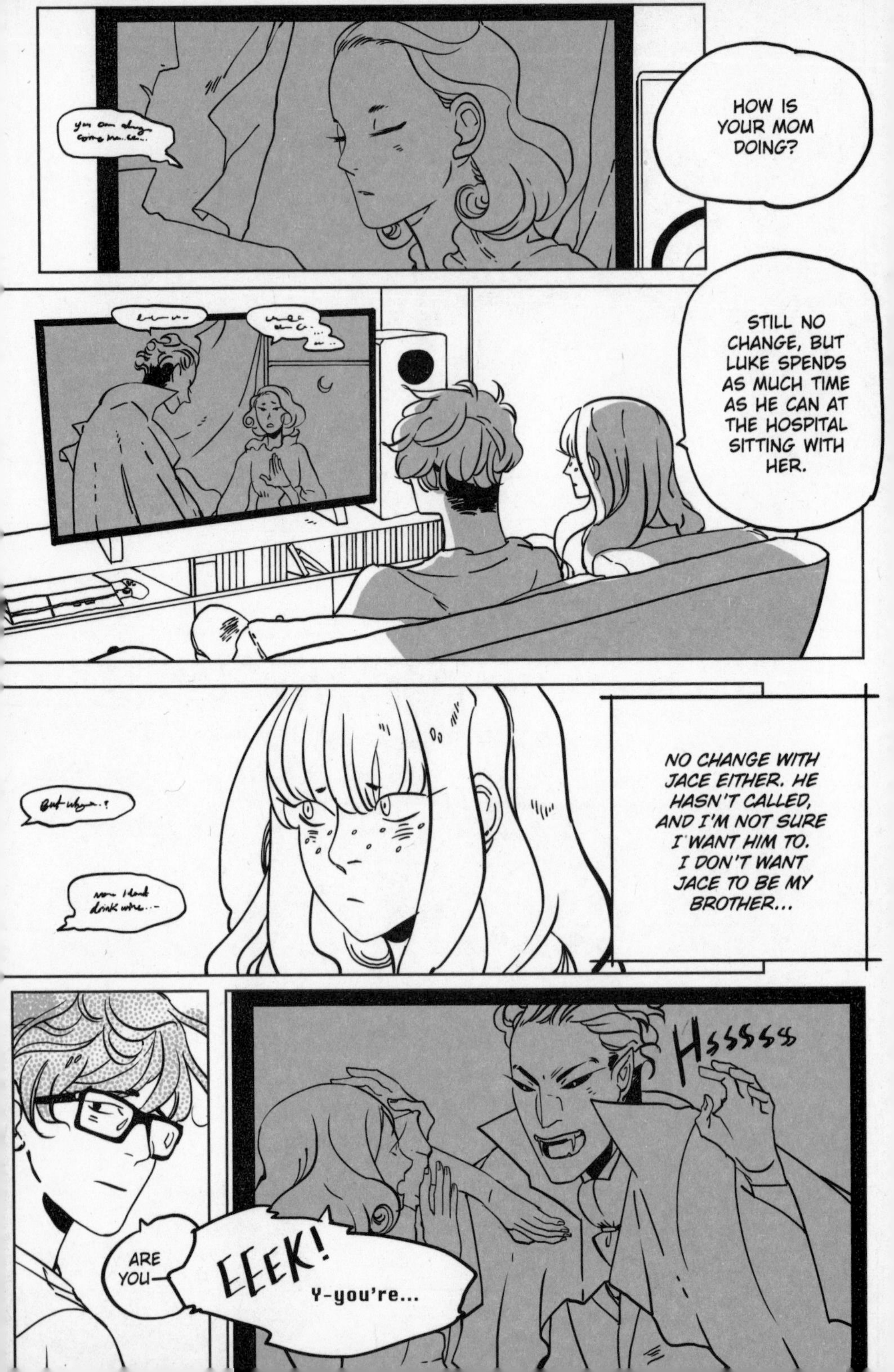
HOW IS YOUR MOM DOING?
STILL NO CHANGE, BUT LUKE SPENDS AS MUCH TIME AS HE CAN AT THE HOSPITAL SITTING WITH HER.
NO CHANGE WITH JACE EITHER. HE HASN'T CALLED, AND I'M NOT SURE I WANT HIM TO. I DON'T WANT JACE TO BE MY BROTHER...
Hsssss
ARE YOU—
EEEK!
Y-you're...

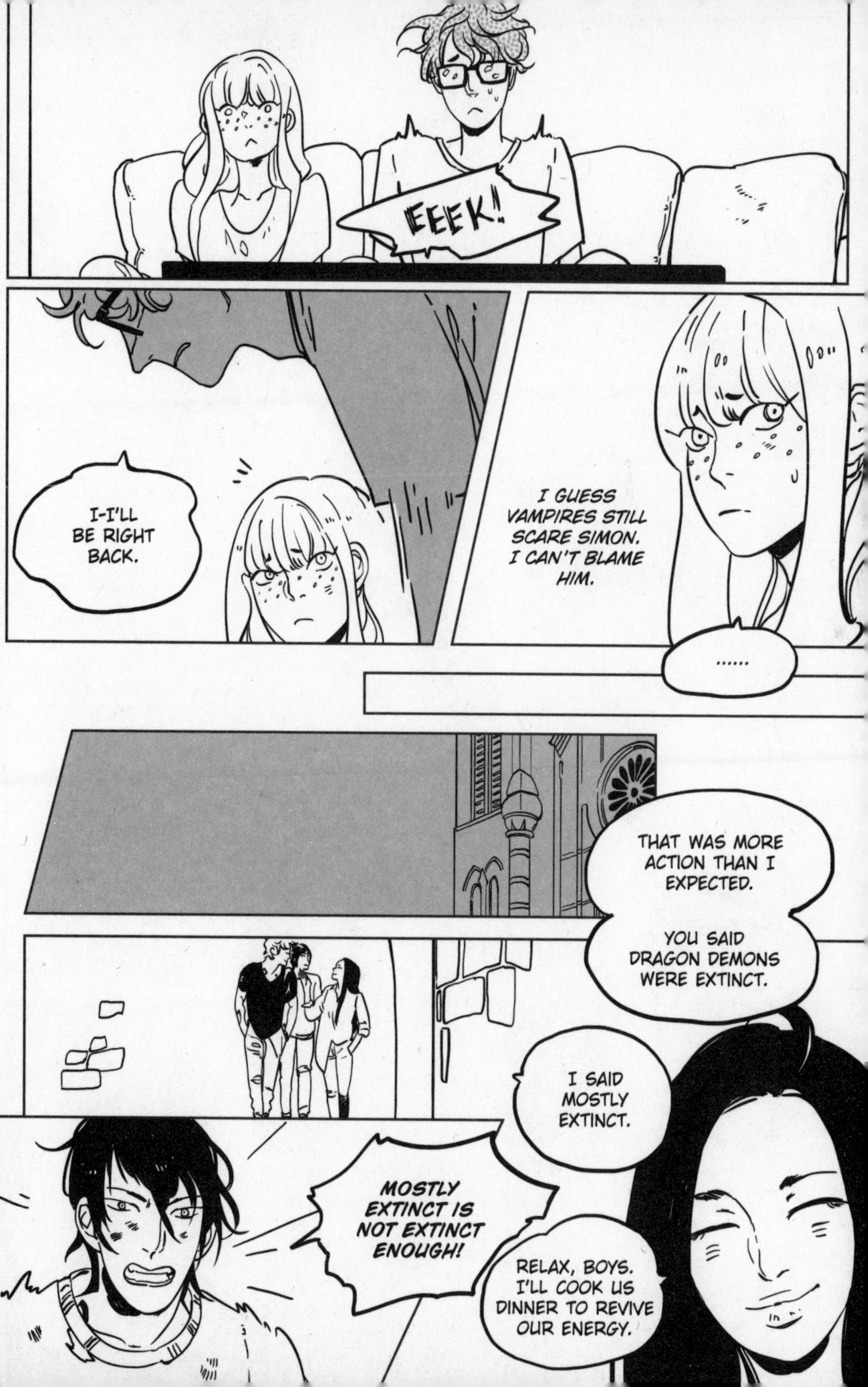
EEEK!
I-I'LL BE RIGHT BACK.
I GUESS VAMPIRES STILL SCARE SIMON. I CAN'T BLAME HIM.
......
THAT WAS MORE ACTION THAN I EXPECTED.
YOU SAID DRAGON DEMONS WERE EXTINCT.
I SAID MOSTLY EXTINCT.
MOSTLY EXTINCT IS NOT EXTINCT ENOUGH!
RELAX, BOYS. I'LL COOK US DINNER TO REVIVE OUR ENERGY.

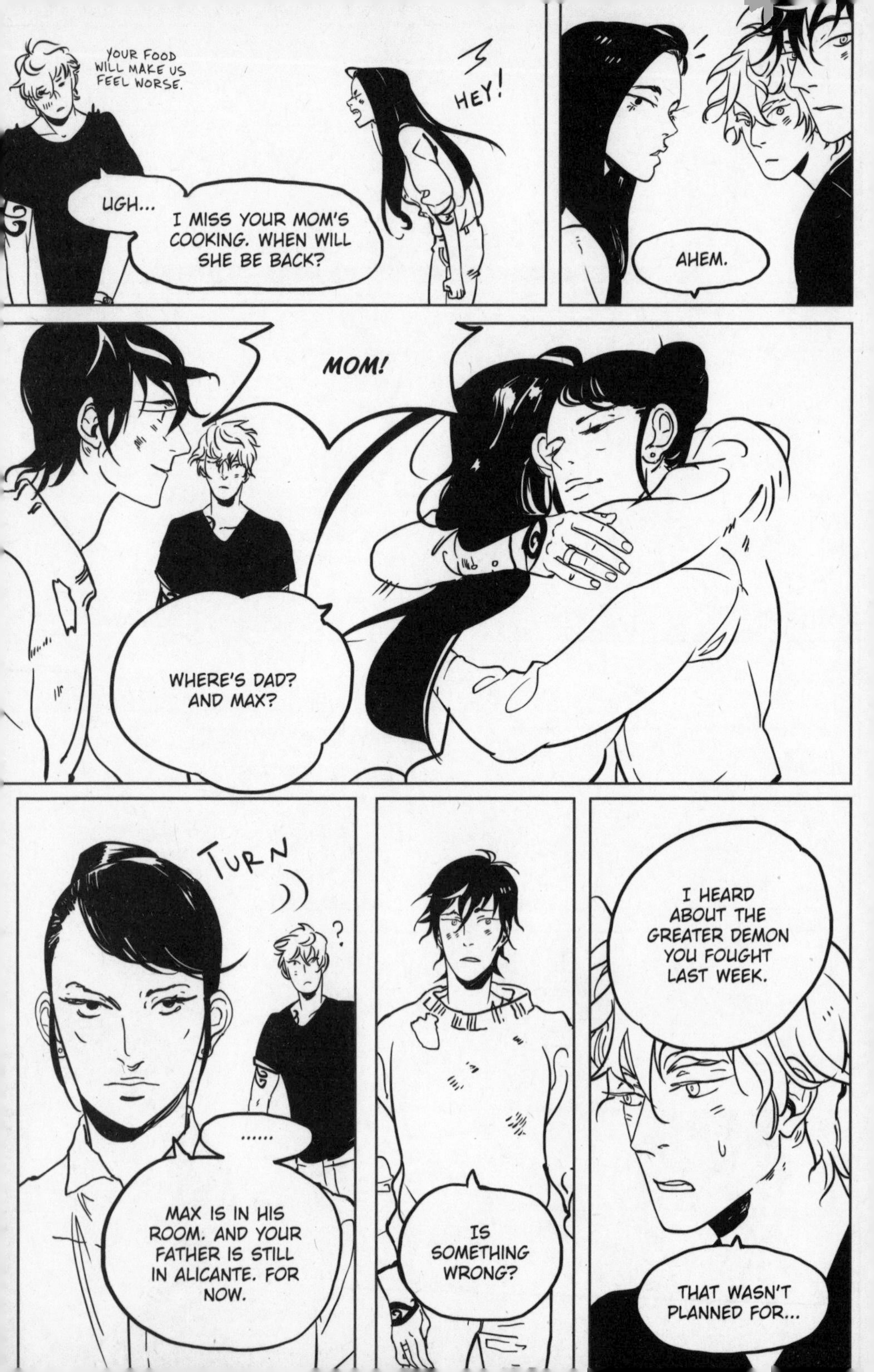
YOUR FOOD WILL MAKE US FEEL WORSE.
HEY!
UGH...
I MISS YOUR MOM'S COOKING. WHEN WILL SHE BE BACK?
AHEM.
MOM!
WHERE'S DAD? AND MAX?
TURN
?
......
MAX IS IN HIS ROOM. AND YOUR FATHER IS STILL IN ALICANTE. FOR NOW.
IS SOMETHING WRONG?
I HEARD ABOUT THE GREATER DEMON YOU FOUGHT LAST WEEK.
THAT WASN'T PLANNED FOR...

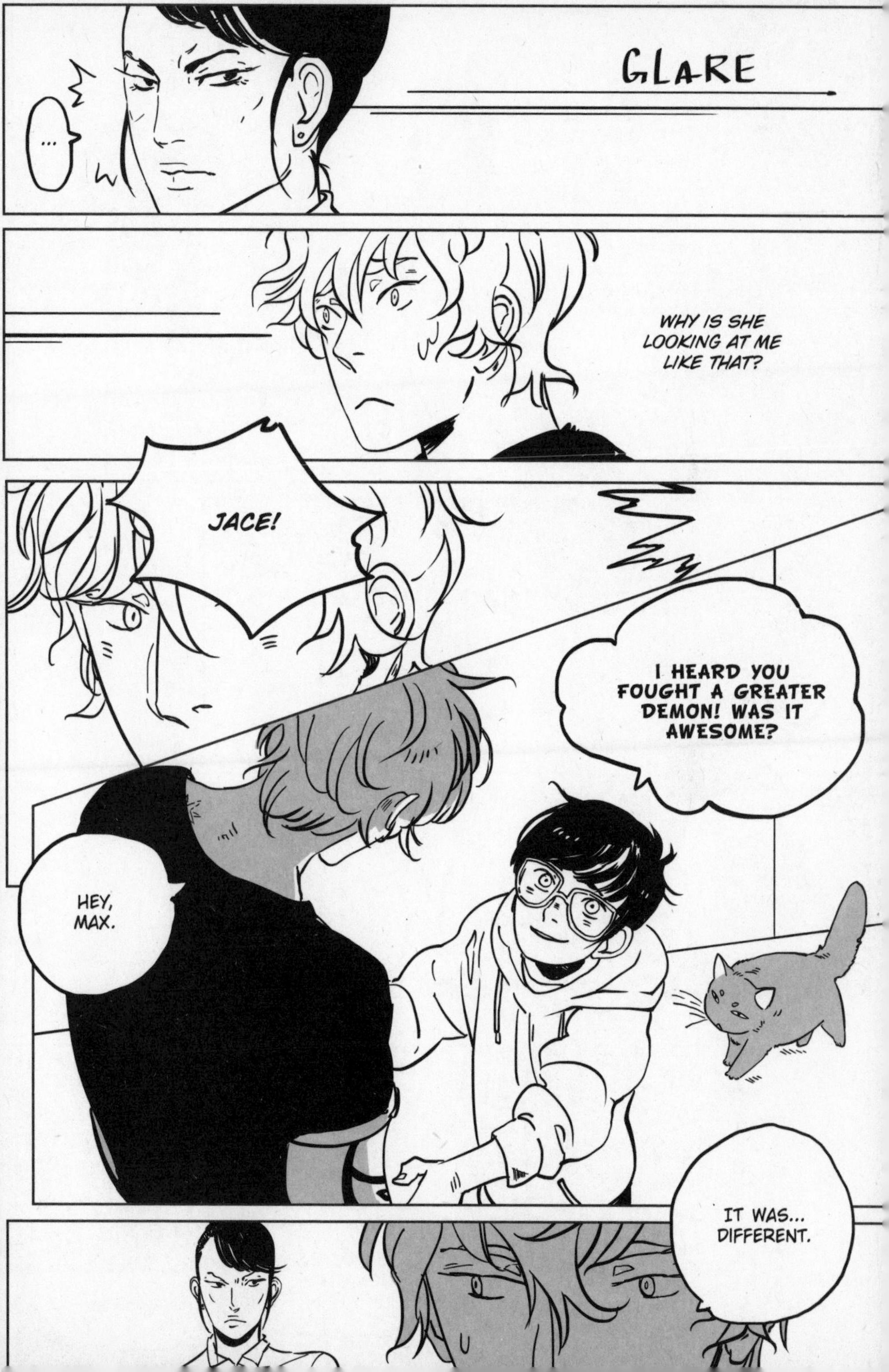
...
GLARE
WHY IS SHE LOOKING AT ME LIKE THAT?
JACE!
I HEARD YOU FOUGHT A GREATER DEMON! WAS IT AWESOME?
HEY, MAX.
IT WAS... DIFFERENT.

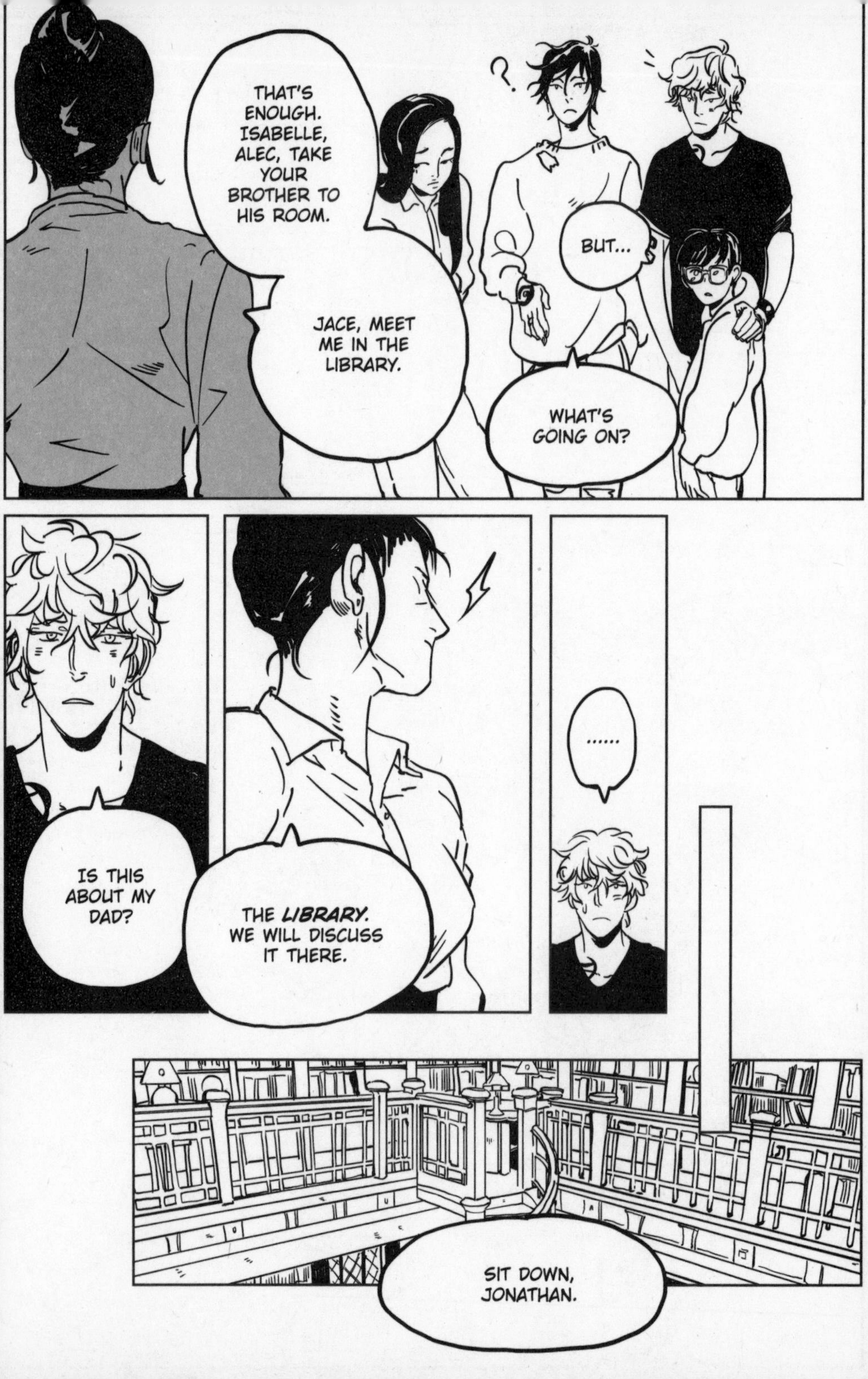
THAT'S ENOUGH. ISABELLE, ALEC, TAKE YOUR BROTHER TO HIS ROOM.
JACE, MEET ME IN THE LIBRARY.
?
BUT...
WHAT'S GOING ON?
IS THIS ABOUT MY DAD?
THE *LIBRARY*. WE WILL DISCUSS IT THERE.
......
SIT DOWN, JONATHAN.

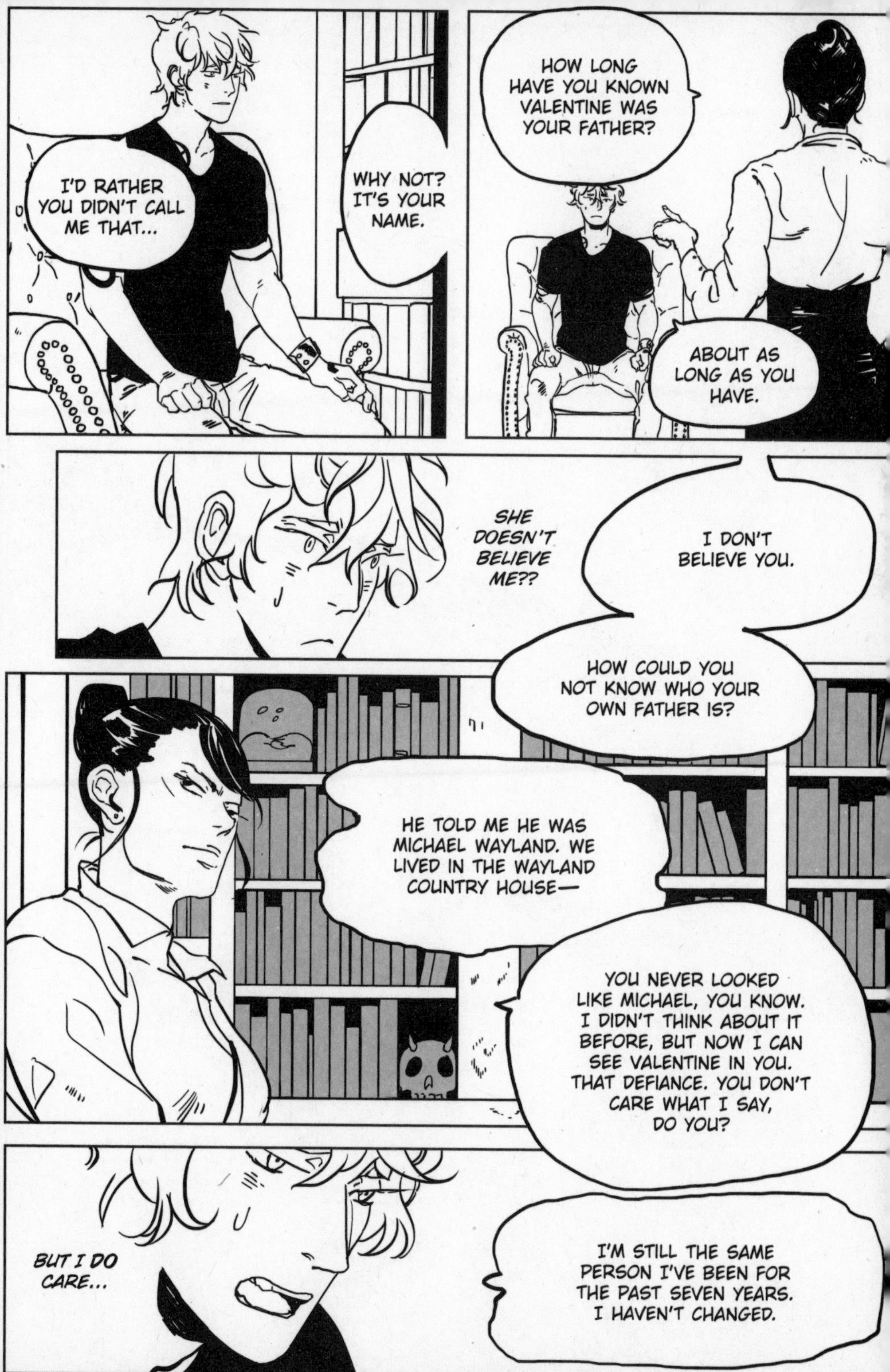
I'D RATHER YOU DIDN'T CALL ME THAT...
WHY NOT? IT'S YOUR NAME.
HOW LONG HAVE YOU KNOWN VALENTINE WAS YOUR FATHER?
ABOUT AS LONG AS YOU HAVE.
SHE DOESN'T BELIEVE ME??
I DON'T BELIEVE YOU.
HOW COULD YOU NOT KNOW WHO YOUR OWN FATHER IS?
HE TOLD ME HE WAS MICHAEL WAYLAND. WE LIVED IN THE WAYLAND COUNTRY HOUSE—
YOU NEVER LOOKED LIKE MICHAEL, YOU KNOW. I DIDN'T THINK ABOUT IT BEFORE, BUT NOW I CAN SEE VALENTINE IN YOU. THAT DEFIANCE. YOU DON'T CARE WHAT I SAY, DO YOU?
BUT I DO CARE...
I'M STILL THE SAME PERSON I'VE BEEN FOR THE PAST SEVEN YEARS. I HAVEN'T CHANGED.

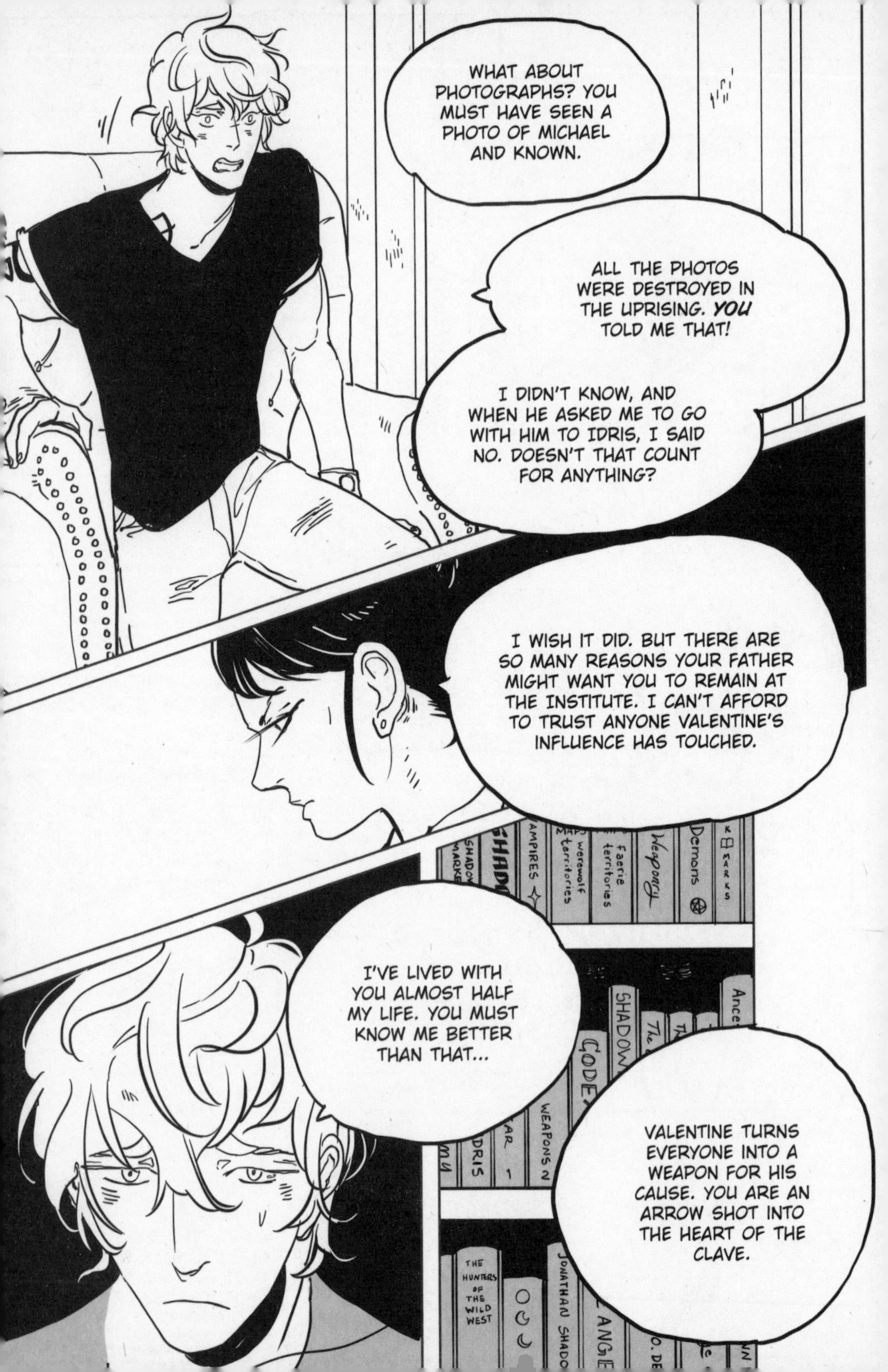
WHAT ABOUT PHOTOGRAPHS? YOU MUST HAVE SEEN A PHOTO OF MICHAEL AND KNOWN.
ALL THE PHOTOS WERE DESTROYED IN THE UPRISING. ***YOU*** TOLD ME THAT!
I DIDN'T KNOW, AND WHEN HE ASKED ME TO GO WITH HIM TO IDRIS, I SAID NO. DOESN'T THAT COUNT FOR ANYTHING?
I WISH IT DID. BUT THERE ARE SO MANY REASONS YOUR FATHER MIGHT WANT YOU TO REMAIN AT THE INSTITUTE. I CAN'T AFFORD TO TRUST ANYONE VALENTINE'S INFLUENCE HAS TOUCHED.
werewolf territories
faerie territories
Weaponry
Demons
I'VE LIVED WITH YOU ALMOST HALF MY LIFE. YOU MUST KNOW ME BETTER THAN THAT...
VALENTINE TURNS EVERYONE INTO A WEAPON FOR HIS CAUSE. YOU ARE AN ARROW SHOT INTO THE HEART OF THE CLAVE.
WEAPONS 2
THE HUNTERS OF THE WILD WEST

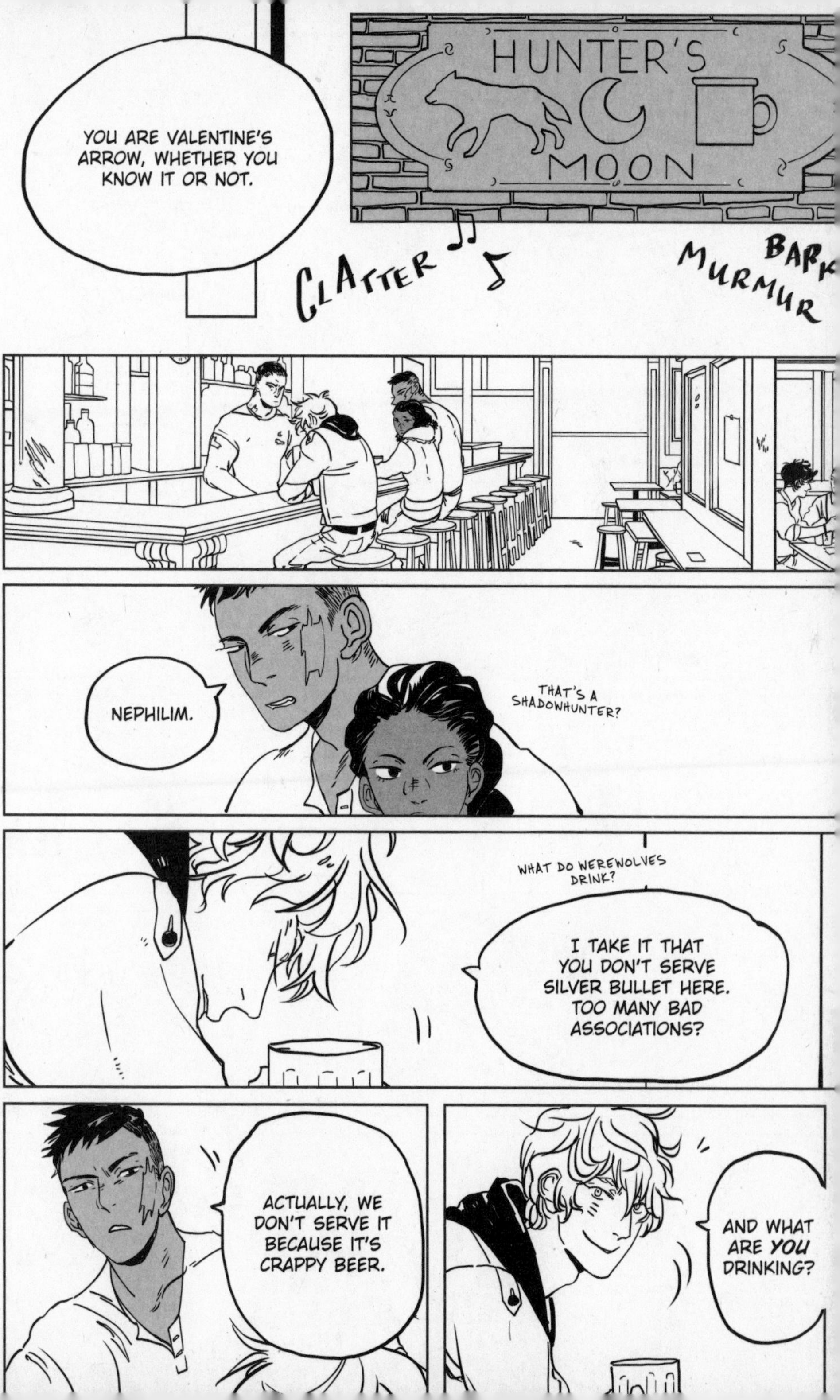
YOU ARE VALENTINE'S ARROW, WHETHER YOU KNOW IT OR NOT.
HUNTER'S MOON
CLATTER
BARK
MURMUR
NEPHILIM.
THAT'S A SHADOWHUNTER?
WHAT DO WEREWOLVES DRINK?
I TAKE IT THAT YOU DON'T SERVE SILVER BULLET HERE. TOO MANY BAD ASSOCIATIONS?
ACTUALLY, WE DON'T SERVE IT BECAUSE IT'S CRAPPY BEER.
AND WHAT ARE *YOU* DRINKING?

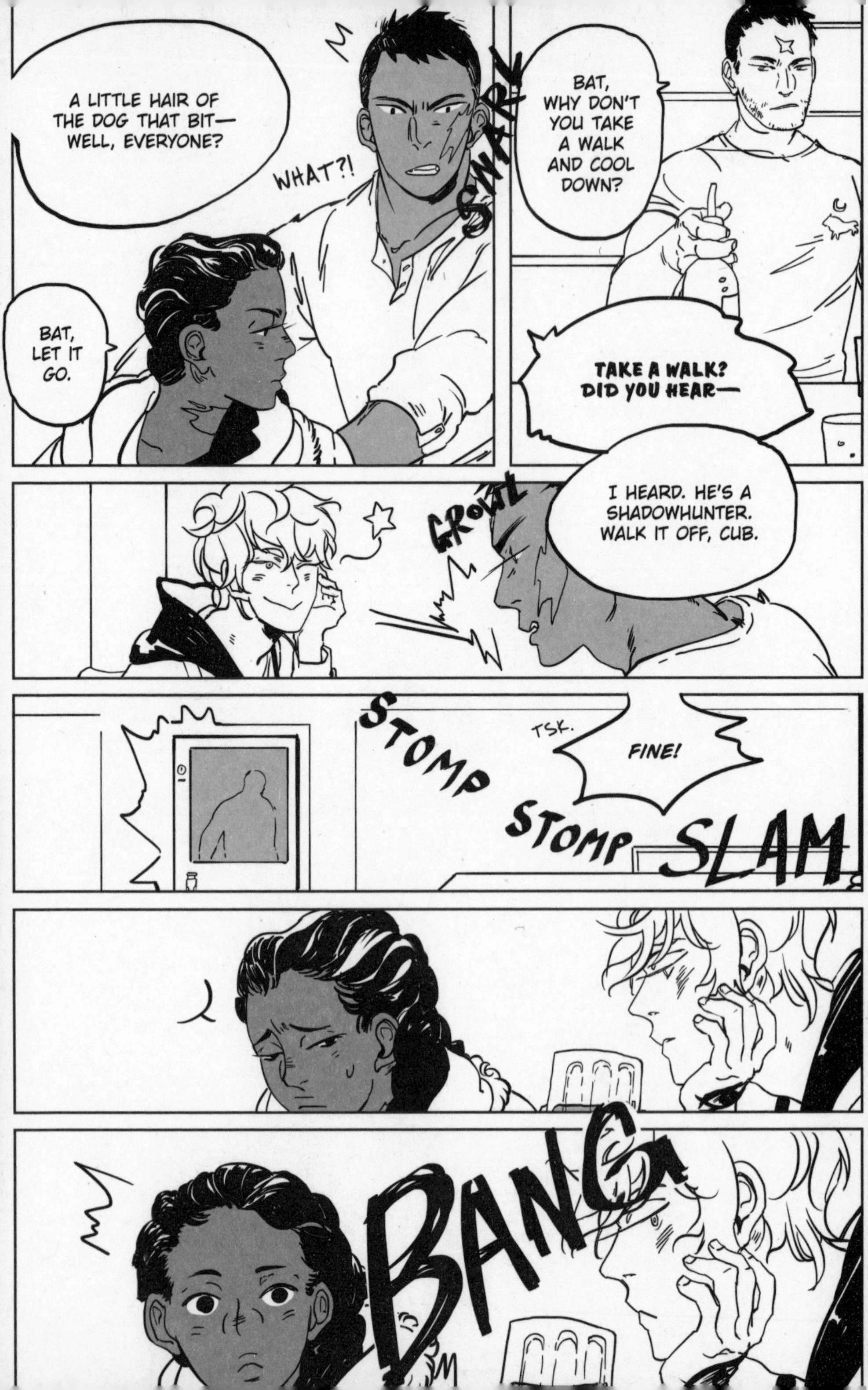
A LITTLE HAIR OF THE DOG THAT BIT— WELL, EVERYONE?
WHAT?!
SNARL
BAT, LET IT GO.
BAT, WHY DON'T YOU TAKE A WALK AND COOL DOWN?
TAKE A WALK? DID YOU HEAR—
GROWL
I HEARD. HE'S A SHADOWHUNTER. WALK IT OFF, CUB.
STOMP
TSK.
FINE!
STOMP
SLAM
BANG

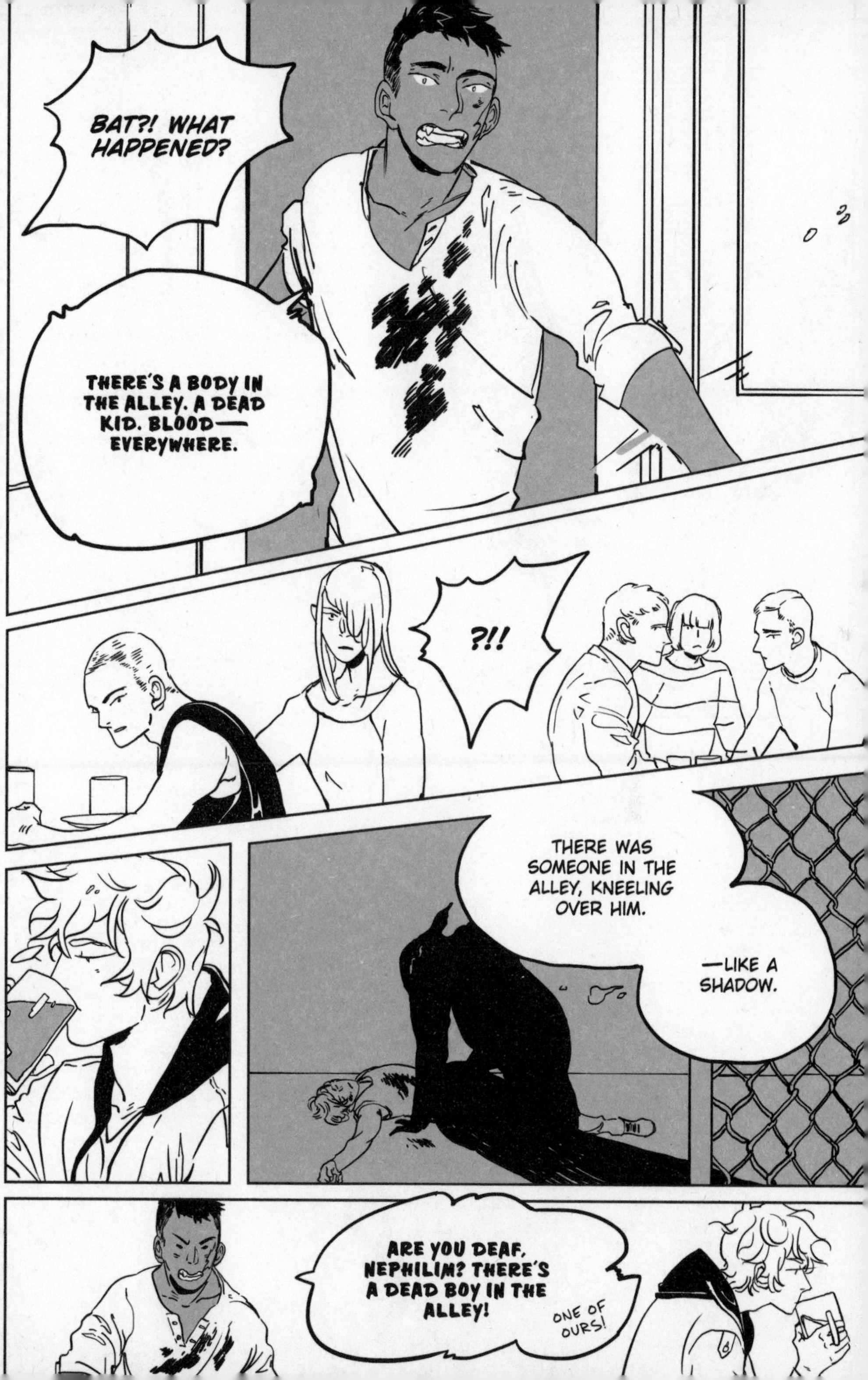
BAT?! WHAT HAPPENED?
THERE'S A BODY IN THE ALLEY. A DEAD KID. BLOOD— EVERYWHERE.
?!!
THERE WAS SOMEONE IN THE ALLEY, KNEELING OVER HIM.
—LIKE A SHADOW.
ARE YOU DEAF, NEPHILIM? THERE'S A DEAD BOY IN THE ALLEY!
ONE OF OURS!

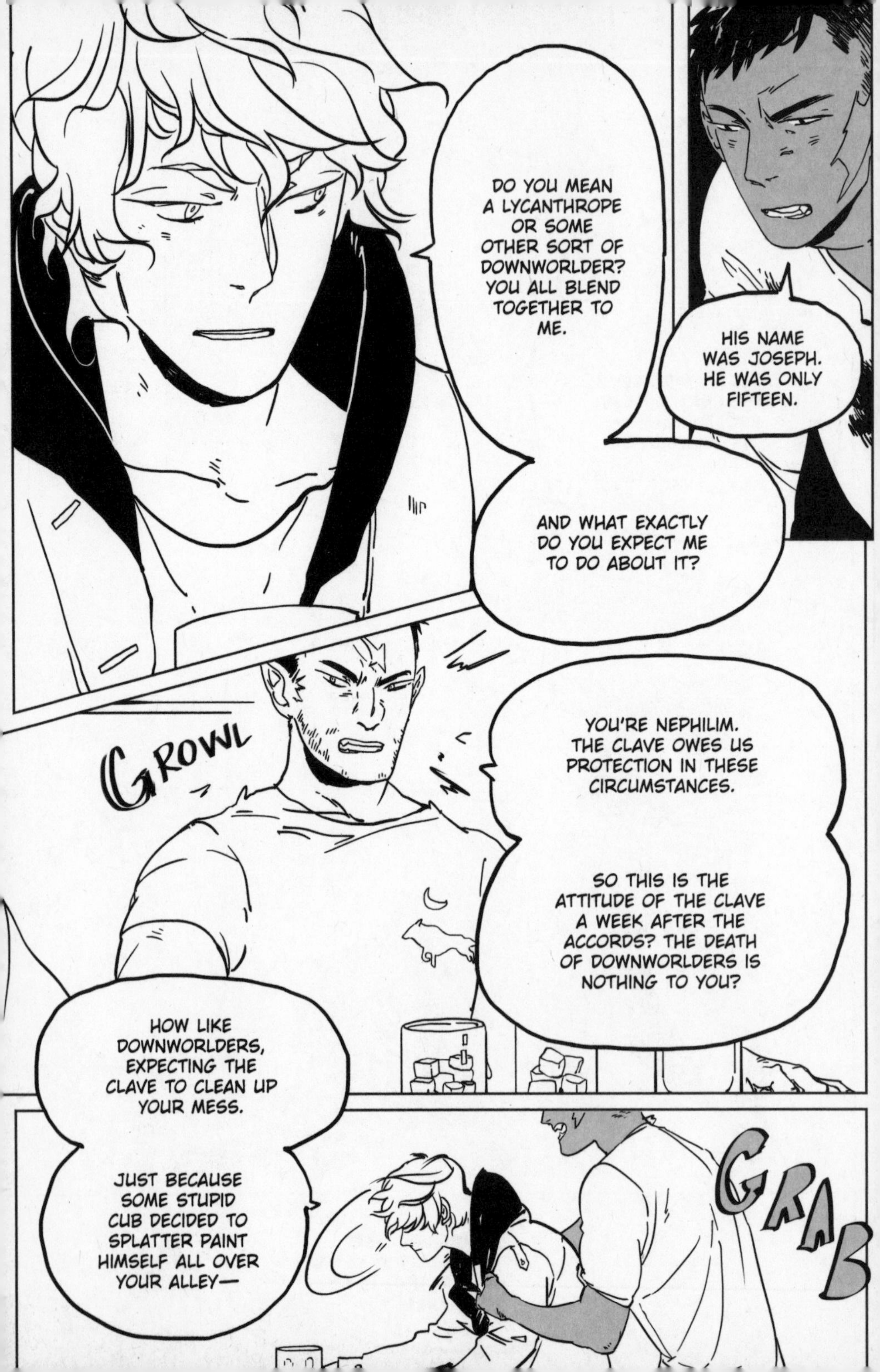
DO YOU MEAN A LYCANTHROPE OR SOME OTHER SORT OF DOWNWORLDER? YOU ALL BLEND TOGETHER TO ME.
HIS NAME WAS JOSEPH. HE WAS ONLY FIFTEEN.
AND WHAT EXACTLY DO YOU EXPECT ME TO DO ABOUT IT?
GROWL
YOU'RE NEPHILIM. THE CLAVE OWES US PROTECTION IN THESE CIRCUMSTANCES.
SO THIS IS THE ATTITUDE OF THE CLAVE A WEEK AFTER THE ACCORDS? THE DEATH OF DOWNWORLDERS IS NOTHING TO YOU?
HOW LIKE DOWNWORLDERS, EXPECTING THE CLAVE TO CLEAN UP YOUR MESS.
JUST BECAUSE SOME STUPID CUB DECIDED TO SPLATTER PAINT HIMSELF ALL OVER YOUR ALLEY—
GRAB

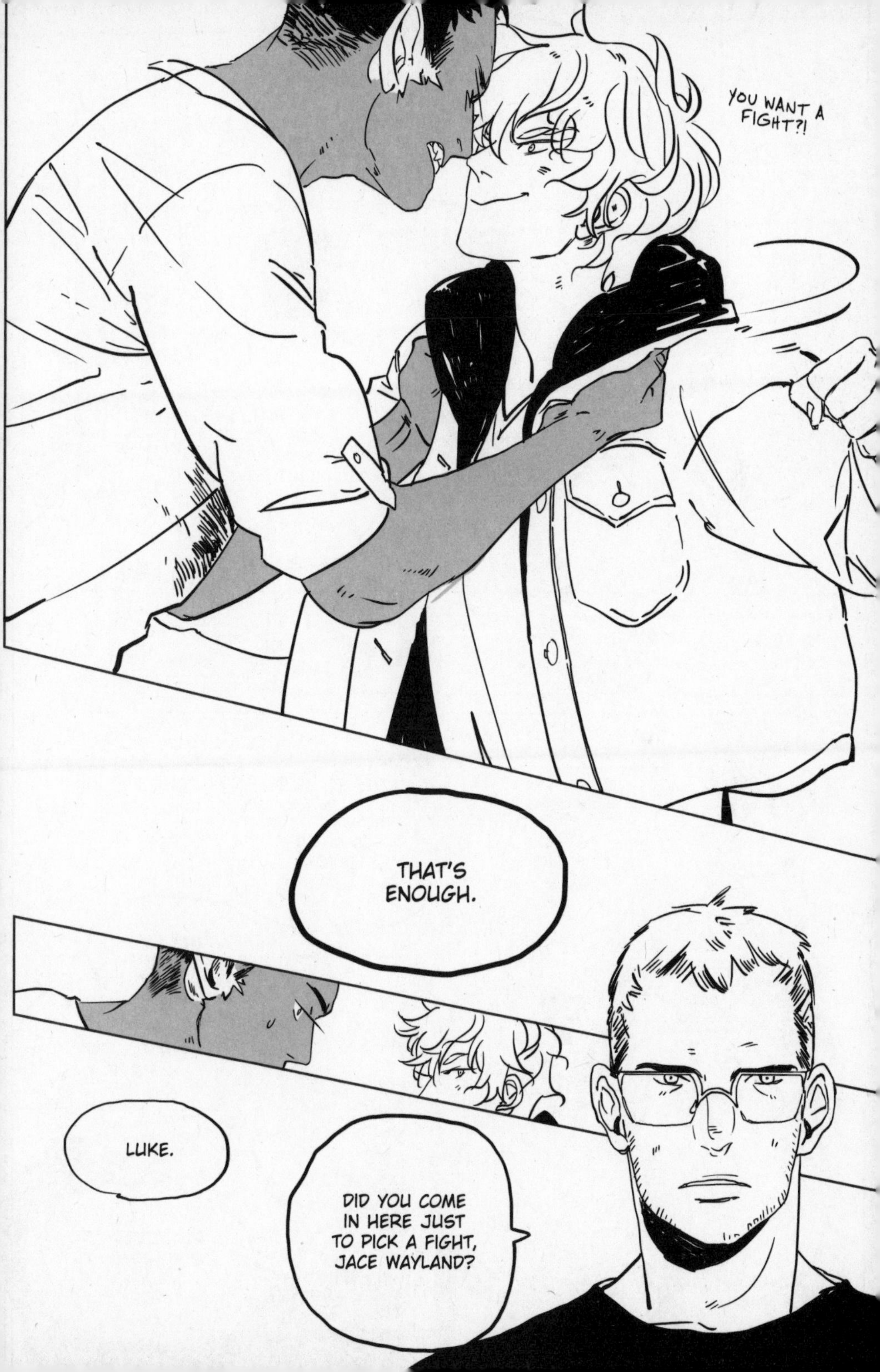
YOU WANT A FIGHT?!
THAT'S ENOUGH.
LUKE.
DID YOU COME IN HERE JUST TO PICK A FIGHT, JACE WAYLAND?

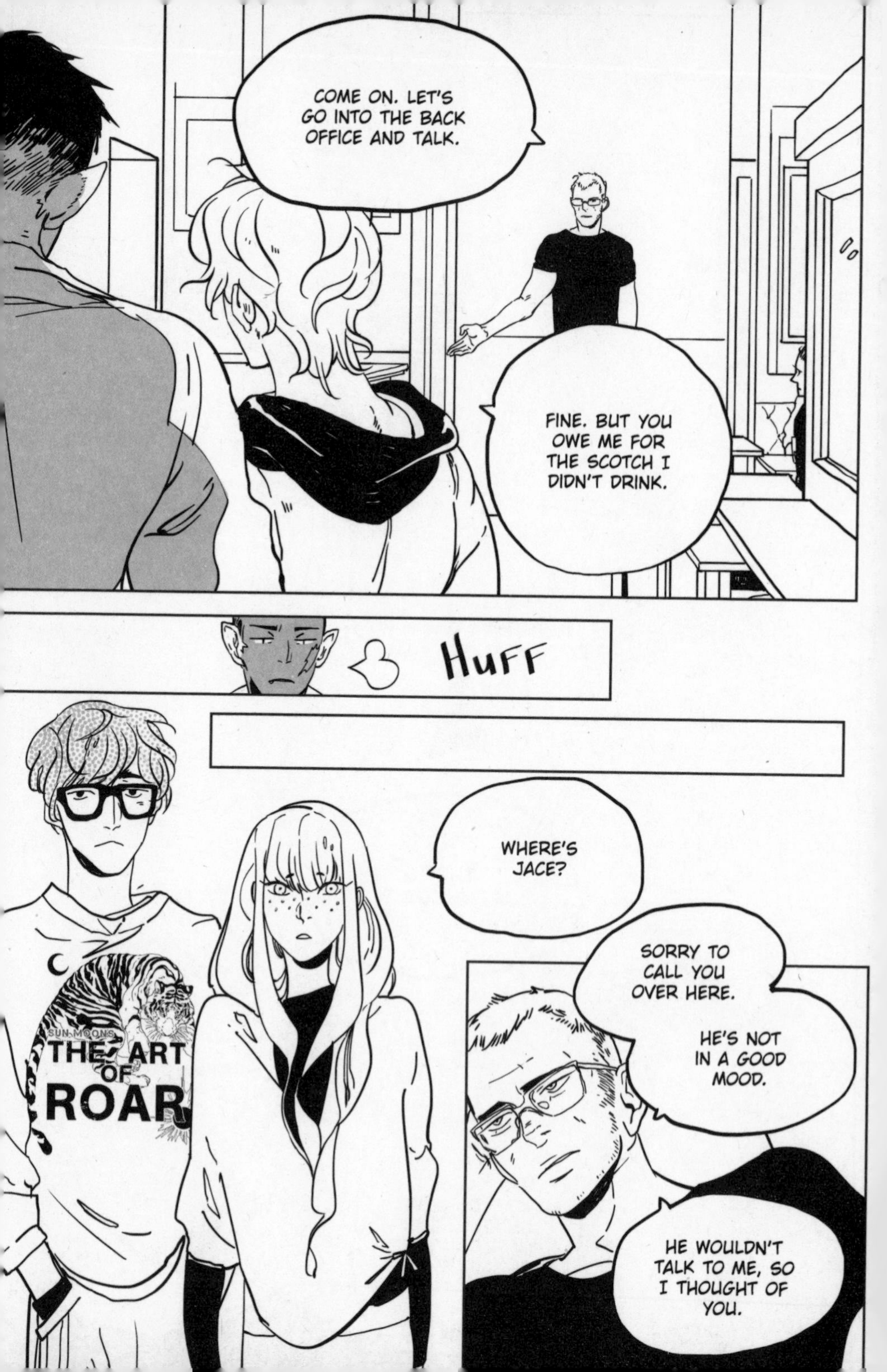
COME ON. LET'S GO INTO THE BACK OFFICE AND TALK.
FINE. BUT YOU OWE ME FOR THE SCOTCH I DIDN'T DRINK.
HUFF
WHERE'S JACE?
SUN MOONS THE ART OF ROAR
SORRY TO CALL YOU OVER HERE.
HE'S NOT IN A GOOD MOOD.
HE WOULDN'T TALK TO ME, SO I THOUGHT OF YOU.

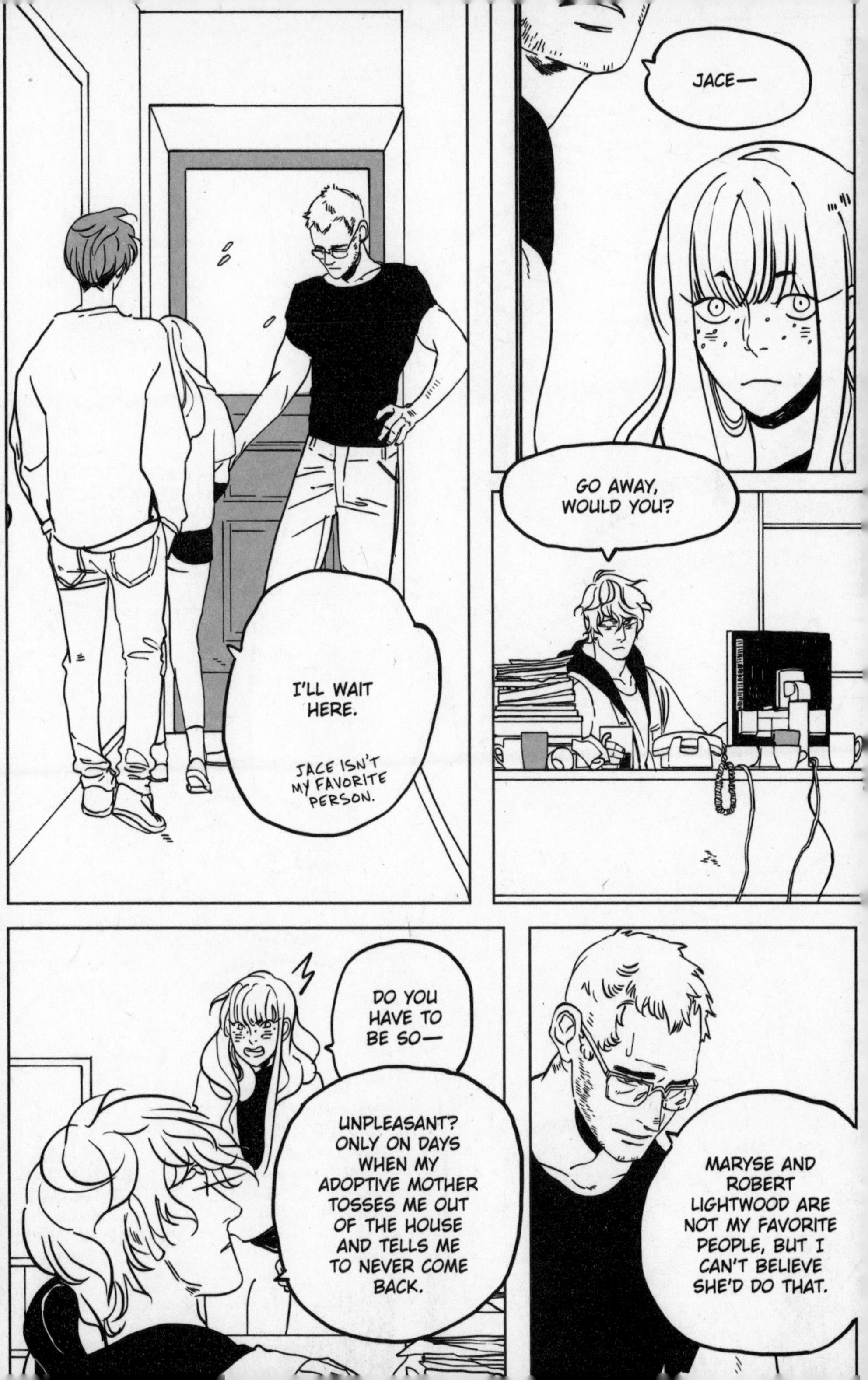
I'LL WAIT HERE.
JACE ISN'T MY FAVORITE PERSON.
JACE—
GO AWAY, WOULD YOU?
DO YOU HAVE TO BE SO—
UNPLEASANT? ONLY ON DAYS WHEN MY ADOPTIVE MOTHER TOSSES ME OUT OF THE HOUSE AND TELLS ME TO NEVER COME BACK.
MARYSE AND ROBERT LIGHTWOOD ARE NOT MY FAVORITE PEOPLE, BUT I CAN'T BELIEVE SHE'D DO THAT.

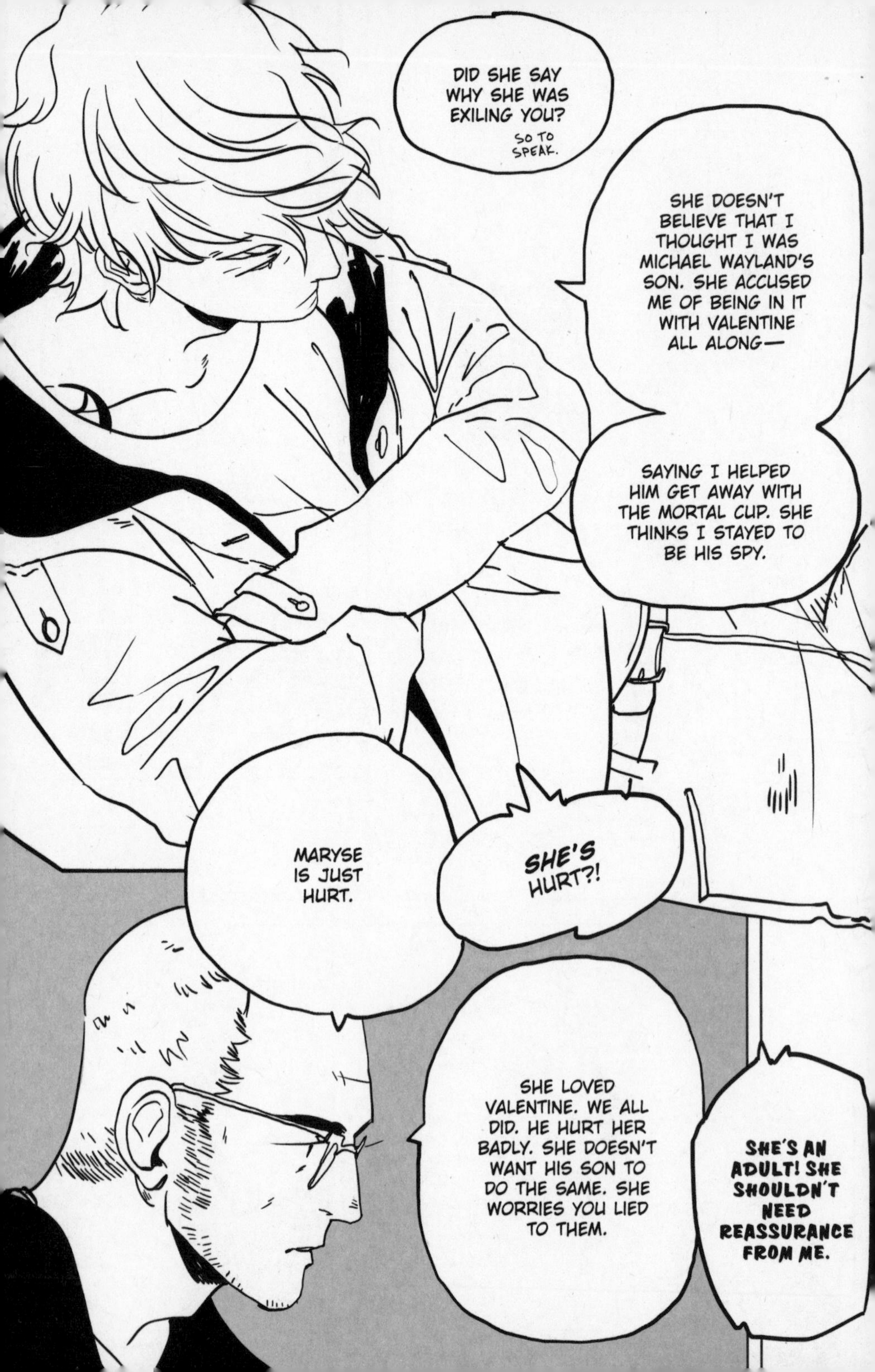
DID SHE SAY WHY SHE WAS EXILING YOU?
SO TO SPEAK.
SHE DOESN'T BELIEVE THAT I THOUGHT I WAS MICHAEL WAYLAND'S SON. SHE ACCUSED ME OF BEING IN IT WITH VALENTINE ALL ALONG—
SAYING I HELPED HIM GET AWAY WITH THE MORTAL CUP. SHE THINKS I STAYED TO BE HIS SPY.
MARYSE IS JUST HURT.
SHE'S HURT?!
SHE LOVED VALENTINE. WE ALL DID. HE HURT HER BADLY. SHE DOESN'T WANT HIS SON TO DO THE SAME. SHE WORRIES YOU LIED TO THEM.
SHE'S AN ADULT! SHE SHOULDN'T NEED REASSURANCE FROM ME.

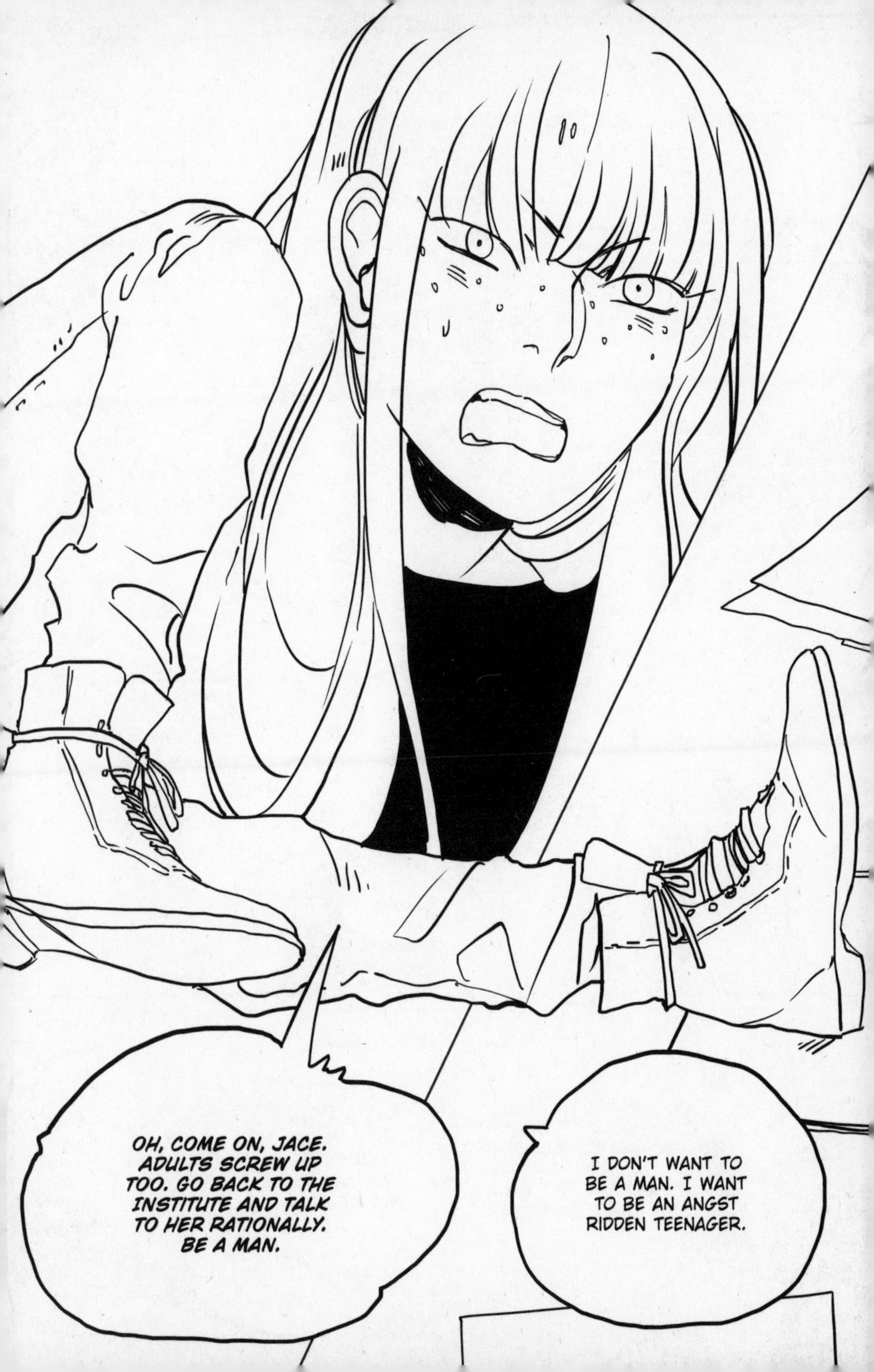
OH, COME ON, JACE. ADULTS SCREW UP TOO. GO BACK TO THE INSTITUTE AND TALK TO HER RATIONALLY. BE A MAN.
I DON'T WANT TO BE A MAN. I WANT TO BE AN ANGST RIDDEN TEENAGER.

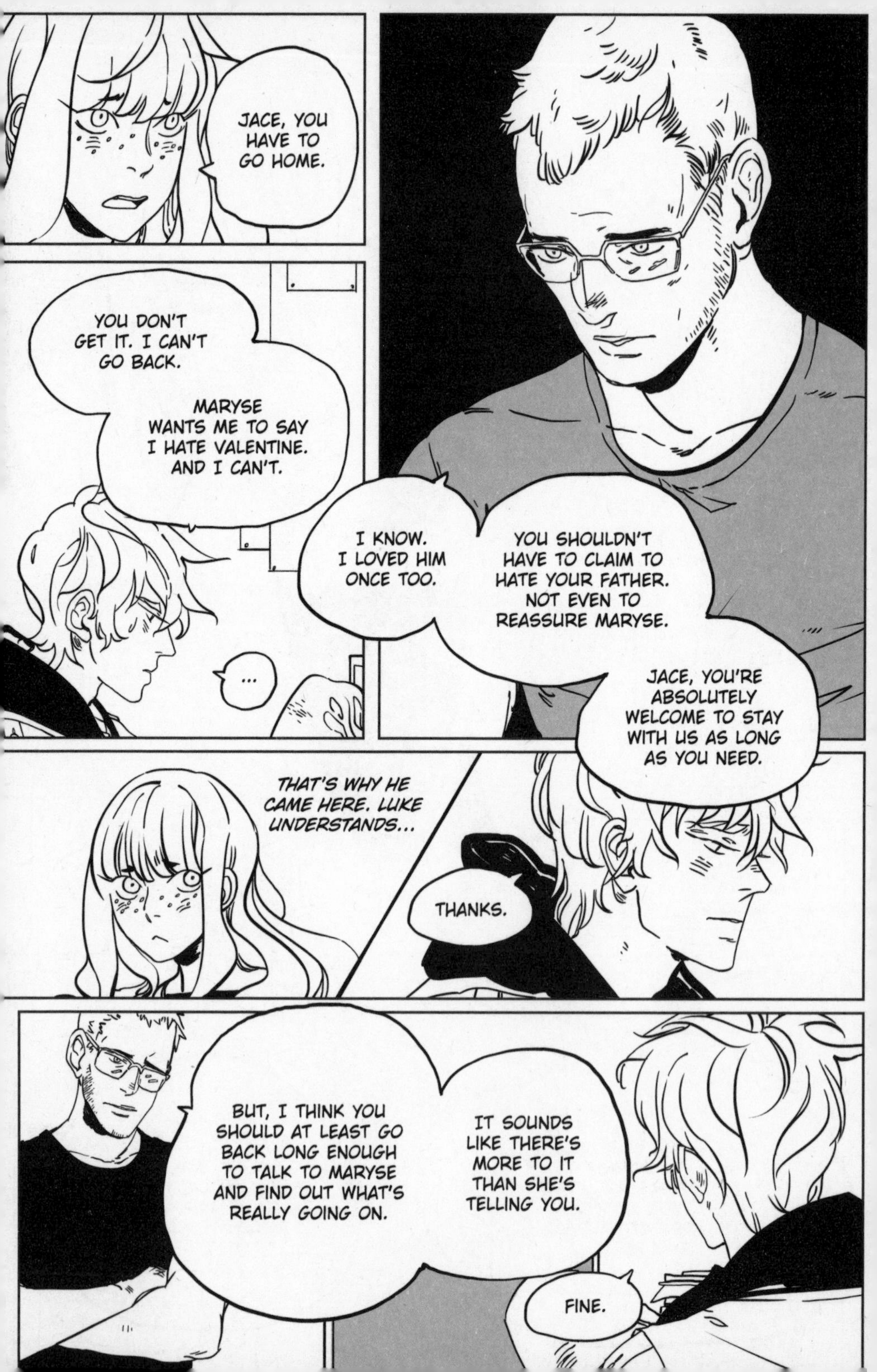
JACE, YOU HAVE TO GO HOME.
YOU DON'T GET IT. I CAN'T GO BACK.
MARYSE WANTS ME TO SAY I HATE VALENTINE. AND I CAN'T.
...
I KNOW. I LOVED HIM ONCE TOO.
YOU SHOULDN'T HAVE TO CLAIM TO HATE YOUR FATHER. NOT EVEN TO REASSURE MARYSE.
JACE, YOU'RE ABSOLUTELY WELCOME TO STAY WITH US AS LONG AS YOU NEED.
THAT'S WHY HE CAME HERE. LUKE UNDERSTANDS...
THANKS.
BUT, I THINK YOU SHOULD AT LEAST GO BACK LONG ENOUGH TO TALK TO MARYSE AND FIND OUT WHAT'S REALLY GOING ON.
IT SOUNDS LIKE THERE'S MORE TO IT THAN SHE'S TELLING YOU.
FINE.

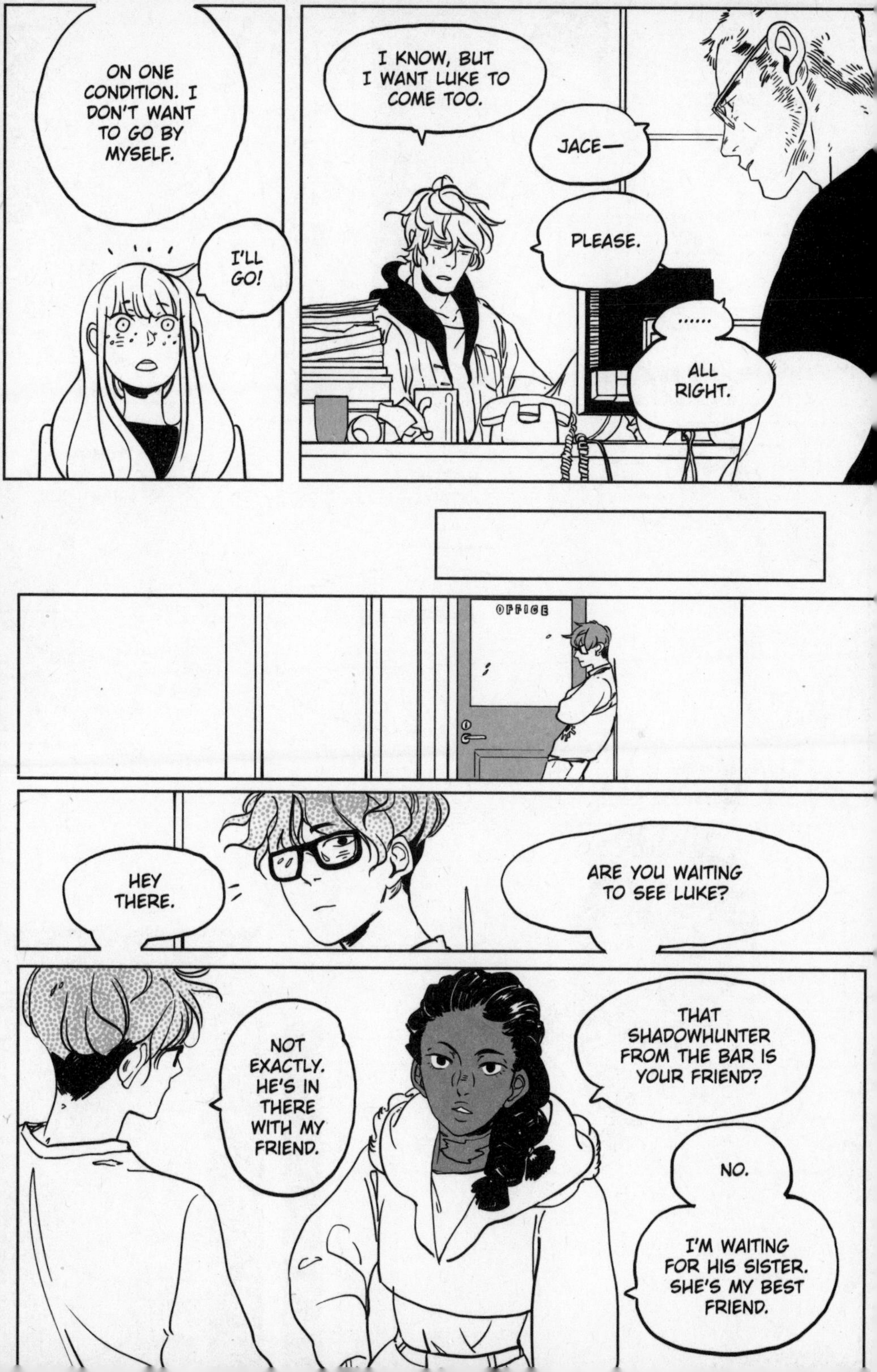
ON ONE CONDITION. I DON'T WANT TO GO BY MYSELF.
I'LL GO!
I KNOW, BUT I WANT LUKE TO COME TOO.
JACE—
PLEASE.
......
ALL RIGHT.
OFFICE
HEY THERE.
ARE YOU WAITING TO SEE LUKE?
NOT EXACTLY. HE'S IN THERE WITH MY FRIEND.
THAT SHADOWHUNTER FROM THE BAR IS YOUR FRIEND?
NO.
I'M WAITING FOR HIS SISTER. SHE'S MY BEST FRIEND.

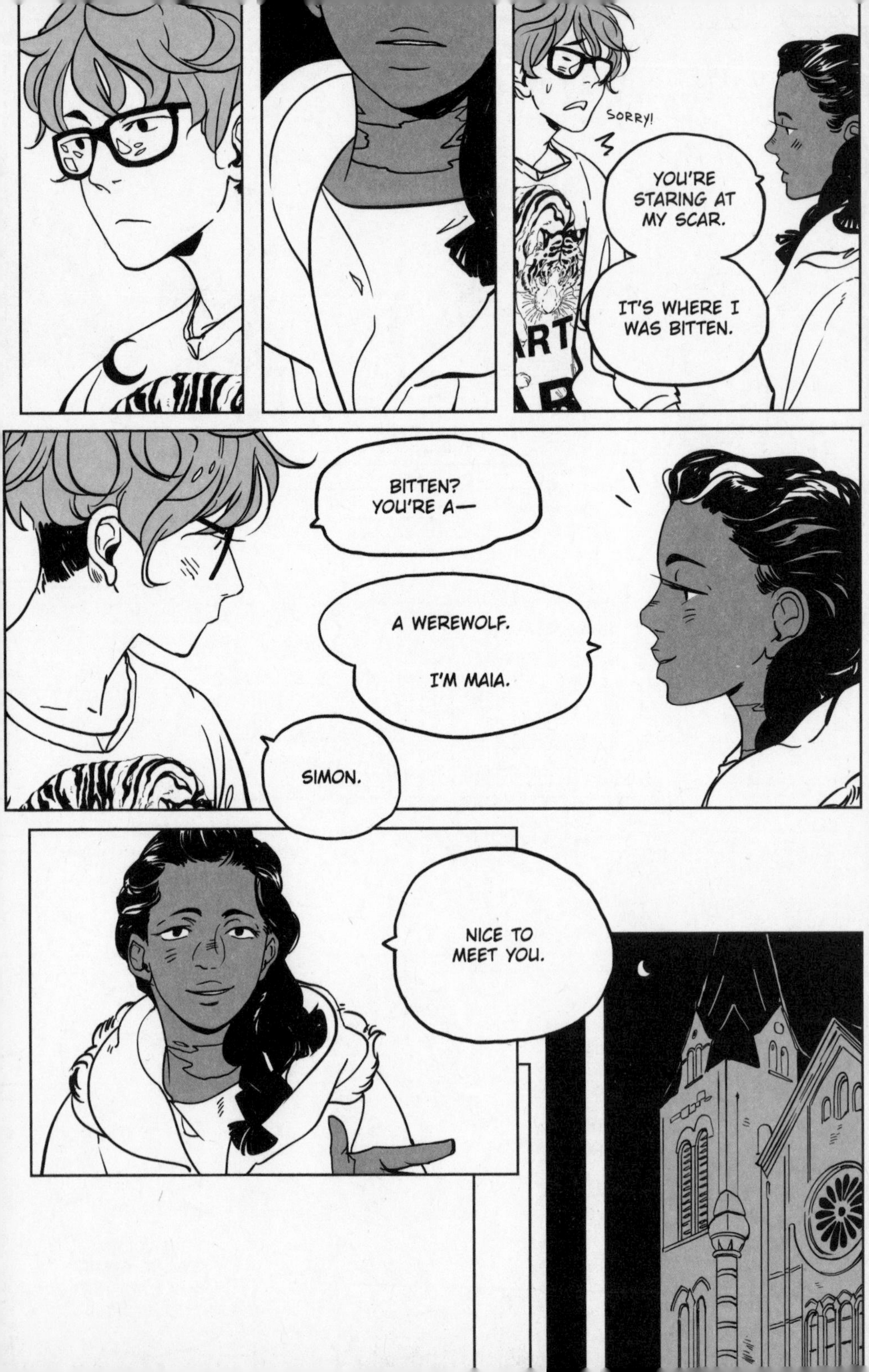
SORRY!
YOU'RE STARING AT MY SCAR.
IT'S WHERE I WAS BITTEN.
BITTEN? YOU'RE A—
A WEREWOLF.
I'M MAIA.
SIMON.
NICE TO MEET YOU.

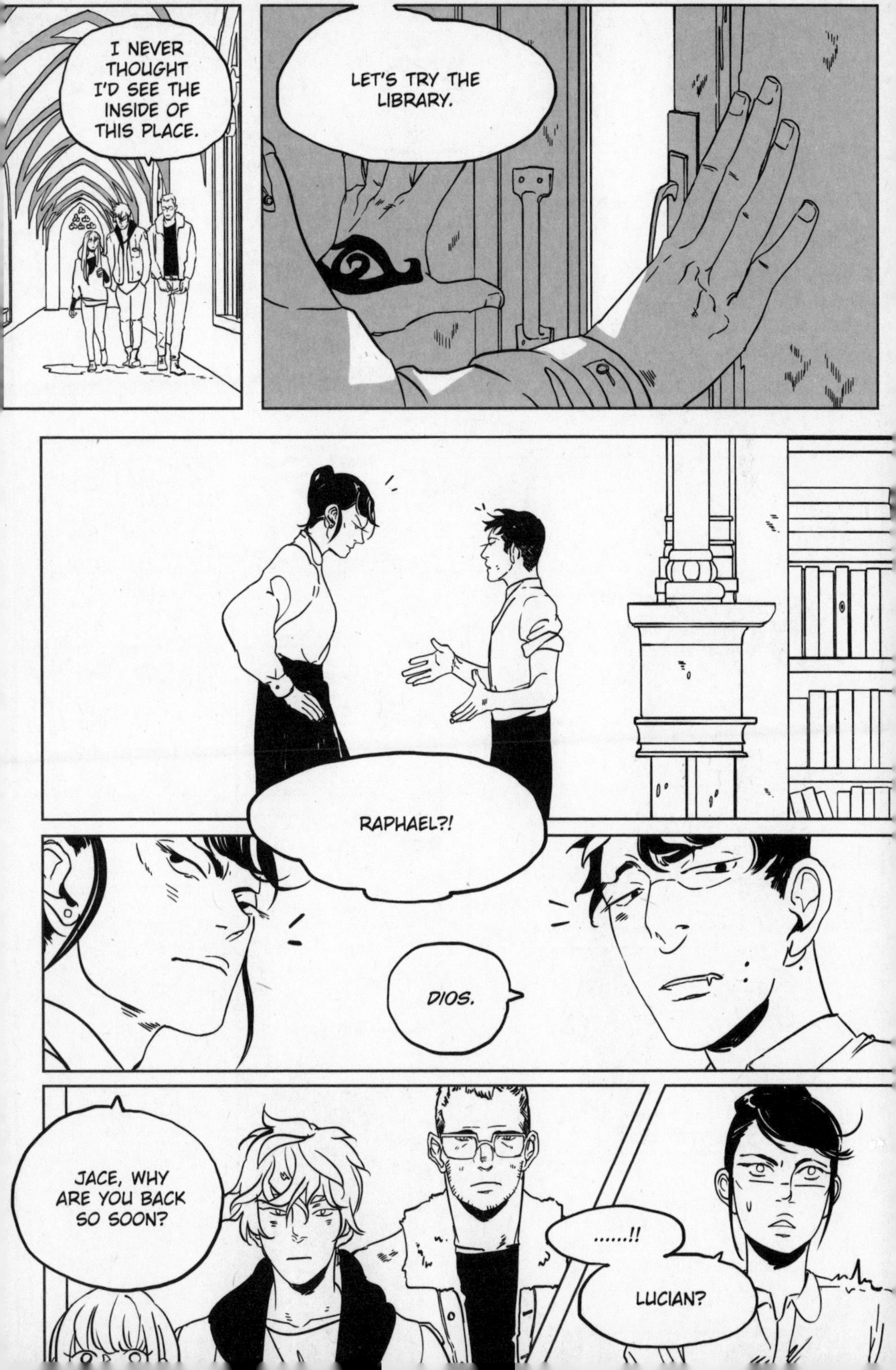
I NEVER THOUGHT I'D SEE THE INSIDE OF THIS PLACE.
LET'S TRY THE LIBRARY.
RAPHAEL?!
DIOS.
JACE, WHY ARE YOU BACK SO SOON?
......!!
LUCIAN?

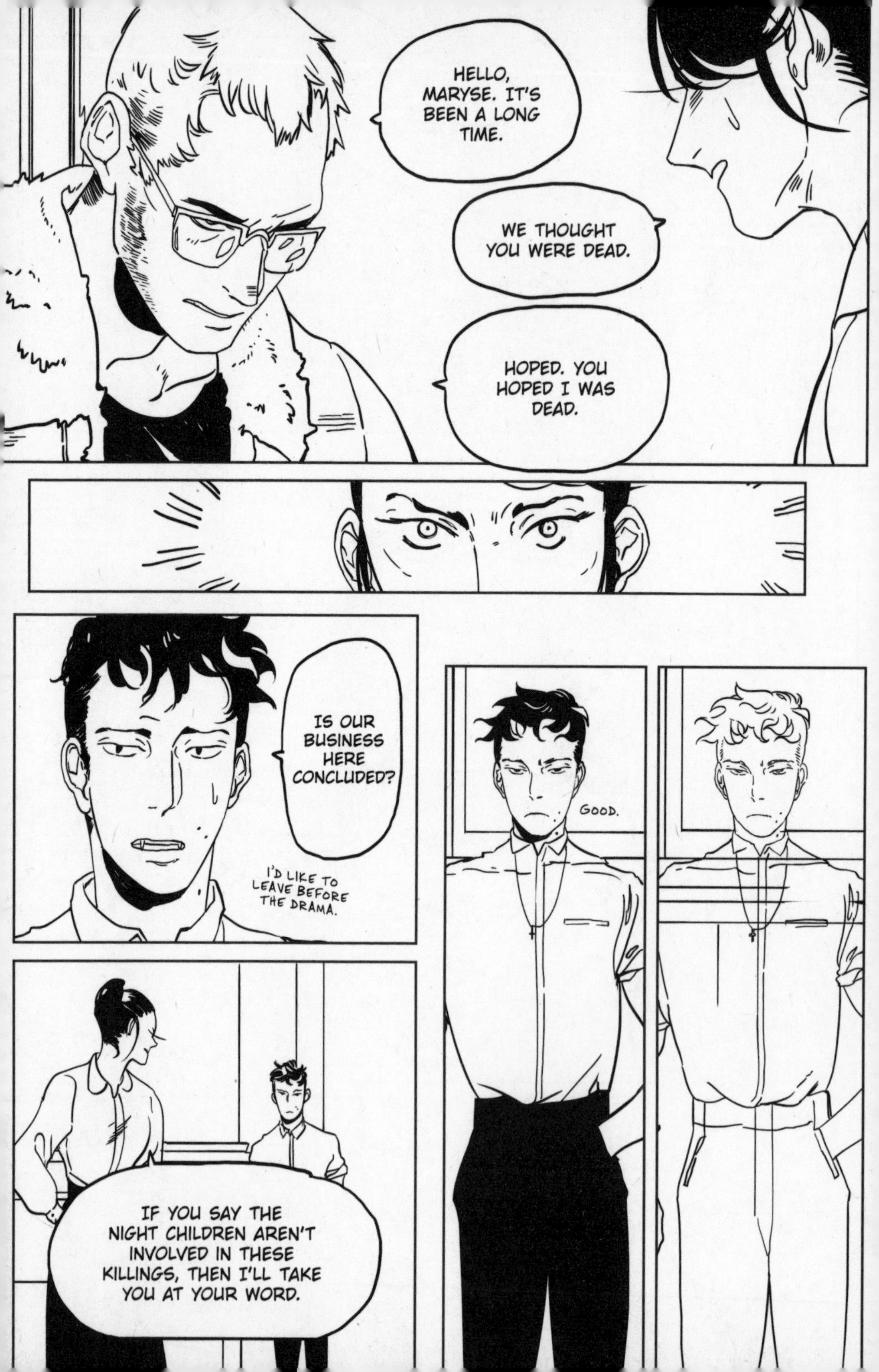
HELLO, MARYSE. IT'S BEEN A LONG TIME.
WE THOUGHT YOU WERE DEAD.
HOPED. YOU HOPED I WAS DEAD.
IS OUR BUSINESS HERE CONCLUDED?
I'D LIKE TO LEAVE BEFORE THE DRAMA.
GOOD.
IF YOU SAY THE NIGHT CHILDREN AREN'T INVOLVED IN THESE KILLINGS, THEN I'LL TAKE YOU AT YOUR WORD.

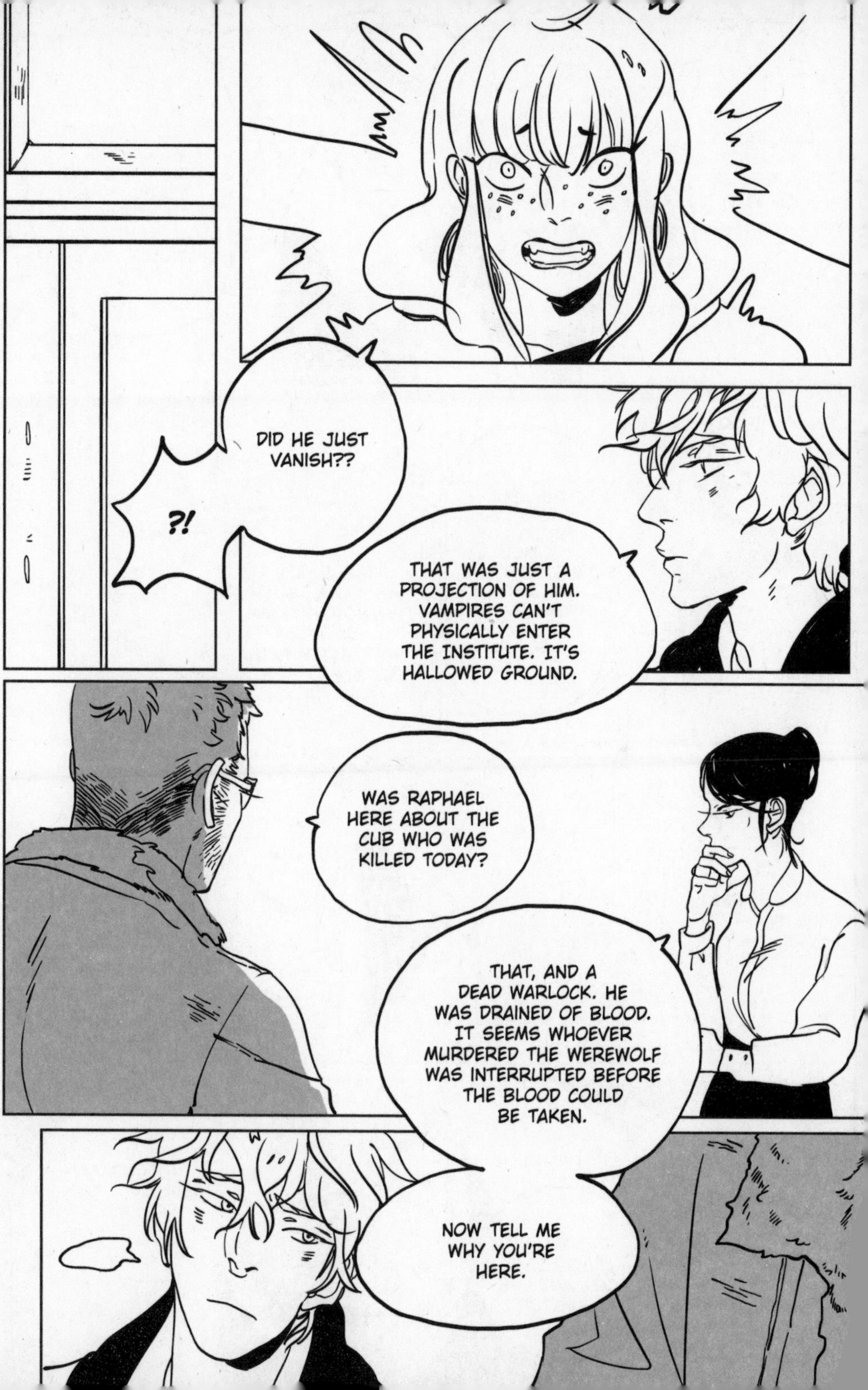
?!
DID HE JUST VANISH??
THAT WAS JUST A PROJECTION OF HIM. VAMPIRES CAN'T PHYSICALLY ENTER THE INSTITUTE. IT'S HALLOWED GROUND.
WAS RAPHAEL HERE ABOUT THE CUB WHO WAS KILLED TODAY?
THAT, AND A DEAD WARLOCK. HE WAS DRAINED OF BLOOD. IT SEEMS WHOEVER MURDERED THE WEREWOLF WAS INTERRUPTED BEFORE THE BLOOD COULD BE TAKEN.
NOW TELL ME WHY YOU'RE HERE.

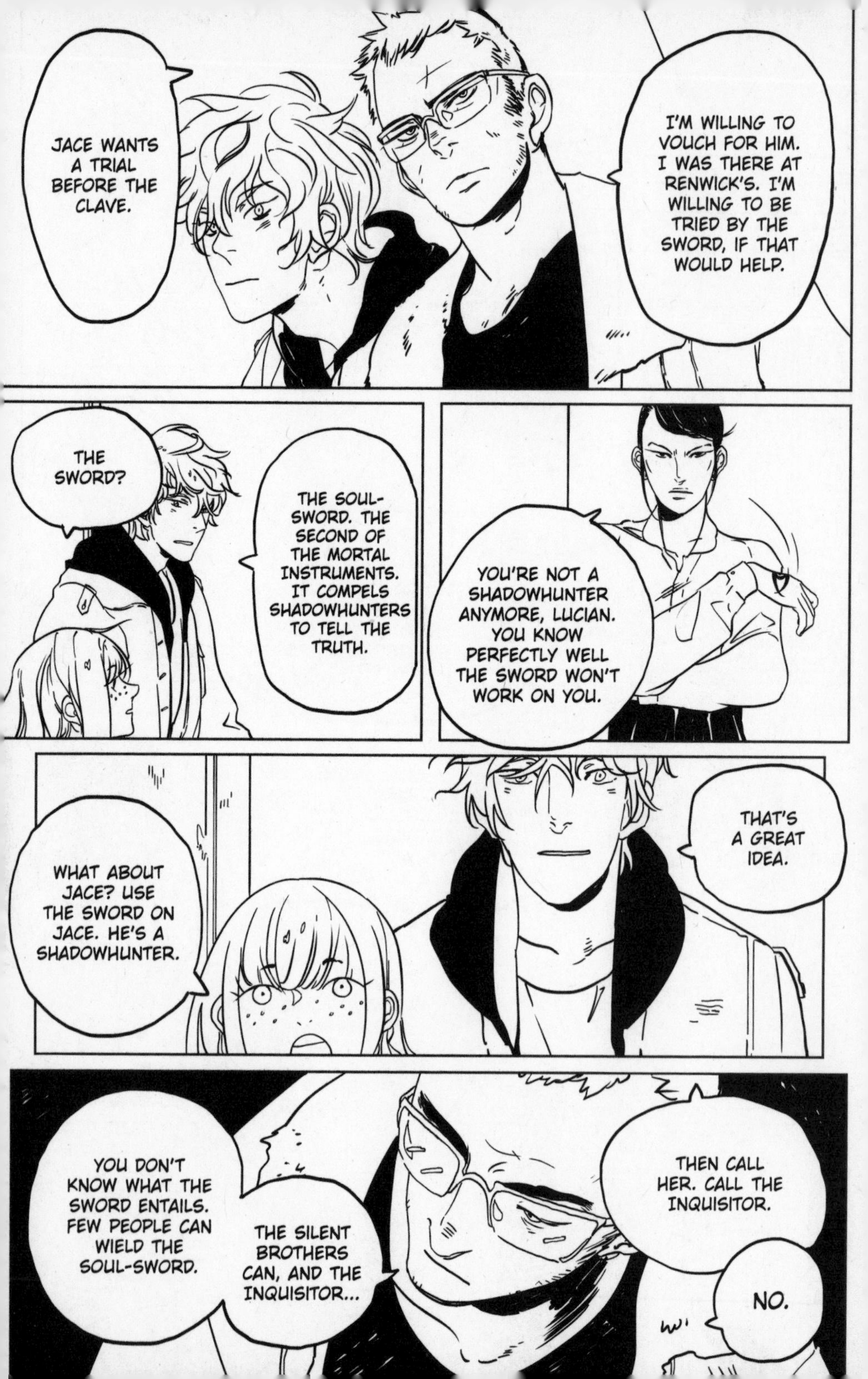
JACE WANTS A TRIAL BEFORE THE CLAVE.
I'M WILLING TO VOUCH FOR HIM. I WAS THERE AT RENWICK'S. I'M WILLING TO BE TRIED BY THE SWORD, IF THAT WOULD HELP.
THE SWORD?
THE SOUL-SWORD. THE SECOND OF THE MORTAL INSTRUMENTS. IT COMPELS SHADOWHUNTERS TO TELL THE TRUTH.
YOU'RE NOT A SHADOWHUNTER ANYMORE, LUCIAN. YOU KNOW PERFECTLY WELL THE SWORD WON'T WORK ON YOU.
WHAT ABOUT JACE? USE THE SWORD ON JACE. HE'S A SHADOWHUNTER.
THAT'S A GREAT IDEA.
YOU DON'T KNOW WHAT THE SWORD ENTAILS. FEW PEOPLE CAN WIELD THE SOUL-SWORD.
THE SILENT BROTHERS CAN, AND THE INQUISITOR...
THEN CALL HER. CALL THE INQUISITOR.
NO.

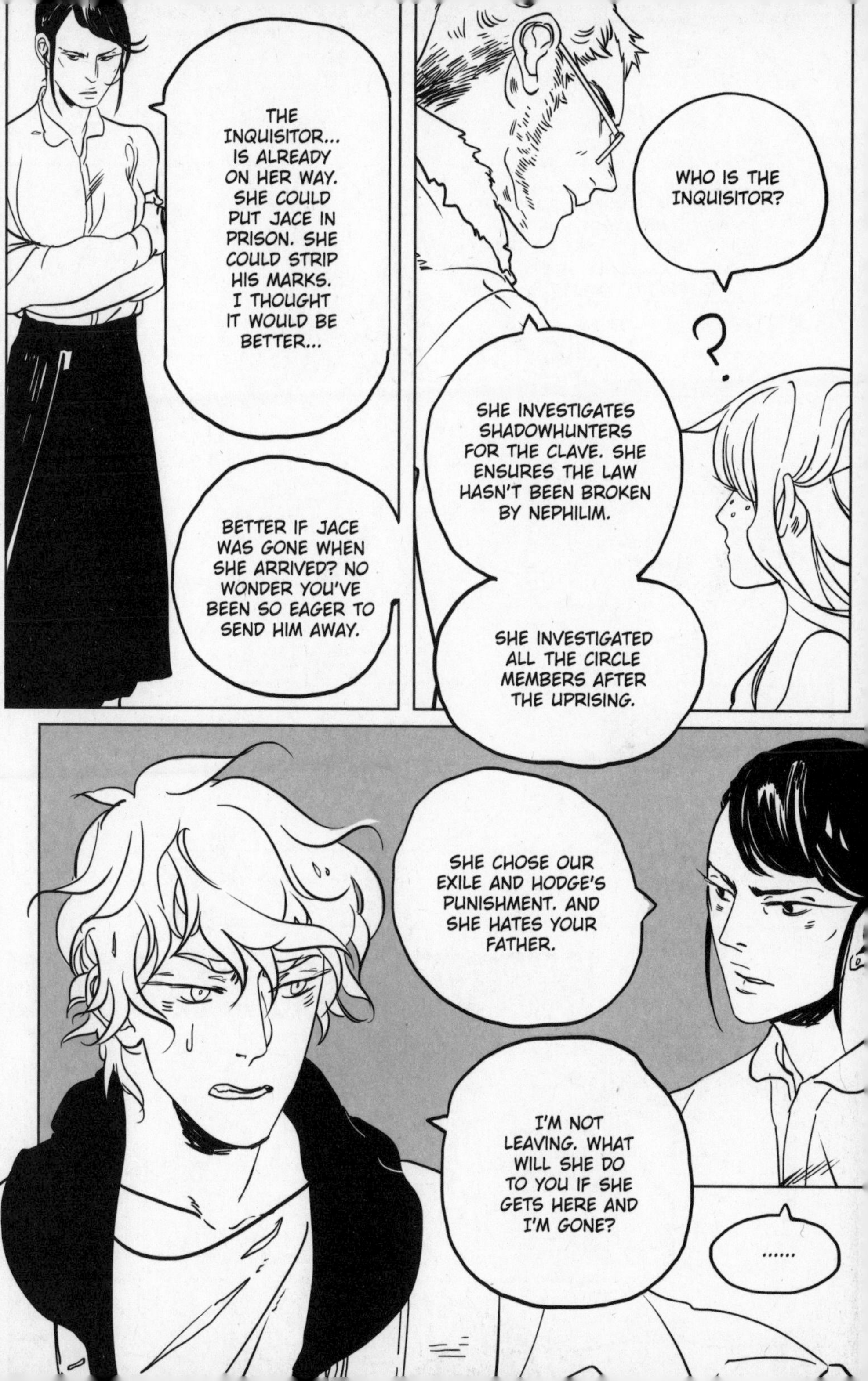
THE INQUISITOR... IS ALREADY ON HER WAY. SHE COULD PUT JACE IN PRISON. SHE COULD STRIP HIS MARKS. I THOUGHT IT WOULD BE BETTER...
BETTER IF JACE WAS GONE WHEN SHE ARRIVED? NO WONDER YOU'VE BEEN SO EAGER TO SEND HIM AWAY.
WHO IS THE INQUISITOR?
?
SHE INVESTIGATES SHADOWHUNTERS FOR THE CLAVE. SHE ENSURES THE LAW HASN'T BEEN BROKEN BY NEPHILIM.
SHE INVESTIGATED ALL THE CIRCLE MEMBERS AFTER THE UPRISING.
SHE CHOSE OUR EXILE AND HODGE'S PUNISHMENT. AND SHE HATES YOUR FATHER.
I'M NOT LEAVING. WHAT WILL SHE DO TO YOU IF SHE GETS HERE AND I'M GONE?
......

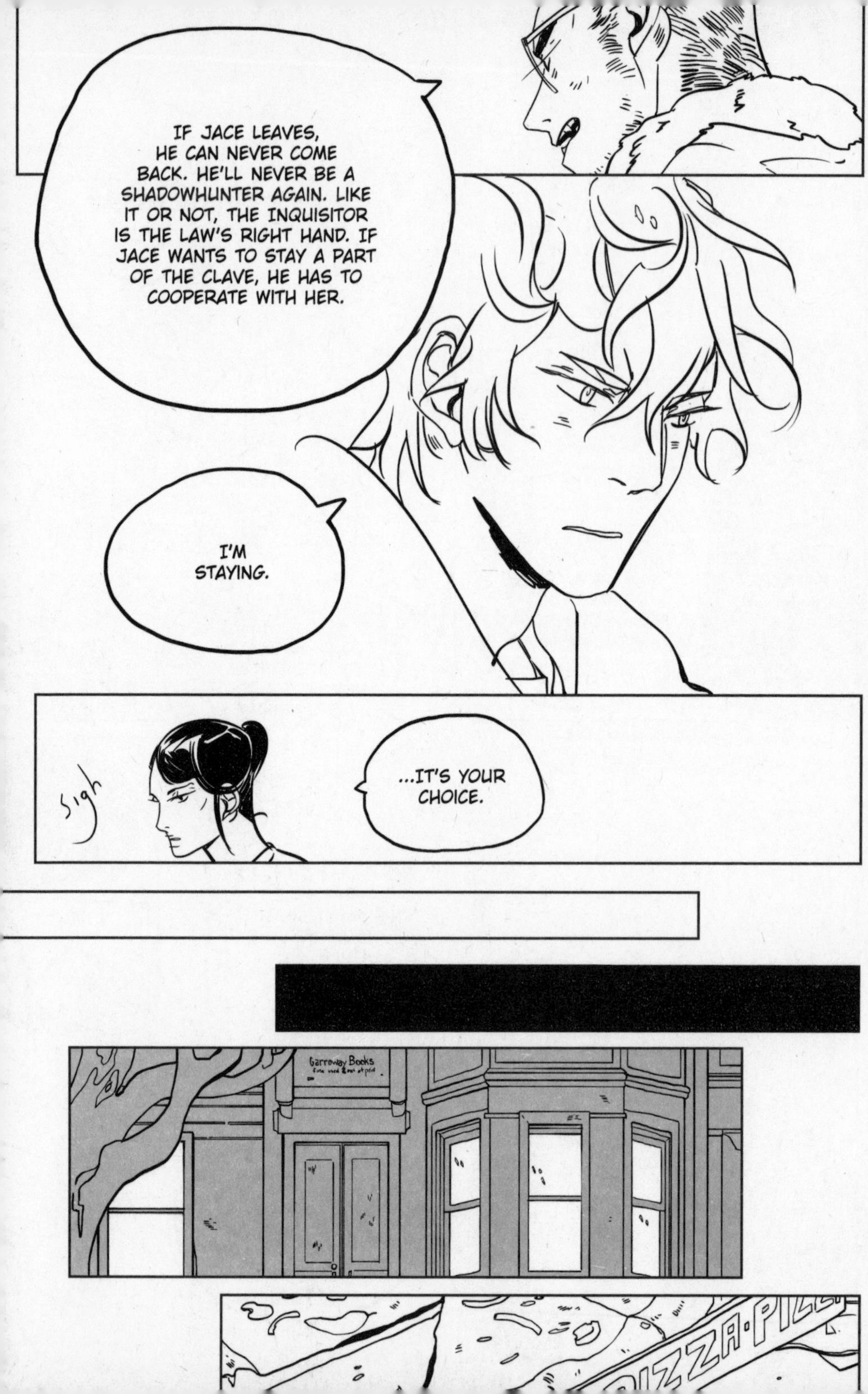

IF JACE LEAVES, HE CAN NEVER COME BACK. HE'LL NEVER BE A SHADOWHUNTER AGAIN. LIKE IT OR NOT, THE INQUISITOR IS THE LAW'S RIGHT HAND. IF JACE WANTS TO STAY A PART OF THE CLAVE, HE HAS TO COOPERATE WITH HER.
I'M STAYING.
sigh
...IT'S YOUR CHOICE.
Garroway Books
PIZZA

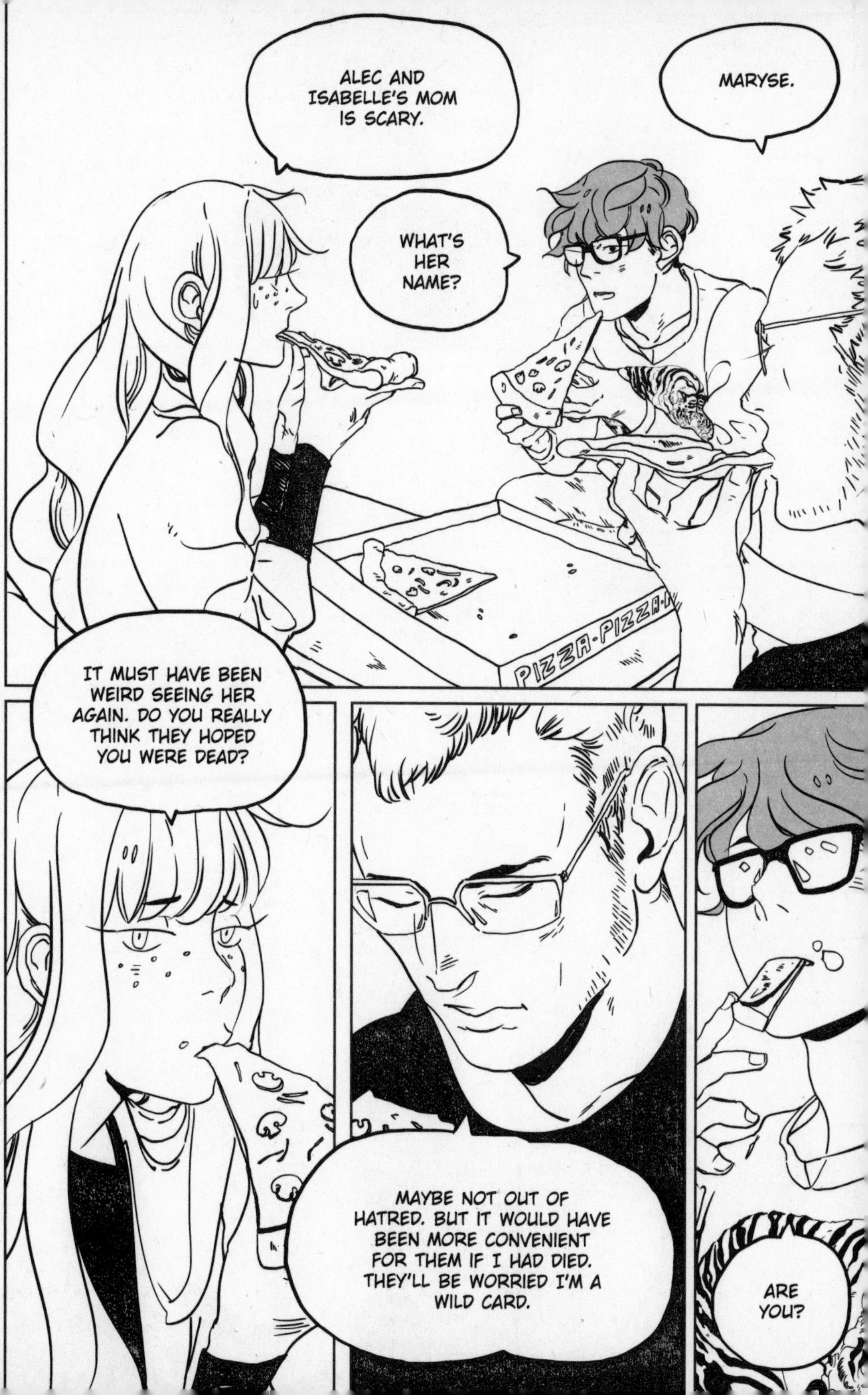
ALEC AND ISABELLE'S MOM IS SCARY.
WHAT'S HER NAME?
MARYSE.
IT MUST HAVE BEEN WEIRD SEEING HER AGAIN. DO YOU REALLY THINK THEY HOPED YOU WERE DEAD?
PIZZA-PIZZA
MAYBE NOT OUT OF HATRED. BUT IT WOULD HAVE BEEN MORE CONVENIENT FOR THEM IF I HAD DIED. THEY'LL BE WORRIED I'M A WILD CARD.
ARE YOU?

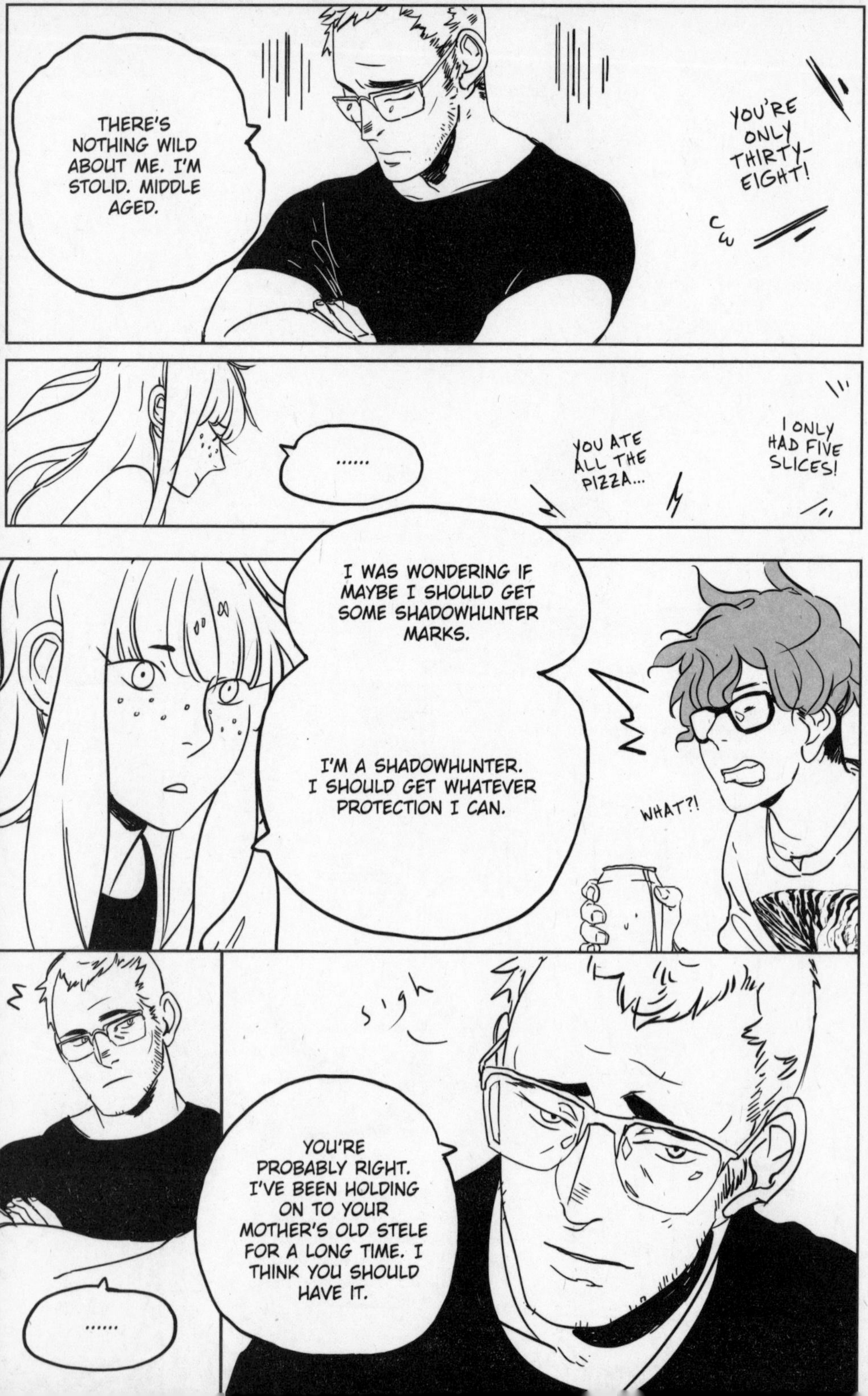
THERE'S NOTHING WILD ABOUT ME. I'M STOLID. MIDDLE AGED.
YOU'RE ONLY THIRTY-EIGHT!
CW
......
YOU ATE ALL THE PIZZA...
I ONLY HAD FIVE SLICES!
I WAS WONDERING IF MAYBE I SHOULD GET SOME SHADOWHUNTER MARKS.
I'M A SHADOWHUNTER. I SHOULD GET WHATEVER PROTECTION I CAN.
WHAT?!
sigh
YOU'RE PROBABLY RIGHT. I'VE BEEN HOLDING ON TO YOUR MOTHER'S OLD STELE FOR A LONG TIME. I THINK YOU SHOULD HAVE IT.
......

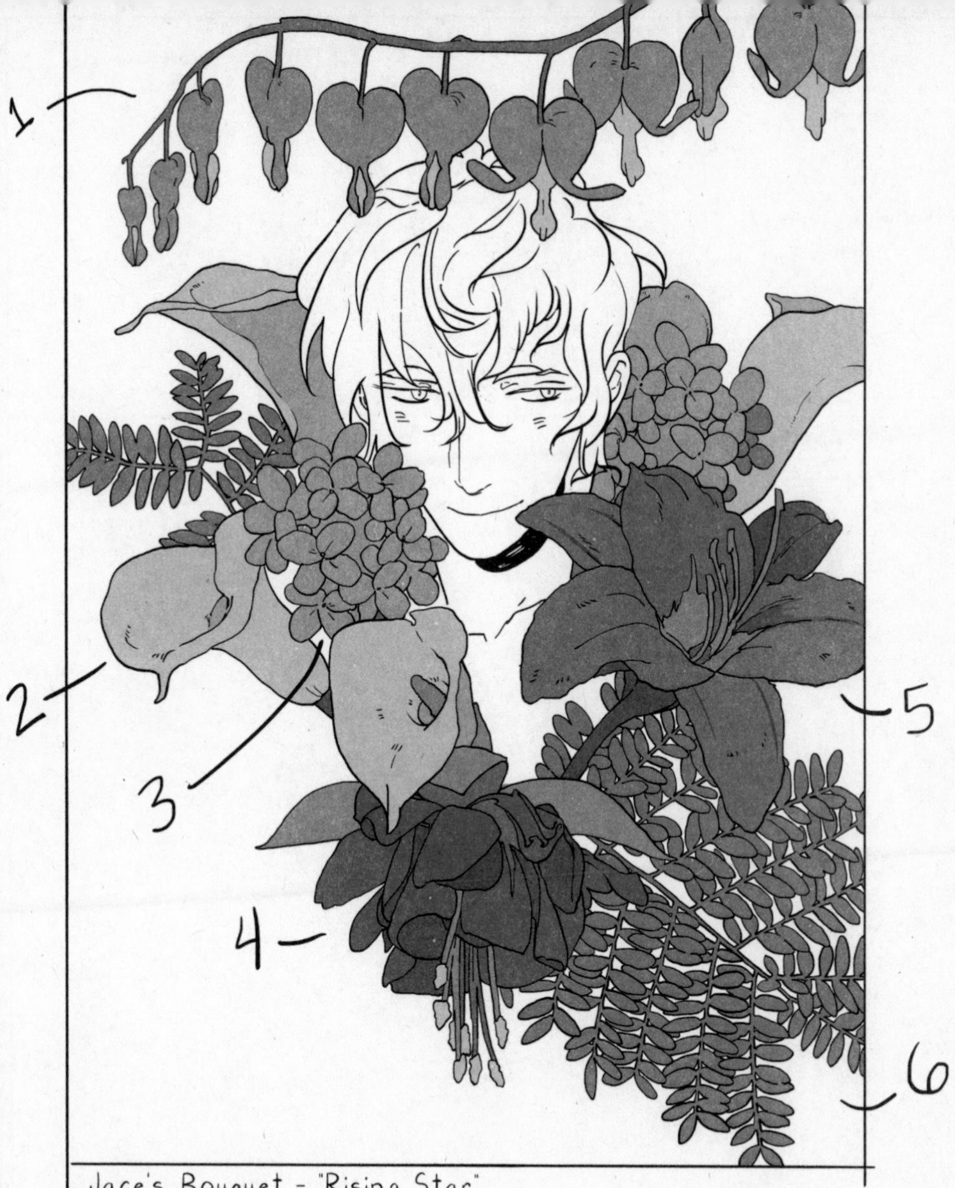
1
2
3
4
5
6

Jace's Bouquet - "Rising Star"

1) Bleeding Heart - Elegance

2) Calla Lily - Panache and Magnificent Beauty

3) Rocket - Vanity

4) Fuchsia - Taste

5) Daylily - Coquetry

6) Honey Locust- Elegance

THE MORTAL INSTRUMENTS

THE GRAPHIC NOVEL

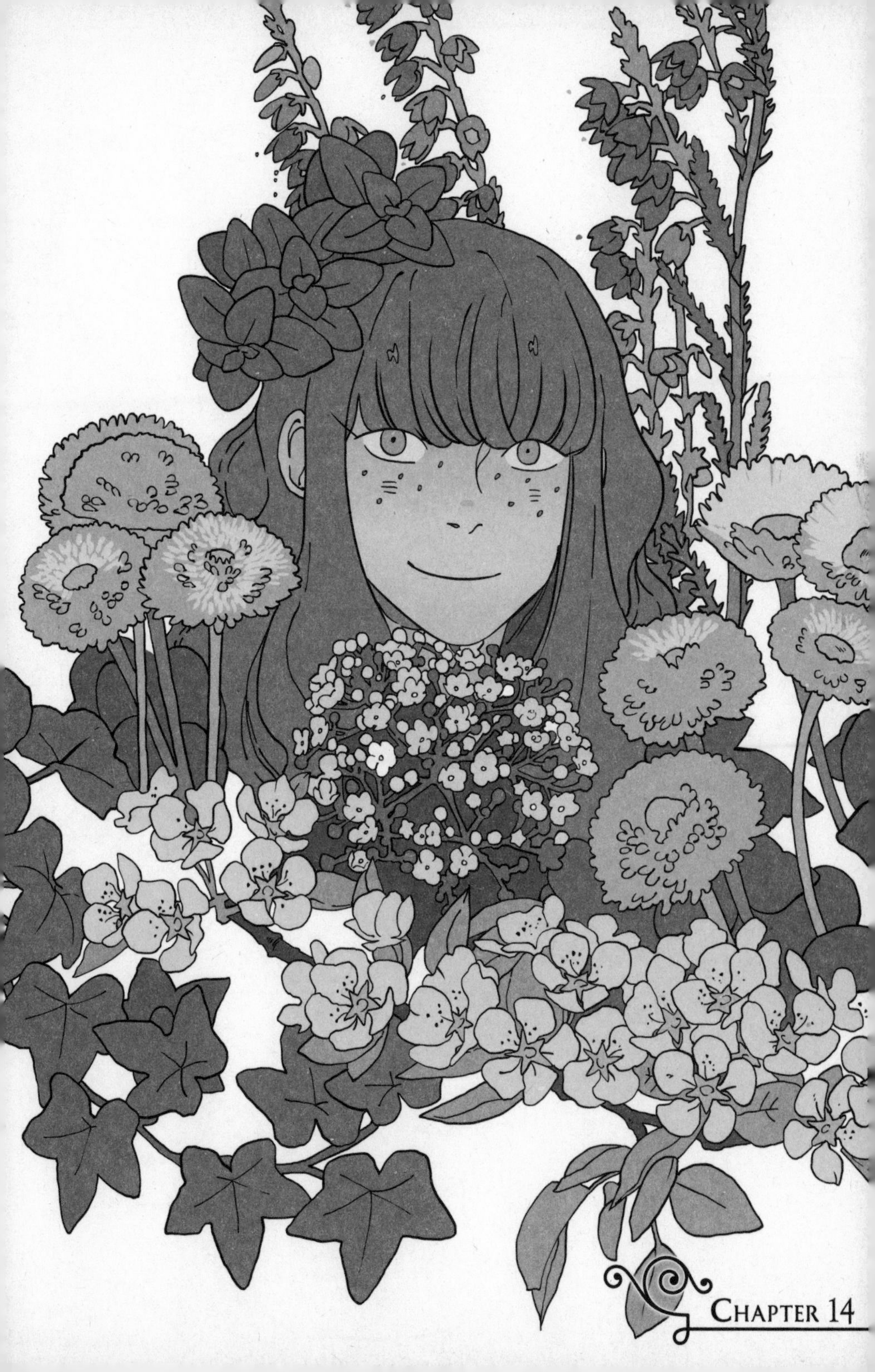

Chapter 14

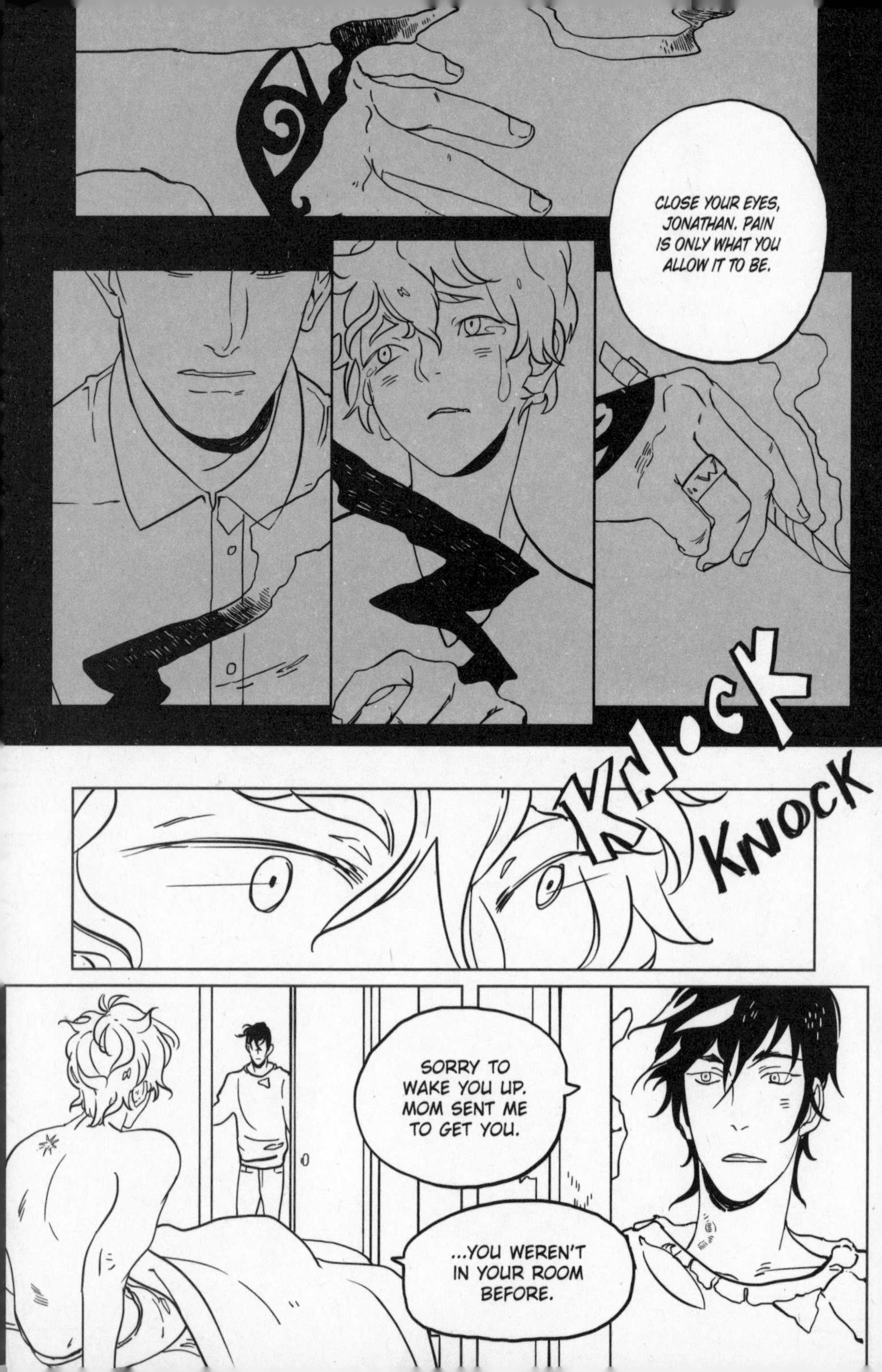
CLOSE YOUR EYES, JONATHAN. PAIN IS ONLY WHAT YOU ALLOW IT TO BE.
KNOCK
KNOCK
SORRY TO WAKE YOU UP. MOM SENT ME TO GET YOU.
...YOU WEREN'T IN YOUR ROOM BEFORE.

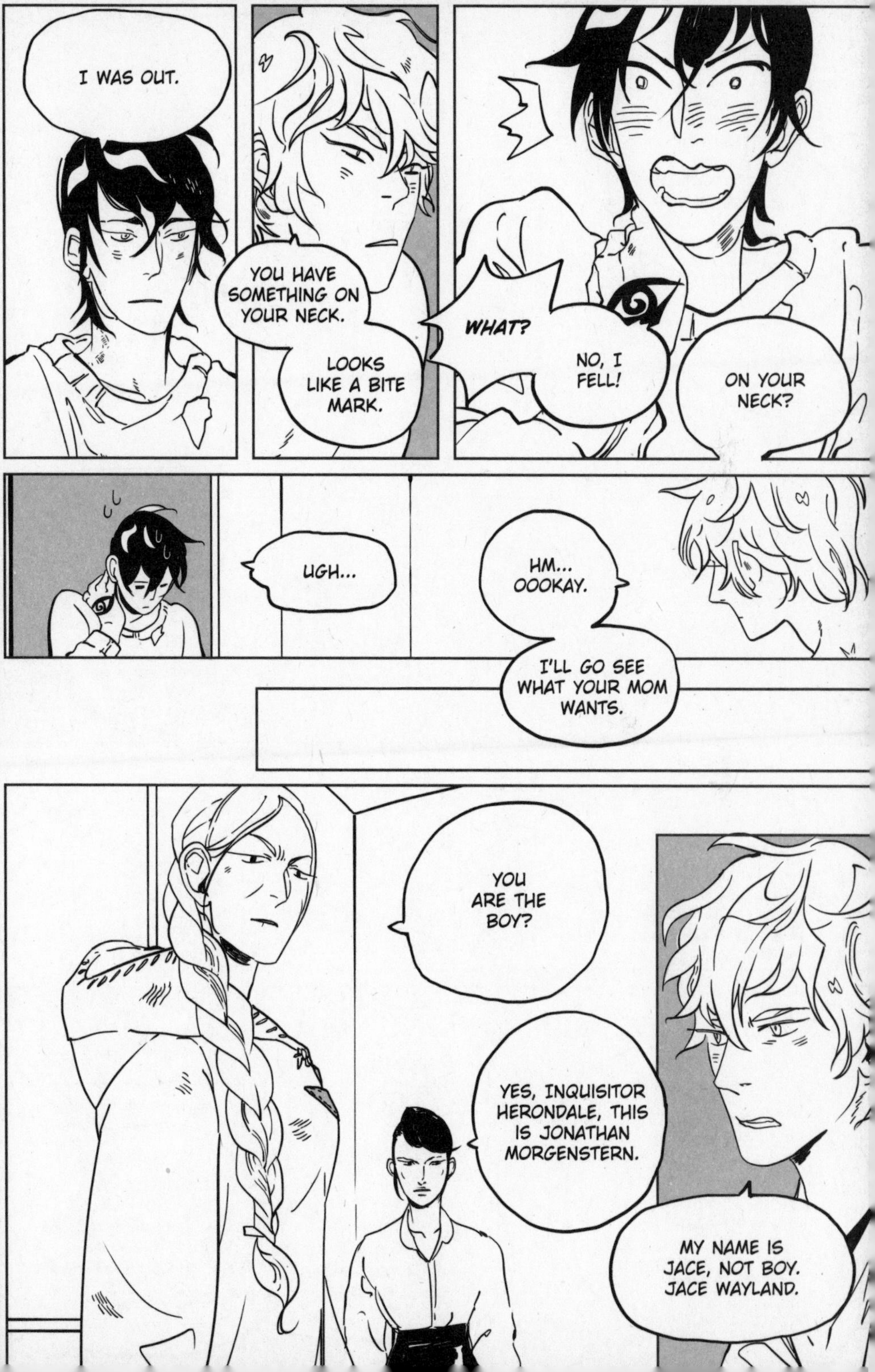
I WAS OUT.
YOU HAVE SOMETHING ON YOUR NECK.
LOOKS LIKE A BITE MARK.
WHAT?
NO, I FELL!
ON YOUR NECK?
UGH...
HM... OOOKAY.
I'LL GO SEE WHAT YOUR MOM WANTS.
YOU ARE THE BOY?
YES, INQUISITOR HERONDALE, THIS IS JONATHAN MORGENSTERN.
MY NAME IS JACE, NOT BOY. JACE WAYLAND.

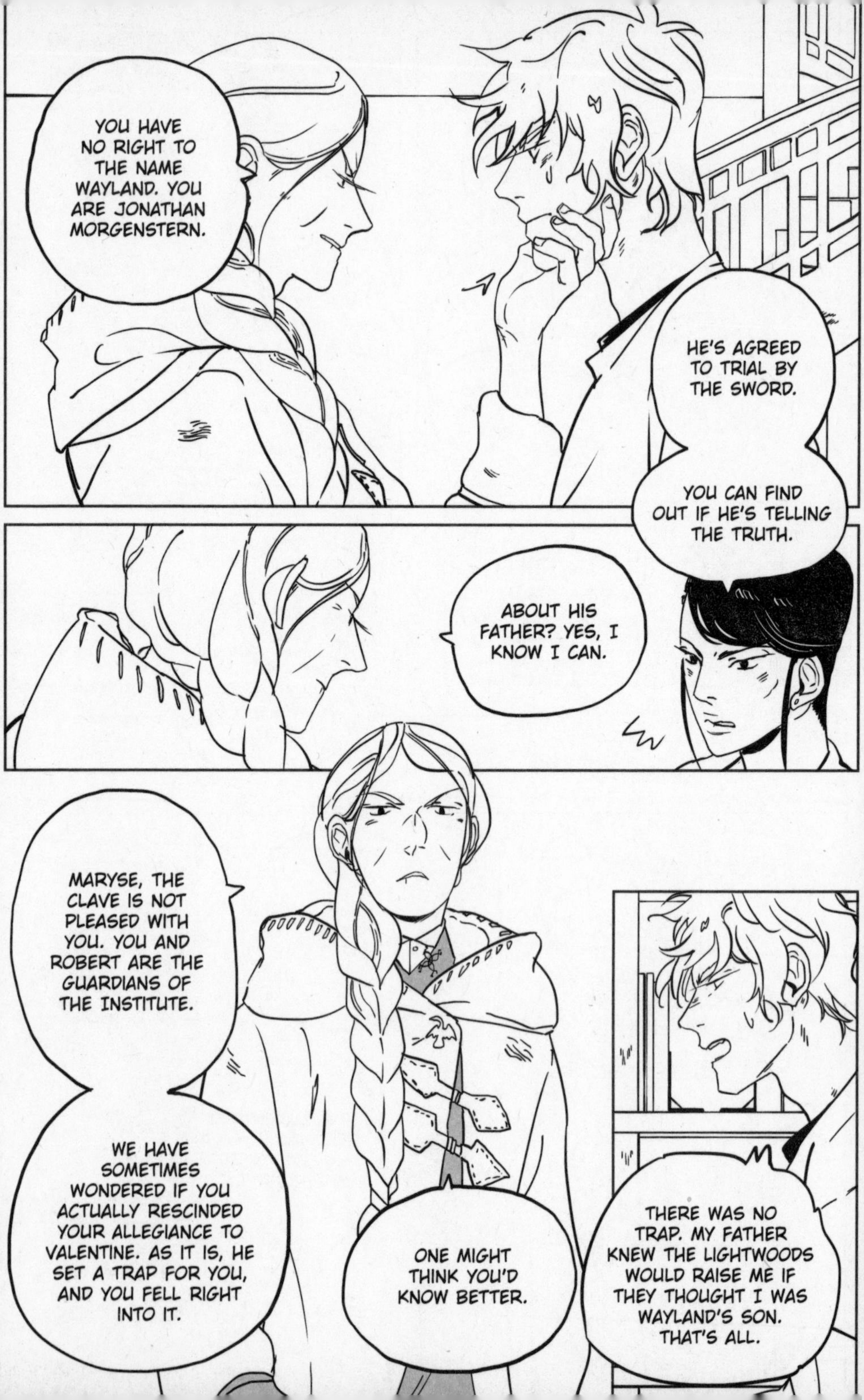
YOU HAVE NO RIGHT TO THE NAME WAYLAND. YOU ARE JONATHAN MORGENSTERN.
HE'S AGREED TO TRIAL BY THE SWORD.
YOU CAN FIND OUT IF HE'S TELLING THE TRUTH.
ABOUT HIS FATHER? YES, I KNOW I CAN.
MARYSE, THE CLAVE IS NOT PLEASED WITH YOU. YOU AND ROBERT ARE THE GUARDIANS OF THE INSTITUTE.
WE HAVE SOMETIMES WONDERED IF YOU ACTUALLY RESCINDED YOUR ALLEGIANCE TO VALENTINE. AS IT IS, HE SET A TRAP FOR YOU, AND YOU FELL RIGHT INTO IT.
ONE MIGHT THINK YOU'D KNOW BETTER.
THERE WAS NO TRAP. MY FATHER KNEW THE LIGHTWOODS WOULD RAISE ME IF THEY THOUGHT I WAS WAYLAND'S SON. THAT'S ALL.

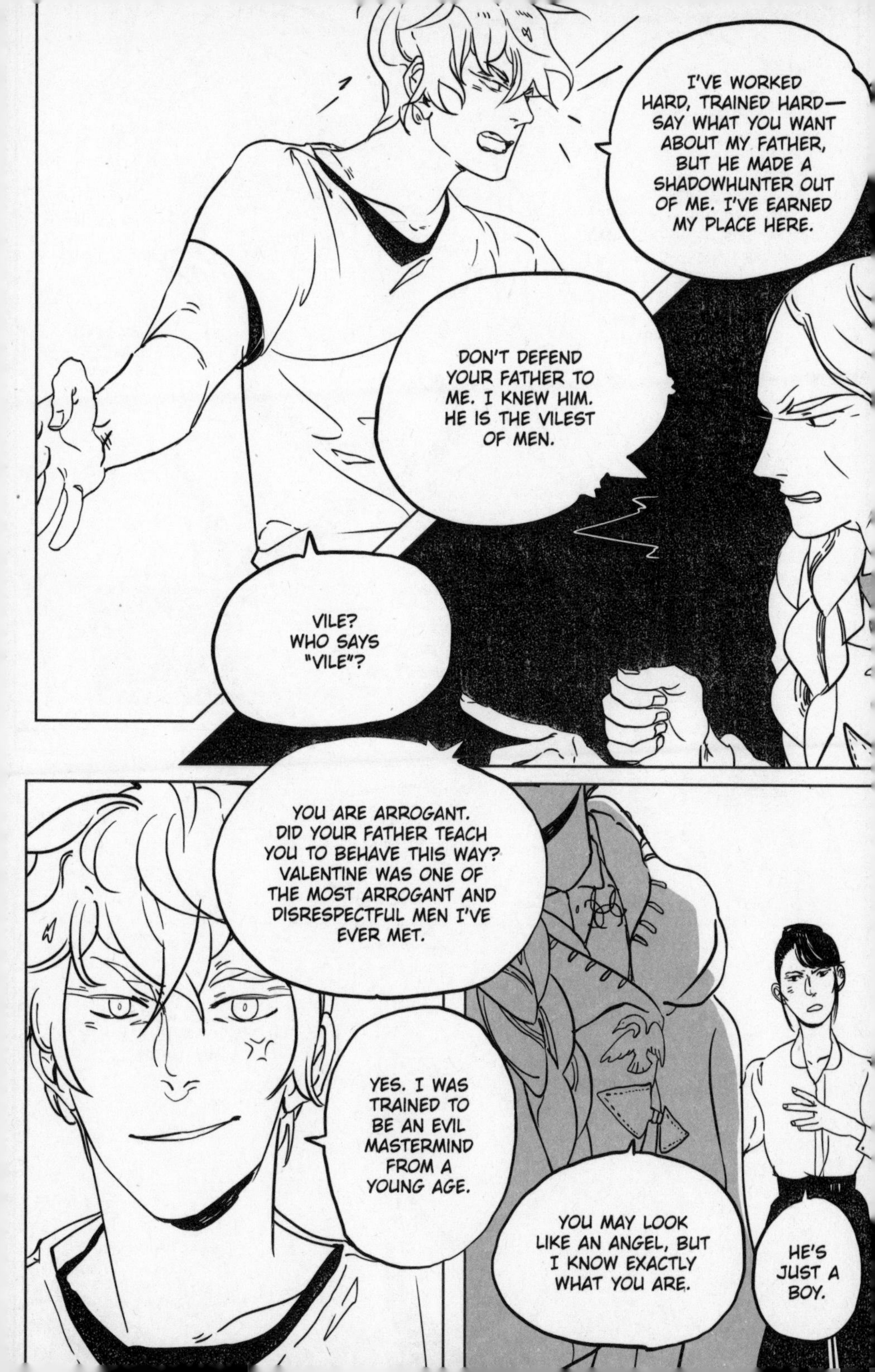
I'VE WORKED HARD, TRAINED HARD—SAY WHAT YOU WANT ABOUT MY FATHER, BUT HE MADE A SHADOWHUNTER OUT OF ME. I'VE EARNED MY PLACE HERE.
DON'T DEFEND YOUR FATHER TO ME. I KNEW HIM. HE IS THE VILEST OF MEN.
VILE? WHO SAYS "VILE"?
YOU ARE ARROGANT. DID YOUR FATHER TEACH YOU TO BEHAVE THIS WAY? VALENTINE WAS ONE OF THE MOST ARROGANT AND DISRESPECTFUL MEN I'VE EVER MET.
YES. I WAS TRAINED TO BE AN EVIL MASTERMIND FROM A YOUNG AGE.
YOU MAY LOOK LIKE AN ANGEL, BUT I KNOW EXACTLY WHAT YOU ARE.
HE'S JUST A BOY.

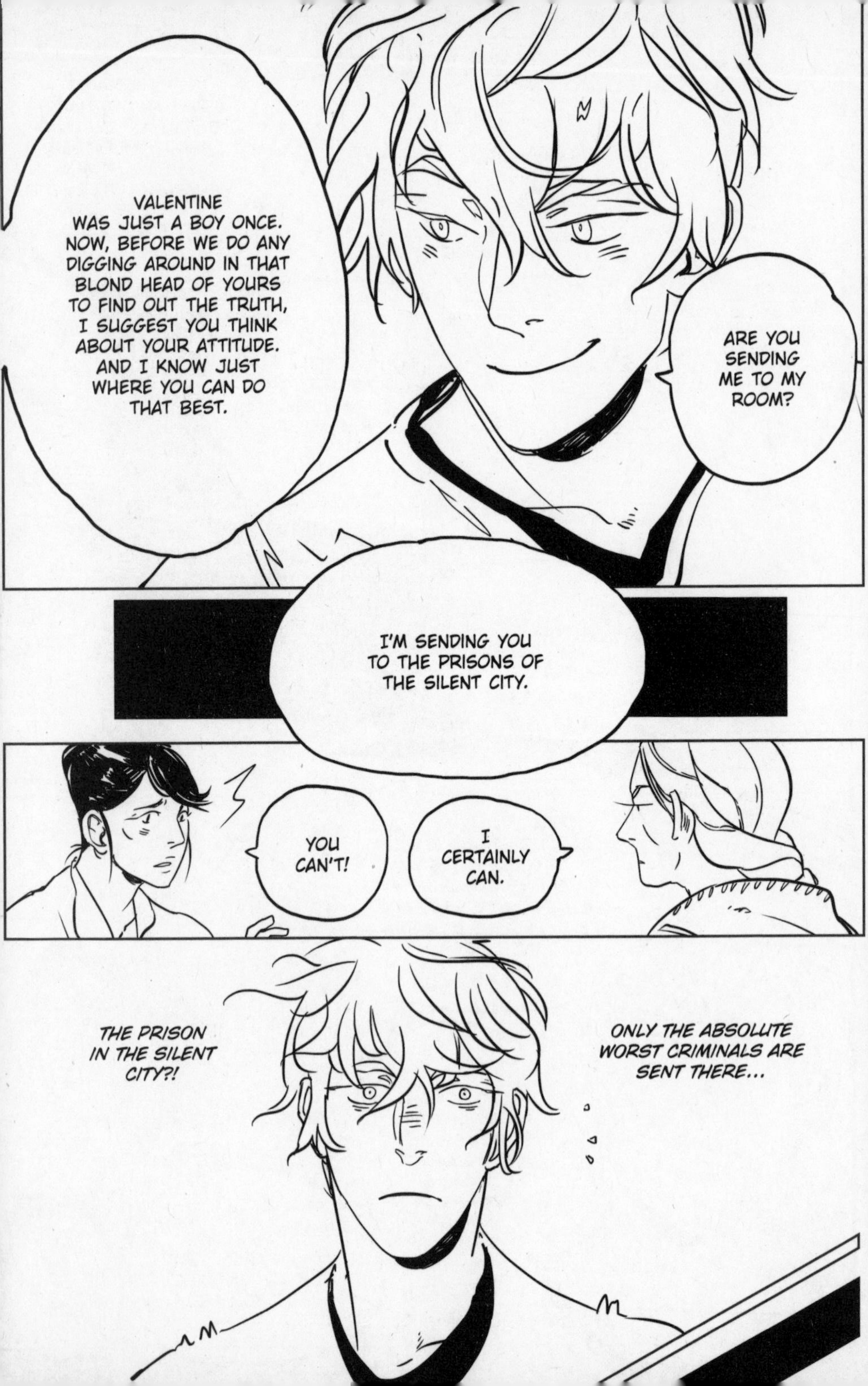
VALENTINE WAS JUST A BOY ONCE. NOW, BEFORE WE DO ANY DIGGING AROUND IN THAT BLOND HEAD OF YOURS TO FIND OUT THE TRUTH, I SUGGEST YOU THINK ABOUT YOUR ATTITUDE. AND I KNOW JUST WHERE YOU CAN DO THAT BEST.
ARE YOU SENDING ME TO MY ROOM?
I'M SENDING YOU TO THE PRISONS OF THE SILENT CITY.
YOU CAN'T!
I CERTAINLY CAN.
THE PRISON IN THE SILENT CITY?!
ONLY THE ABSOLUTE WORST CRIMINALS ARE SENT THERE...

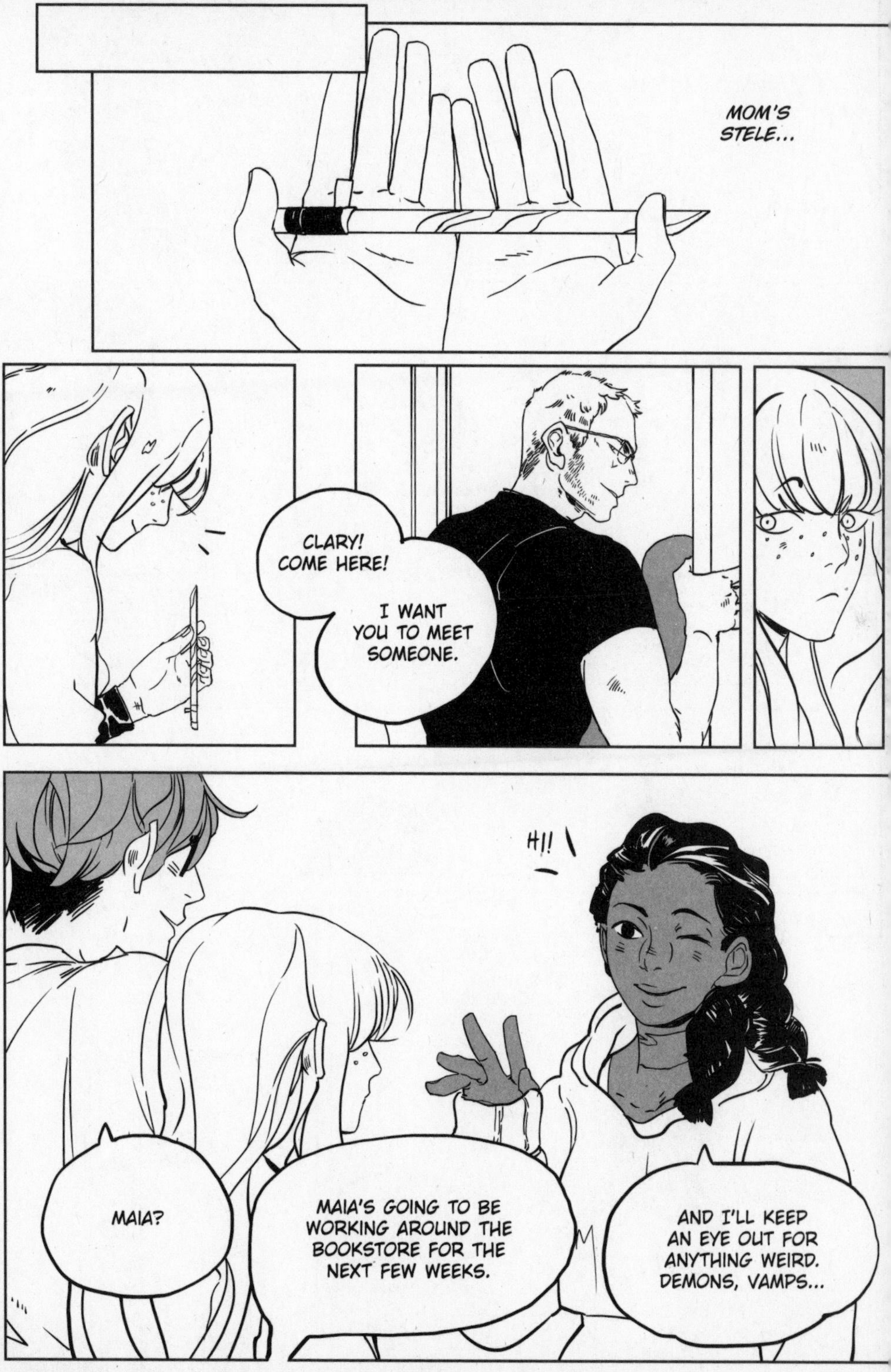
MOM'S STELE...
CLARY! COME HERE!
I WANT YOU TO MEET SOMEONE.
HI!
MAIA?
MAIA'S GOING TO BE WORKING AROUND THE BOOKSTORE FOR THE NEXT FEW WEEKS.
AND I'LL KEEP AN EYE OUT FOR ANYTHING WEIRD. DEMONS, VAMPS...

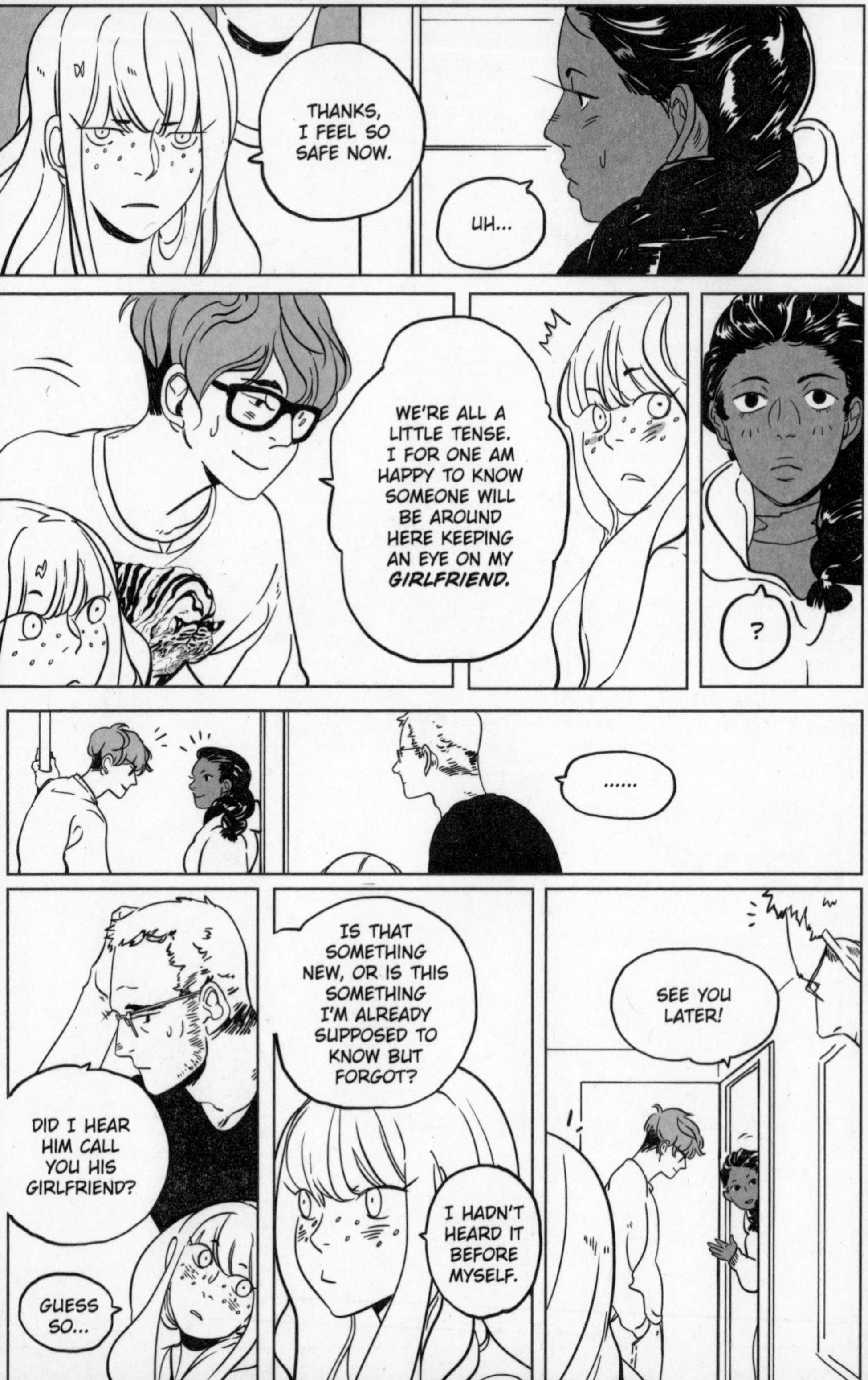
THANKS, I FEEL SO SAFE NOW.
UH...
WE'RE ALL A LITTLE TENSE. I FOR ONE AM HAPPY TO KNOW SOMEONE WILL BE AROUND HERE KEEPING AN EYE ON MY *GIRLFRIEND.*
?
......
DID I HEAR HIM CALL YOU HIS GIRLFRIEND?
GUESS SO...
IS THAT SOMETHING NEW, OR IS THIS SOMETHING I'M ALREADY SUPPOSED TO KNOW BUT FORGOT?
I HADN'T HEARD IT BEFORE MYSELF.
SEE YOU LATER!

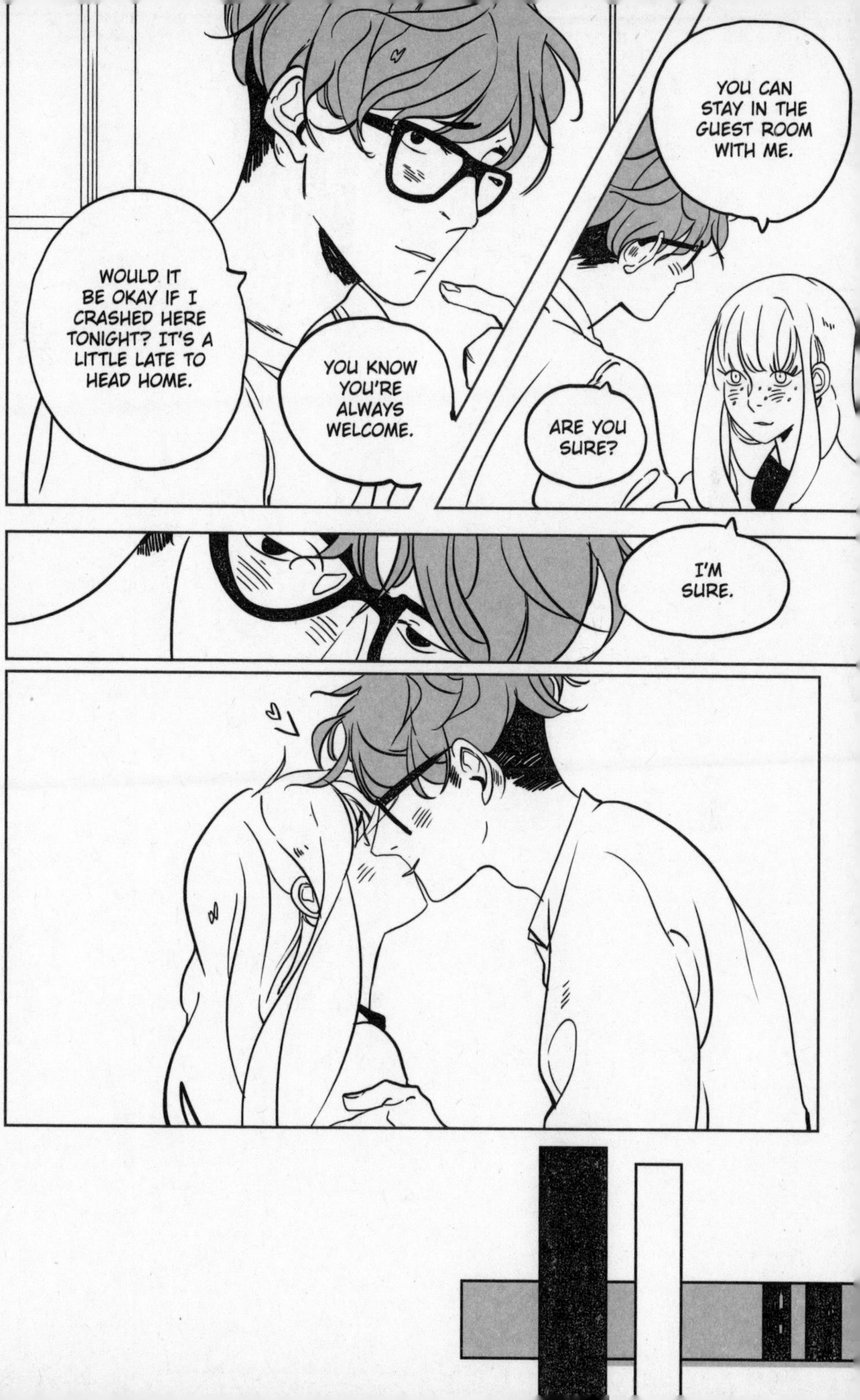
WOULD IT BE OKAY IF I CRASHED HERE TONIGHT? IT'S A LITTLE LATE TO HEAD HOME.
YOU KNOW YOU'RE ALWAYS WELCOME.
YOU CAN STAY IN THE GUEST ROOM WITH ME.
ARE YOU SURE?
I'M SURE.

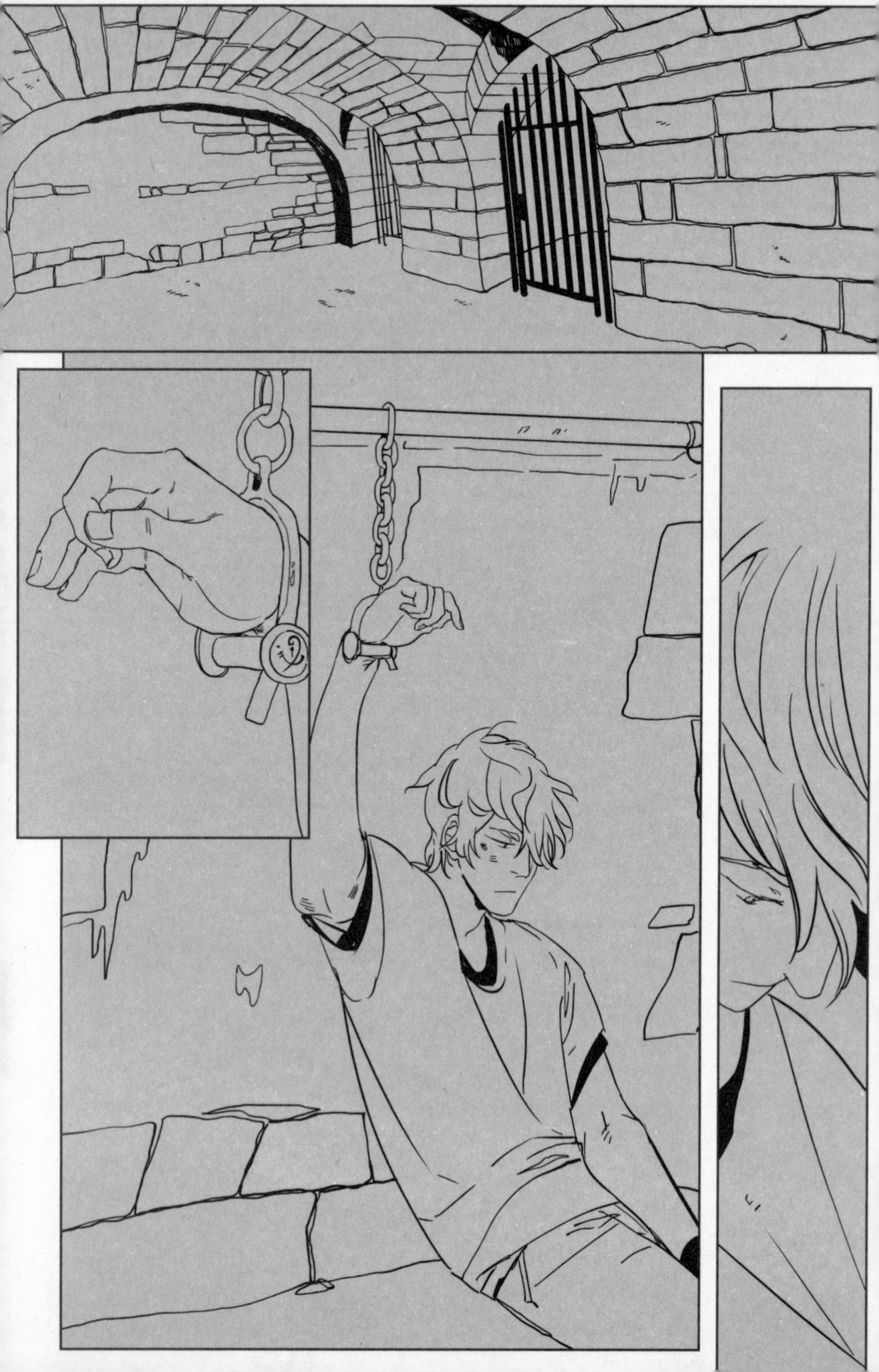

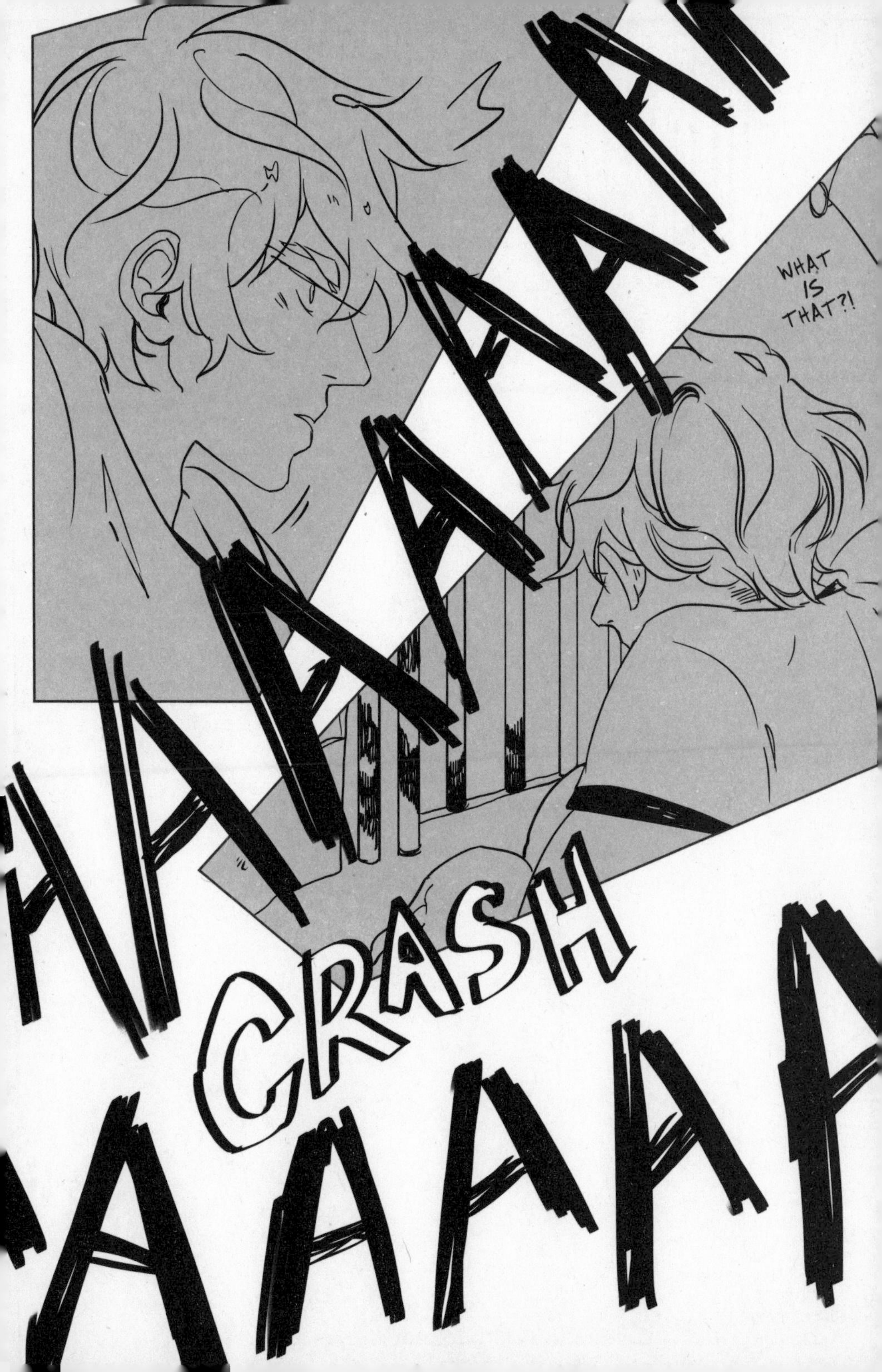
WHAT IS THAT?!
CRASH

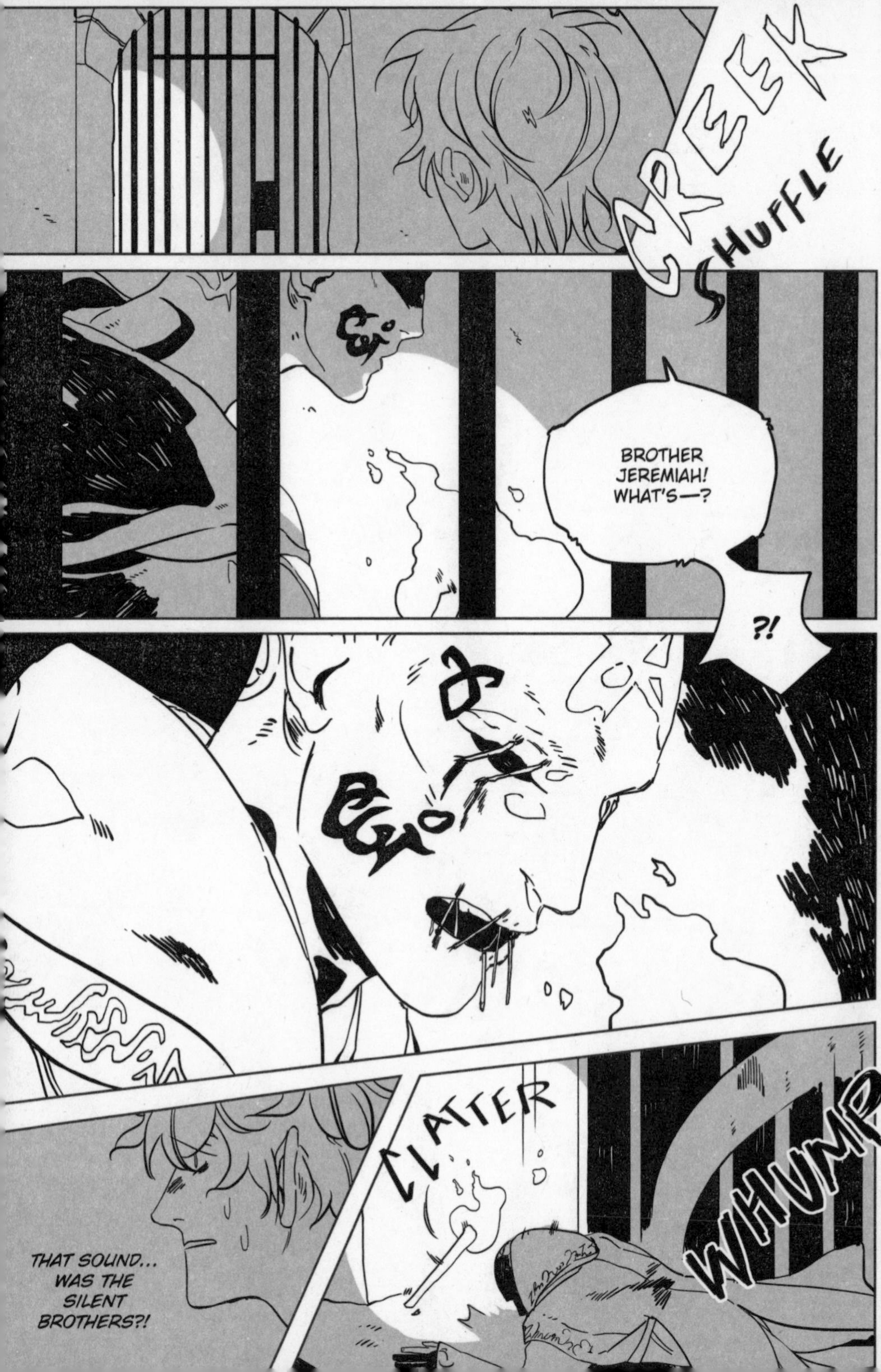
CREEK
SHUFFLE
BROTHER JEREMIAH! WHAT'S—?
?!
CLATTER
WHUMP
THAT SOUND... WAS THE SILENT BROTHERS?!

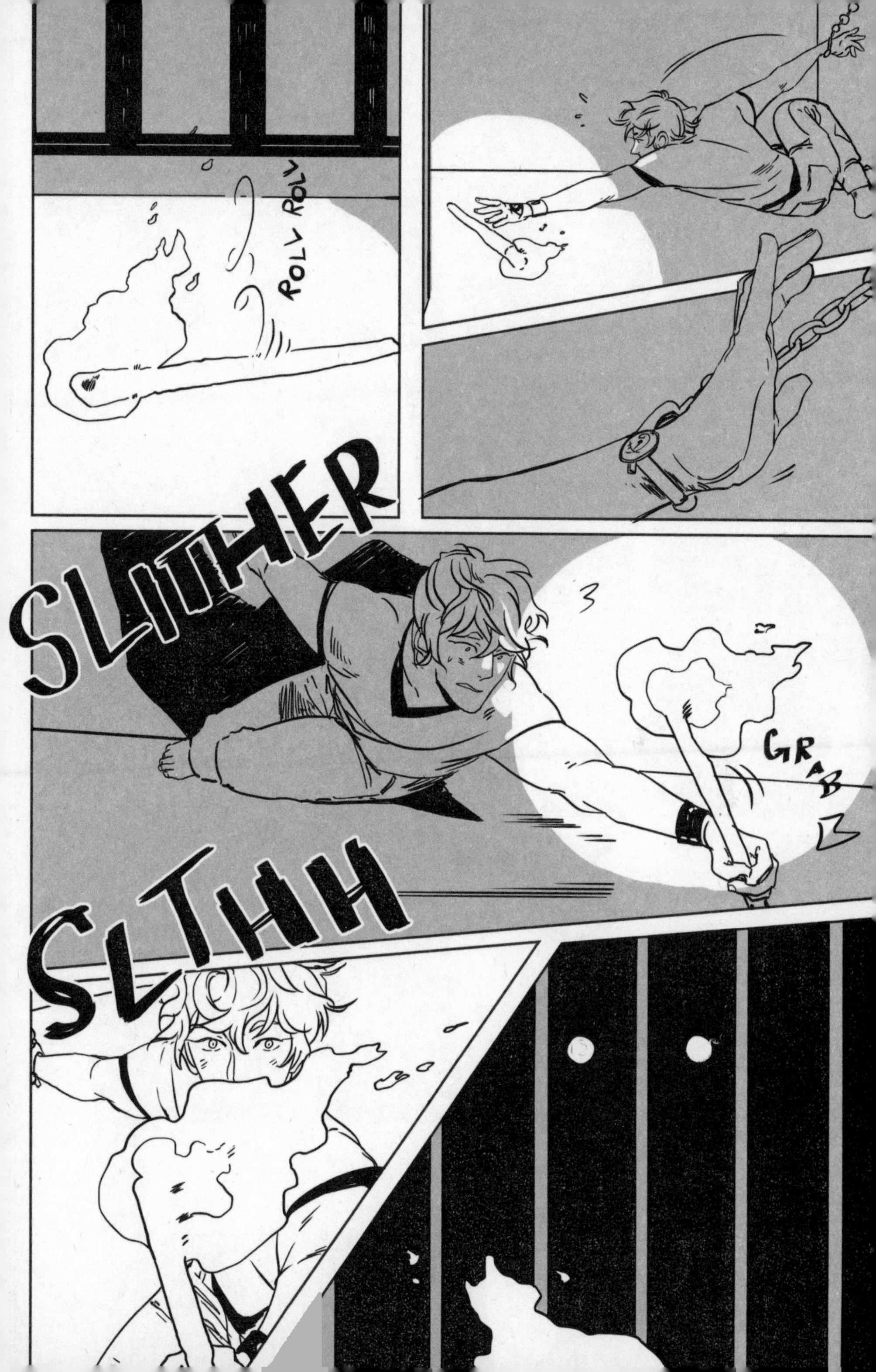
ROLL ROLL
SLITHER
GRAB
SLTHH

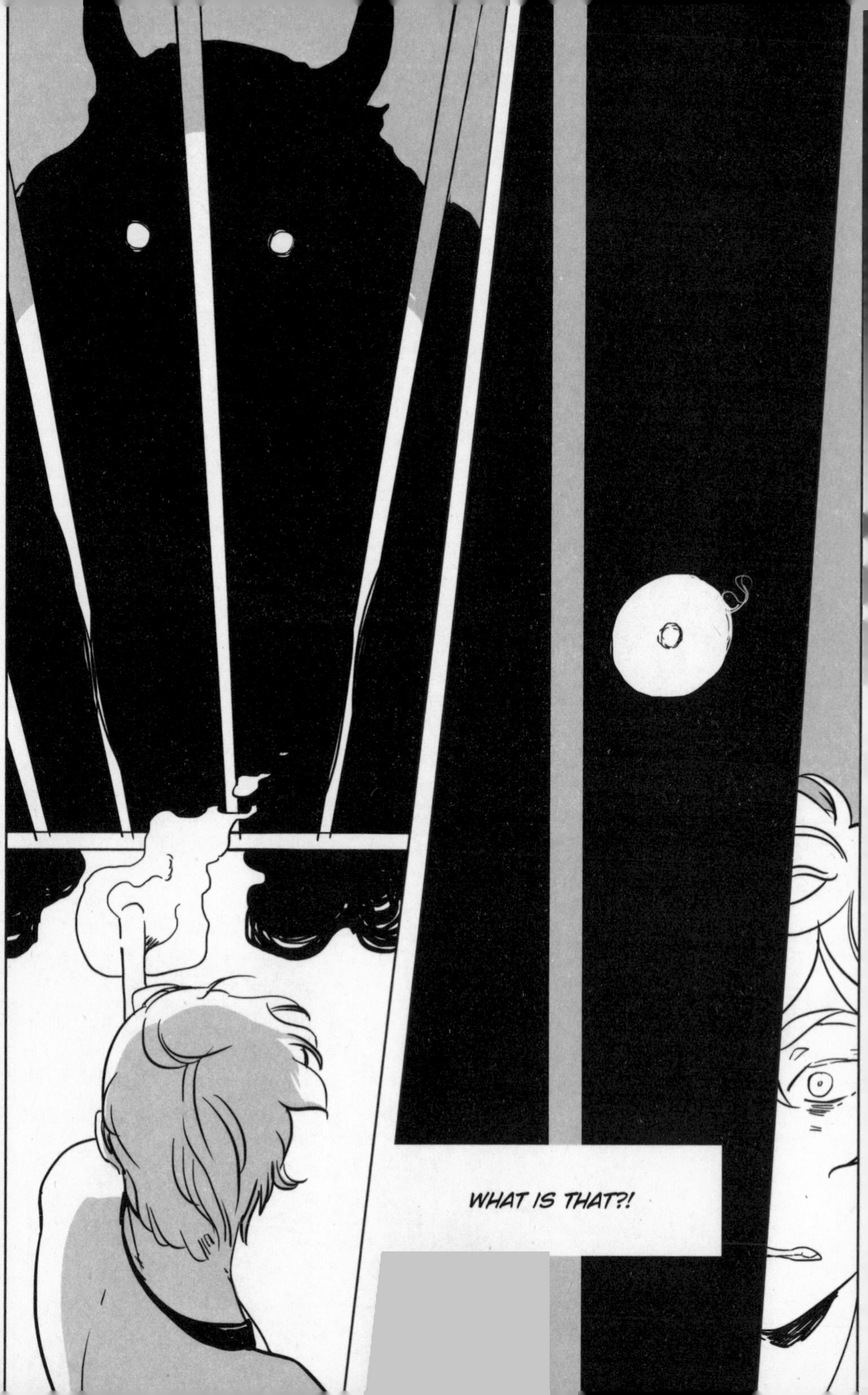
WHAT IS THAT?!

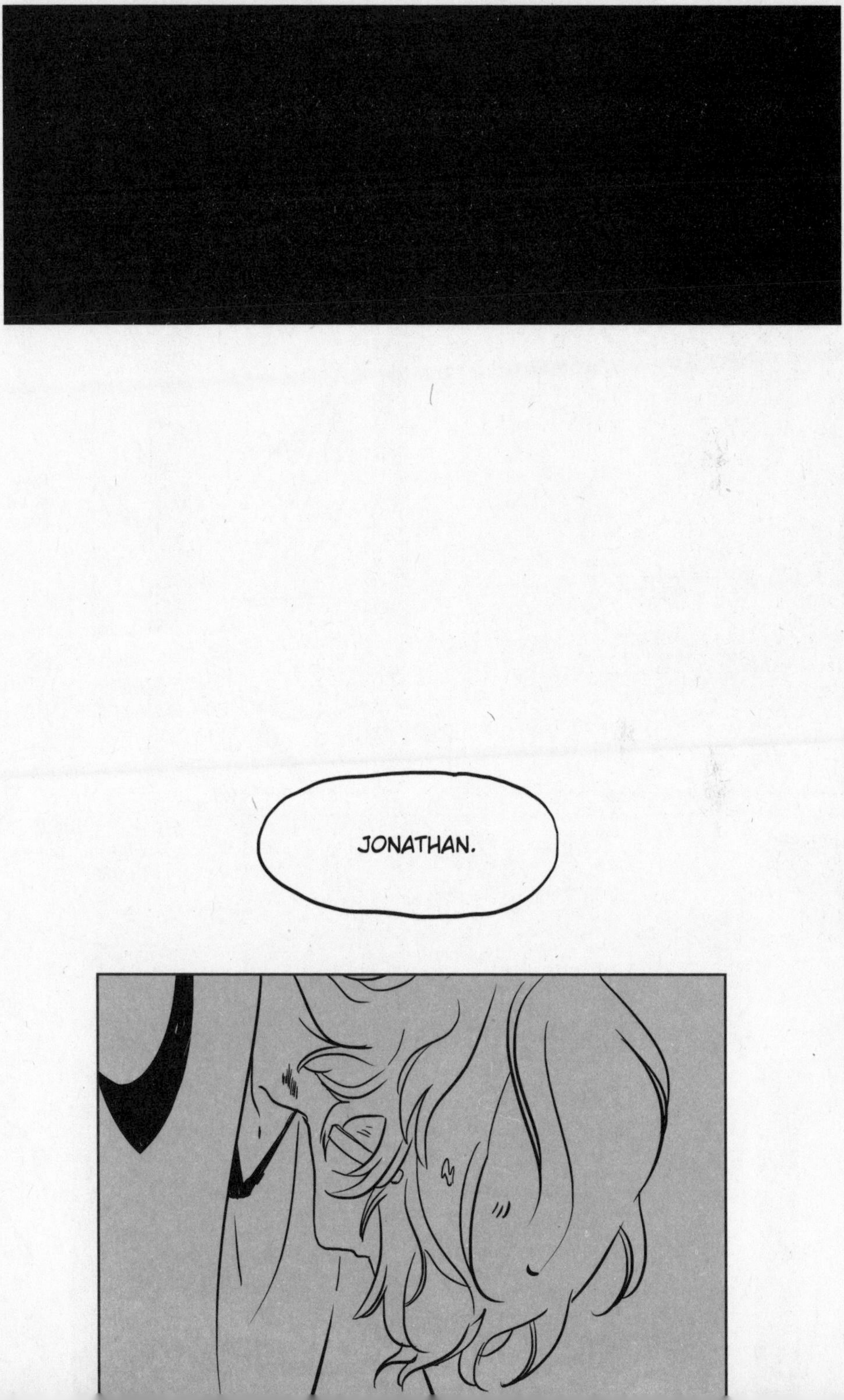
JONATHAN.

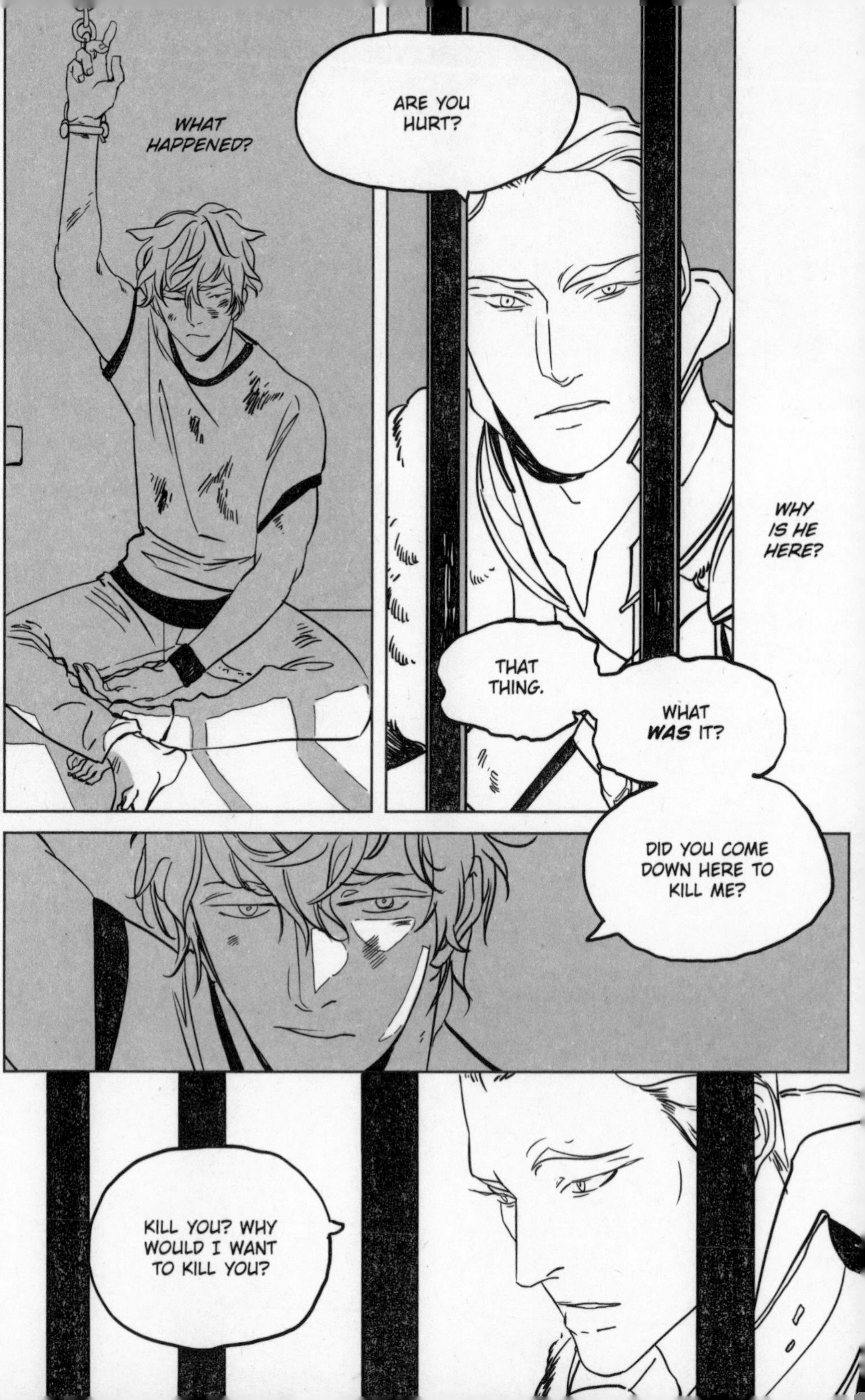
WHAT HAPPENED?
ARE YOU HURT?
WHY IS HE HERE?
THAT THING.
WHAT *WAS* IT?
DID YOU COME DOWN HERE TO KILL ME?
KILL YOU? WHY WOULD I WANT TO KILL YOU?

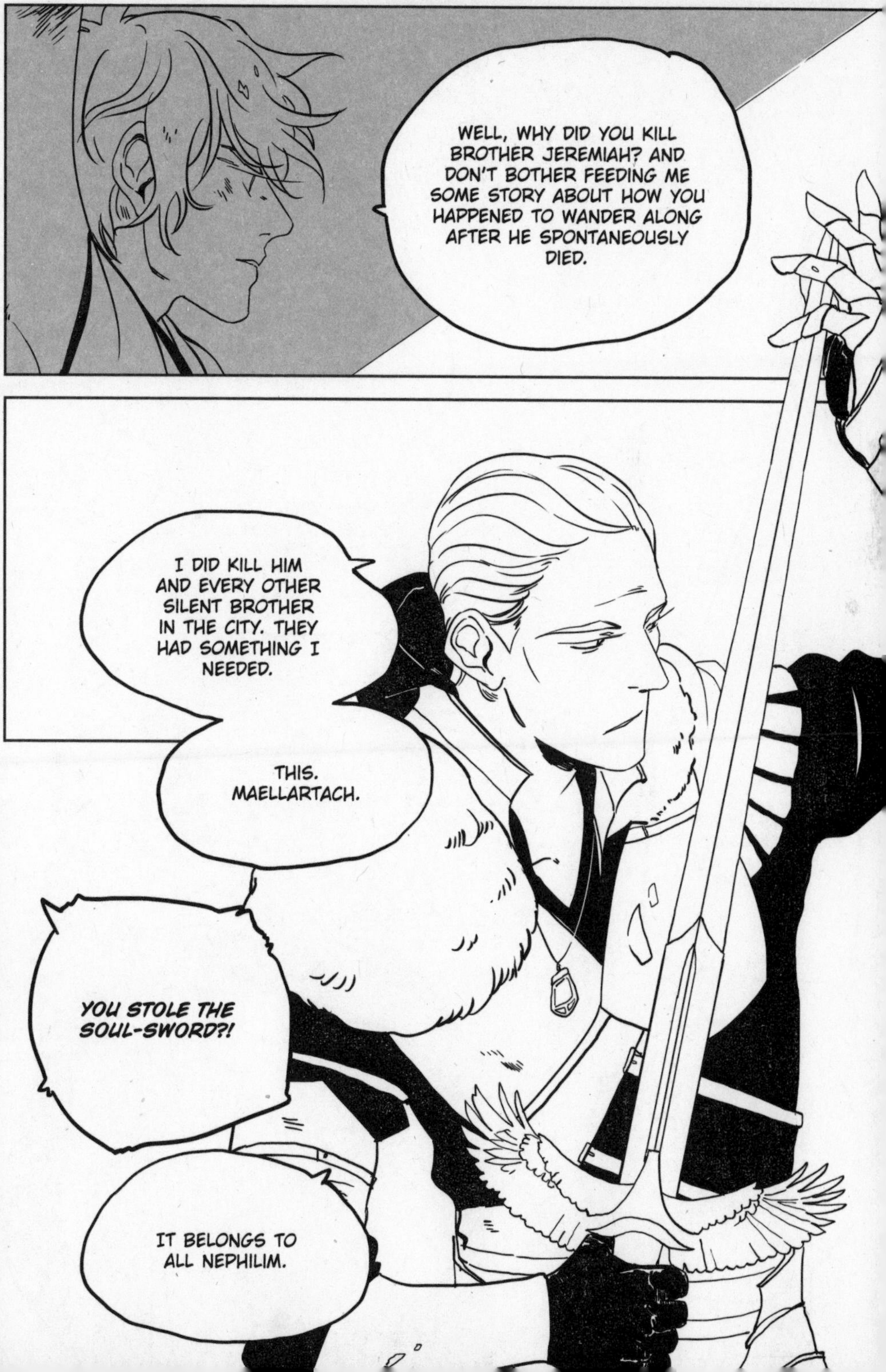
WELL, WHY DID YOU KILL BROTHER JEREMIAH? AND DON'T BOTHER FEEDING ME SOME STORY ABOUT HOW YOU HAPPENED TO WANDER ALONG AFTER HE SPONTANEOUSLY DIED.
I DID KILL HIM AND EVERY OTHER SILENT BROTHER IN THE CITY. THEY HAD SOMETHING I NEEDED.
THIS. MAELLARTACH.
YOU STOLE THE SOUL-SWORD?!
IT BELONGS TO ALL NEPHILIM.

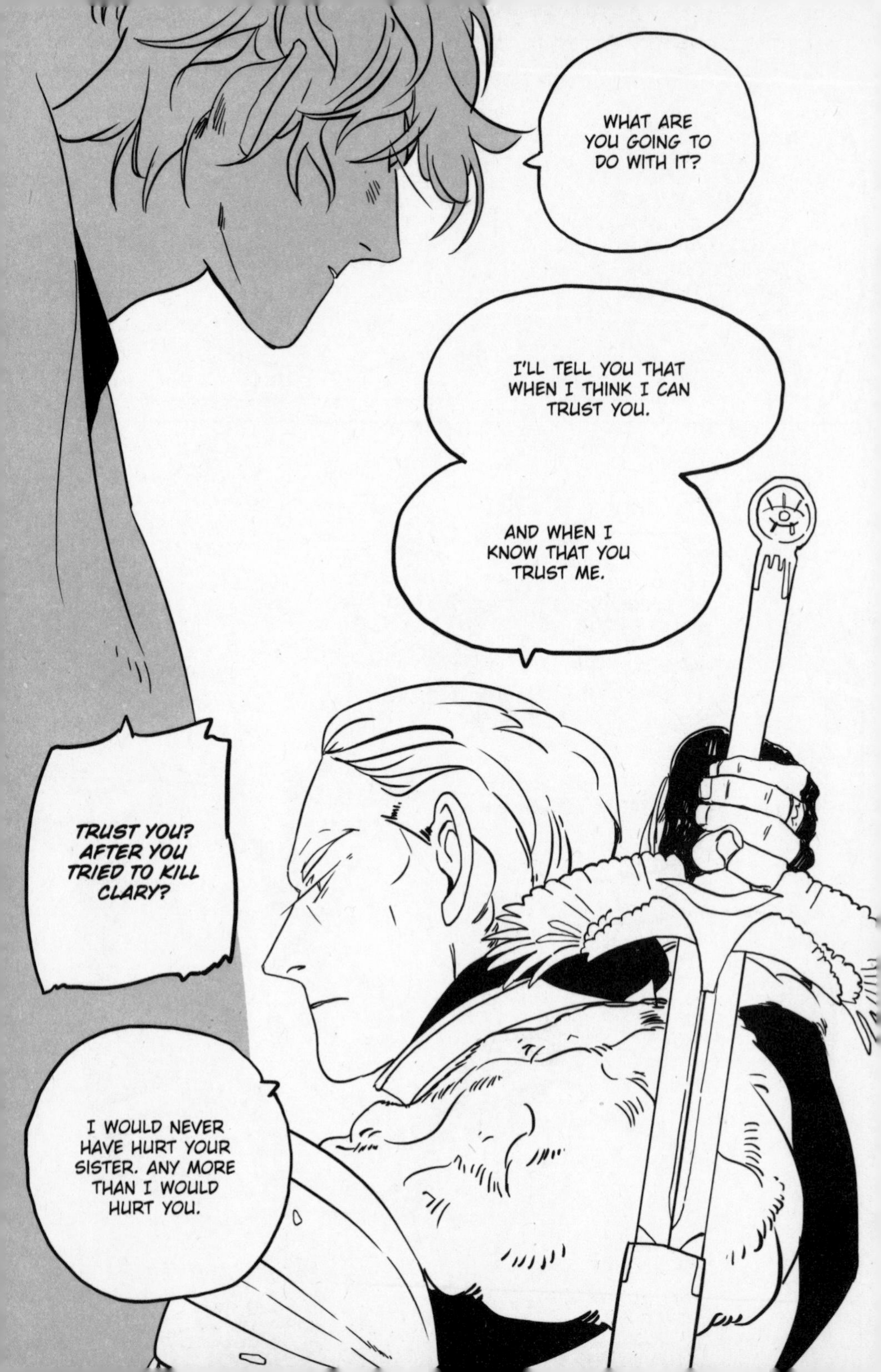
WHAT ARE YOU GOING TO DO WITH IT?
I'LL TELL YOU THAT WHEN I THINK I CAN TRUST YOU.
AND WHEN I KNOW THAT YOU TRUST ME.
TRUST YOU? AFTER YOU TRIED TO KILL CLARY?
I WOULD NEVER HAVE HURT YOUR SISTER. ANY MORE THAN I WOULD HURT YOU.

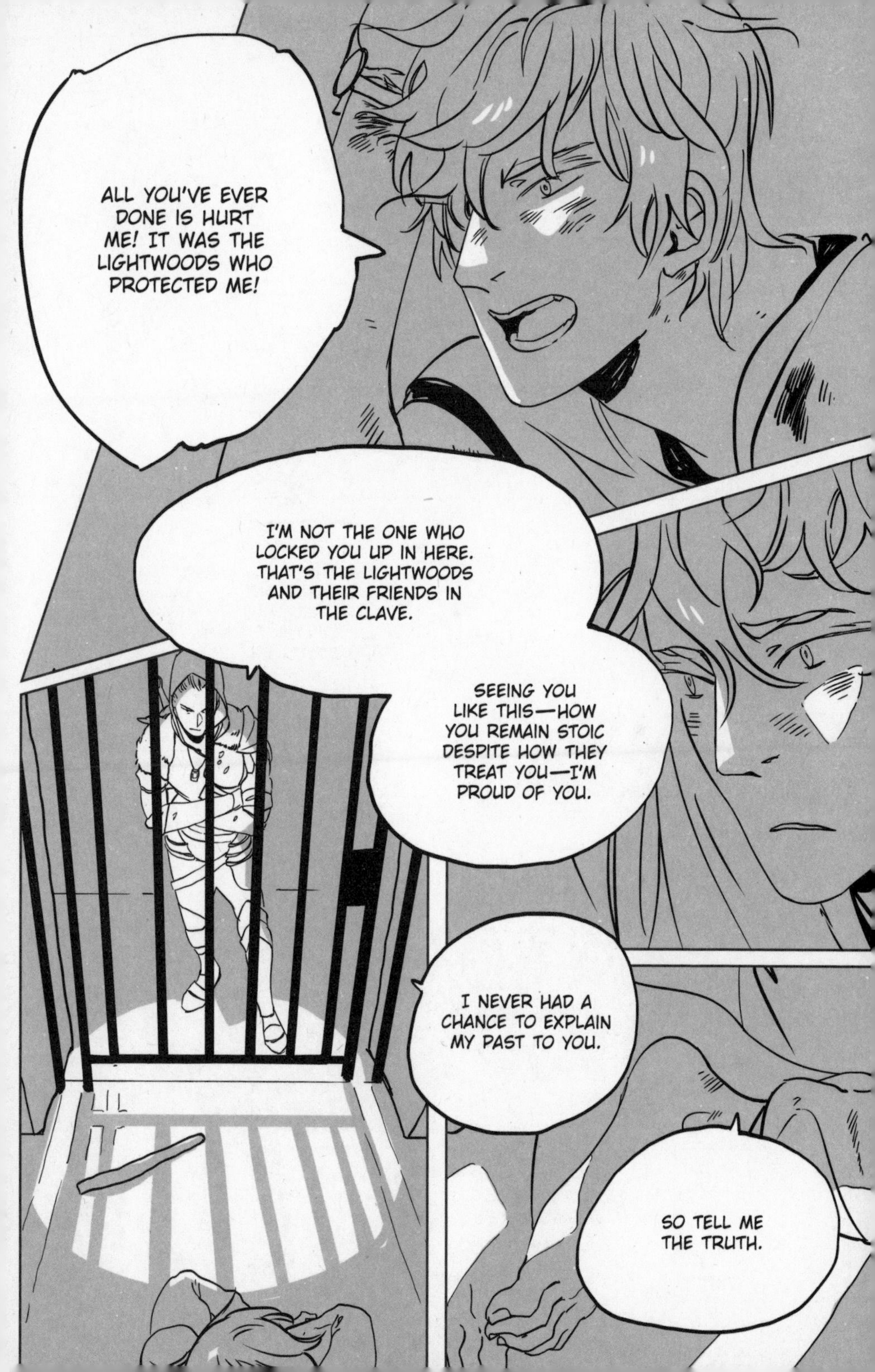
ALL YOU'VE EVER DONE IS HURT ME! IT WAS THE LIGHTWOODS WHO PROTECTED ME!
I'M NOT THE ONE WHO LOCKED YOU UP IN HERE. THAT'S THE LIGHTWOODS AND THEIR FRIENDS IN THE CLAVE.
SEEING YOU LIKE THIS—HOW YOU REMAIN STOIC DESPITE HOW THEY TREAT YOU—I'M PROUD OF YOU.
I NEVER HAD A CHANCE TO EXPLAIN MY PAST TO YOU.
SO TELL ME THE TRUTH.

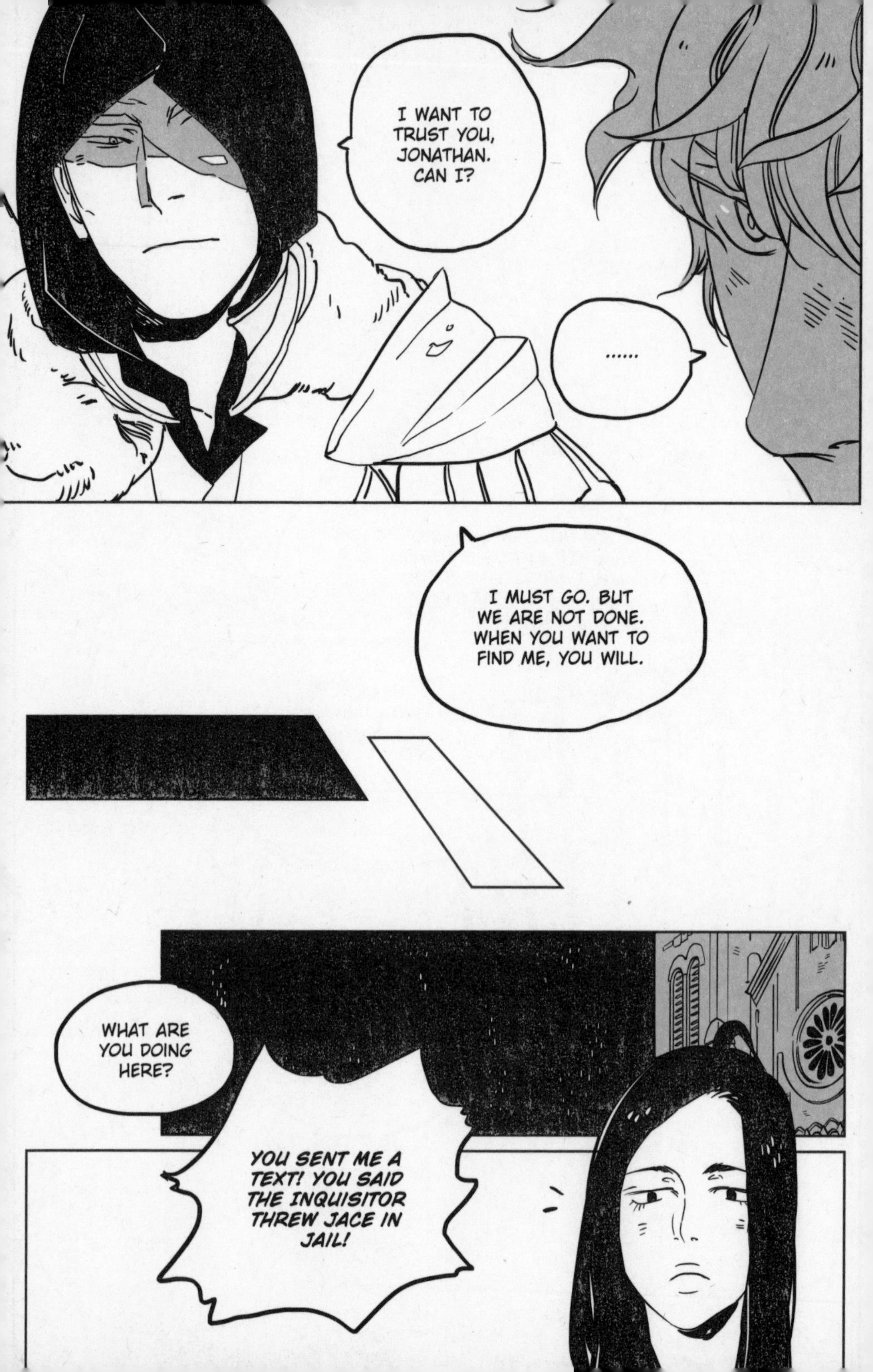
I WANT TO TRUST YOU, JONATHAN. CAN I?
......
I MUST GO. BUT WE ARE NOT DONE. WHEN YOU WANT TO FIND ME, YOU WILL.
WHAT ARE YOU DOING HERE?
YOU SENT ME A TEXT! YOU SAID THE INQUISITOR THREW JACE IN JAIL!

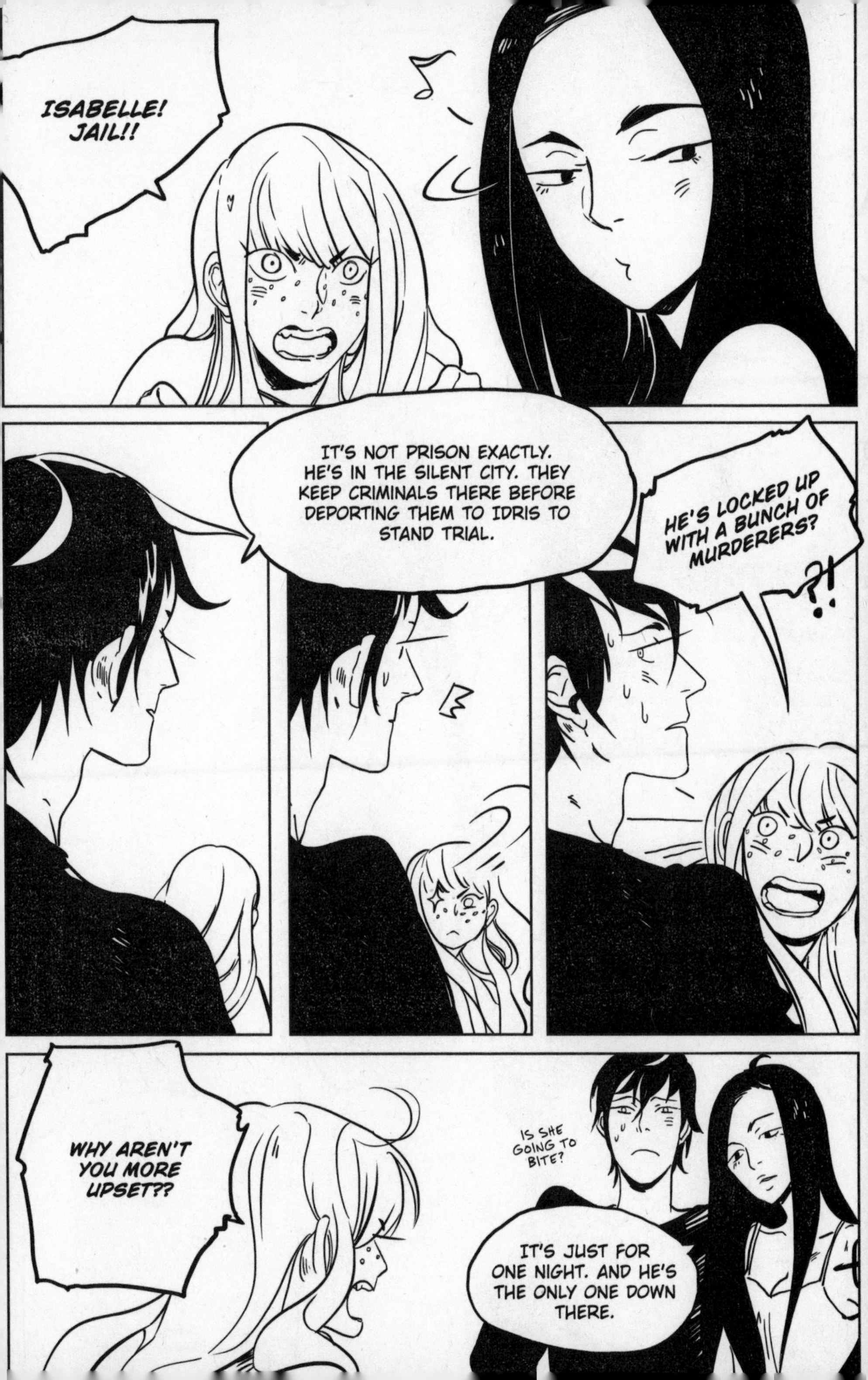
ISABELLE! JAIL!!
IT'S NOT PRISON EXACTLY. HE'S IN THE SILENT CITY. THEY KEEP CRIMINALS THERE BEFORE DEPORTING THEM TO IDRIS TO STAND TRIAL.
HE'S LOCKED UP WITH A BUNCH OF MURDERERS?
?!
WHY AREN'T YOU MORE UPSET??
IS SHE GOING TO BITE?
IT'S JUST FOR ONE NIGHT. AND HE'S THE ONLY ONE DOWN THERE.

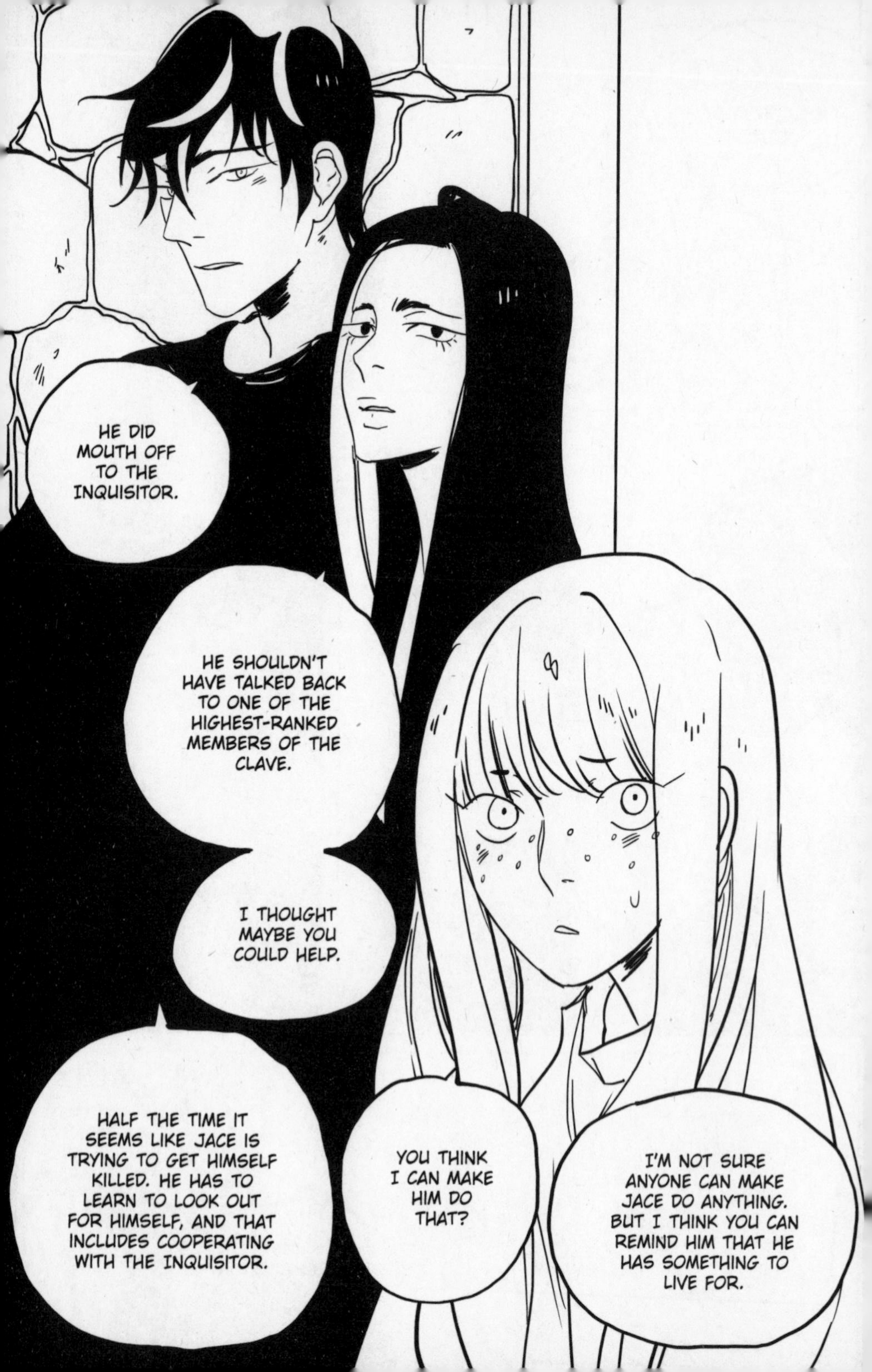
HE DID MOUTH OFF TO THE INQUISITOR.
HE SHOULDN'T HAVE TALKED BACK TO ONE OF THE HIGHEST-RANKED MEMBERS OF THE CLAVE.
I THOUGHT MAYBE YOU COULD HELP.
HALF THE TIME IT SEEMS LIKE JACE IS TRYING TO GET HIMSELF KILLED. HE HAS TO LEARN TO LOOK OUT FOR HIMSELF, AND THAT INCLUDES COOPERATING WITH THE INQUISITOR.
YOU THINK I CAN MAKE HIM DO THAT?
I'M NOT SURE ANYONE CAN MAKE JACE DO ANYTHING. BUT I THINK YOU CAN REMIND HIM THAT HE HAS SOMETHING TO LIVE FOR.

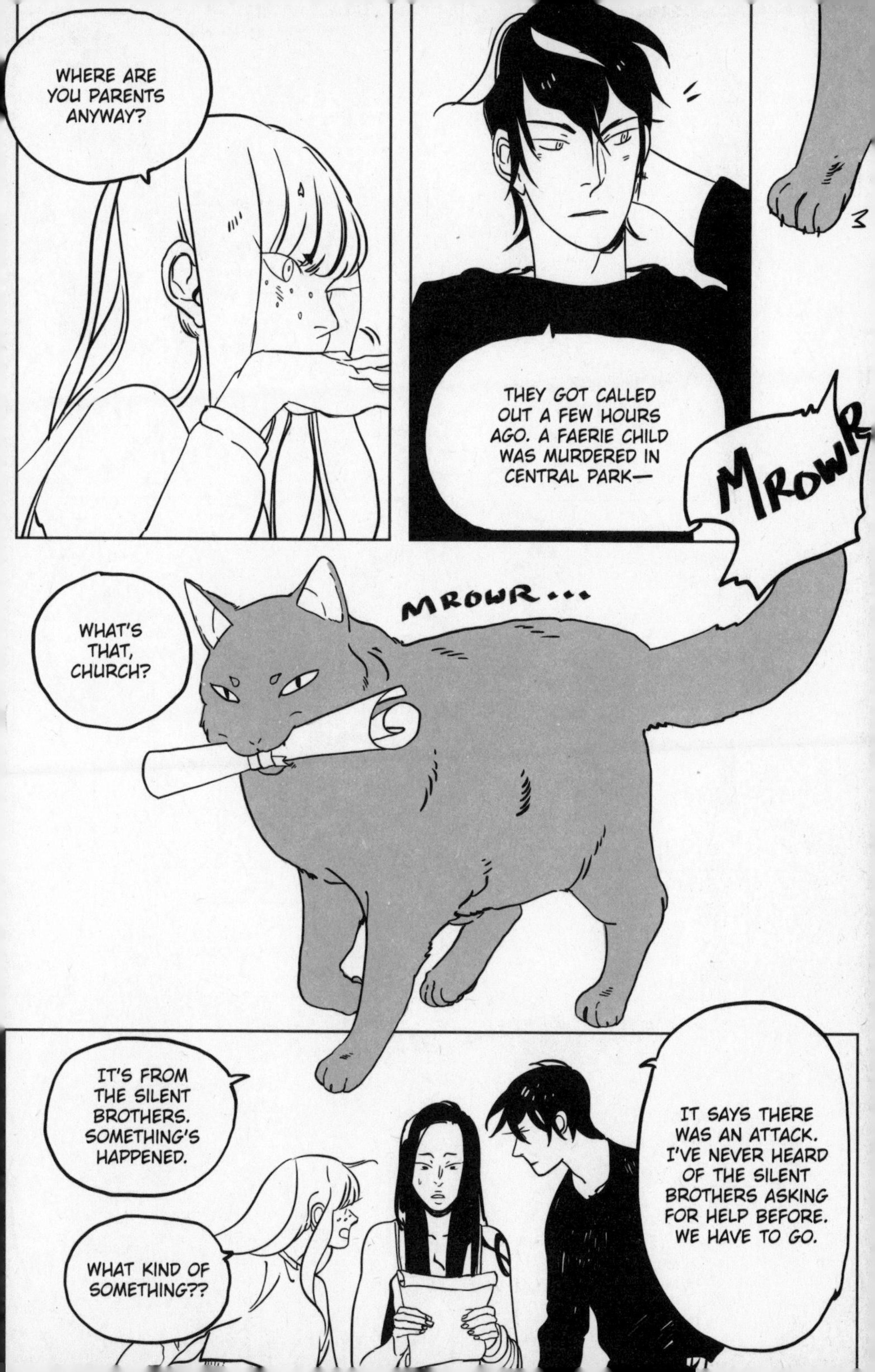
WHERE ARE YOU PARENTS ANYWAY?
THEY GOT CALLED OUT A FEW HOURS AGO. A FAERIE CHILD WAS MURDERED IN CENTRAL PARK—
MROWR
WHAT'S THAT, CHURCH?
MROWR...
IT'S FROM THE SILENT BROTHERS. SOMETHING'S HAPPENED.
WHAT KIND OF SOMETHING??
IT SAYS THERE WAS AN ATTACK. I'VE NEVER HEARD OF THE SILENT BROTHERS ASKING FOR HELP BEFORE. WE HAVE TO GO.

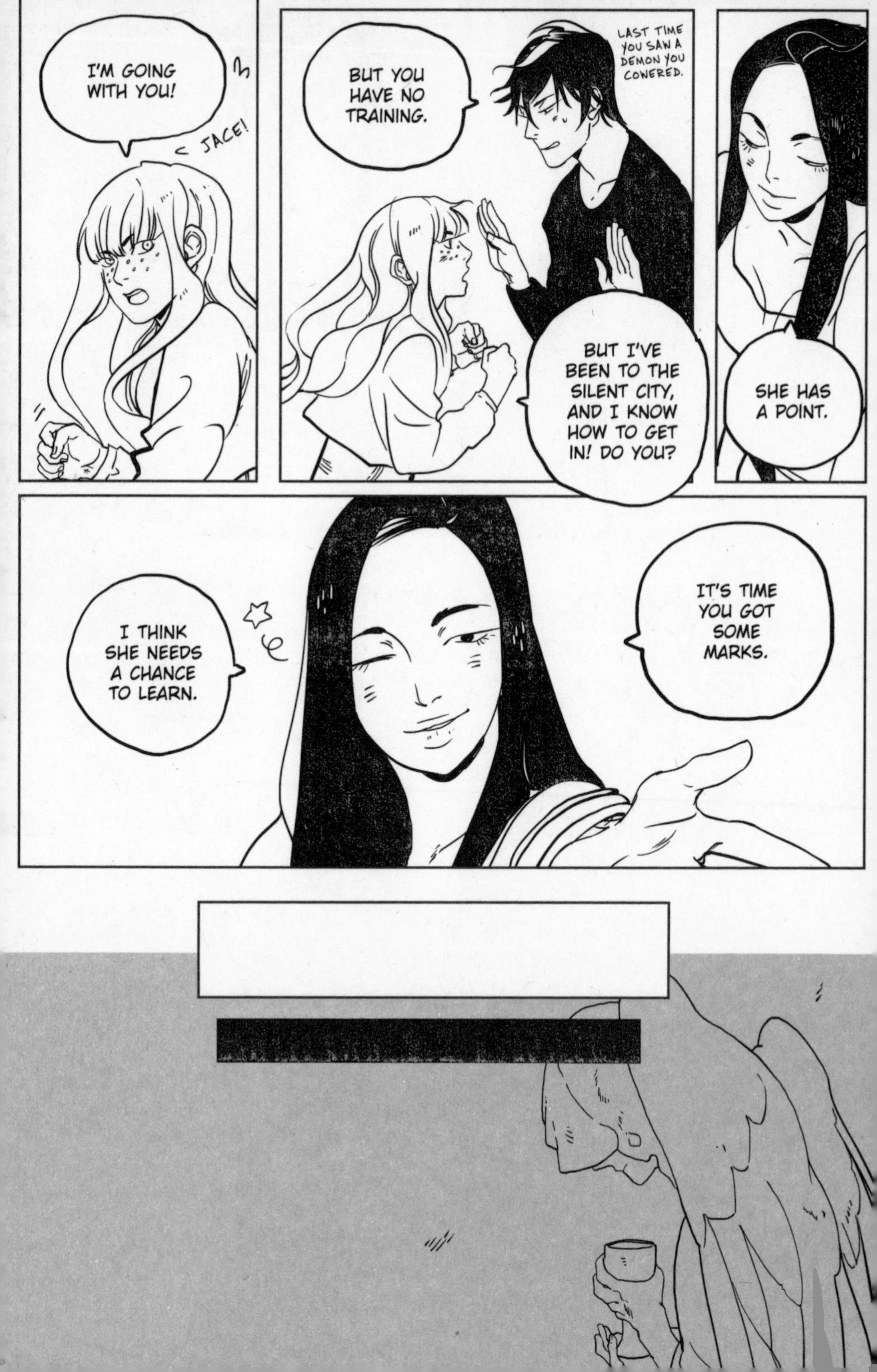
I'M GOING WITH YOU!
JACE!
BUT YOU HAVE NO TRAINING.
LAST TIME YOU SAW A DEMON YOU COWERED.
BUT I'VE BEEN TO THE SILENT CITY, AND I KNOW HOW TO GET IN! DO YOU?
SHE HAS A POINT.
I THINK SHE NEEDS A CHANCE TO LEARN.
IT'S TIME YOU GOT SOME MARKS.

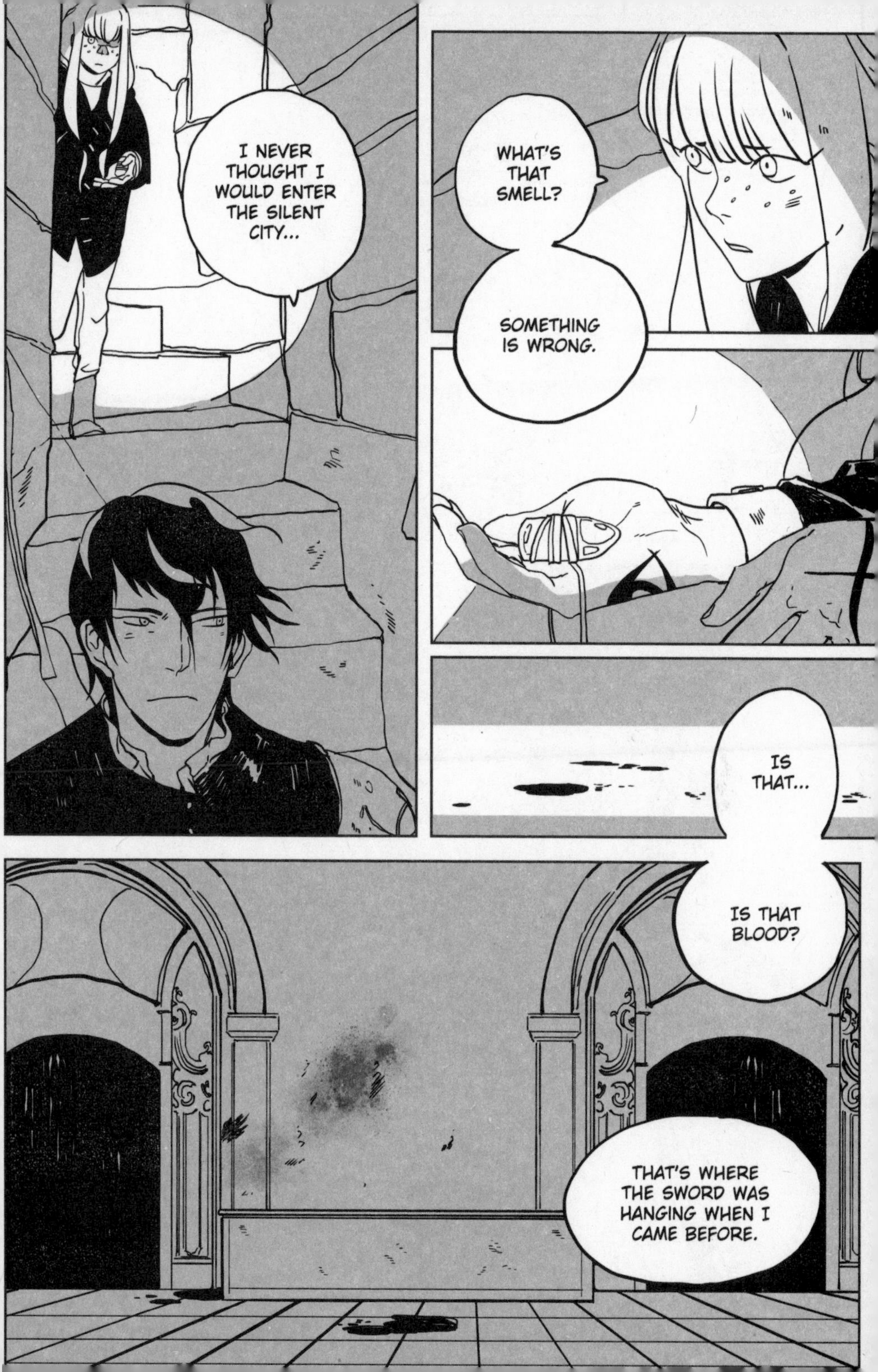
I NEVER THOUGHT I WOULD ENTER THE SILENT CITY...
WHAT'S THAT SMELL?
SOMETHING IS WRONG.
IS THAT...
IS THAT BLOOD?
THAT'S WHERE THE SWORD WAS HANGING WHEN I CAME BEFORE.

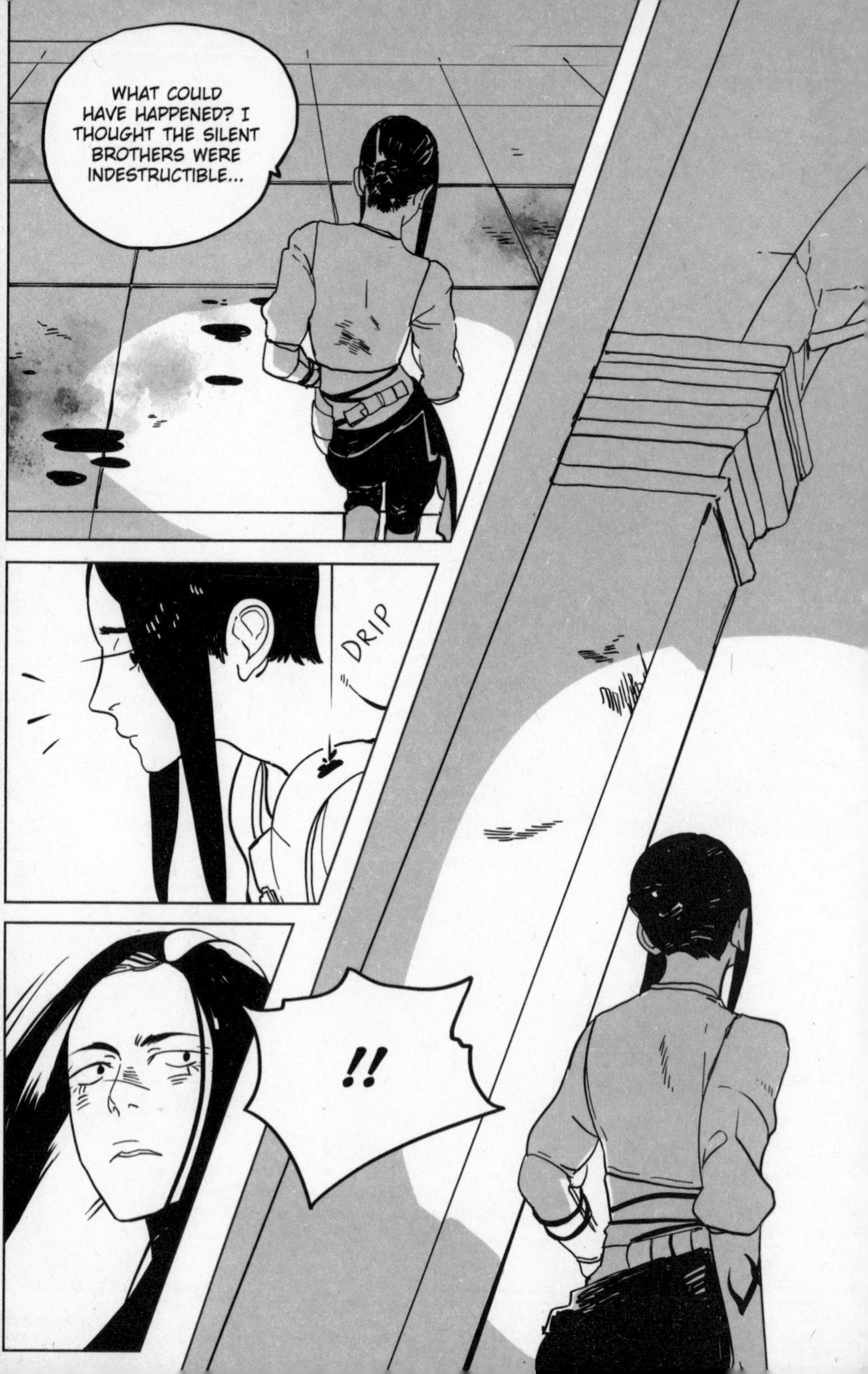
WHAT COULD HAVE HAPPENED? I THOUGHT THE SILENT BROTHERS WERE INDESTRUCTIBLE...
DRIP
!!

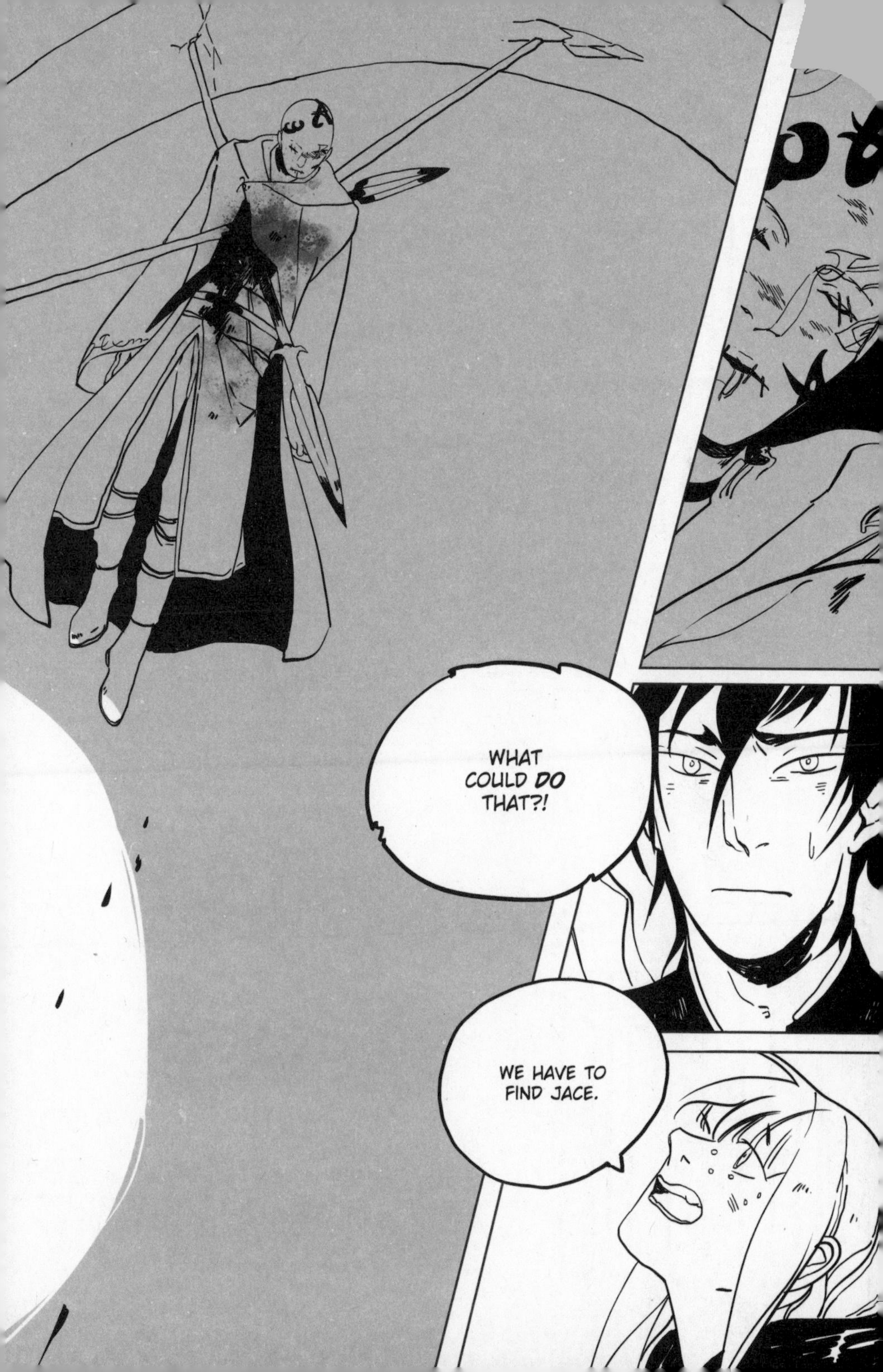
WHAT COULD DO THAT?!
WE HAVE TO FIND JACE.

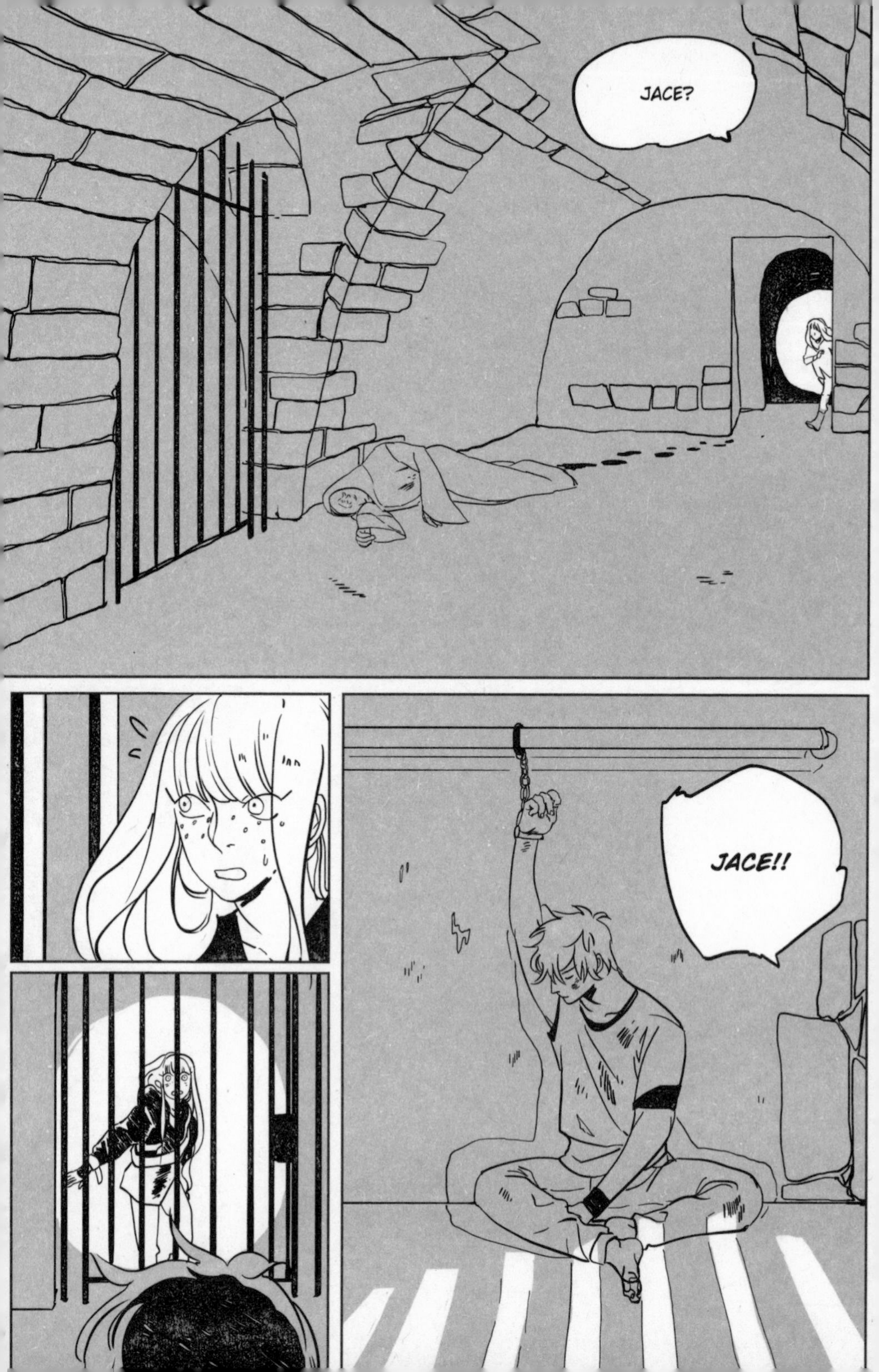
JACE?
JACE!!

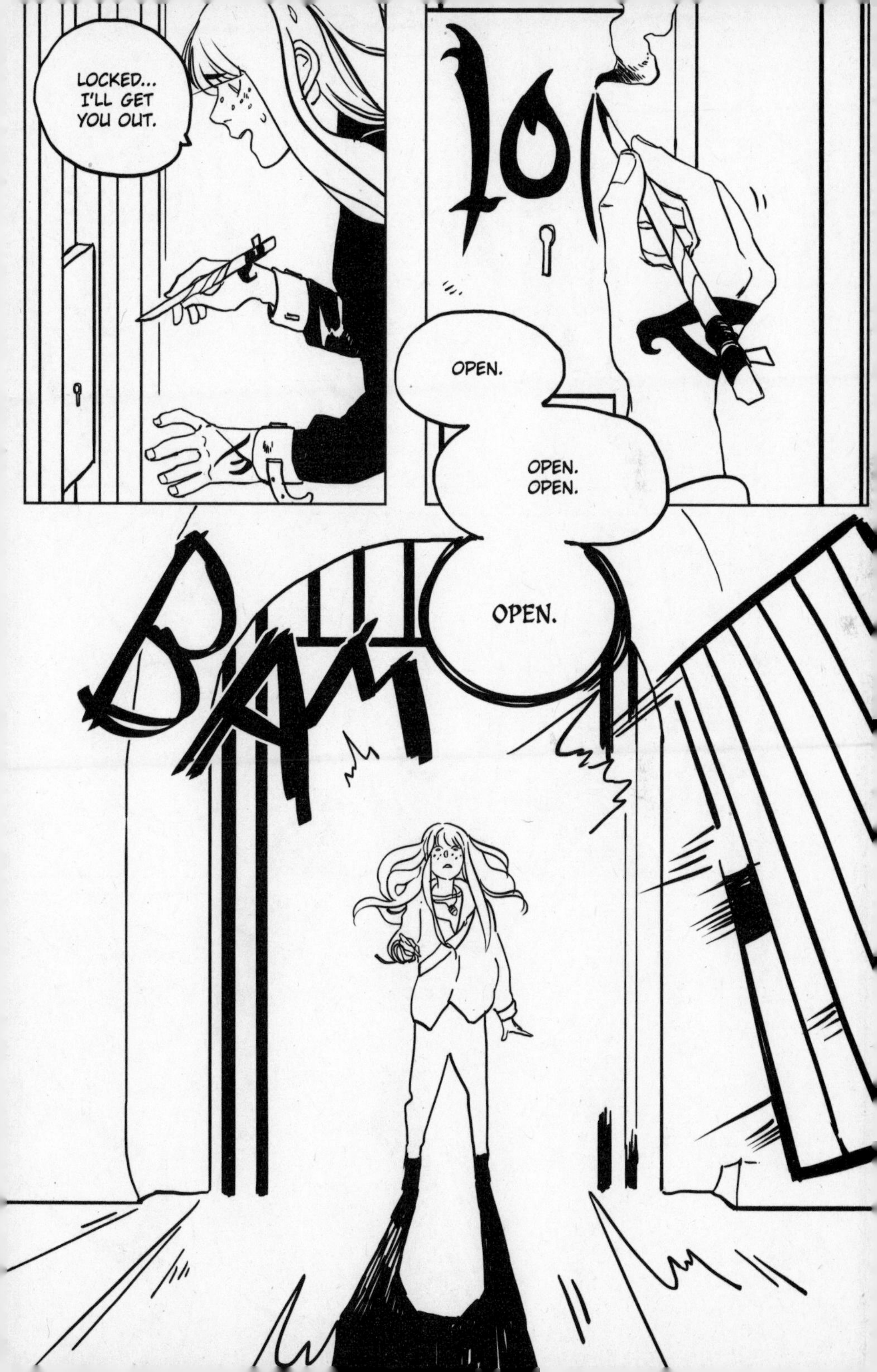
LOCKED... I'LL GET YOU OUT.
OPEN.
OPEN. OPEN.
OPEN.
BAM

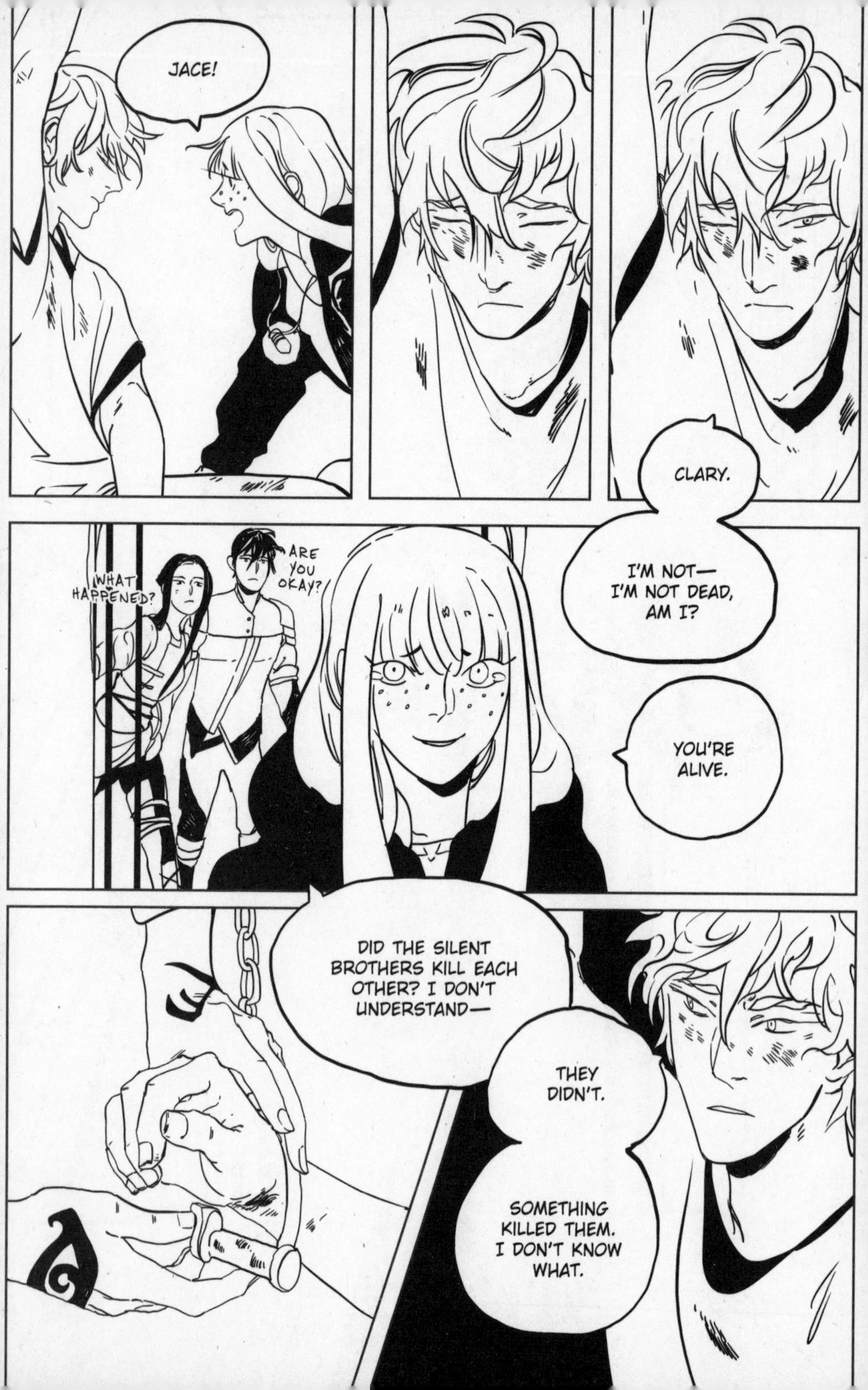
JACE!
CLARY.
I'M NOT— I'M NOT DEAD, AM I?
WHAT HAPPENED?
ARE YOU OKAY?
YOU'RE ALIVE.
DID THE SILENT BROTHERS KILL EACH OTHER? I DON'T UNDERSTAND—
THEY DIDN'T.
SOMETHING KILLED THEM. I DON'T KNOW WHAT.

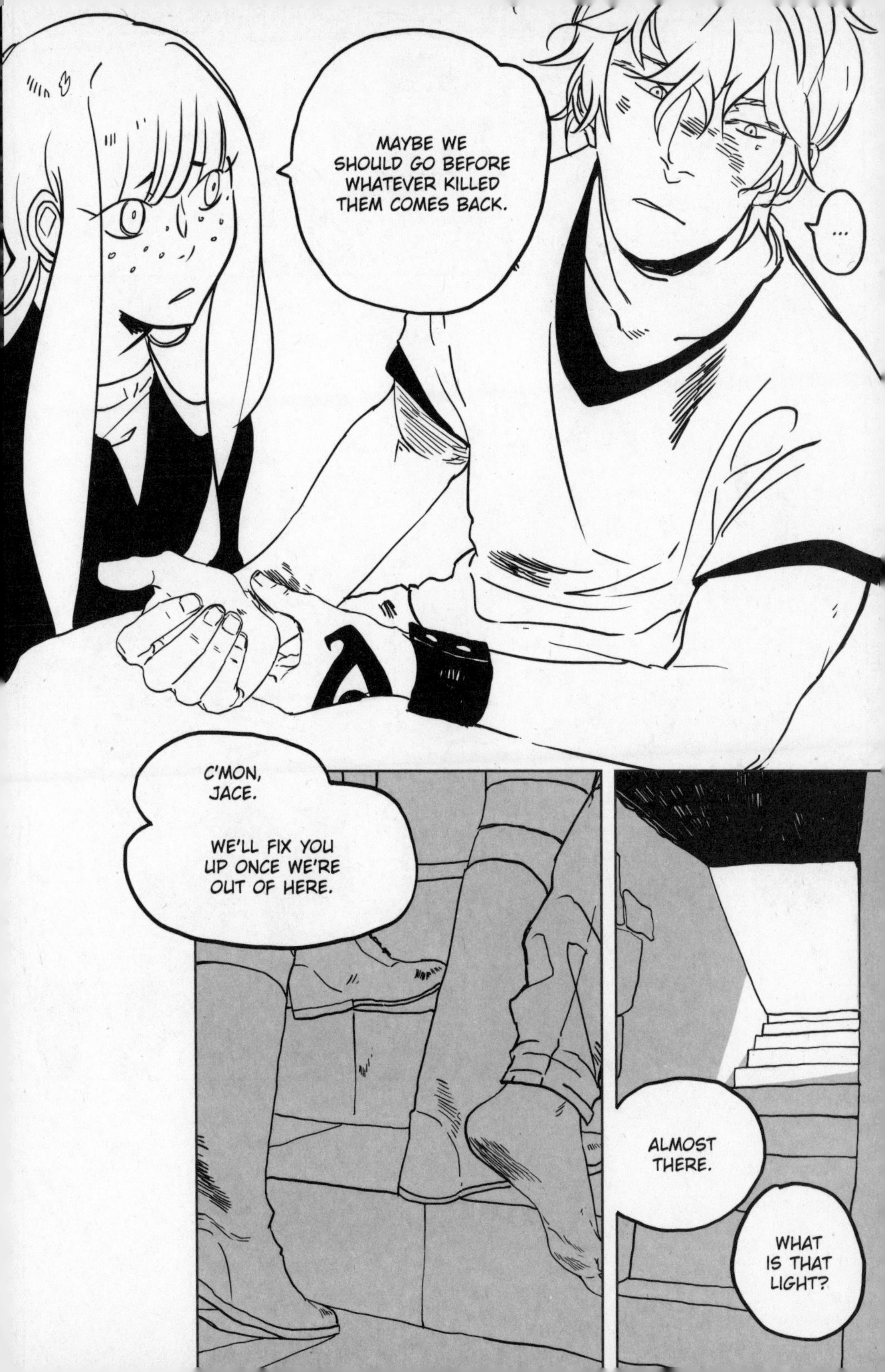
MAYBE WE SHOULD GO BEFORE WHATEVER KILLED THEM COMES BACK.
...
C'MON, JACE.
WE'LL FIX YOU UP ONCE WE'RE OUT OF HERE.
ALMOST THERE.
WHAT IS THAT LIGHT?

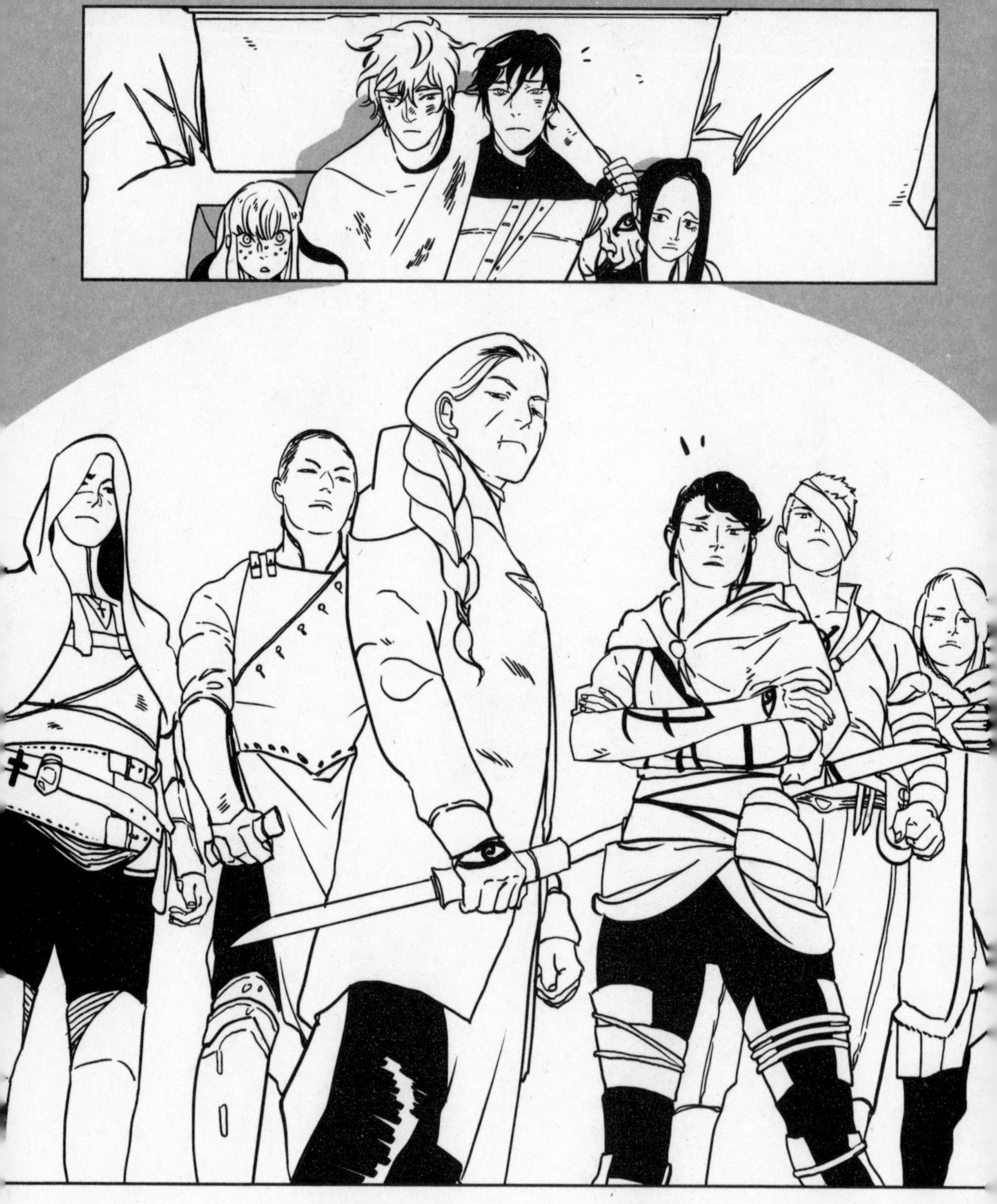

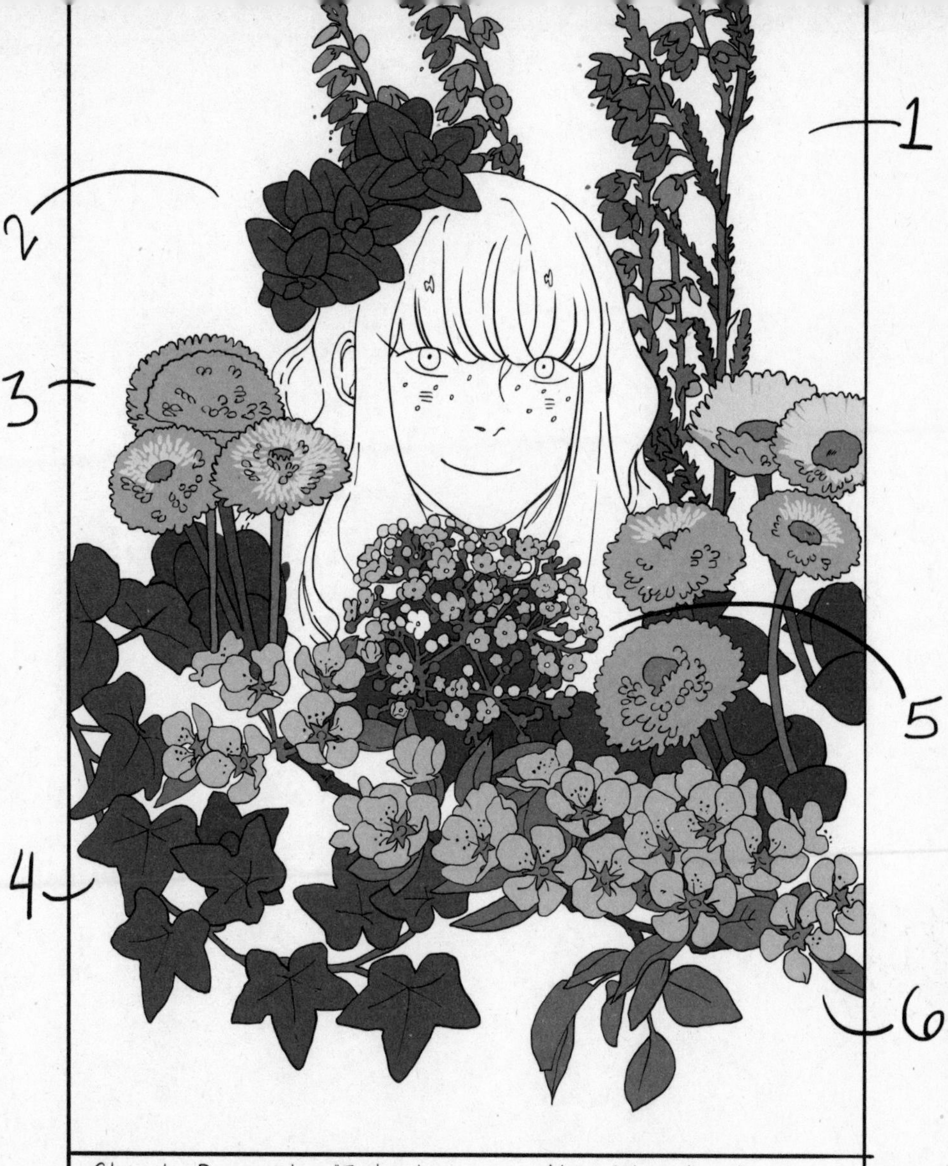
1
2
3
4
5
6

Clary's Bouquet - "Embarking on a New Adventure"

1) Heather - Protection from Danger

2) Sweet Marjoram - Kindness

3) English Daisy - Cheerfulness

4) Ivy - Trustfulness

5) Laurustinus - Thoughts of Heaven

6) Pear Blossoms - Hope

THE MORTAL INSTRUMENTS

THE GRAPHIC NOVEL

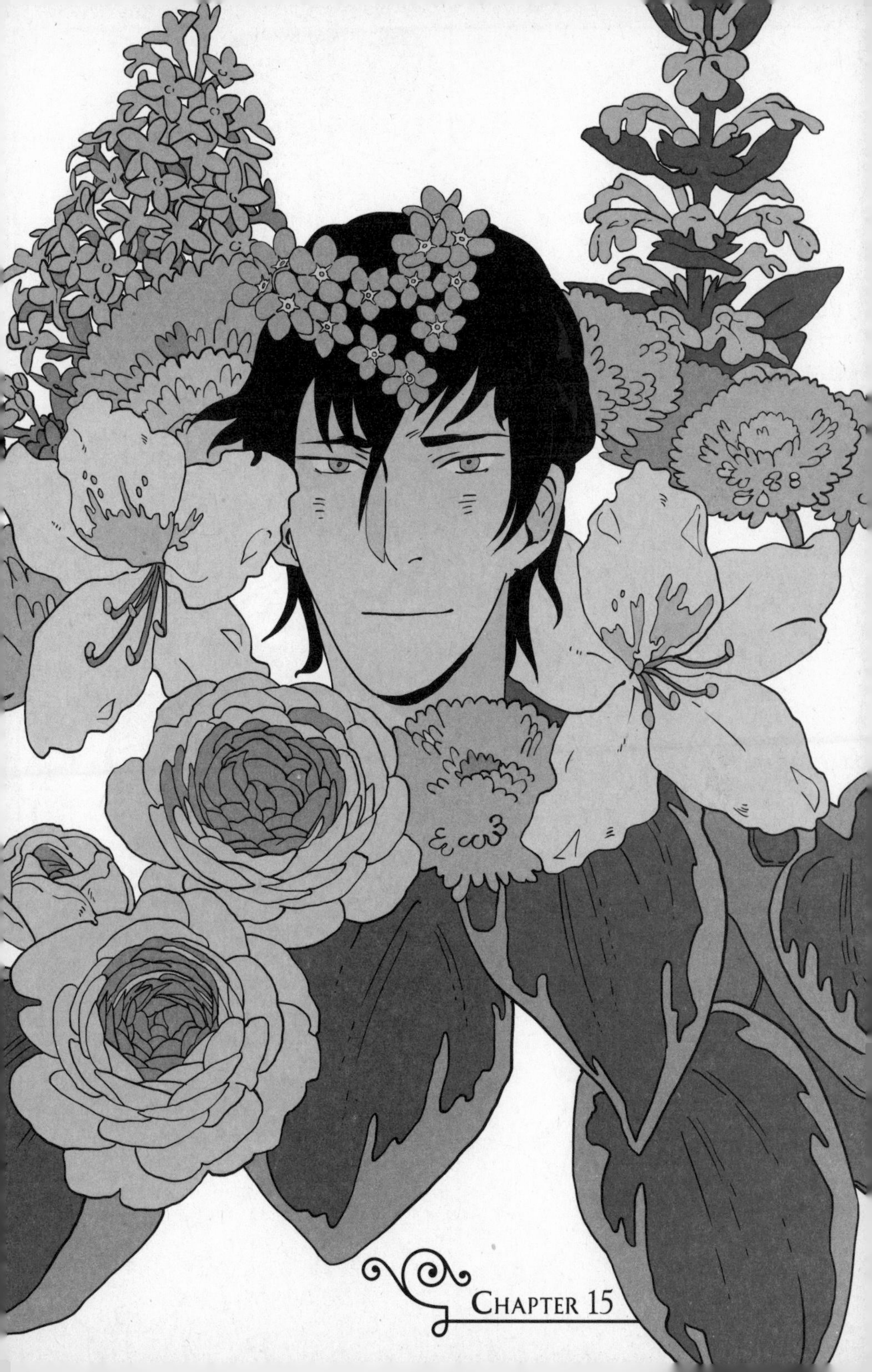

CHAPTER 15

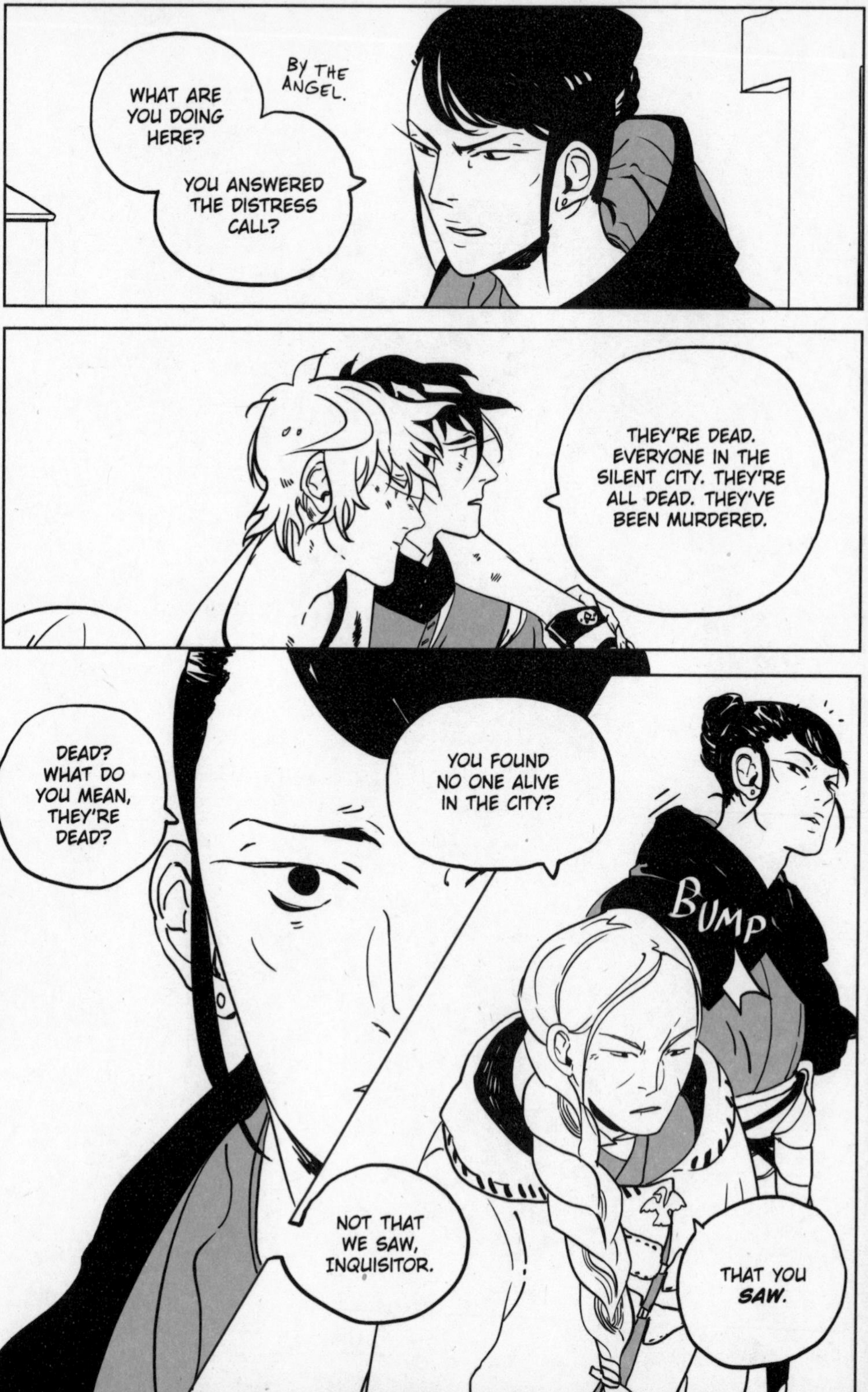
WHAT ARE YOU DOING HERE?
YOU ANSWERED THE DISTRESS CALL?
BY THE ANGEL.
THEY'RE DEAD. EVERYONE IN THE SILENT CITY. THEY'RE ALL DEAD. THEY'VE BEEN MURDERED.
DEAD? WHAT DO YOU MEAN, THEY'RE DEAD?
YOU FOUND NO ONE ALIVE IN THE CITY?
BUMP
NOT THAT WE SAW, INQUISITOR.
THAT YOU SAW.

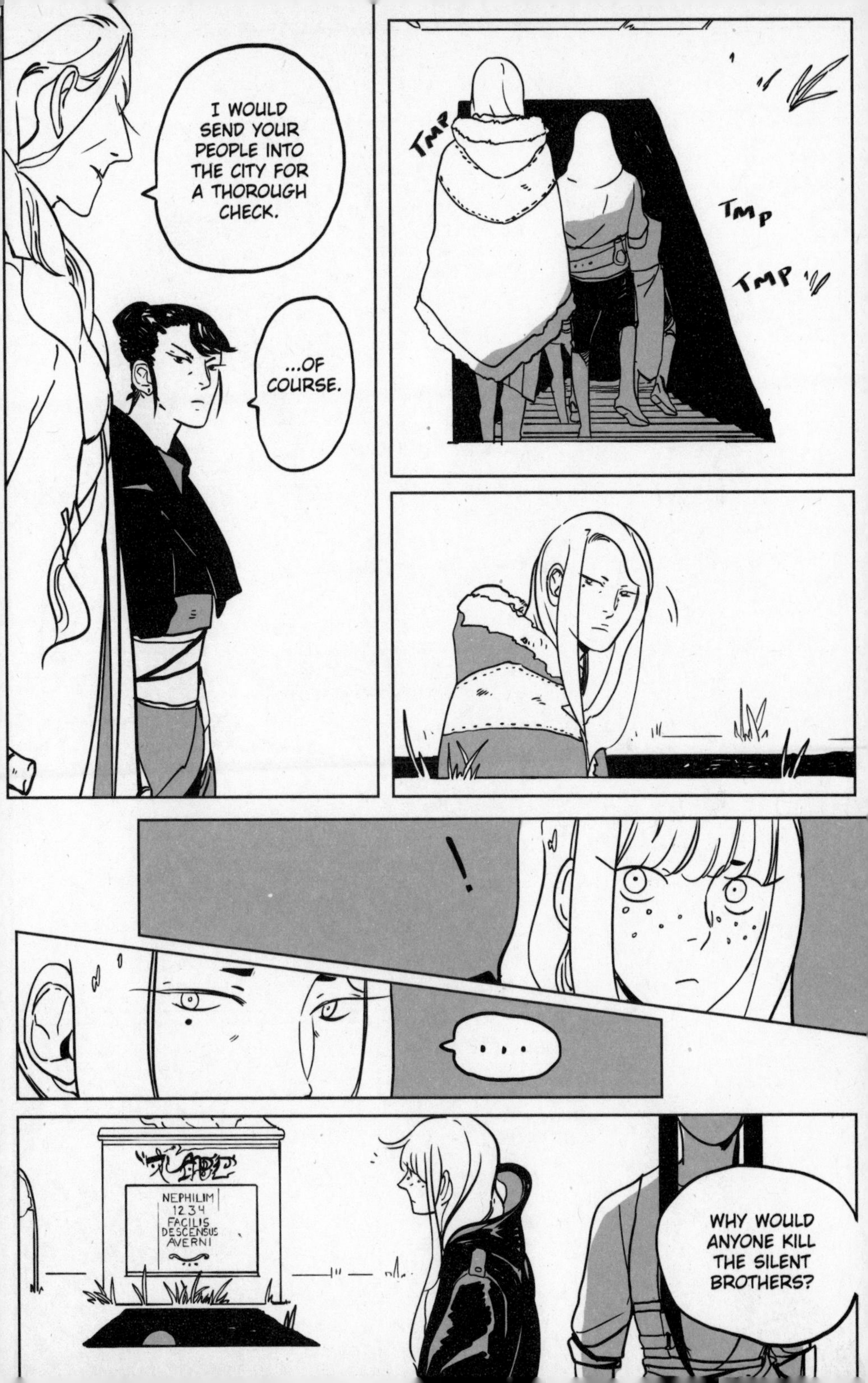
I WOULD SEND YOUR PEOPLE INTO THE CITY FOR A THOROUGH CHECK.
...OF COURSE.
TMP
TMP
TMP
!
...
NEPHILIM
12.3.4
FACILIS DESCENSUS AVERNI
WHY WOULD ANYONE KILL THE SILENT BROTHERS?

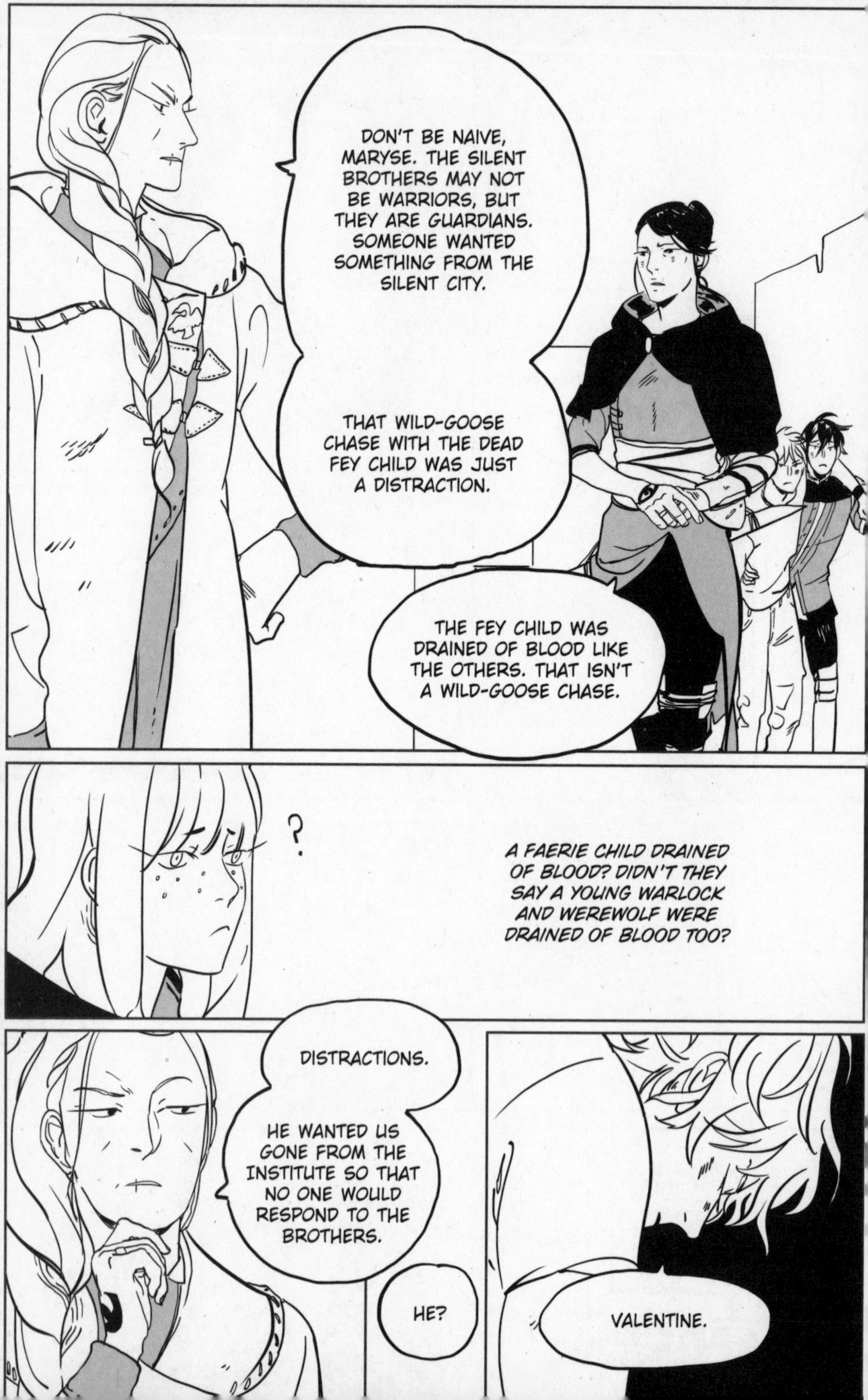
DON'T BE NAIVE, MARYSE. THE SILENT BROTHERS MAY NOT BE WARRIORS, BUT THEY ARE GUARDIANS. SOMEONE WANTED SOMETHING FROM THE SILENT CITY.
THAT WILD-GOOSE CHASE WITH THE DEAD FEY CHILD WAS JUST A DISTRACTION.
THE FEY CHILD WAS DRAINED OF BLOOD LIKE THE OTHERS. THAT ISN'T A WILD-GOOSE CHASE.
?
A FAERIE CHILD DRAINED OF BLOOD? DIDN'T THEY SAY A YOUNG WARLOCK AND WEREWOLF WERE DRAINED OF BLOOD TOO?
DISTRACTIONS.
HE WANTED US GONE FROM THE INSTITUTE SO THAT NO ONE WOULD RESPOND TO THE BROTHERS.
HE?
VALENTINE.

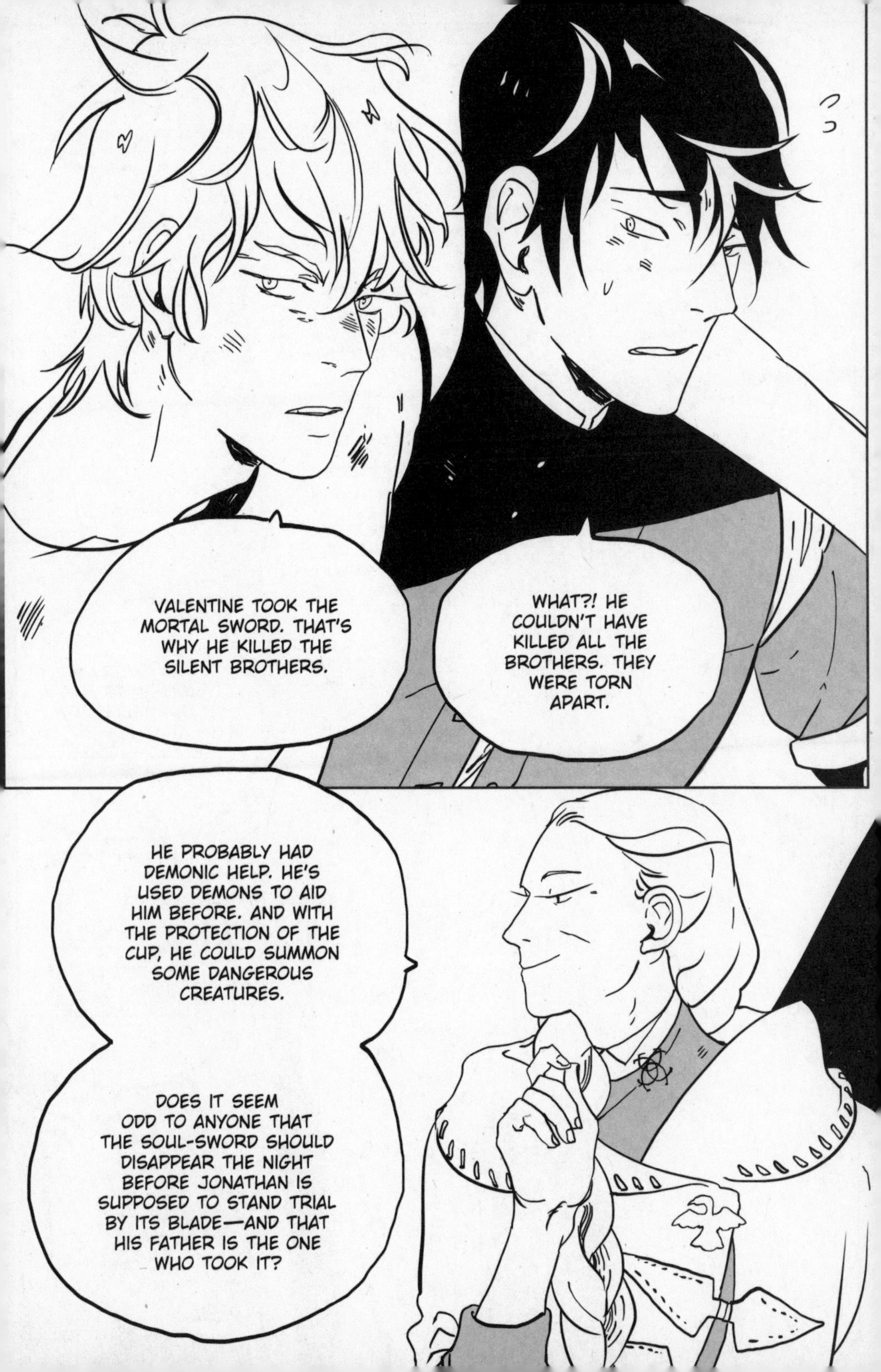
VALENTINE TOOK THE MORTAL SWORD. THAT'S WHY HE KILLED THE SILENT BROTHERS.
WHAT?! HE COULDN'T HAVE KILLED ALL THE BROTHERS. THEY WERE TORN APART.
HE PROBABLY HAD DEMONIC HELP. HE'S USED DEMONS TO AID HIM BEFORE. AND WITH THE PROTECTION OF THE CUP, HE COULD SUMMON SOME DANGEROUS CREATURES.
DOES IT SEEM ODD TO ANYONE THAT THE SOUL-SWORD SHOULD DISAPPEAR THE NIGHT BEFORE JONATHAN IS SUPPOSED TO STAND TRIAL BY ITS BLADE—AND THAT HIS FATHER IS THE ONE WHO TOOK IT?

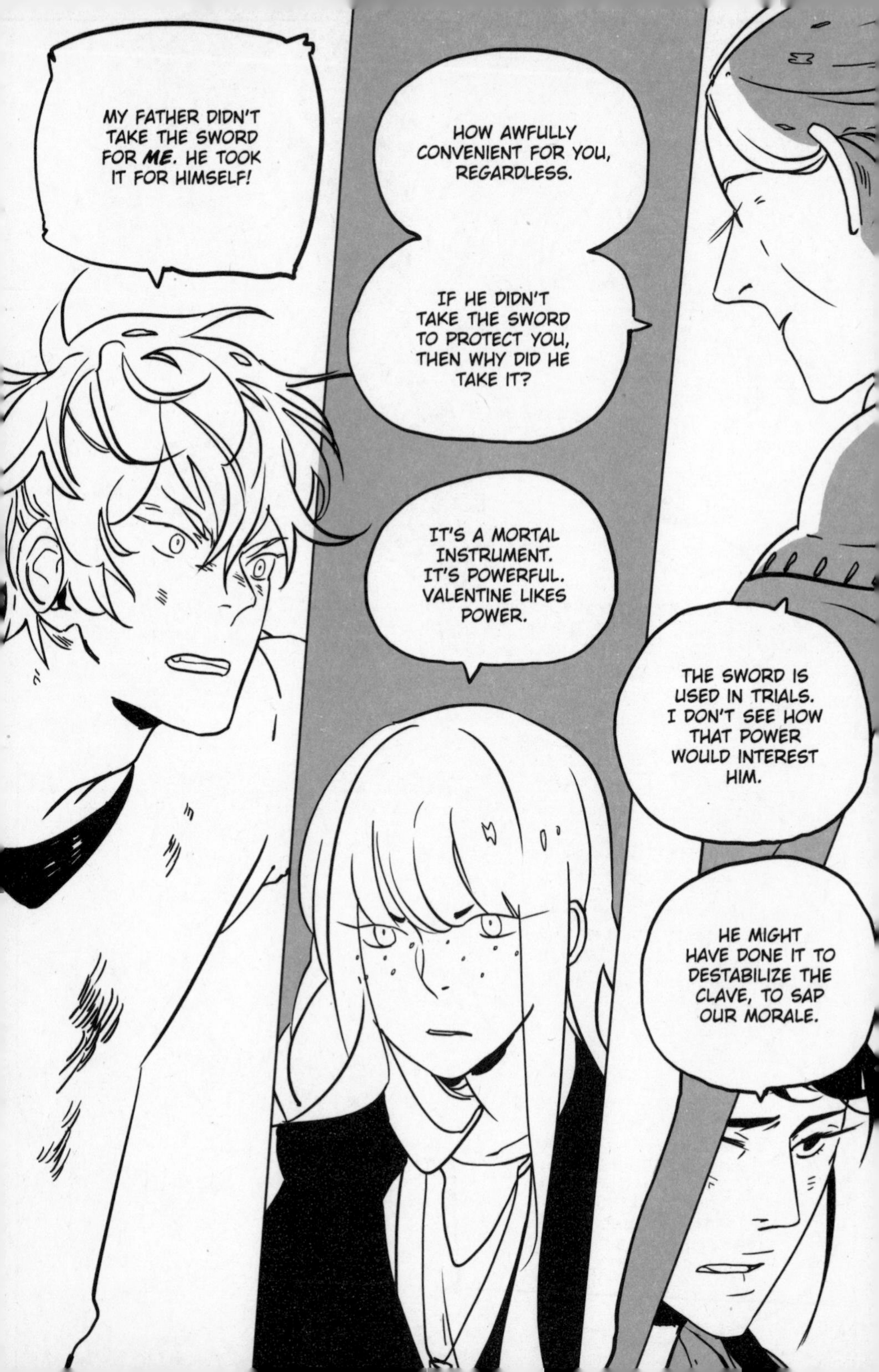
MY FATHER DIDN'T TAKE THE SWORD FOR *ME*. HE TOOK IT FOR HIMSELF!
HOW AWFULLY CONVENIENT FOR YOU, REGARDLESS.
IF HE DIDN'T TAKE THE SWORD TO PROTECT YOU, THEN WHY DID HE TAKE IT?
IT'S A MORTAL INSTRUMENT. IT'S POWERFUL. VALENTINE LIKES POWER.
THE SWORD IS USED IN TRIALS. I DON'T SEE HOW THAT POWER WOULD INTEREST HIM.
HE MIGHT HAVE DONE IT TO DESTABILIZE THE CLAVE, TO SAP OUR MORALE.

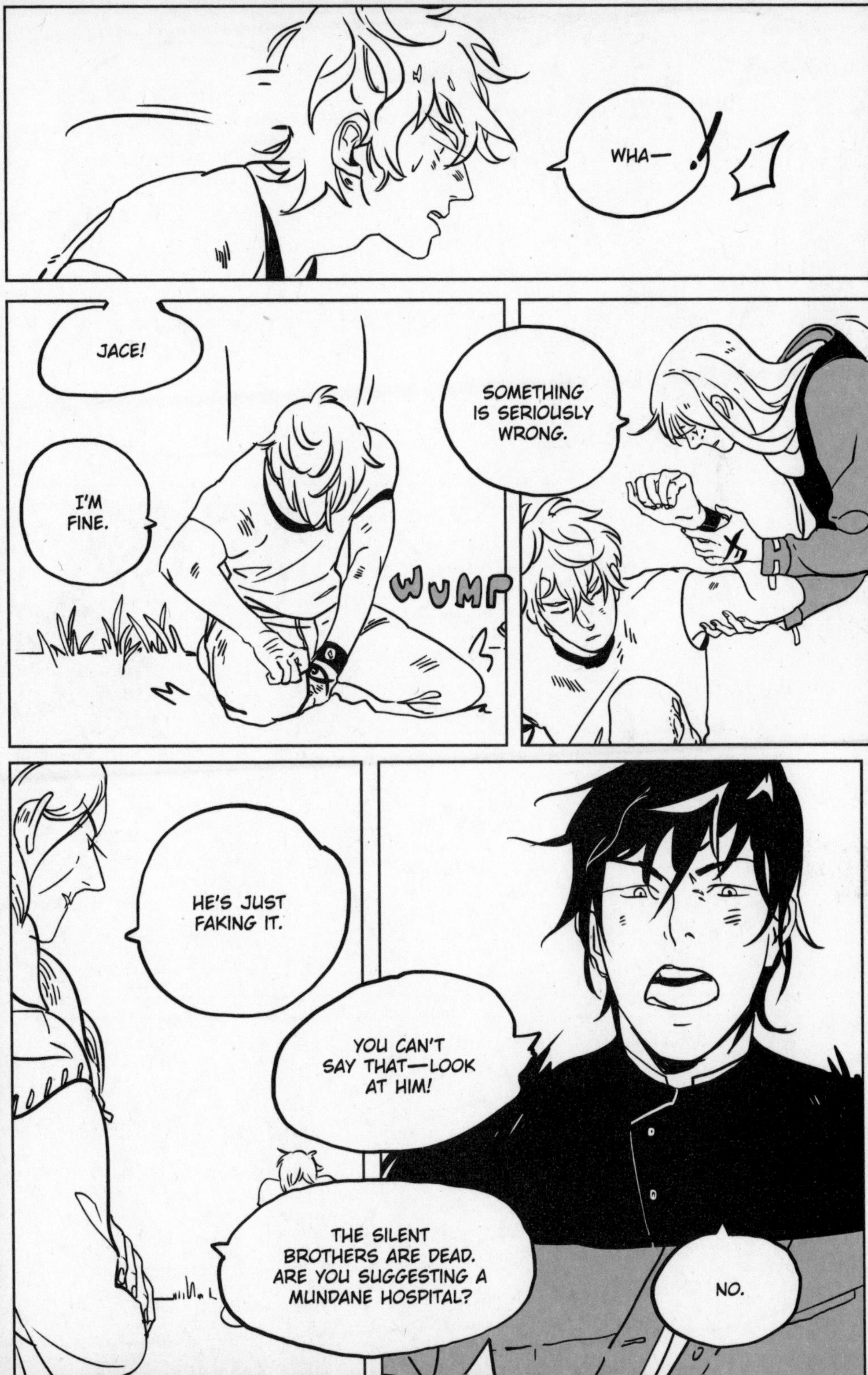
WHA—
JACE!
I'M FINE.
WUMP
SOMETHING IS SERIOUSLY WRONG.
HE'S JUST FAKING IT.
YOU CAN'T SAY THAT—LOOK AT HIM!
THE SILENT BROTHERS ARE DEAD. ARE YOU SUGGESTING A MUNDANE HOSPITAL?
NO.

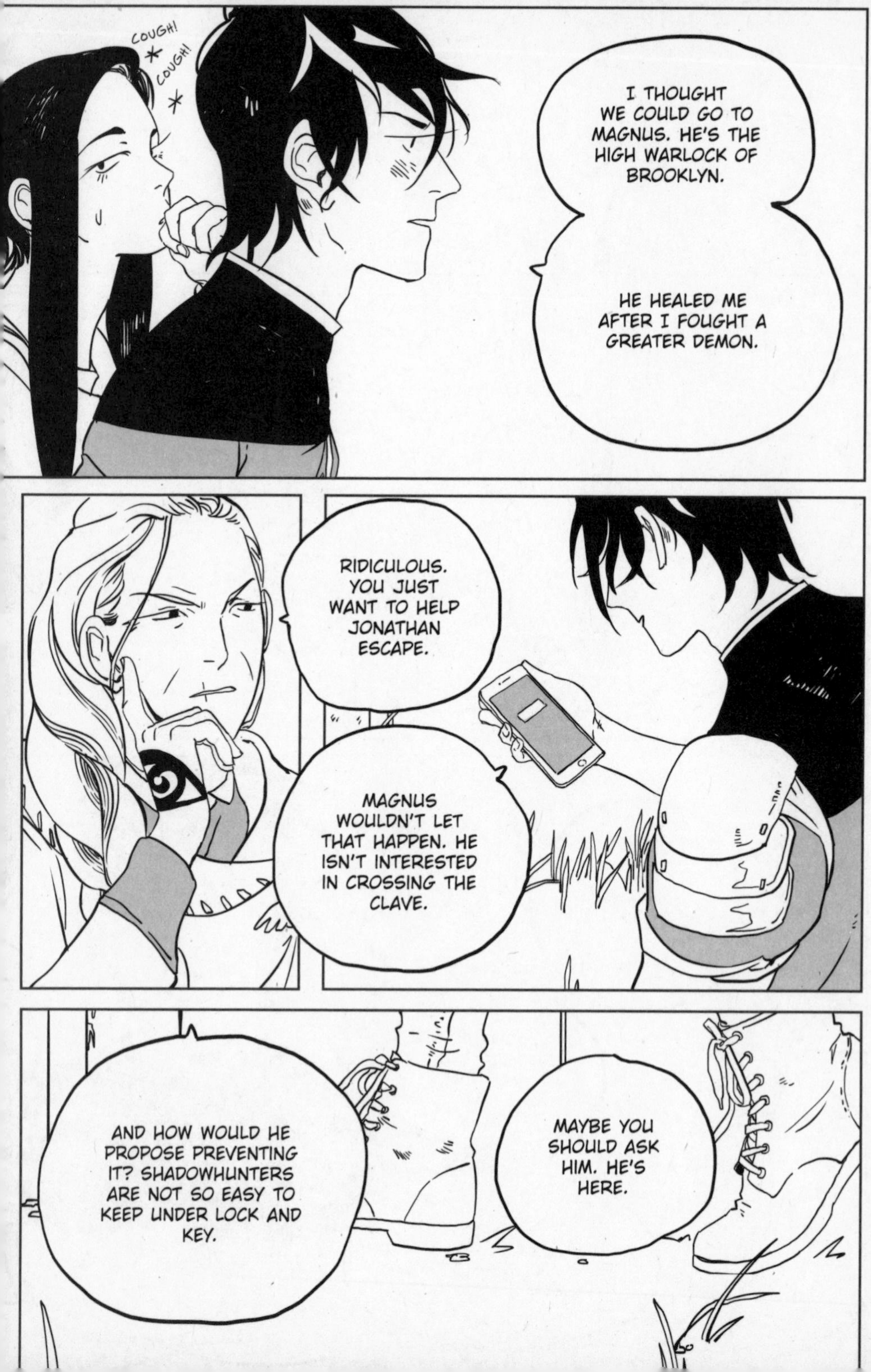
COUGH!
COUGH!
I THOUGHT WE COULD GO TO MAGNUS. HE'S THE HIGH WARLOCK OF BROOKLYN.
HE HEALED ME AFTER I FOUGHT A GREATER DEMON.
RIDICULOUS. YOU JUST WANT TO HELP JONATHAN ESCAPE.
MAGNUS WOULDN'T LET THAT HAPPEN. HE ISN'T INTERESTED IN CROSSING THE CLAVE.
AND HOW WOULD HE PROPOSE PREVENTING IT? SHADOWHUNTERS ARE NOT SO EASY TO KEEP UNDER LOCK AND KEY.
MAYBE YOU SHOULD ASK HIM. HE'S HERE.

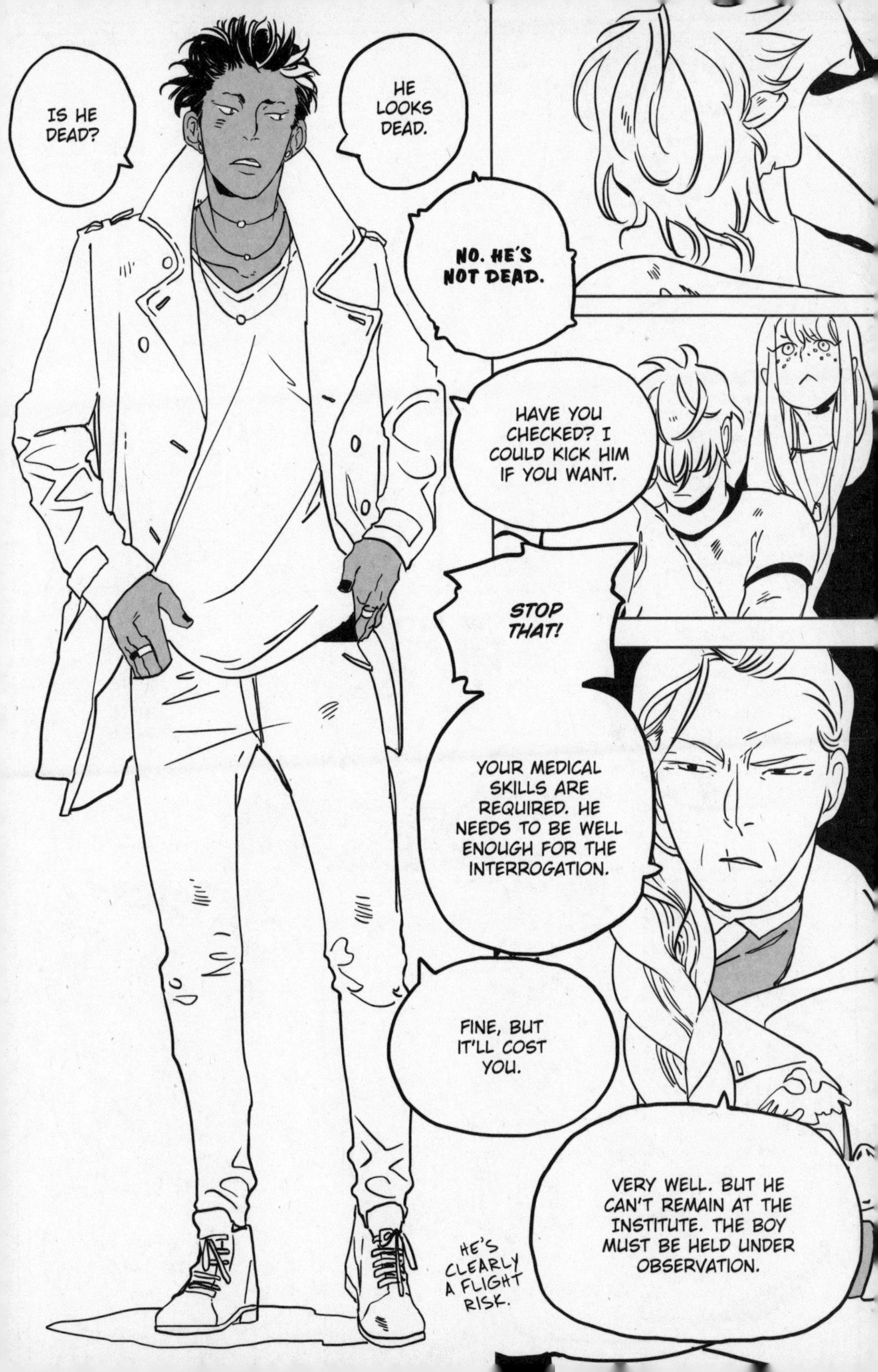
IS HE DEAD?
HE LOOKS DEAD.
NO. HE'S NOT DEAD.
HAVE YOU CHECKED? I COULD KICK HIM IF YOU WANT.
STOP THAT!
YOUR MEDICAL SKILLS ARE REQUIRED. HE NEEDS TO BE WELL ENOUGH FOR THE INTERROGATION.
FINE, BUT IT'LL COST YOU.
VERY WELL. BUT HE CAN'T REMAIN AT THE INSTITUTE. THE BOY MUST BE HELD UNDER OBSERVATION.
HE'S CLEARLY A FLIGHT RISK.

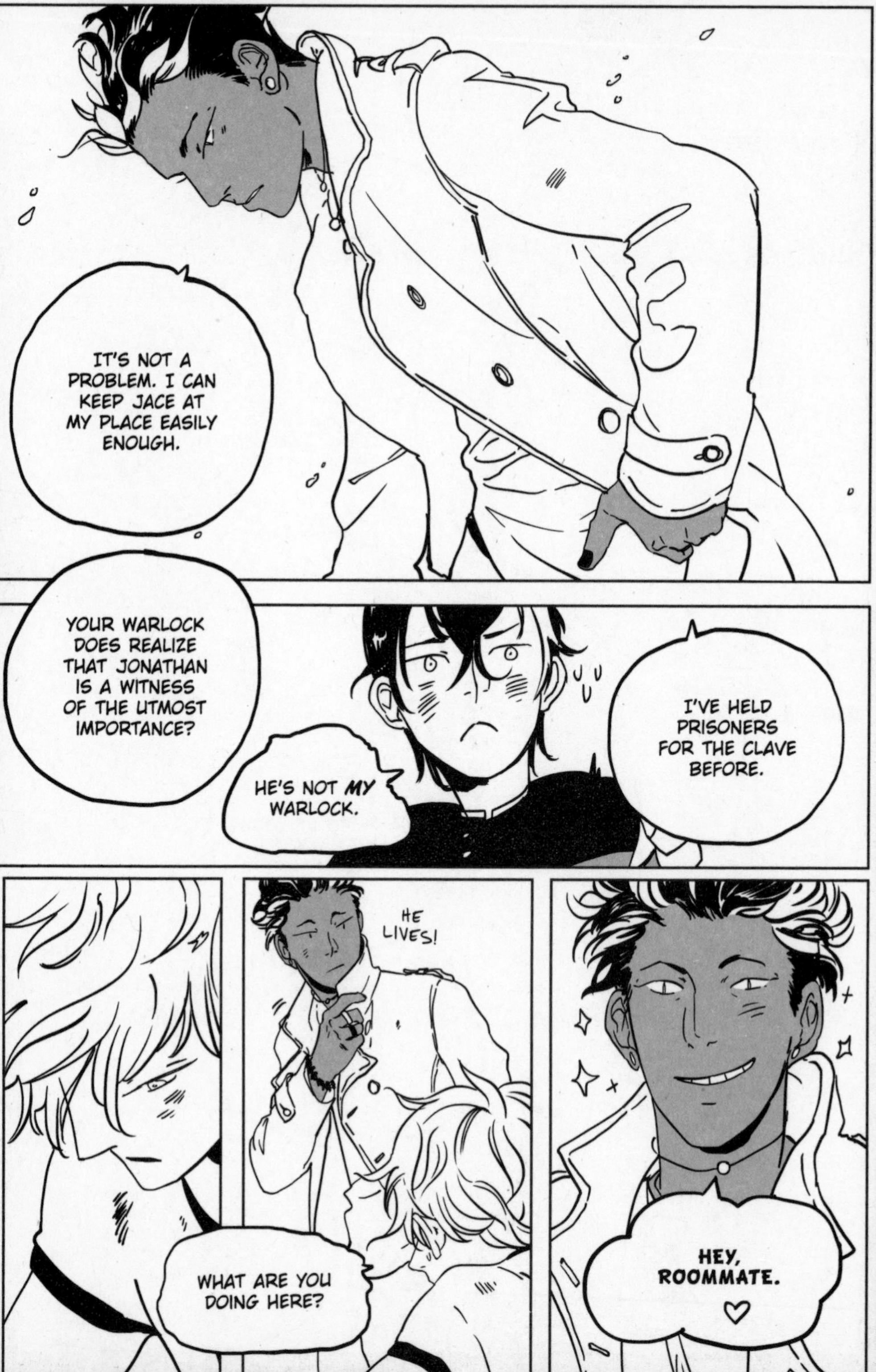
IT'S NOT A PROBLEM. I CAN KEEP JACE AT MY PLACE EASILY ENOUGH.
YOUR WARLOCK DOES REALIZE THAT JONATHAN IS A WITNESS OF THE UTMOST IMPORTANCE?
HE'S NOT MY WARLOCK.
I'VE HELD PRISONERS FOR THE CLAVE BEFORE.
WHAT ARE YOU DOING HERE?
HE LIVES!
HEY, ROOMMATE. ♡

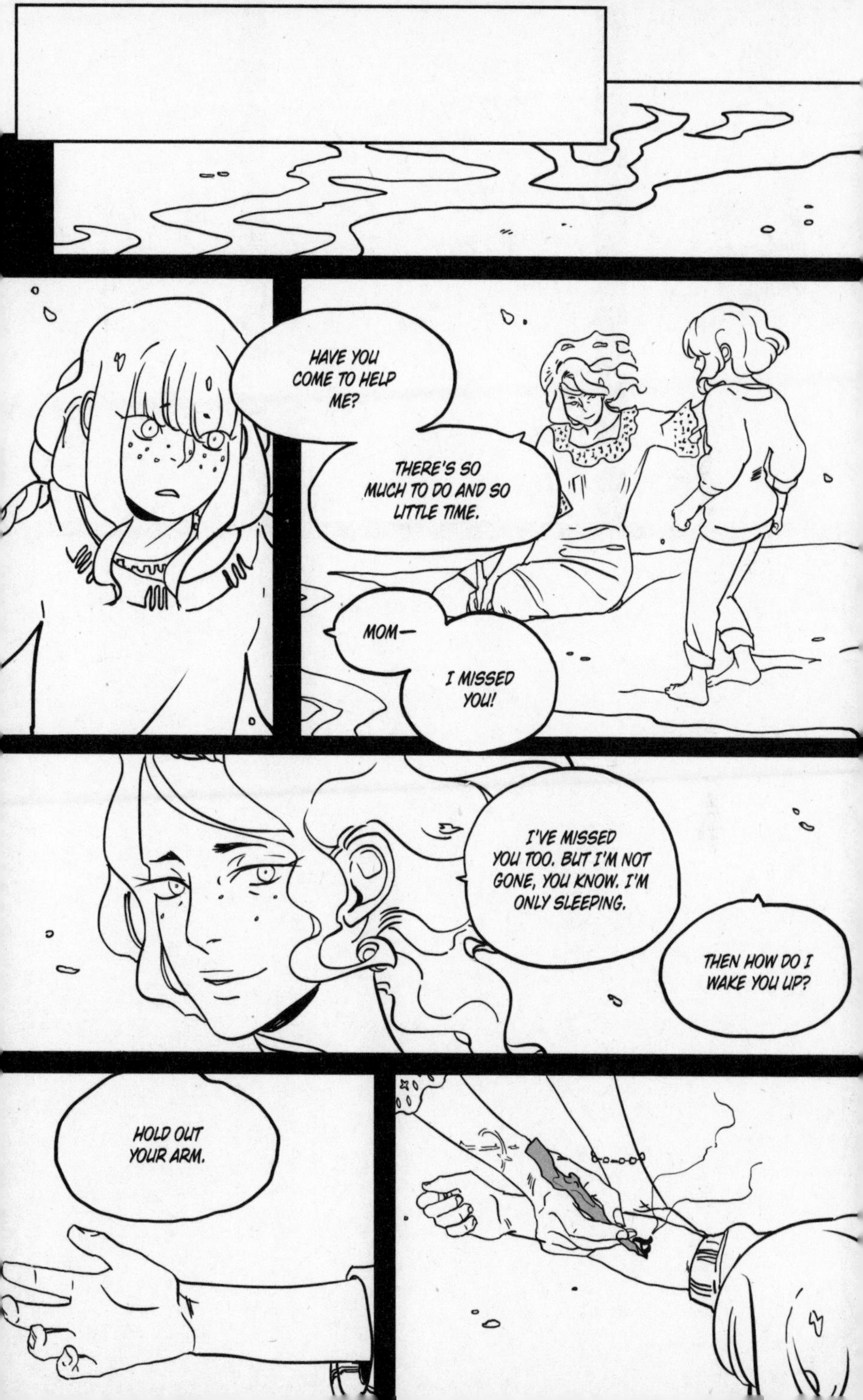
HAVE YOU COME TO HELP ME?
THERE'S SO MUCH TO DO AND SO LITTLE TIME.
MOM—
I MISSED YOU!
I'VE MISSED YOU TOO. BUT I'M NOT GONE, YOU KNOW. I'M ONLY SLEEPING.
THEN HOW DO I WAKE YOU UP?
HOLD OUT YOUR ARM.

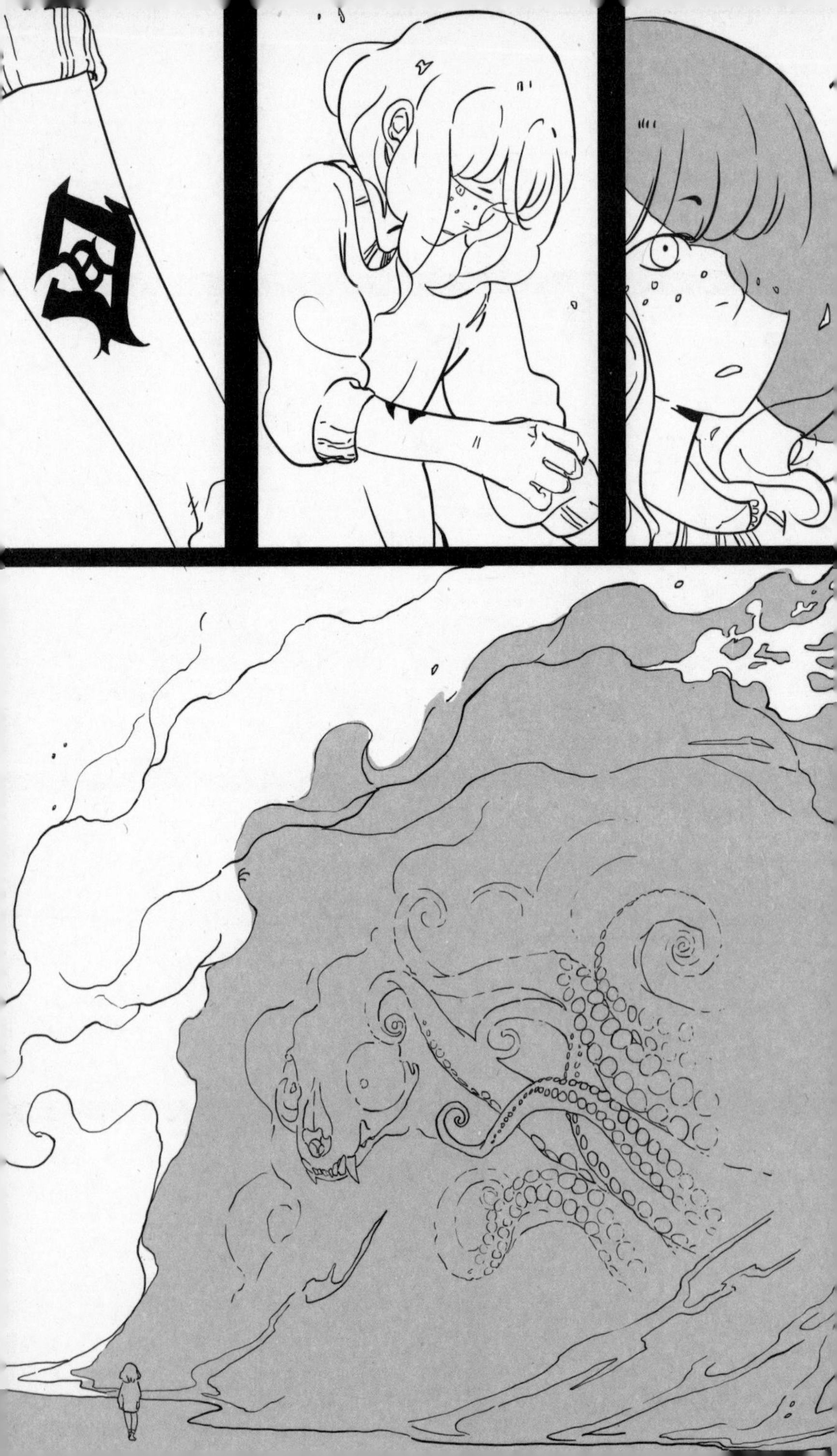

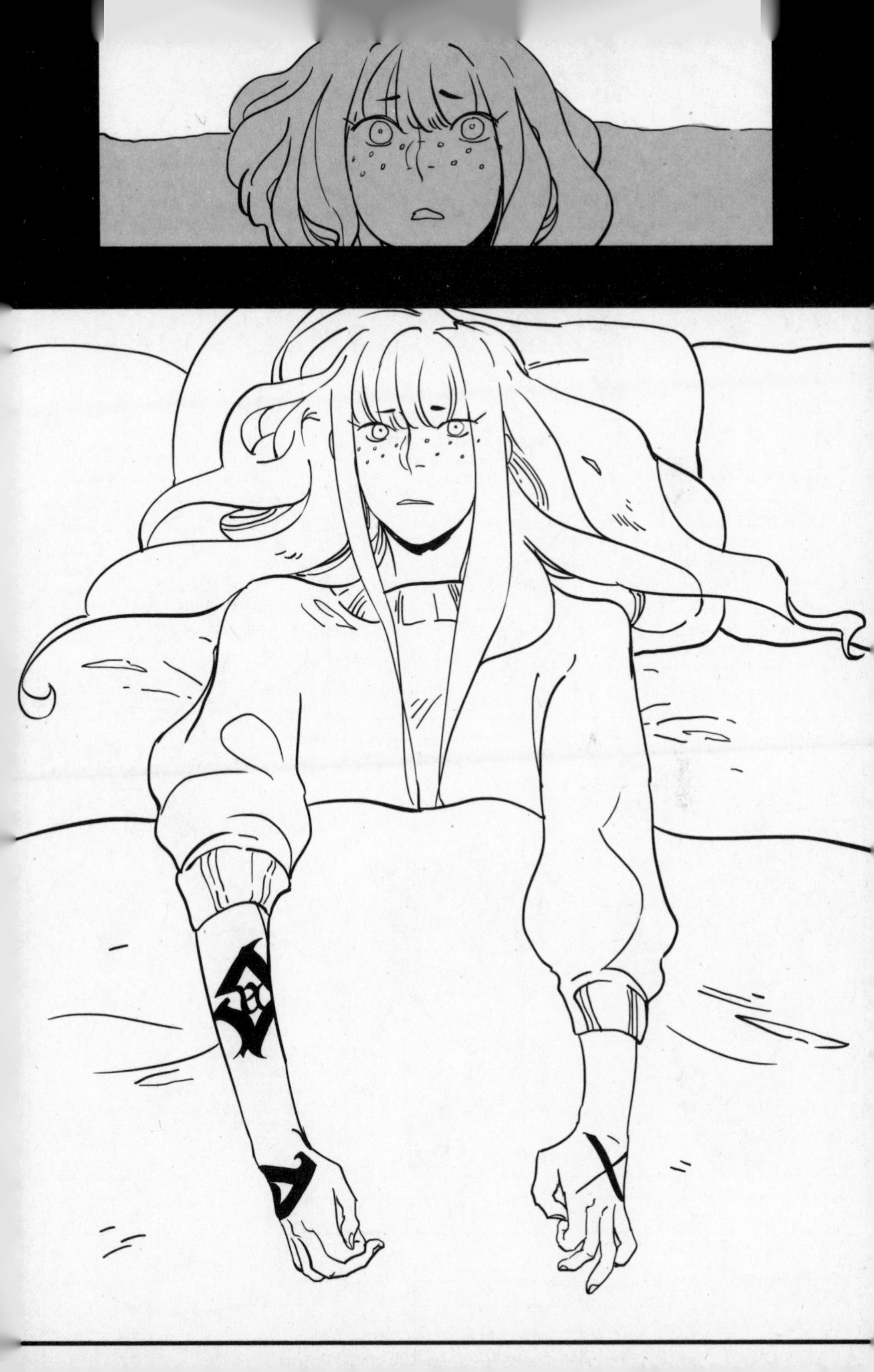

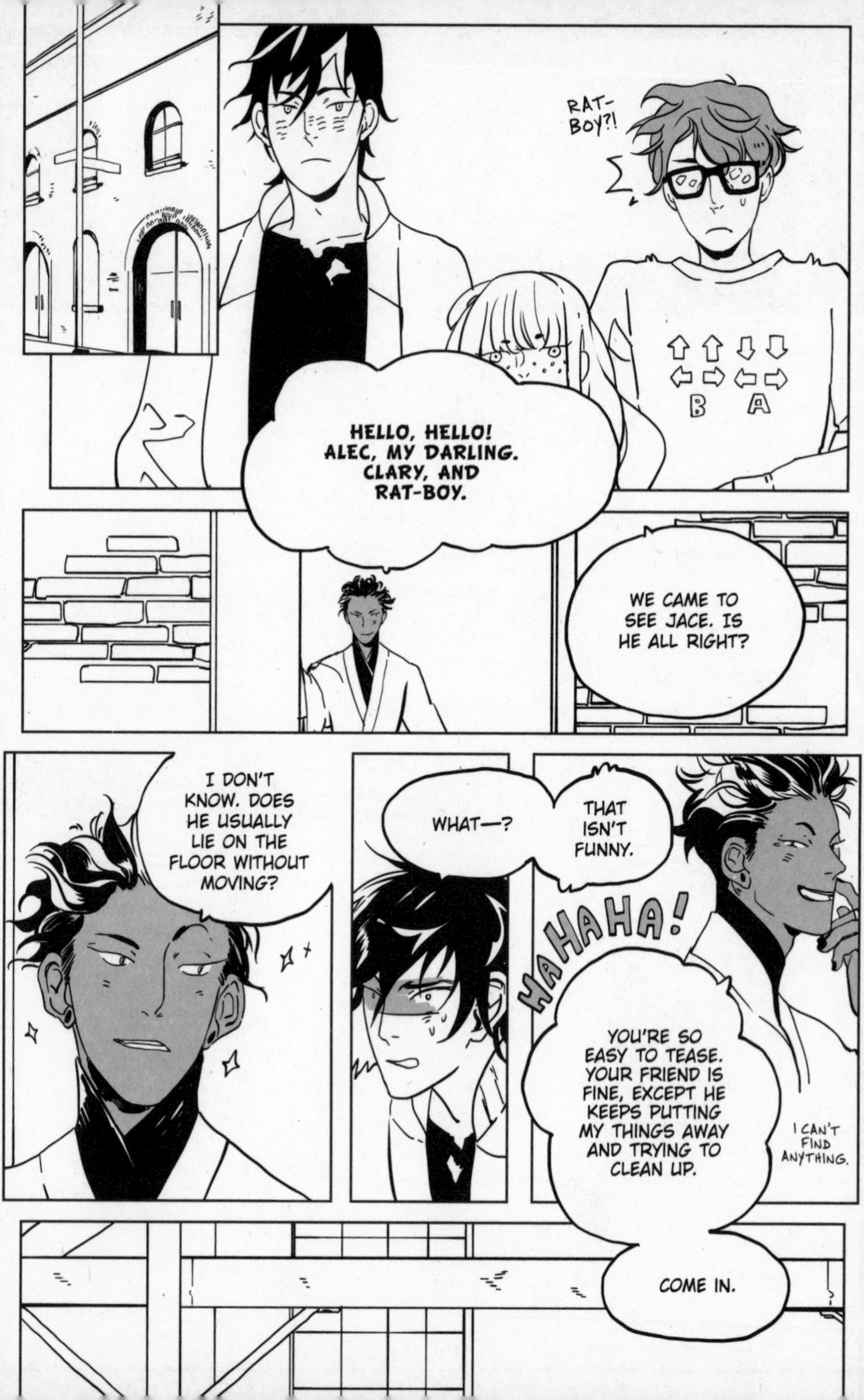
RAT-BOY?!
HELLO, HELLO! ALEC, MY DARLING. CLARY, AND RAT-BOY.
WE CAME TO SEE JACE. IS HE ALL RIGHT?
I DON'T KNOW. DOES HE USUALLY LIE ON THE FLOOR WITHOUT MOVING?
WHAT—?
THAT ISN'T FUNNY.
HAHAHAHA!
YOU'RE SO EASY TO TEASE. YOUR FRIEND IS FINE, EXCEPT HE KEEPS PUTTING MY THINGS AWAY AND TRYING TO CLEAN UP.
I CAN'T FIND ANYTHING.
COME IN.

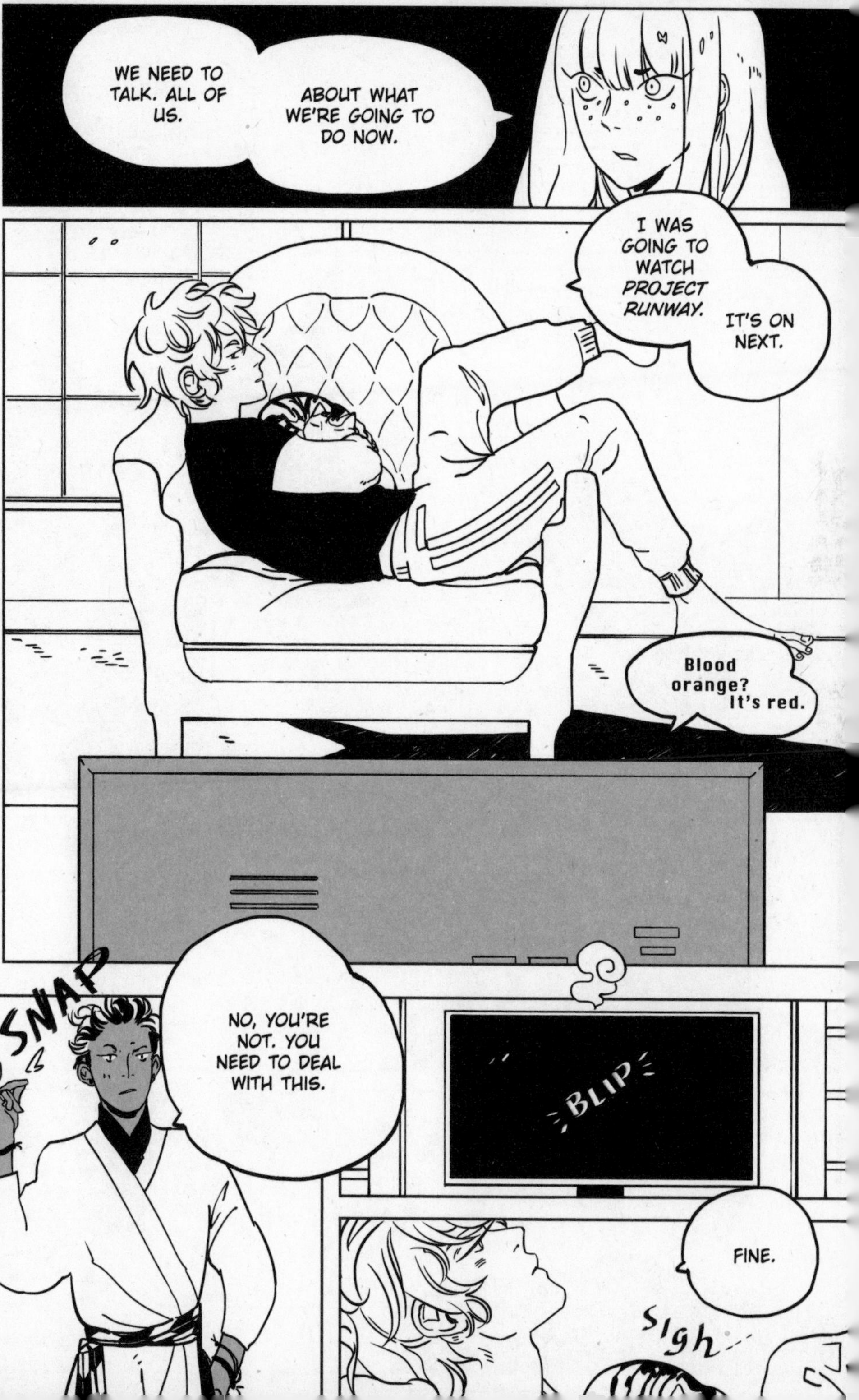
WE NEED TO TALK. ALL OF US.
ABOUT WHAT WE'RE GOING TO DO NOW.
I WAS GOING TO WATCH PROJECT RUNWAY.
IT'S ON NEXT.
Blood orange? It's red.
SNAP
NO, YOU'RE NOT. YOU NEED TO DEAL WITH THIS.
BLIP
FINE.
Sigh

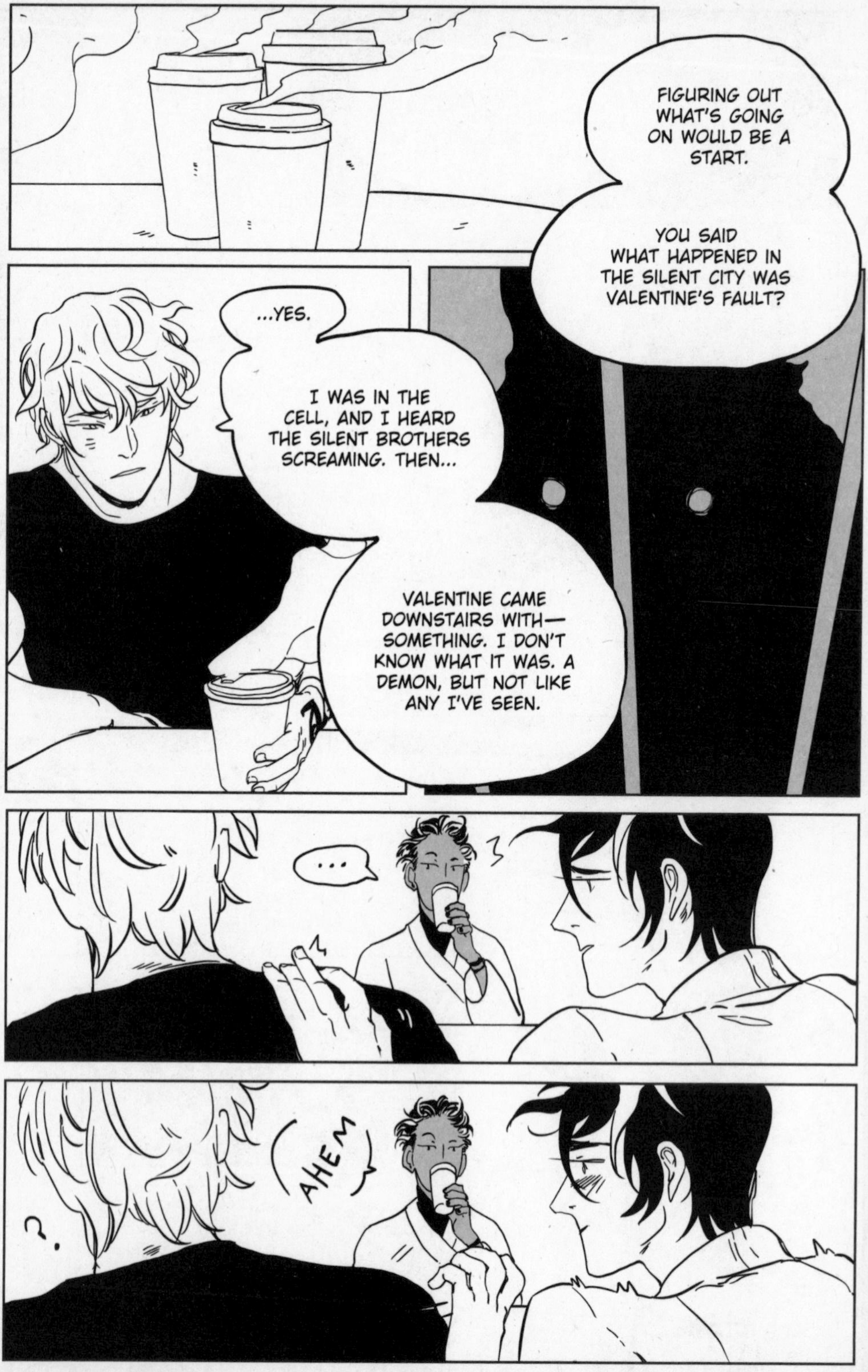
FIGURING OUT WHAT'S GOING ON WOULD BE A START.
YOU SAID WHAT HAPPENED IN THE SILENT CITY WAS VALENTINE'S FAULT?
...YES.
I WAS IN THE CELL, AND I HEARD THE SILENT BROTHERS SCREAMING. THEN...
VALENTINE CAME DOWNSTAIRS WITH— SOMETHING. I DON'T KNOW WHAT IT WAS. A DEMON, BUT NOT LIKE ANY I'VE SEEN.
...
AHEM
?

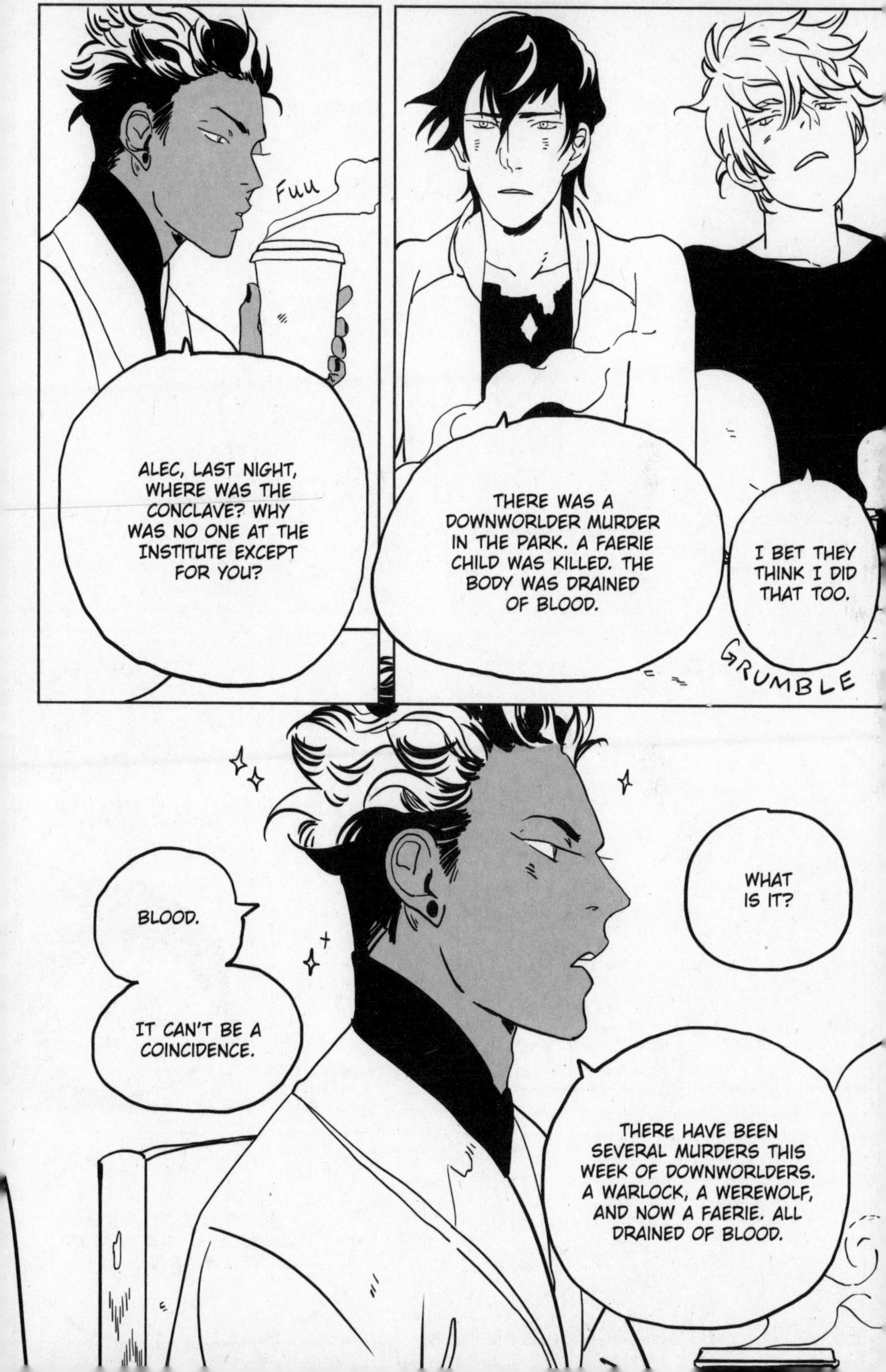
FUU
ALEC, LAST NIGHT, WHERE WAS THE CONCLAVE? WHY WAS NO ONE AT THE INSTITUTE EXCEPT FOR YOU?
THERE WAS A DOWNWORLDER MURDER IN THE PARK. A FAERIE CHILD WAS KILLED. THE BODY WAS DRAINED OF BLOOD.
I BET THEY THINK I DID THAT TOO.
GRUMBLE
BLOOD.
IT CAN'T BE A COINCIDENCE.
WHAT IS IT?
THERE HAVE BEEN SEVERAL MURDERS THIS WEEK OF DOWNWORLDERS. A WARLOCK, A WEREWOLF, AND NOW A FAERIE. ALL DRAINED OF BLOOD.

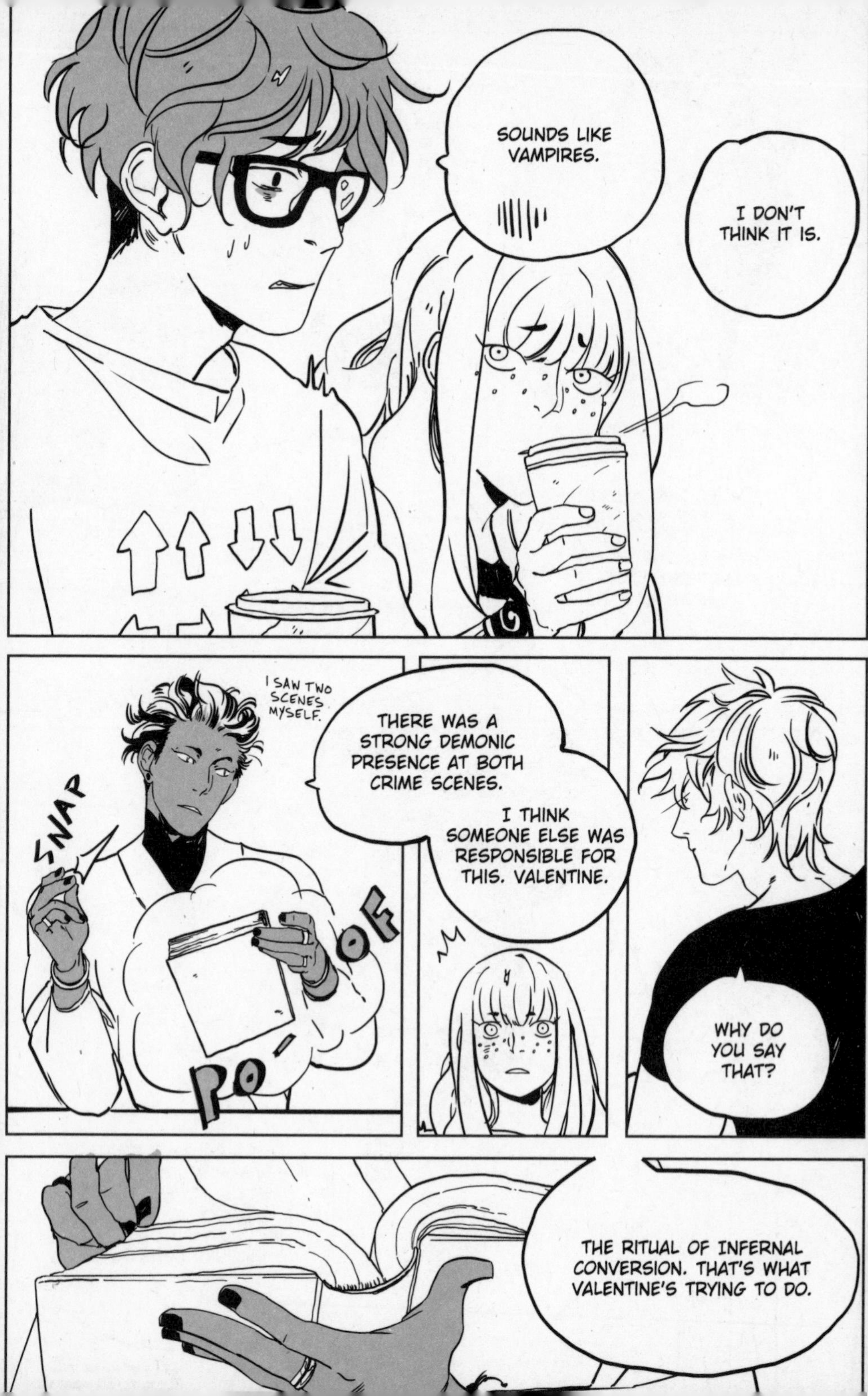
SOUNDS LIKE VAMPIRES.
I DON'T THINK IT IS.
I SAW TWO SCENES MYSELF.
SNAP
POOF
THERE WAS A STRONG DEMONIC PRESENCE AT BOTH CRIME SCENES.
I THINK SOMEONE ELSE WAS RESPONSIBLE FOR THIS. VALENTINE.
WHY DO YOU SAY THAT?
THE RITUAL OF INFERNAL CONVERSION. THAT'S WHAT VALENTINE'S TRYING TO DO.

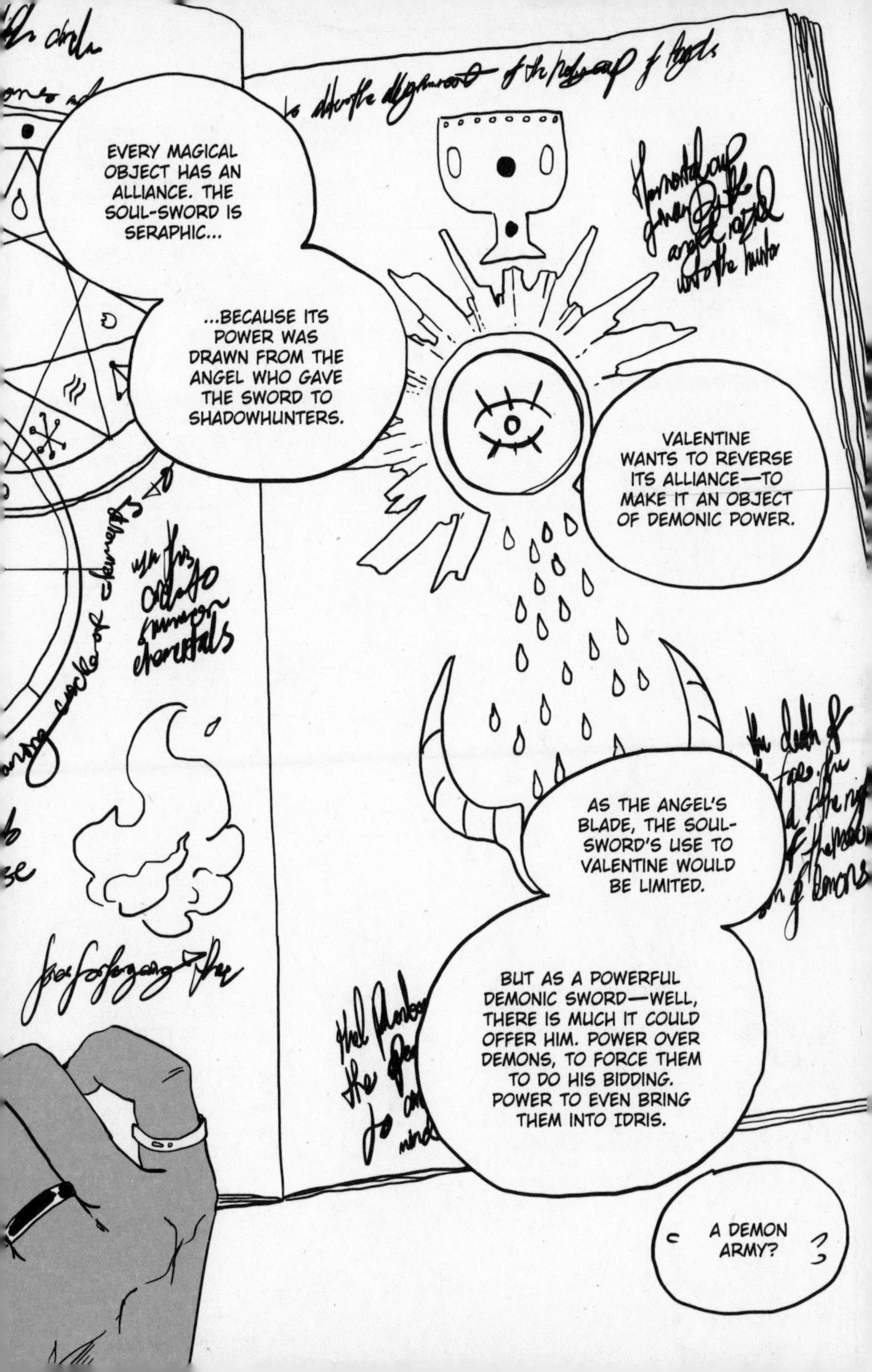
EVERY MAGICAL OBJECT HAS AN ALLIANCE. THE SOUL-SWORD IS SERAPHIC...
...BECAUSE ITS POWER WAS DRAWN FROM THE ANGEL WHO GAVE THE SWORD TO SHADOWHUNTERS.
VALENTINE WANTS TO REVERSE ITS ALLIANCE—TO MAKE IT AN OBJECT OF DEMONIC POWER.
AS THE ANGEL'S BLADE, THE SOUL-SWORD'S USE TO VALENTINE WOULD BE LIMITED.
BUT AS A POWERFUL DEMONIC SWORD—WELL, THERE IS MUCH IT COULD OFFER HIM. POWER OVER DEMONS, TO FORCE THEM TO DO HIS BIDDING. POWER TO EVEN BRING THEM INTO IDRIS.
A DEMON ARMY?

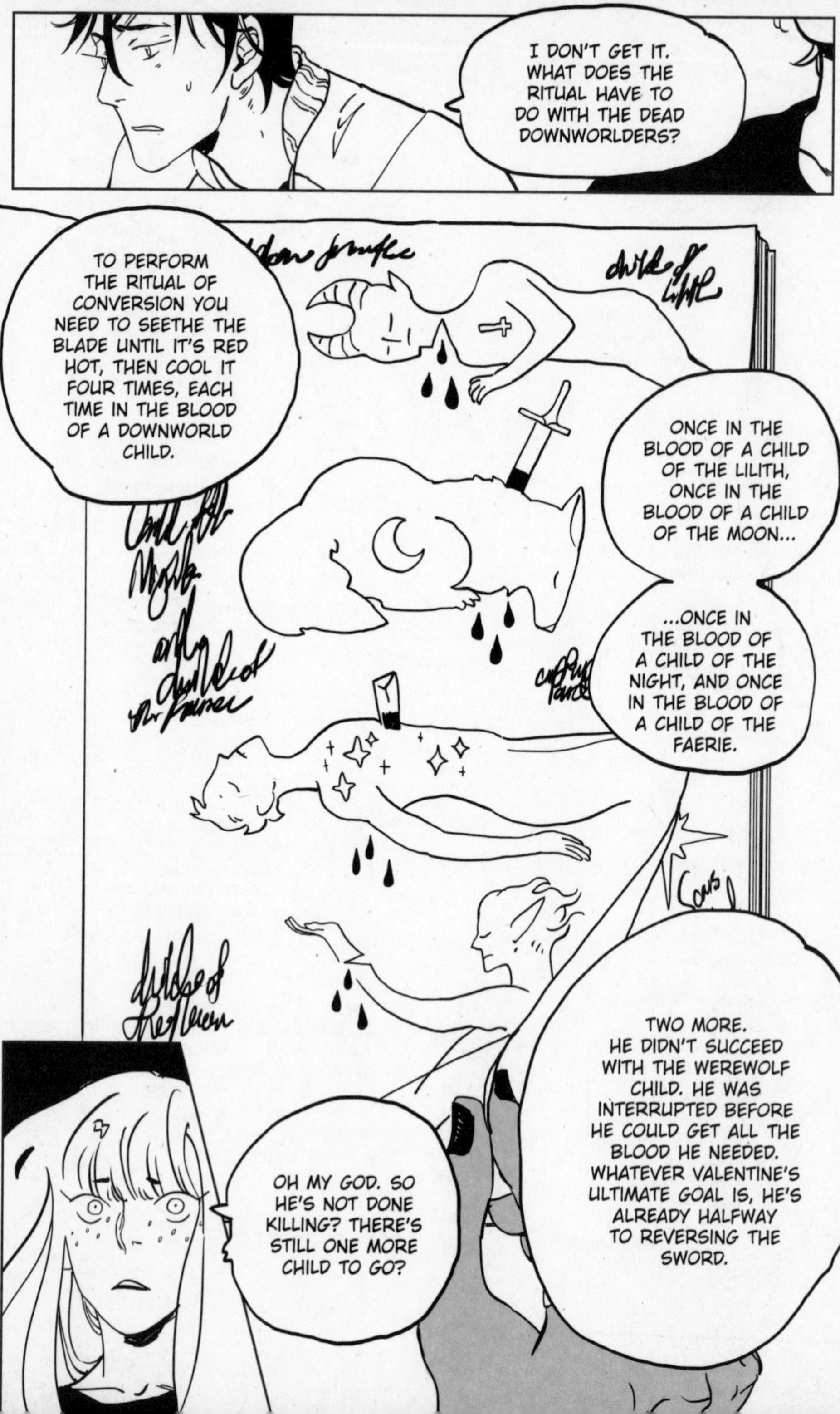
I DON'T GET IT. WHAT DOES THE RITUAL HAVE TO DO WITH THE DEAD DOWNWORLDERS?
TO PERFORM THE RITUAL OF CONVERSION YOU NEED TO SEETHE THE BLADE UNTIL IT'S RED HOT, THEN COOL IT FOUR TIMES, EACH TIME IN THE BLOOD OF A DOWNWORLD CHILD.
ONCE IN THE BLOOD OF A CHILD OF THE LILITH, ONCE IN THE BLOOD OF A CHILD OF THE MOON...
...ONCE IN THE BLOOD OF A CHILD OF THE NIGHT, AND ONCE IN THE BLOOD OF A CHILD OF THE FAERIE.
OH MY GOD. SO HE'S NOT DONE KILLING? THERE'S STILL ONE MORE CHILD TO GO?
TWO MORE. HE DIDN'T SUCCEED WITH THE WEREWOLF CHILD. HE WAS INTERRUPTED BEFORE HE COULD GET ALL THE BLOOD HE NEEDED. WHATEVER VALENTINE'S ULTIMATE GOAL IS, HE'S ALREADY HALFWAY TO REVERSING THE SWORD.

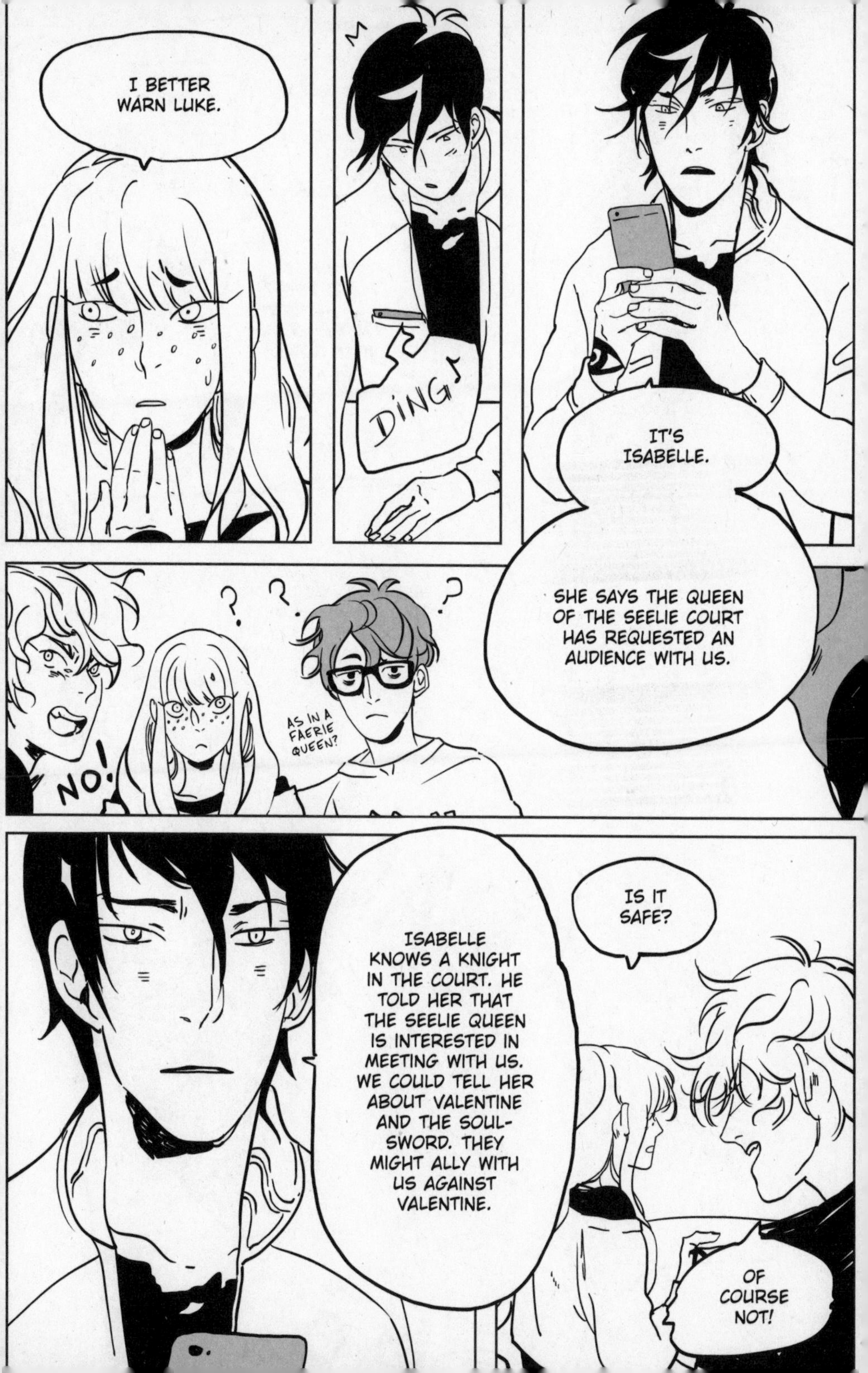
I BETTER WARN LUKE.
DING
IT'S ISABELLE.
SHE SAYS THE QUEEN OF THE SEELIE COURT HAS REQUESTED AN AUDIENCE WITH US.
NO!
AS IN A FAERIE QUEEN?
ISABELLE KNOWS A KNIGHT IN THE COURT. HE TOLD HER THAT THE SEELIE QUEEN IS INTERESTED IN MEETING WITH US. WE COULD TELL HER ABOUT VALENTINE AND THE SOUL-SWORD. THEY MIGHT ALLY WITH US AGAINST VALENTINE.
IS IT SAFE?
OF COURSE NOT!

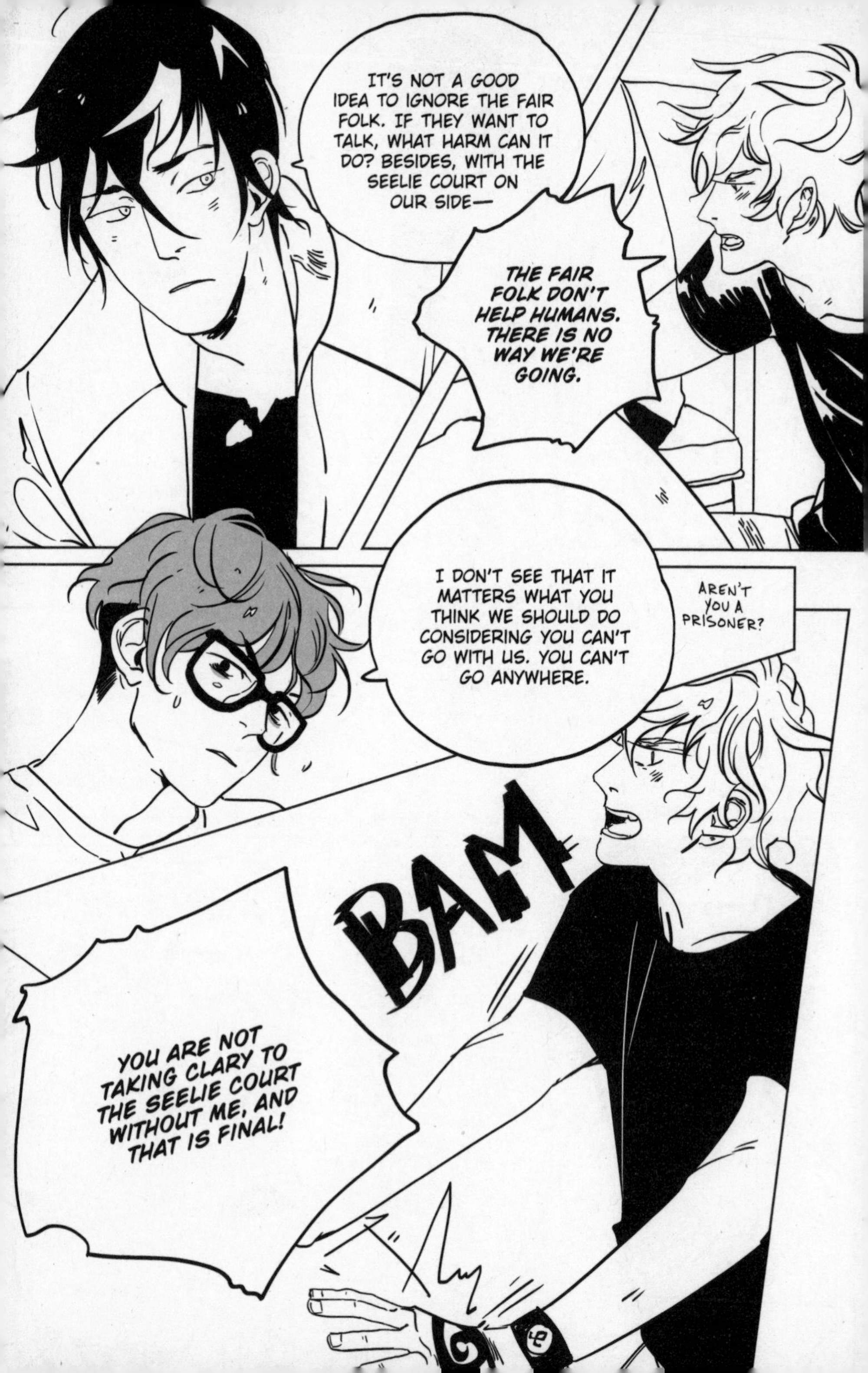
IT'S NOT A GOOD IDEA TO IGNORE THE FAIR FOLK. IF THEY WANT TO TALK, WHAT HARM CAN IT DO? BESIDES, WITH THE SEELIE COURT ON OUR SIDE—
THE FAIR FOLK DON'T HELP HUMANS. THERE IS NO WAY WE'RE GOING.
I DON'T SEE THAT IT MATTERS WHAT YOU THINK WE SHOULD DO CONSIDERING YOU CAN'T GO WITH US. YOU CAN'T GO ANYWHERE.
AREN'T YOU A PRISONER?
BAM
YOU ARE NOT TAKING CLARY TO THE SEELIE COURT WITHOUT ME, AND THAT IS FINAL!

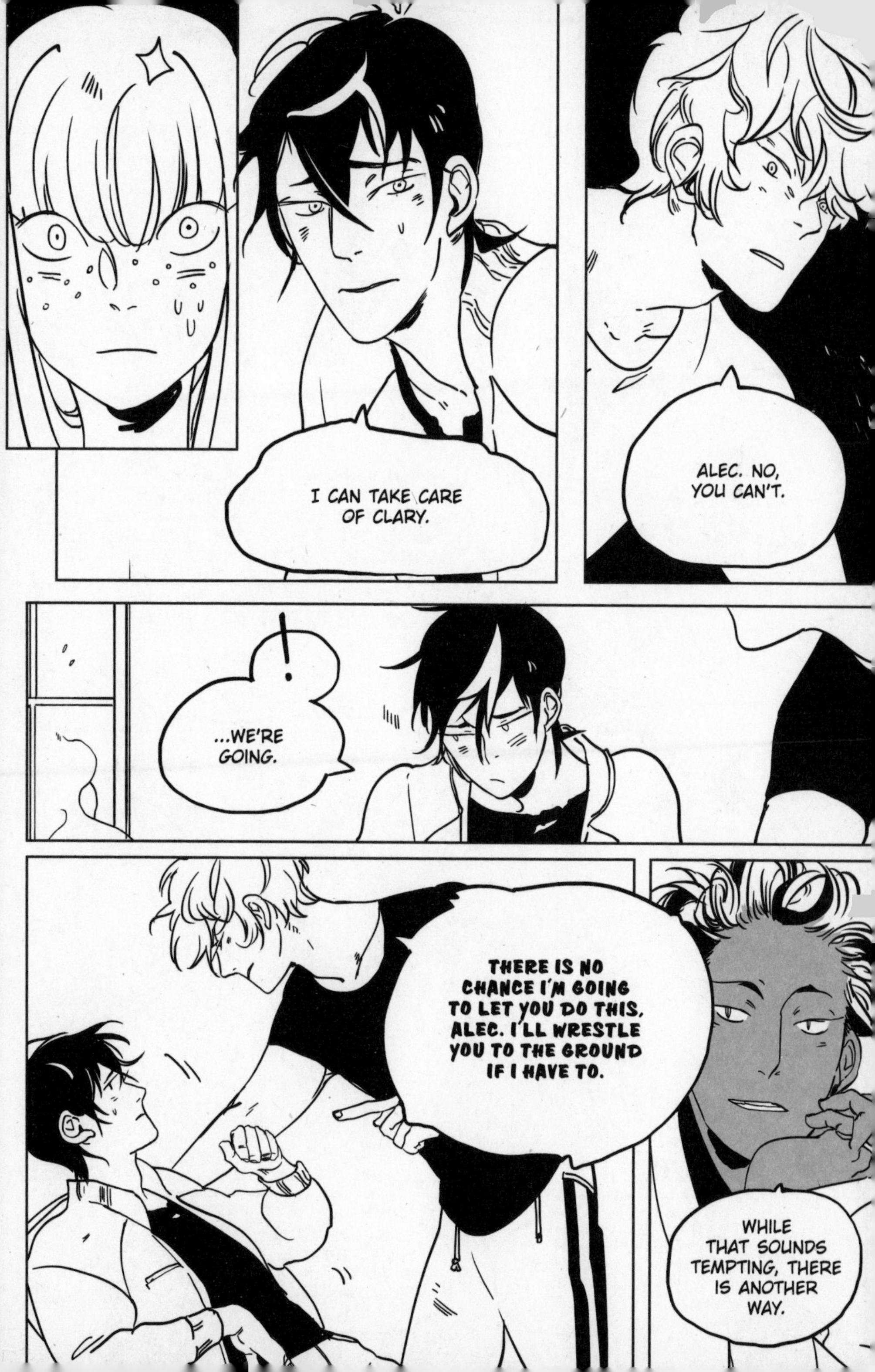
I CAN TAKE CARE OF CLARY.
ALEC. NO, YOU CAN'T.
!
...WE'RE GOING.
THERE IS NO CHANCE I'M GOING TO LET YOU DO THIS, ALEC. I'LL WRESTLE YOU TO THE GROUND IF I HAVE TO.
WHILE THAT SOUNDS TEMPTING, THERE IS ANOTHER WAY.

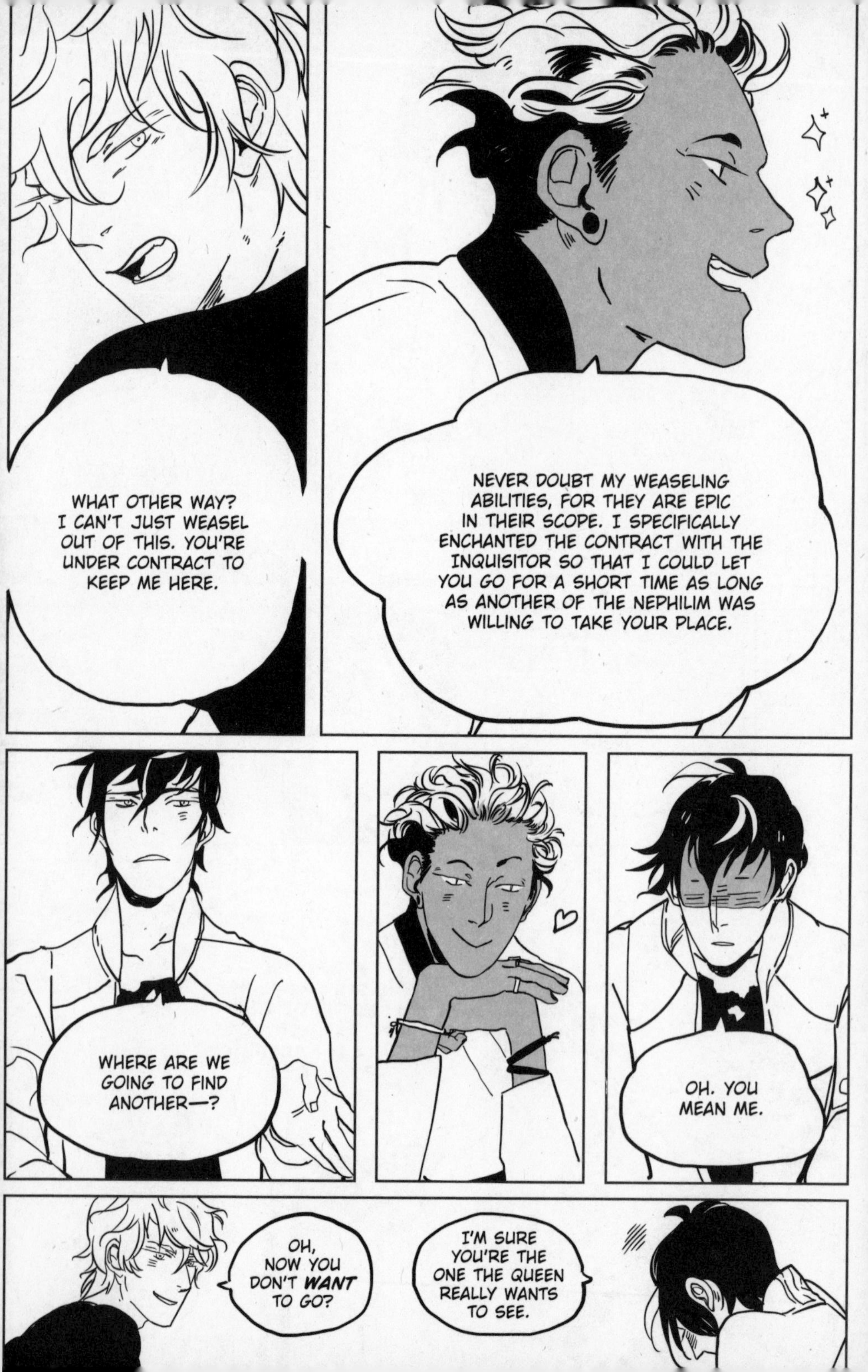
WHAT OTHER WAY? I CAN'T JUST WEASEL OUT OF THIS. YOU'RE UNDER CONTRACT TO KEEP ME HERE.
NEVER DOUBT MY WEASELING ABILITIES, FOR THEY ARE EPIC IN THEIR SCOPE. I SPECIFICALLY ENCHANTED THE CONTRACT WITH THE INQUISITOR SO THAT I COULD LET YOU GO FOR A SHORT TIME AS LONG AS ANOTHER OF THE NEPHILIM WAS WILLING TO TAKE YOUR PLACE.
WHERE ARE WE GOING TO FIND ANOTHER—?
OH. YOU MEAN ME.
OH, NOW YOU DON'T *WANT* TO GO?
I'M SURE YOU'RE THE ONE THE QUEEN REALLY WANTS TO SEE.

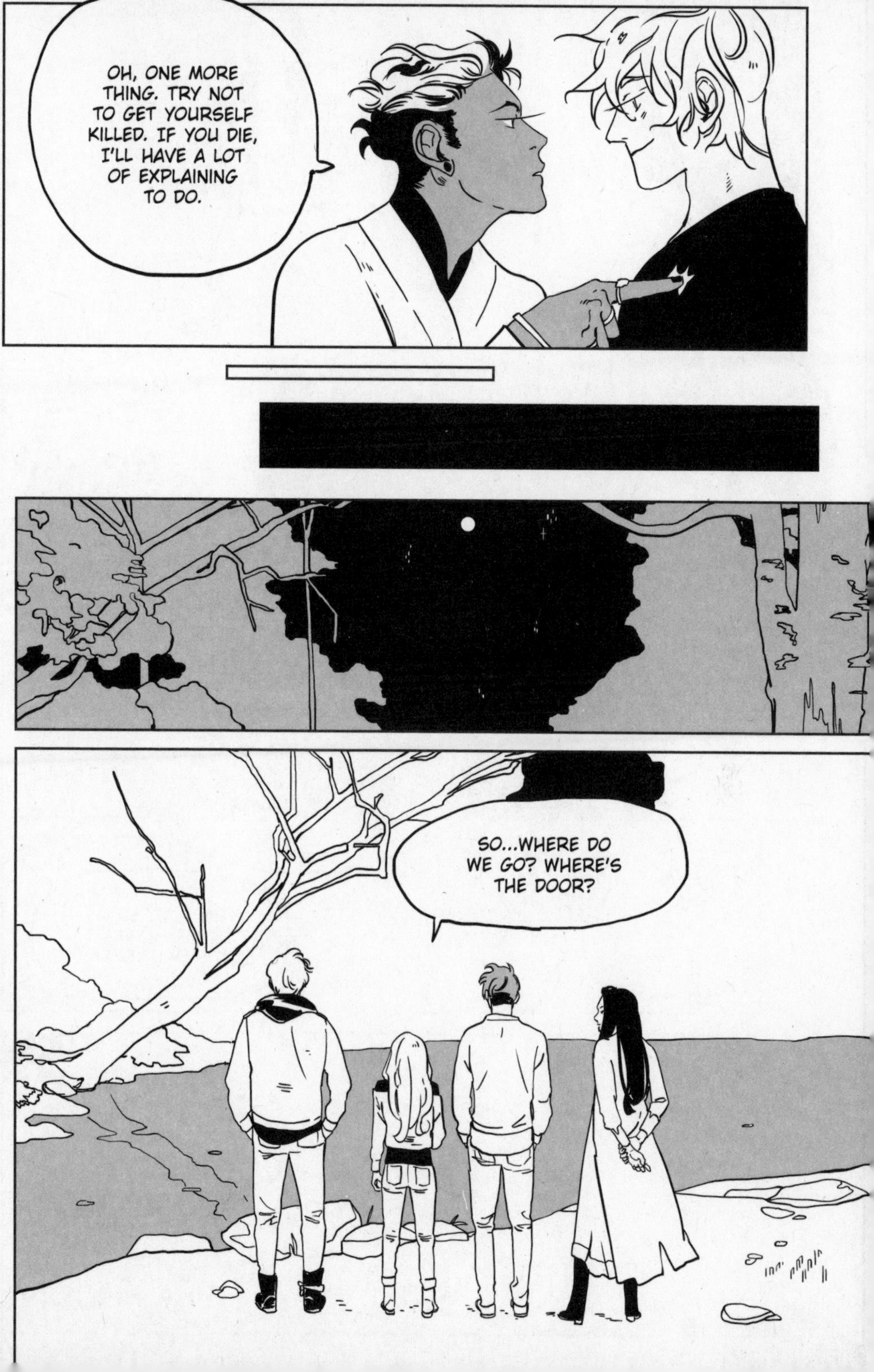
OH, ONE MORE THING. TRY NOT TO GET YOURSELF KILLED. IF YOU DIE, I'LL HAVE A LOT OF EXPLAINING TO DO.
SO...WHERE DO WE GO? WHERE'S THE DOOR?

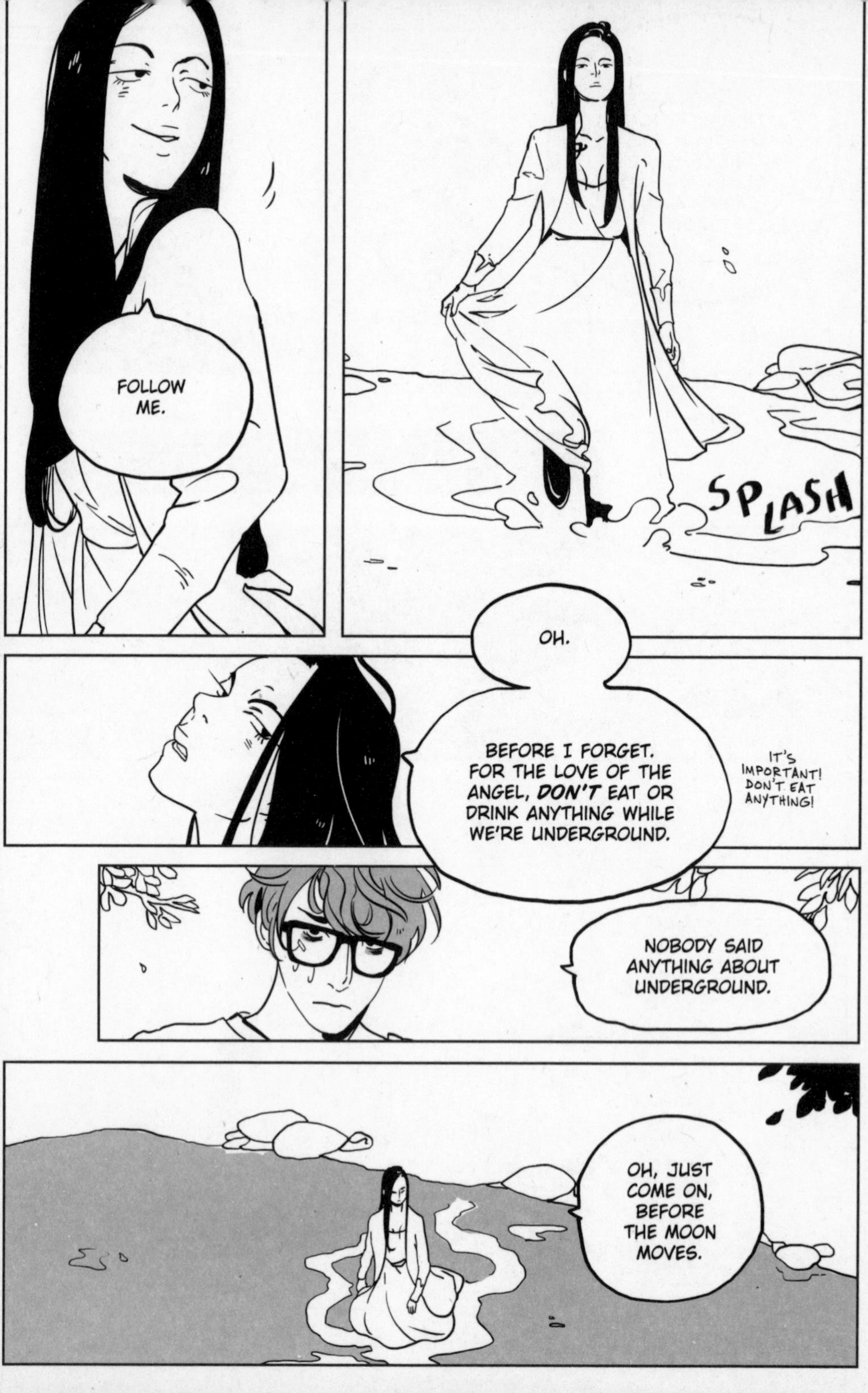
FOLLOW ME.
SPLASH
OH.
BEFORE I FORGET. FOR THE LOVE OF THE ANGEL, ***DON'T*** EAT OR DRINK ANYTHING WHILE WE'RE UNDERGROUND.
IT'S IMPORTANT! DON'T EAT ANYTHING!
NOBODY SAID ANYTHING ABOUT UNDERGROUND.
OH, JUST COME ON, BEFORE THE MOON MOVES.

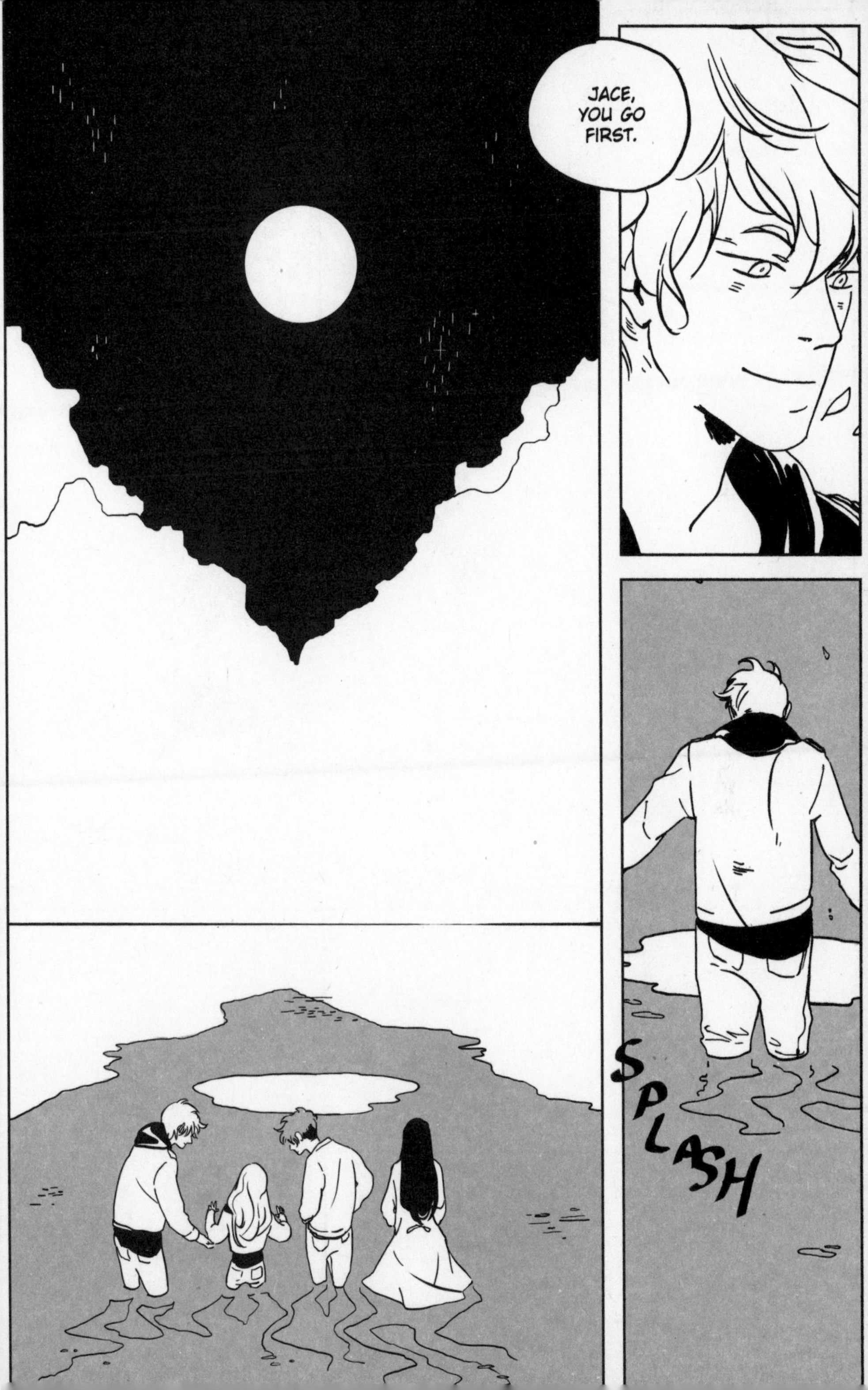
JACE, YOU GO FIRST.
SPLASH

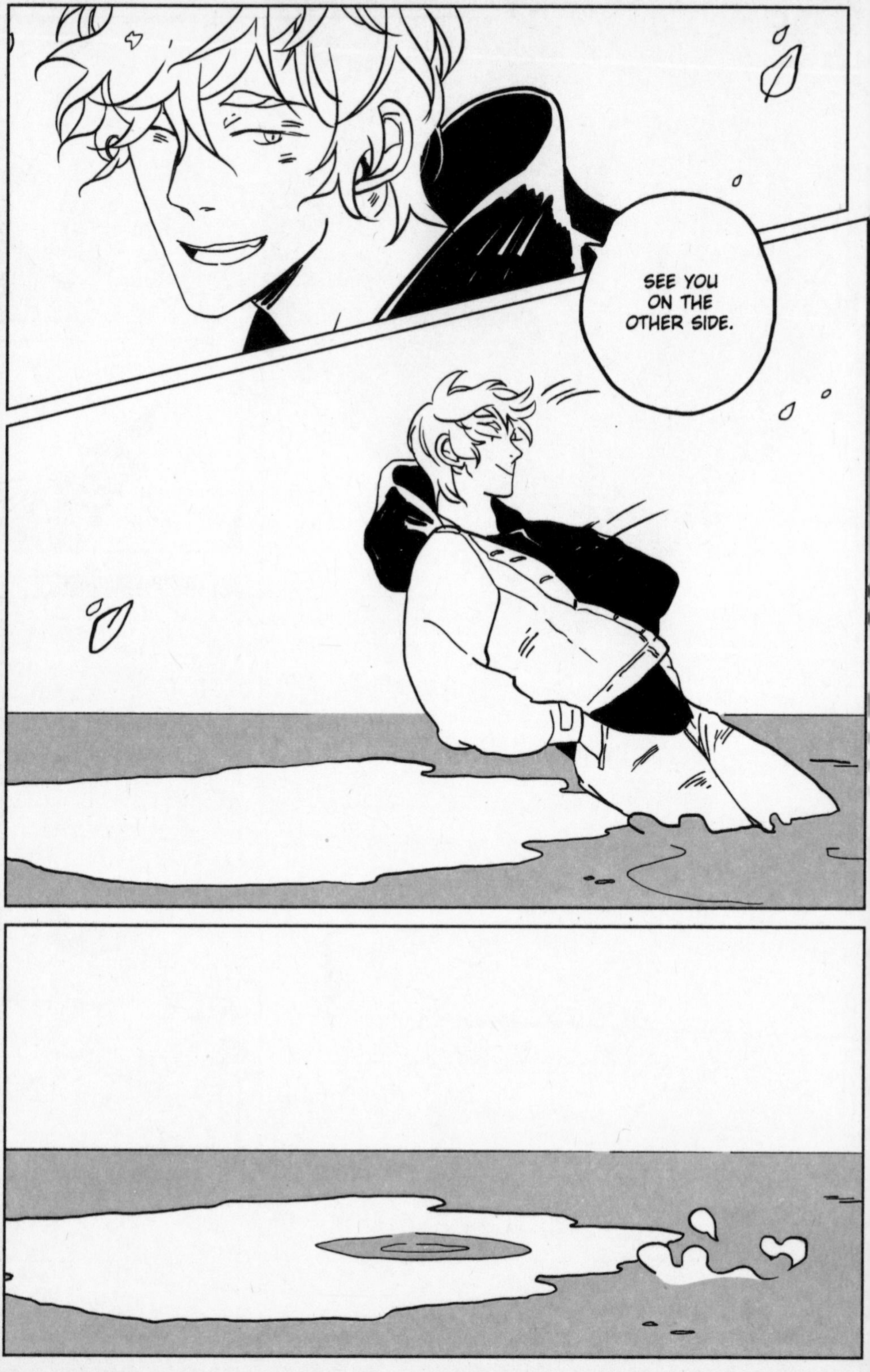
SEE YOU ON THE OTHER SIDE.

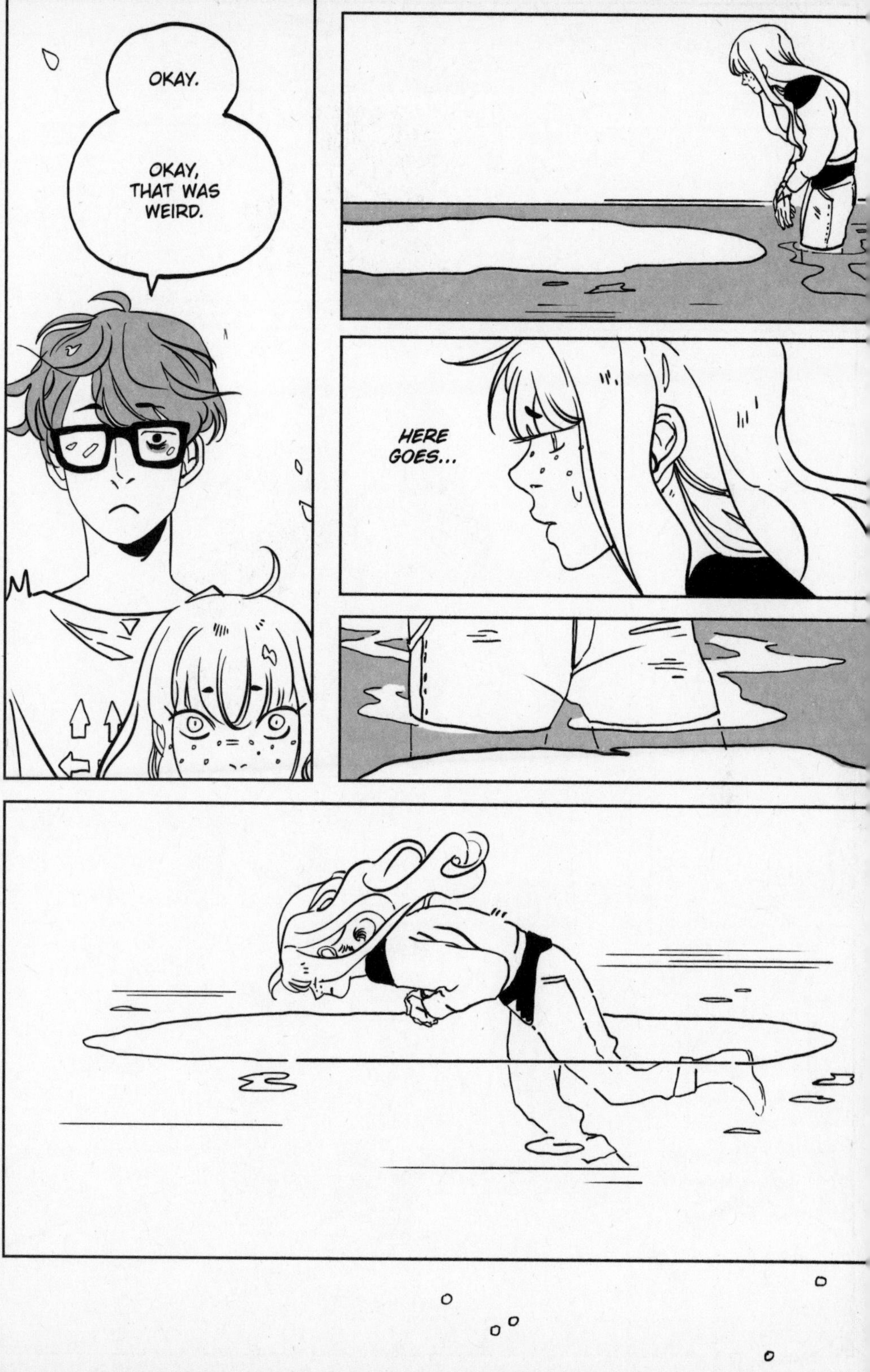
OKAY.
OKAY, THAT WAS WEIRD.
HERE GOES...

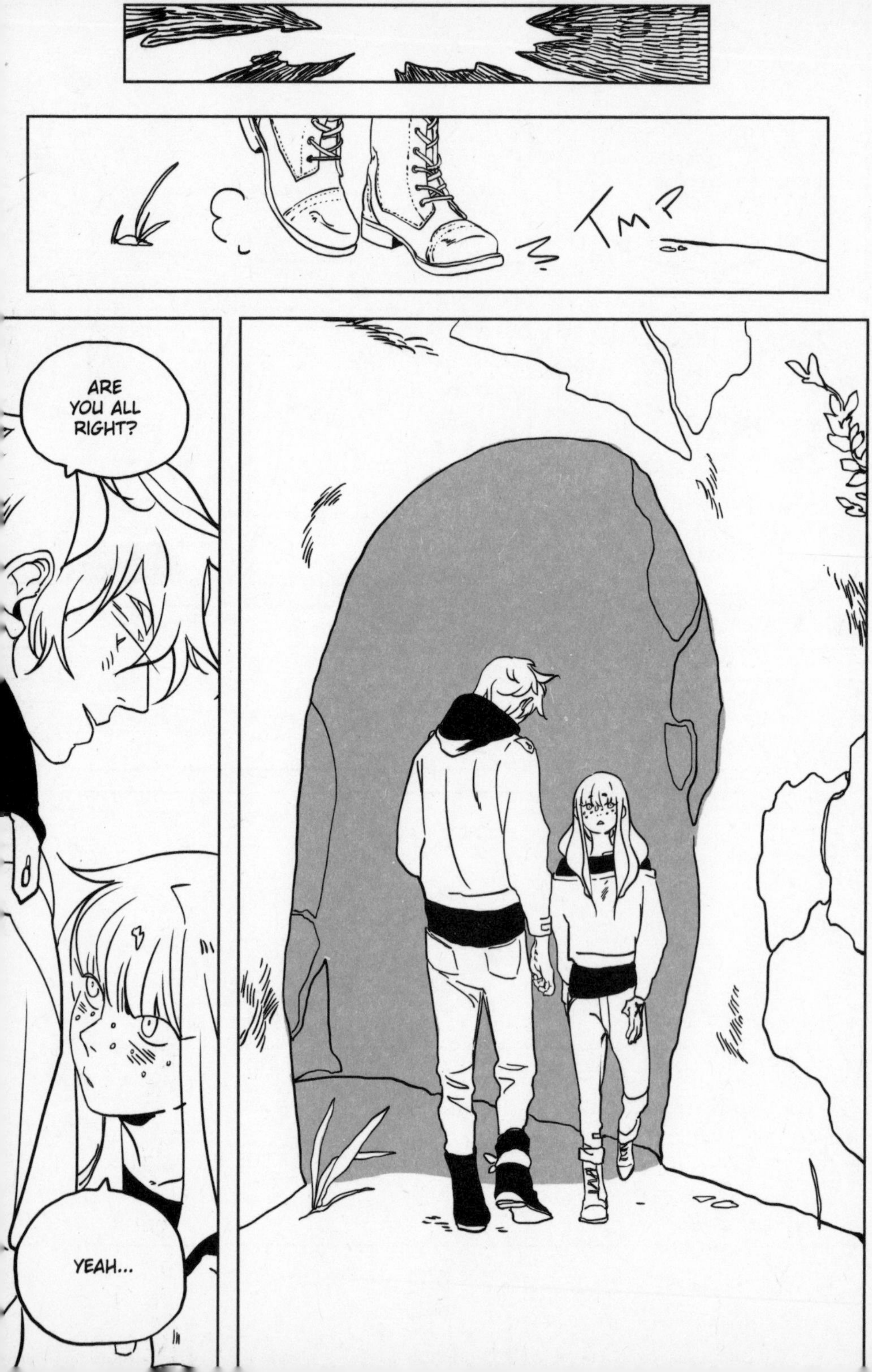
TMP
ARE YOU ALL RIGHT?
YEAH...

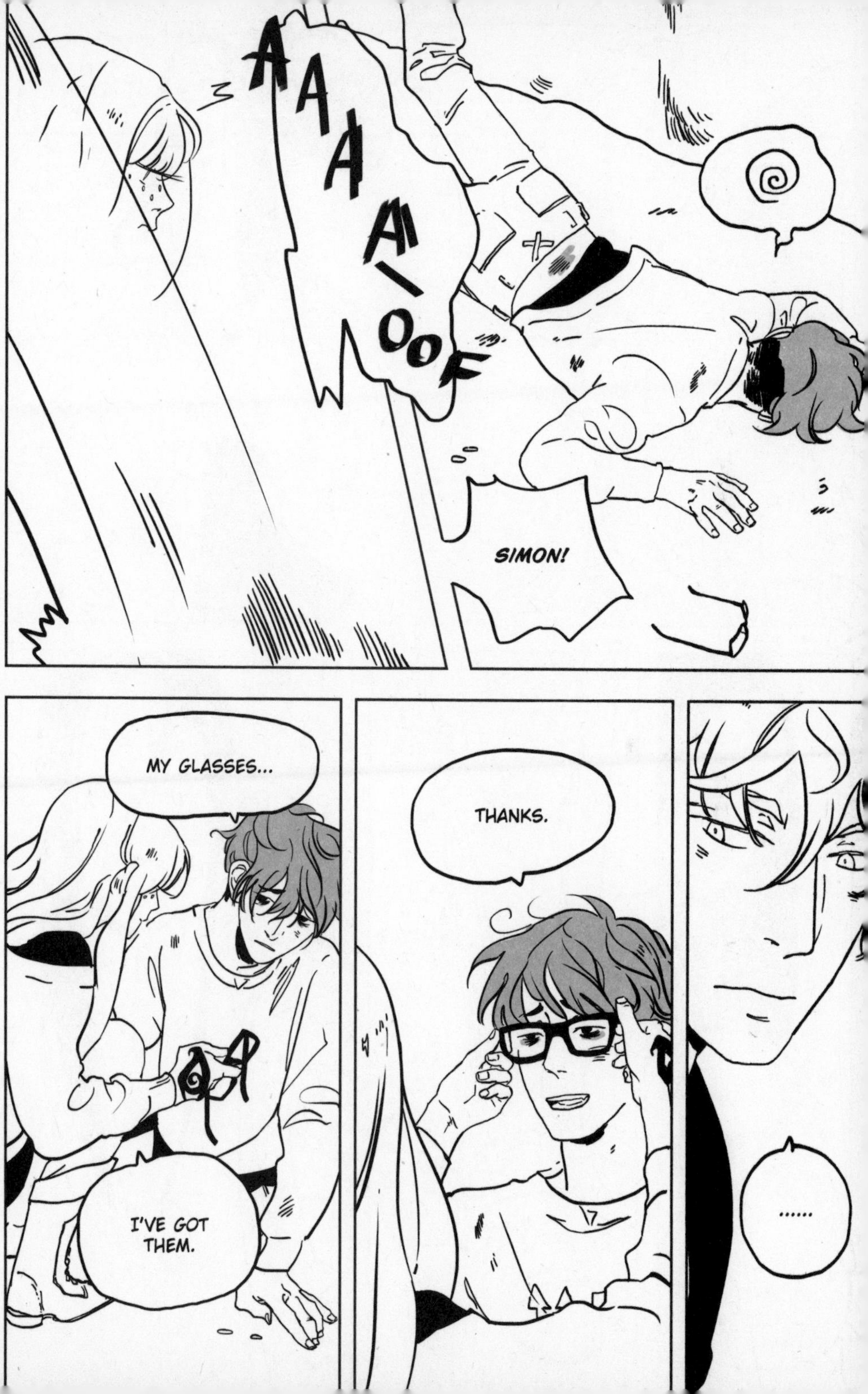
AAAAA—OOF
SIMON!
MY GLASSES...
I'VE GOT THEM.
THANKS.
......

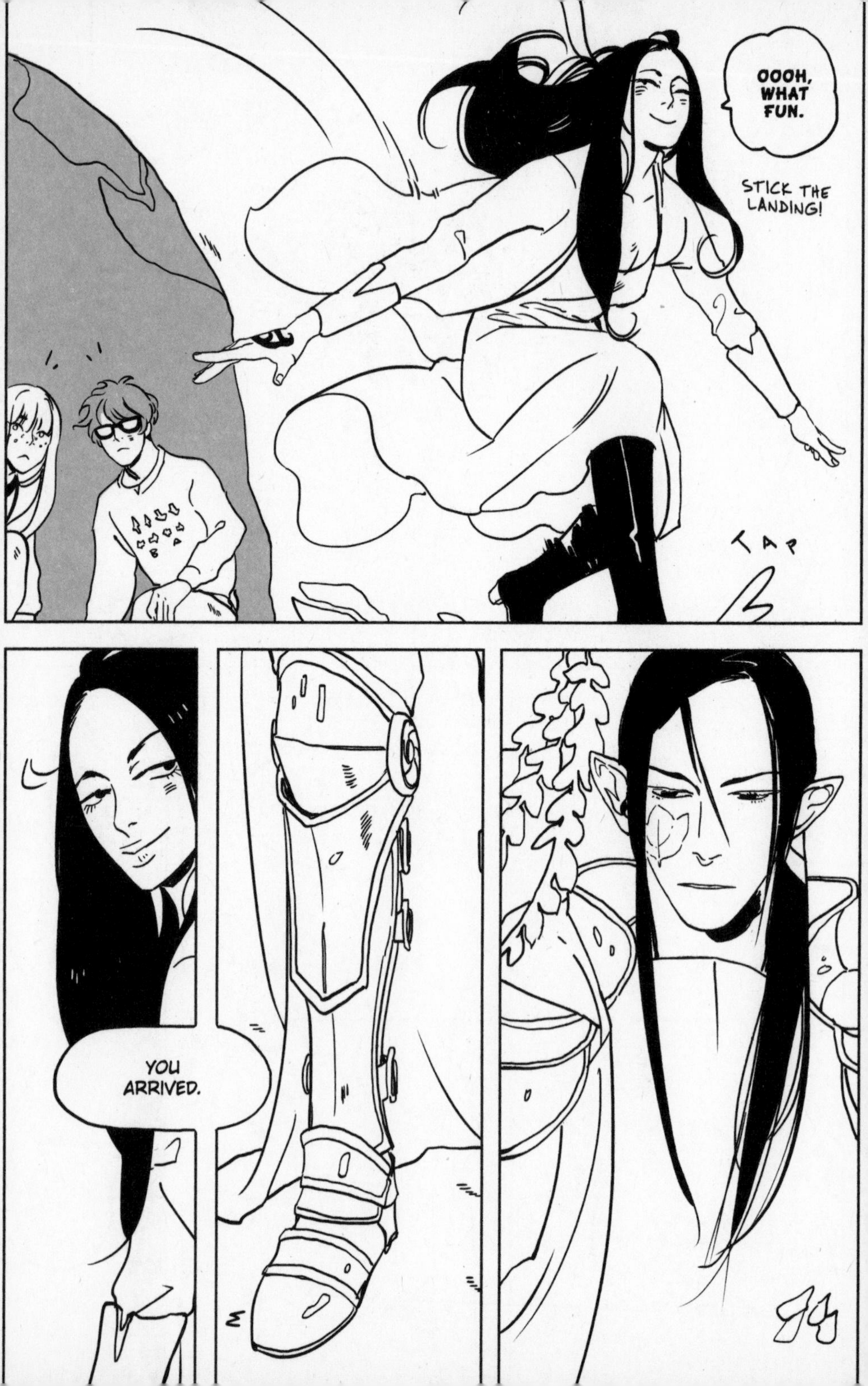
OOOH, WHAT FUN.
STICK THE LANDING!
TAP
YOU ARRIVED.

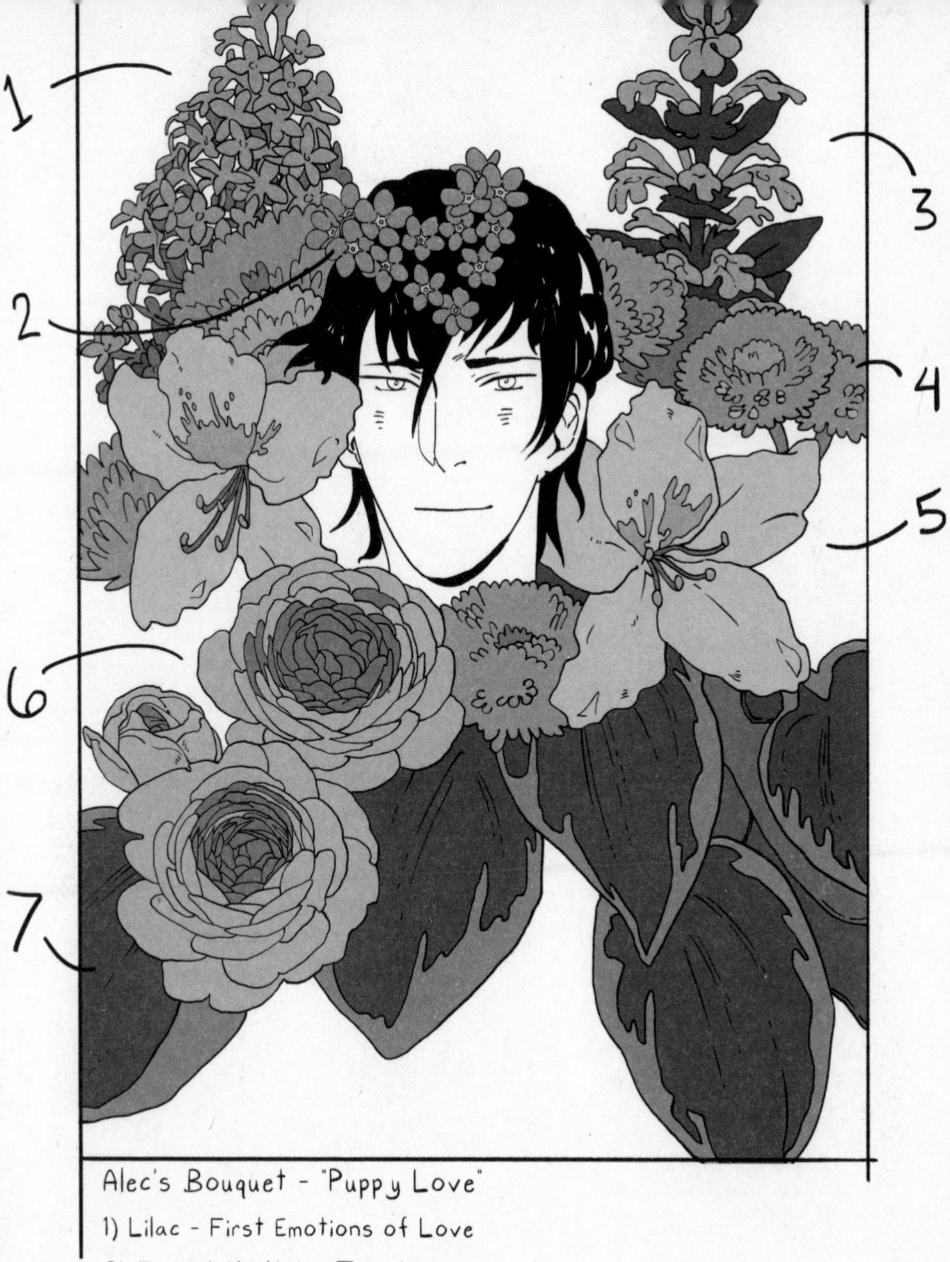
1
2
3
4
5
6
7

Alec's Bouquet - "Puppy Love"

1) Lilac - First Emotions of Love

2) Forget Me Not - True Love

3) Bugle - Most Lovable

4) English Daisy - Innocence

5) White Azalea - First Love

6) Thornless Rose - Early Attachment

7) Hosta - Devotion

THE MORTAL INSTRUMENTS

THE GRAPHIC NOVEL

Chapter 16

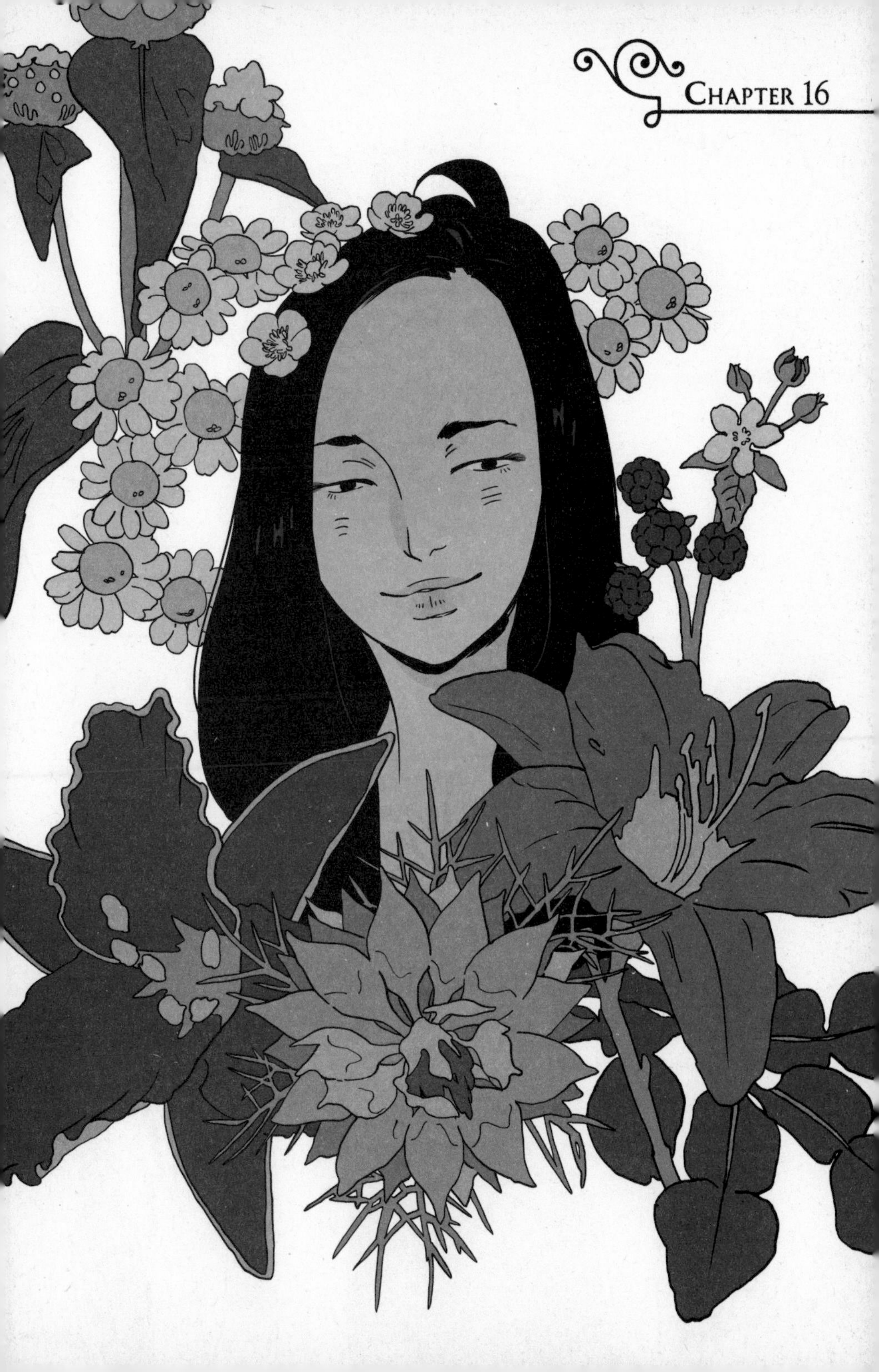

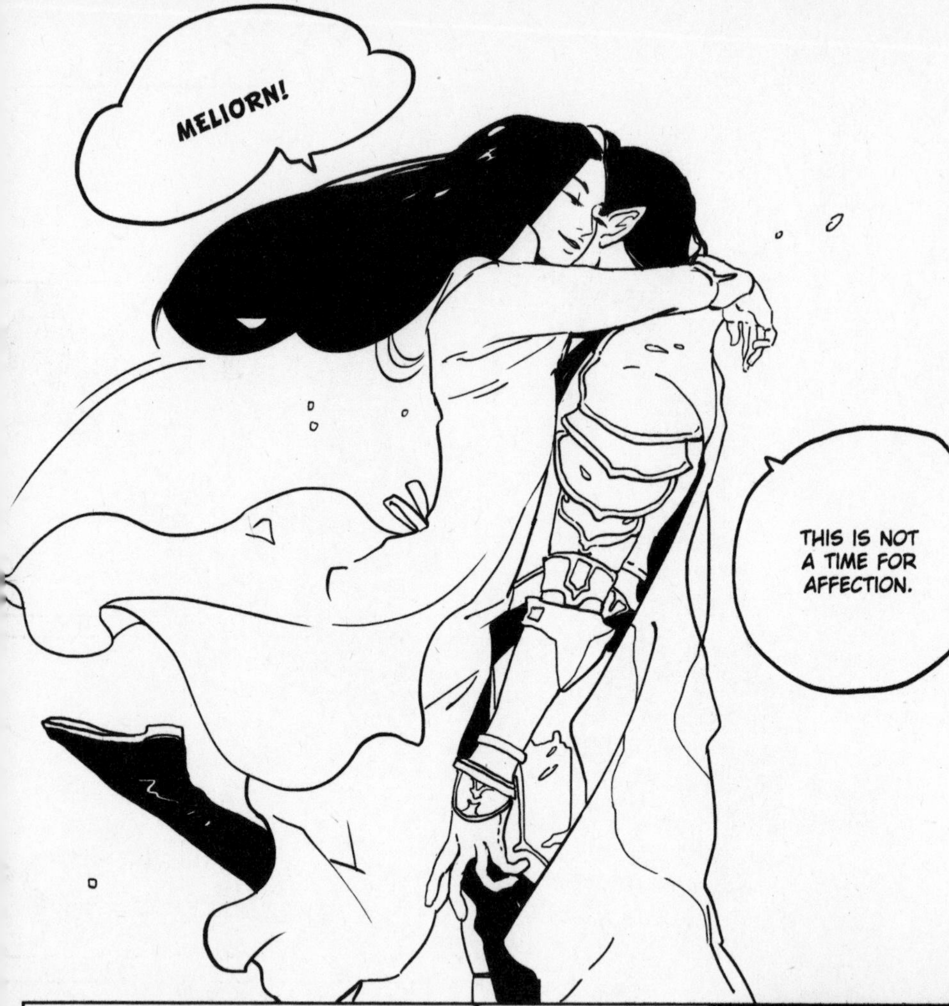
MELIORN!
THIS IS NOT A TIME FOR AFFECTION.

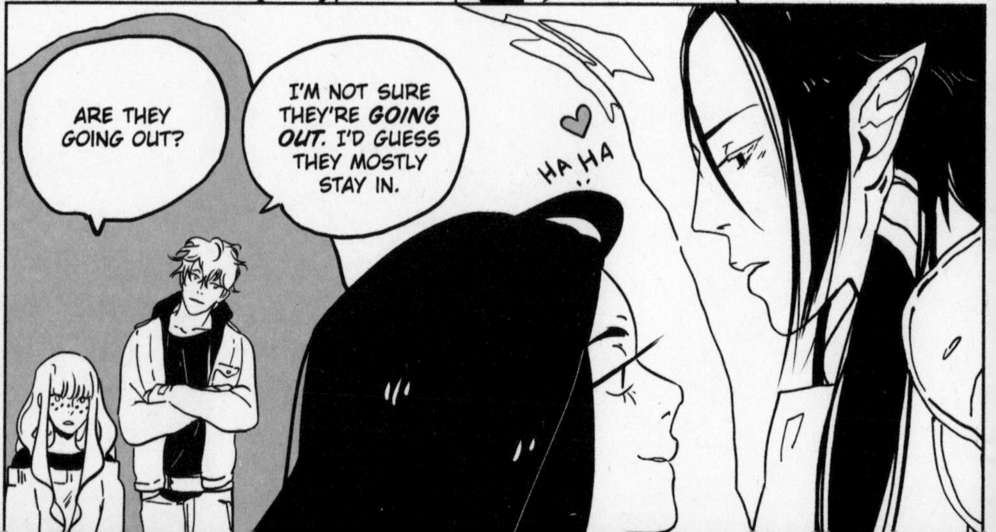
ARE THEY GOING OUT?
I'M NOT SURE THEY'RE ***GOING OUT***. I'D GUESS THEY MOSTLY STAY IN.
HA HA

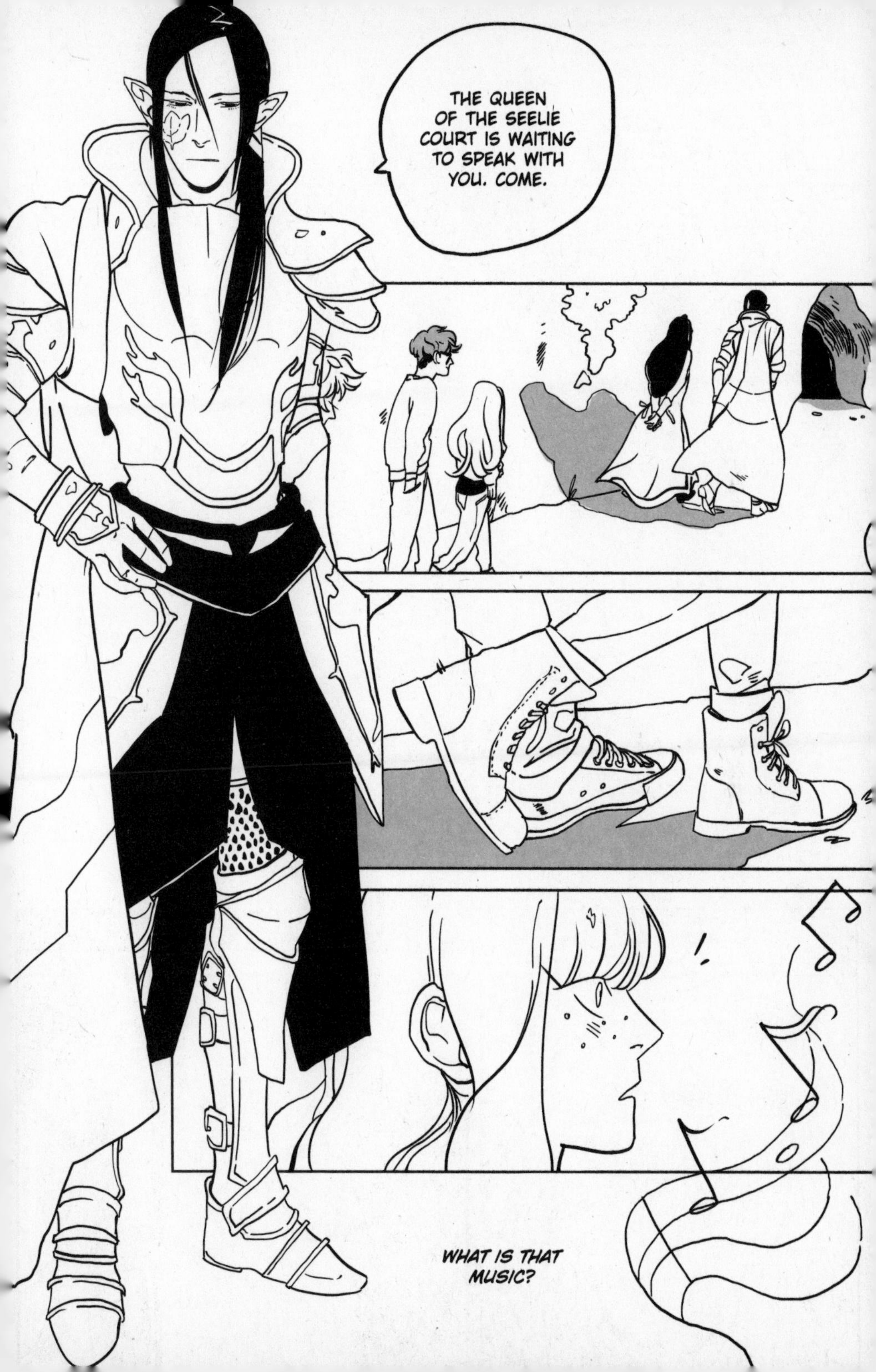
THE QUEEN OF THE SEELIE COURT IS WAITING TO SPEAK WITH YOU. COME.
WHAT IS THAT MUSIC?

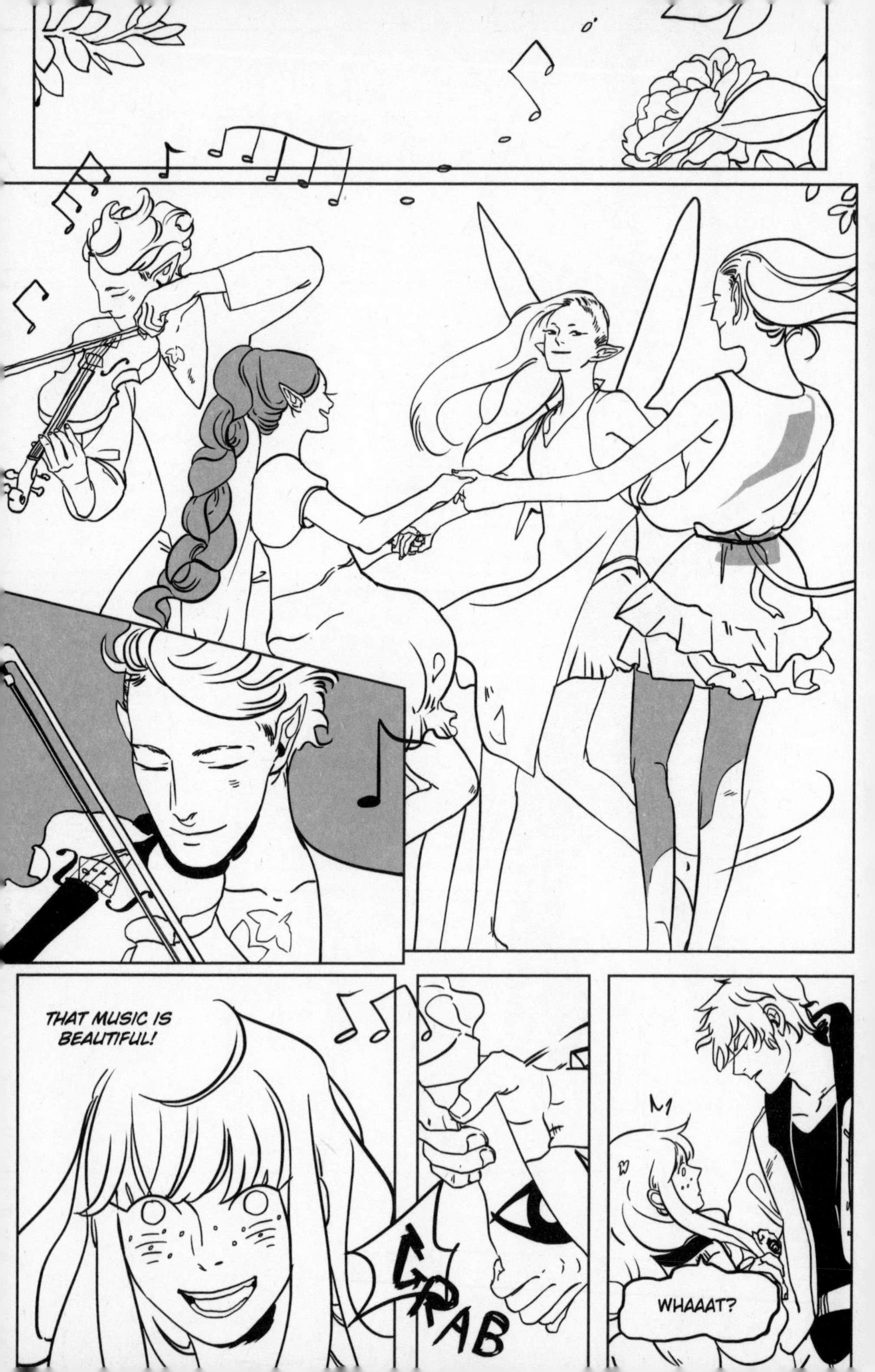
THAT MUSIC IS BEAUTIFUL!
GRAB
WHAAAT?

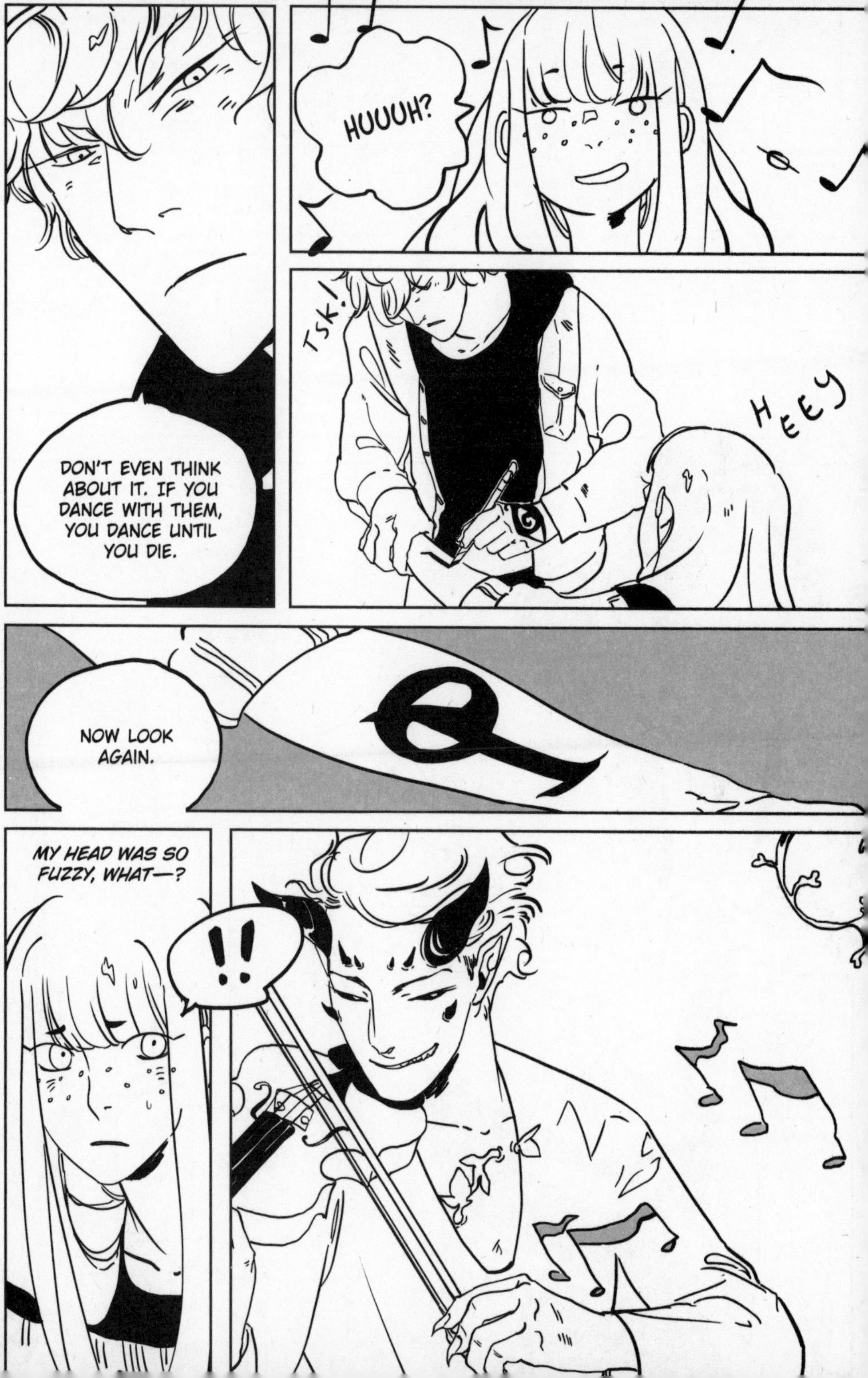
HUUUH?
DON'T EVEN THINK ABOUT IT. IF YOU DANCE WITH THEM, YOU DANCE UNTIL YOU DIE.
TSK!
HEEY
NOW LOOK AGAIN.
MY HEAD WAS SO FUZZY, WHAT—?
!!

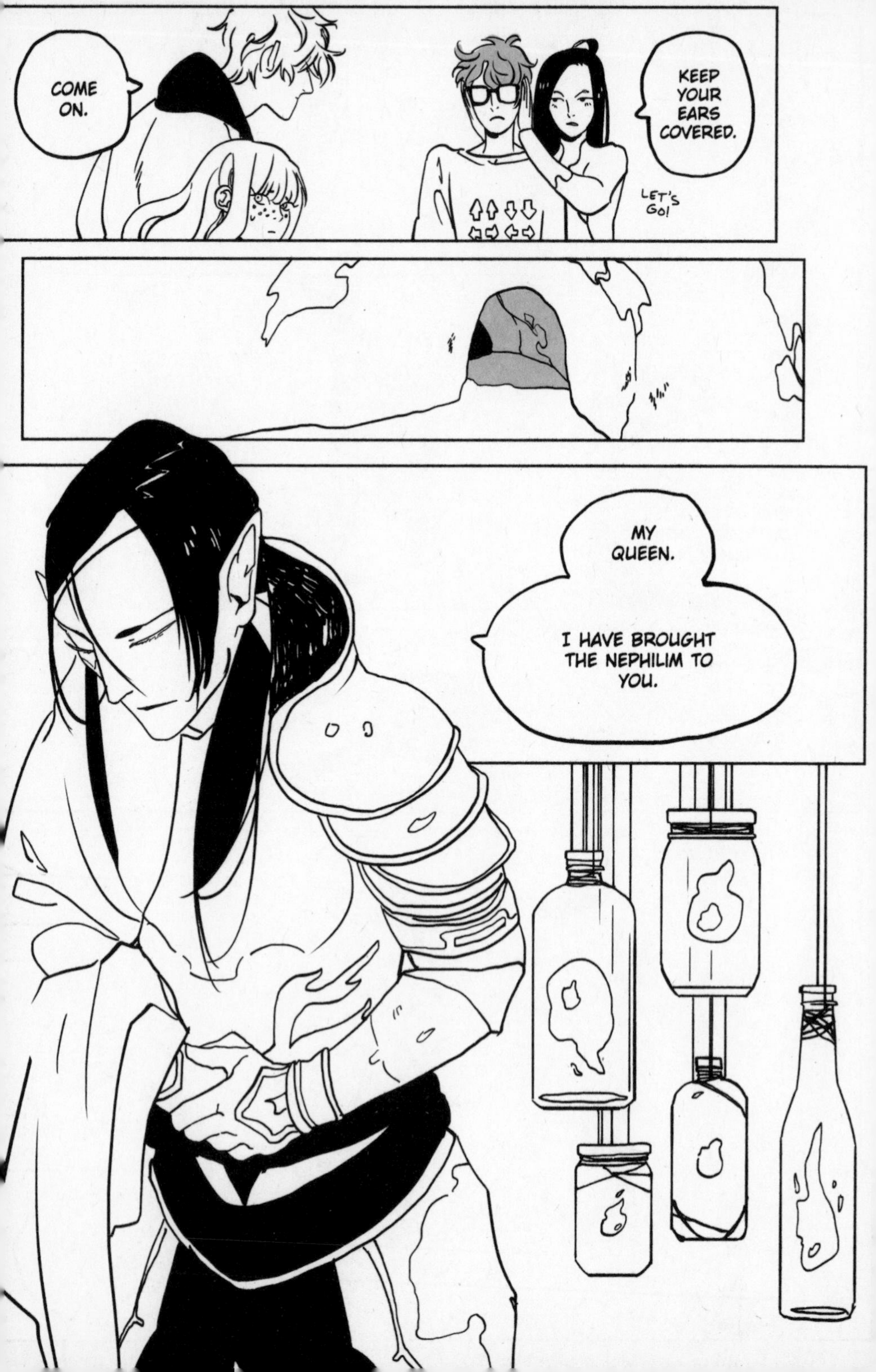
COME ON.
KEEP YOUR EARS COVERED.
LET'S GO!
MY QUEEN.
I HAVE BROUGHT THE NEPHILIM TO YOU.

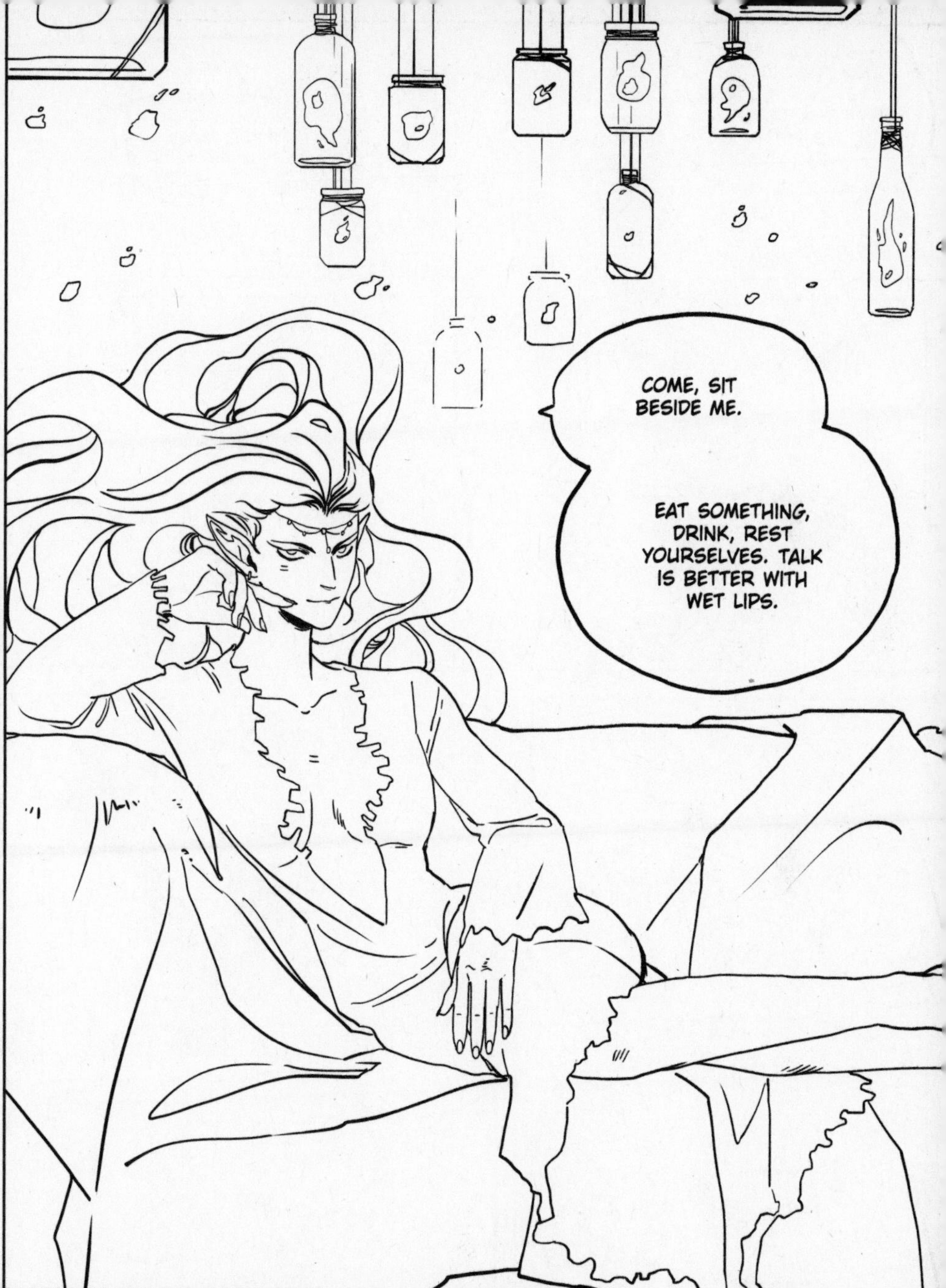
COME, SIT BESIDE ME.
EAT SOMETHING, DRINK, REST YOURSELVES. TALK IS BETTER WITH WET LIPS.

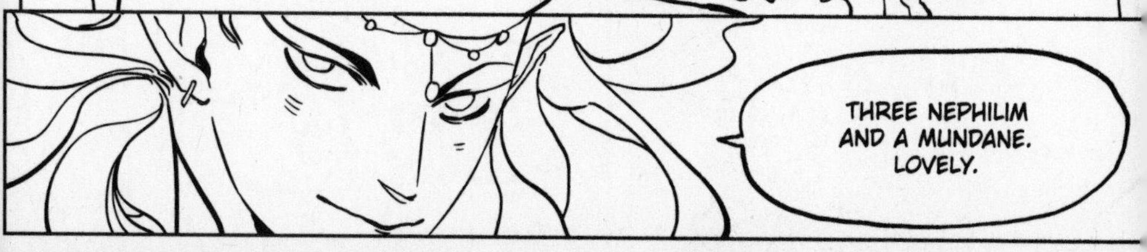
THREE NEPHILIM AND A MUNDANE. LOVELY.

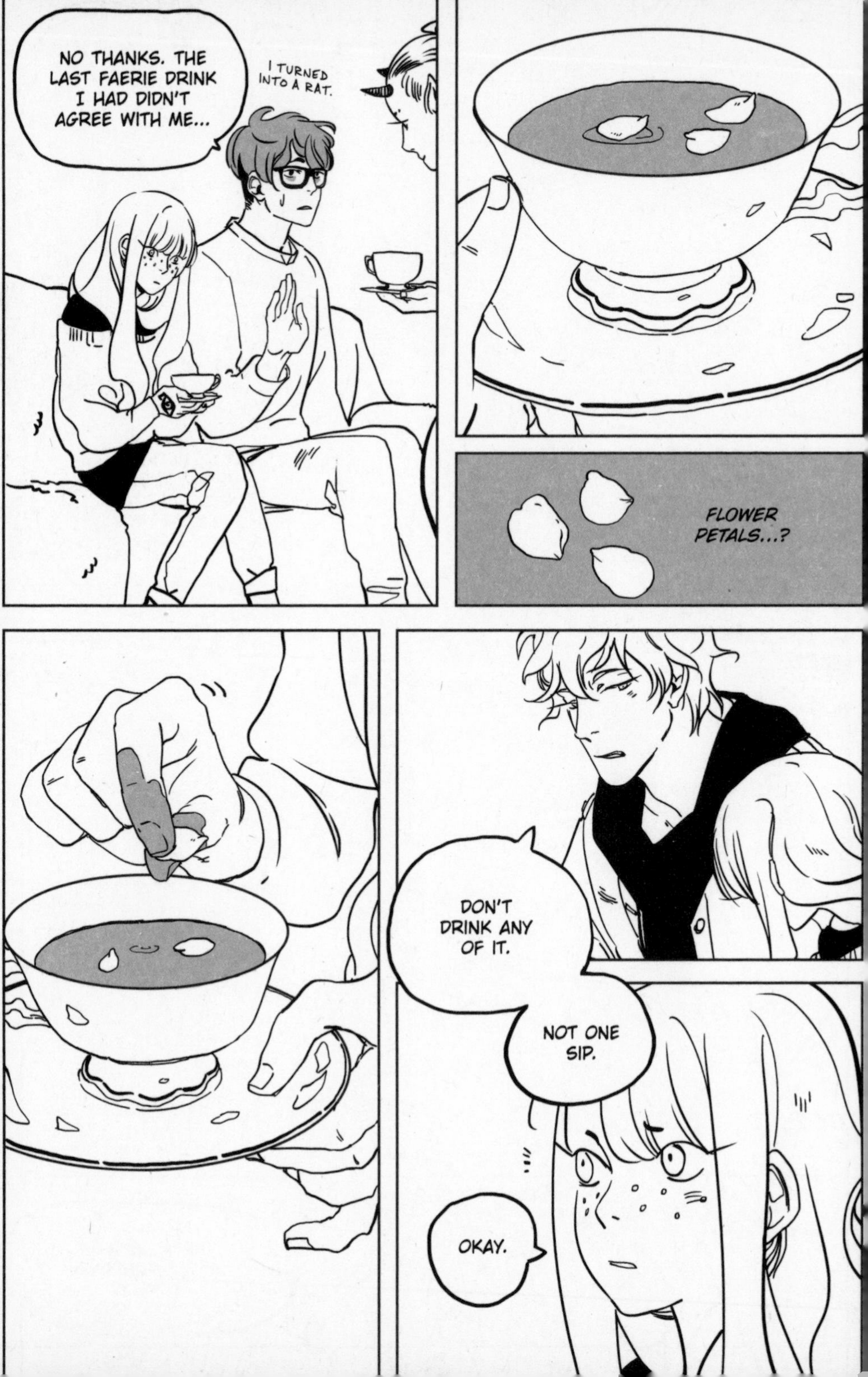
NO THANKS. THE LAST FAERIE DRINK I HAD DIDN'T AGREE WITH ME...
I TURNED INTO A RAT.
FLOWER PETALS...?
DON'T DRINK ANY OF IT.
NOT ONE SIP.
OKAY.

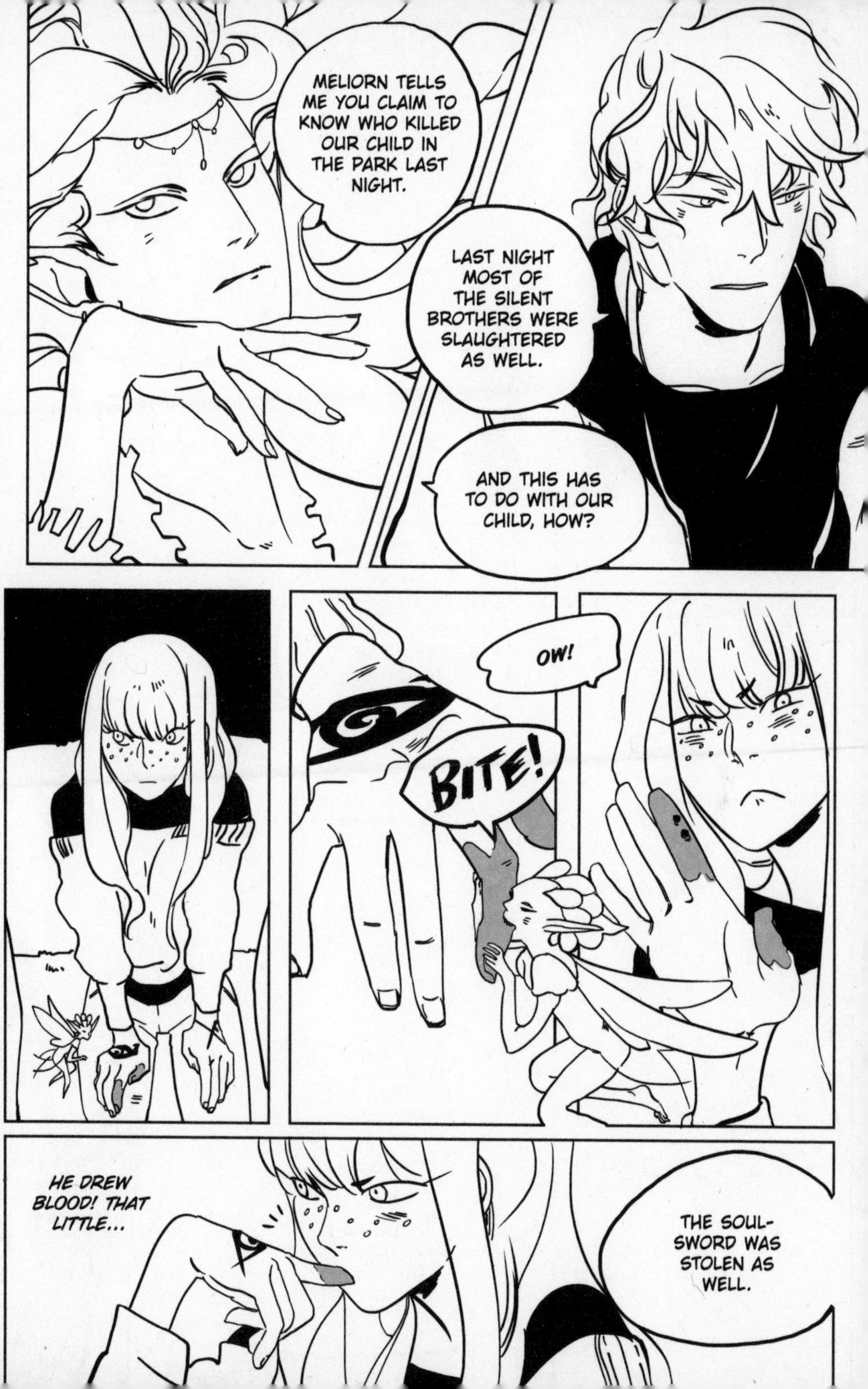
MELIORN TELLS ME YOU CLAIM TO KNOW WHO KILLED OUR CHILD IN THE PARK LAST NIGHT.
LAST NIGHT MOST OF THE SILENT BROTHERS WERE SLAUGHTERED AS WELL.
AND THIS HAS TO DO WITH OUR CHILD, HOW?
BITE!
OW!
HE DREW BLOOD! THAT LITTLE...
THE SOUL-SWORD WAS STOLEN AS WELL.

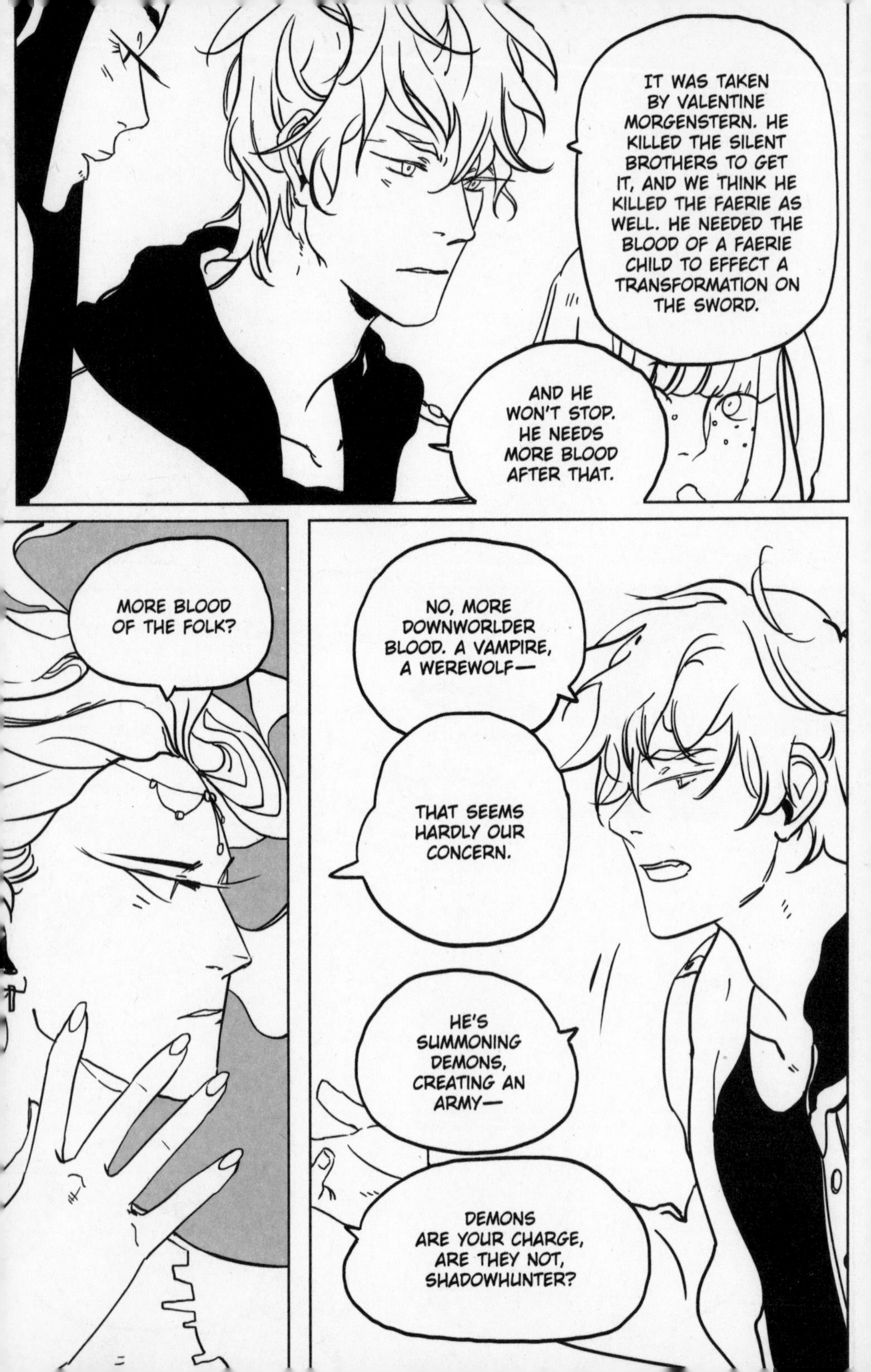
IT WAS TAKEN BY VALENTINE MORGENSTERN. HE KILLED THE SILENT BROTHERS TO GET IT, AND WE THINK HE KILLED THE FAERIE AS WELL. HE NEEDED THE BLOOD OF A FAERIE CHILD TO EFFECT A TRANSFORMATION ON THE SWORD.
AND HE WON'T STOP. HE NEEDS MORE BLOOD AFTER THAT.
MORE BLOOD OF THE FOLK?
NO, MORE DOWNWORLDER BLOOD. A VAMPIRE, A WEREWOLF—
THAT SEEMS HARDLY OUR CONCERN.
HE'S SUMMONING DEMONS, CREATING AN ARMY—
DEMONS ARE YOUR CHARGE, ARE THEY NOT, SHADOWHUNTER?

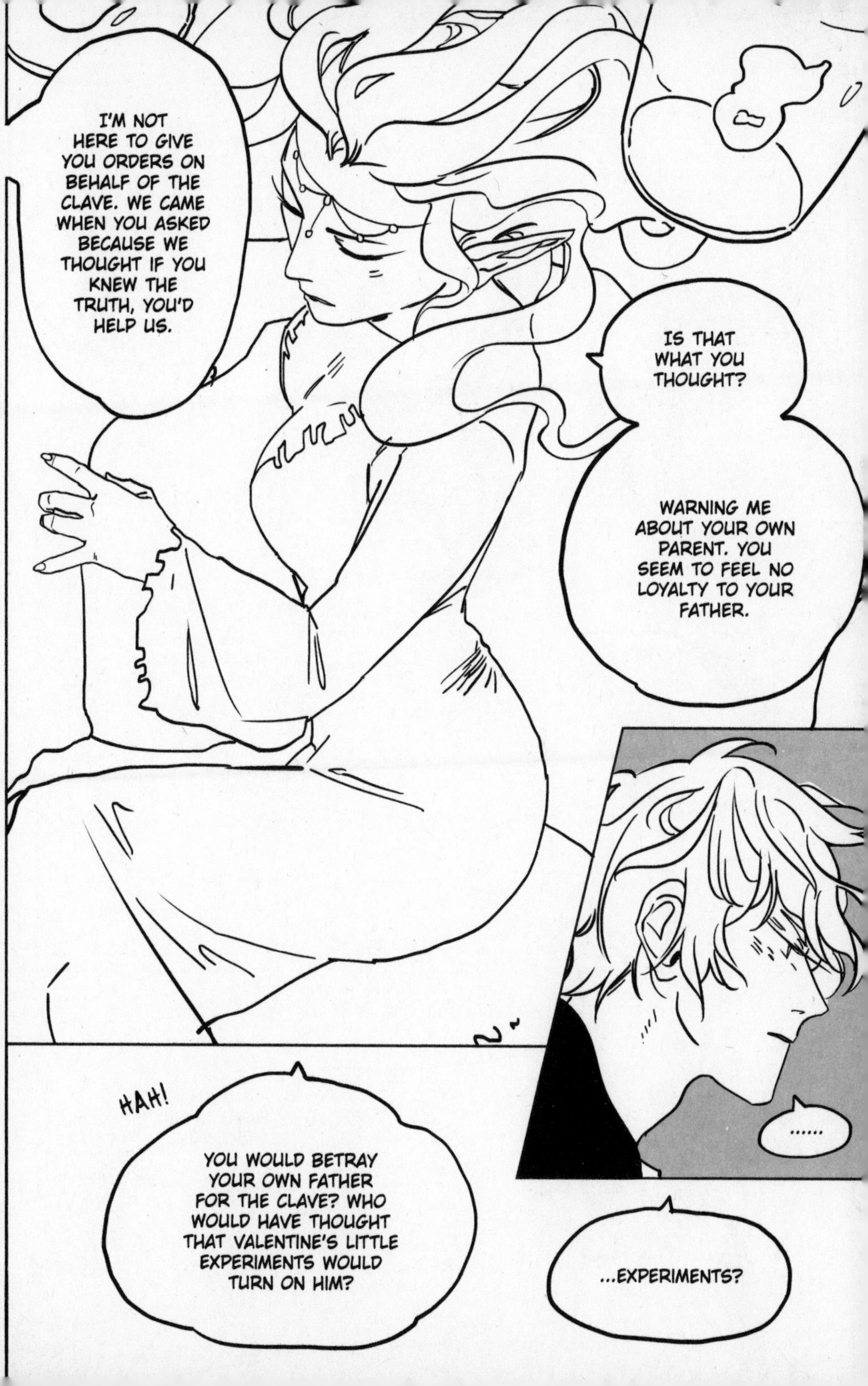
I'M NOT HERE TO GIVE YOU ORDERS ON BEHALF OF THE CLAVE. WE CAME WHEN YOU ASKED BECAUSE WE THOUGHT IF YOU KNEW THE TRUTH, YOU'D HELP US.
IS THAT WHAT YOU THOUGHT?
WARNING ME ABOUT YOUR OWN PARENT. YOU SEEM TO FEEL NO LOYALTY TO YOUR FATHER.
HAH!
YOU WOULD BETRAY YOUR OWN FATHER FOR THE CLAVE? WHO WOULD HAVE THOUGHT THAT VALENTINE'S LITTLE EXPERIMENTS WOULD TURN ON HIM?
......
...EXPERIMENTS?

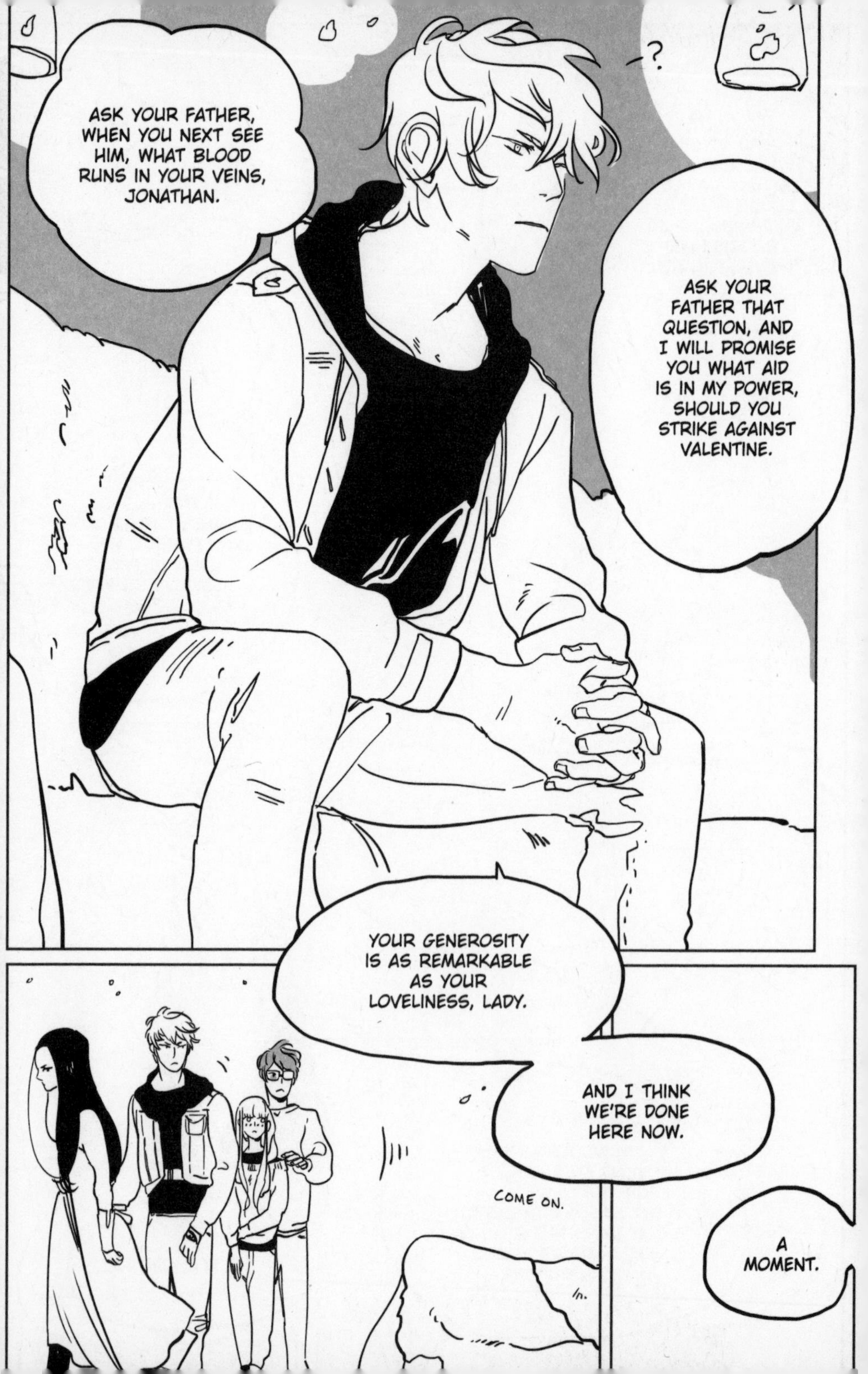
ASK YOUR FATHER, WHEN YOU NEXT SEE HIM, WHAT BLOOD RUNS IN YOUR VEINS, JONATHAN.
?
ASK YOUR FATHER THAT QUESTION, AND I WILL PROMISE YOU WHAT AID IS IN MY POWER, SHOULD YOU STRIKE AGAINST VALENTINE.
YOUR GENEROSITY IS AS REMARKABLE AS YOUR LOVELINESS, LADY.
AND I THINK WE'RE DONE HERE NOW.
COME ON.
A MOMENT.

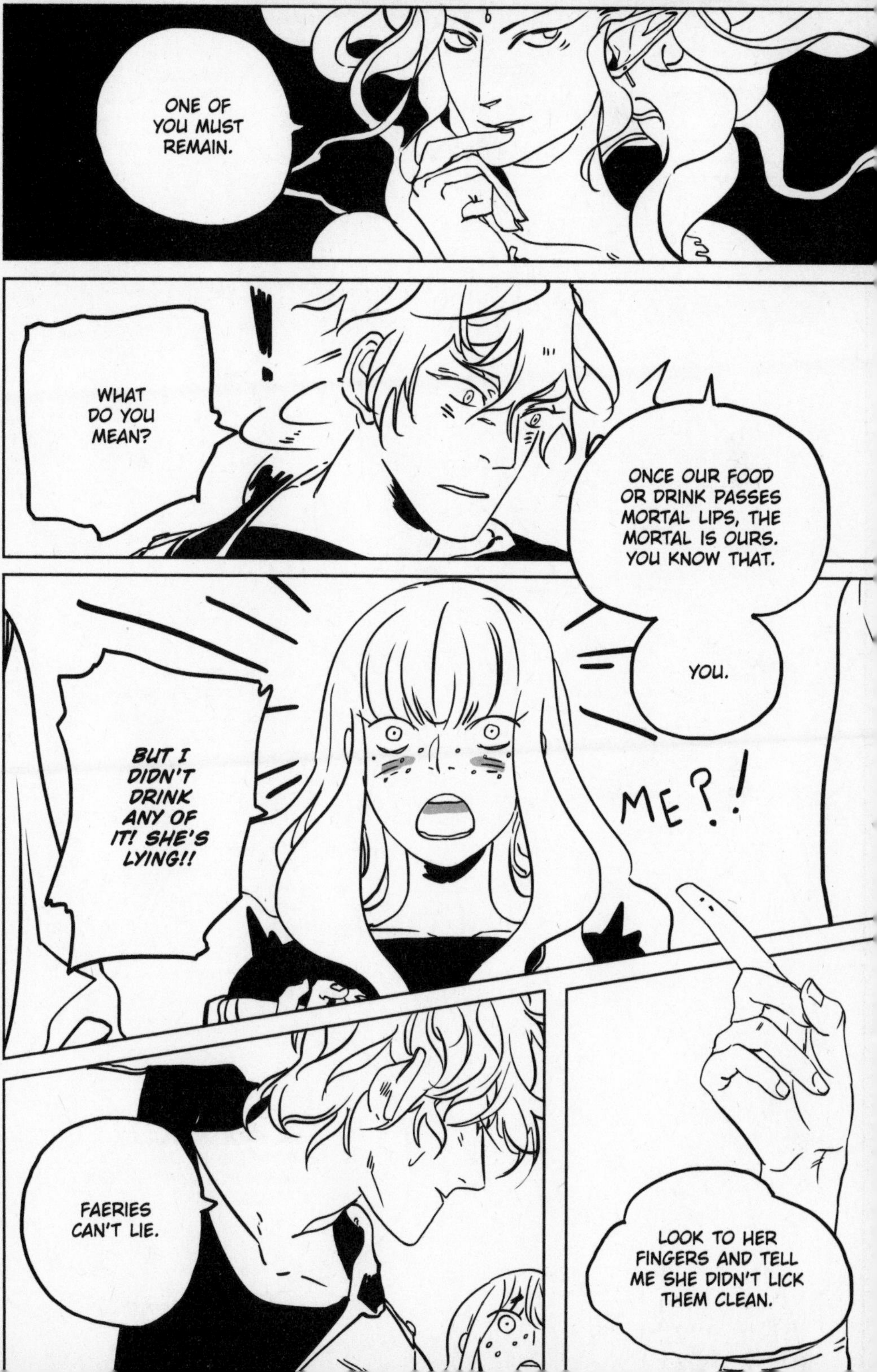
ONE OF YOU MUST REMAIN.
!
WHAT DO YOU MEAN?
ONCE OUR FOOD OR DRINK PASSES MORTAL LIPS, THE MORTAL IS OURS. YOU KNOW THAT.
YOU.
BUT I DIDN'T DRINK ANY OF IT! SHE'S LYING!!
ME?!
FAERIES CAN'T LIE.
LOOK TO HER FINGERS AND TELL ME SHE DIDN'T LICK THEM CLEAN.

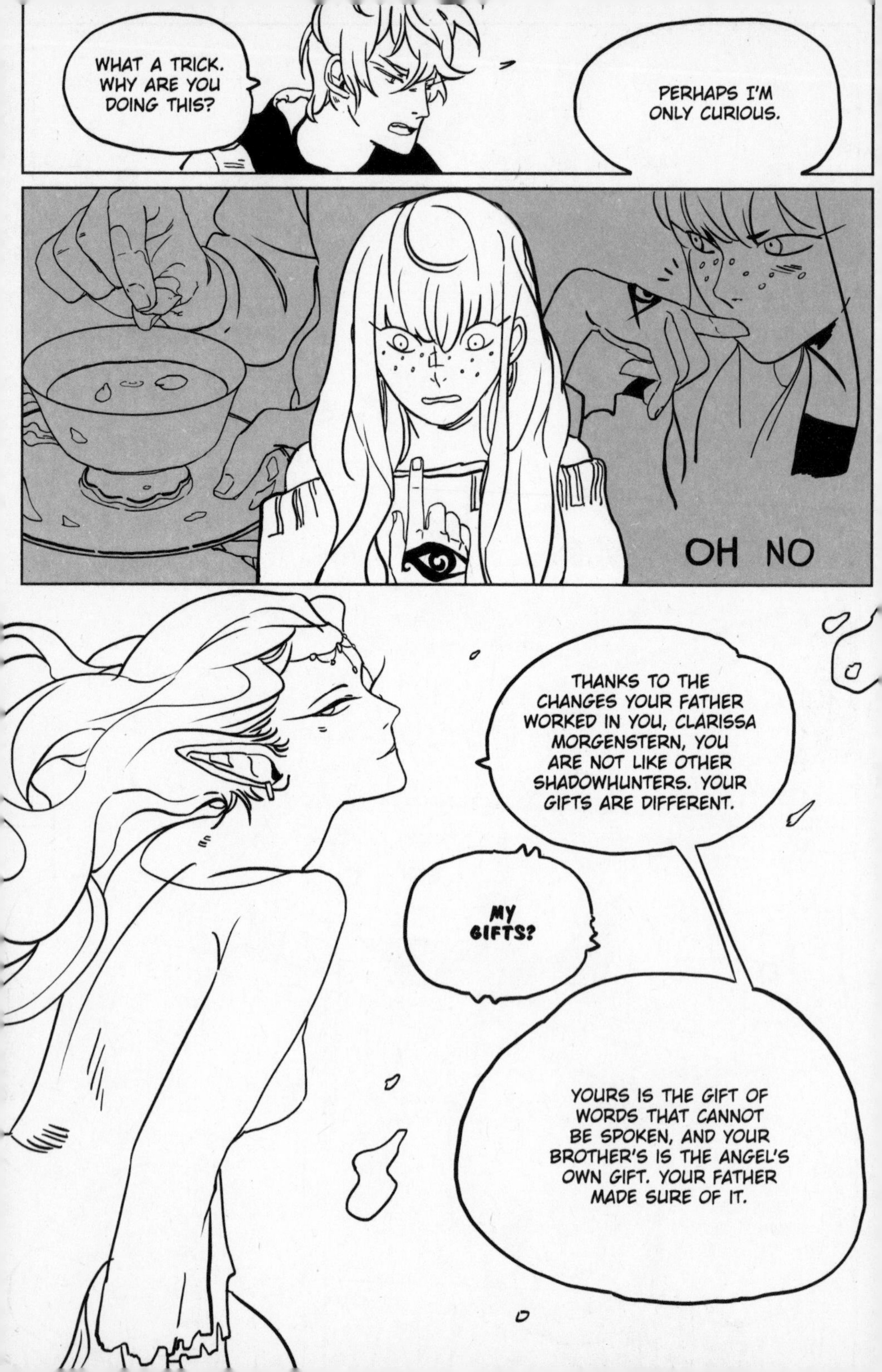
WHAT A TRICK. WHY ARE YOU DOING THIS?
PERHAPS I'M ONLY CURIOUS.
OH NO
THANKS TO THE CHANGES YOUR FATHER WORKED IN YOU, CLARISSA MORGENSTERN, YOU ARE NOT LIKE OTHER SHADOWHUNTERS. YOUR GIFTS ARE DIFFERENT.
MY GIFTS?
YOURS IS THE GIFT OF WORDS THAT CANNOT BE SPOKEN, AND YOUR BROTHER'S IS THE ANGEL'S OWN GIFT. YOUR FATHER MADE SURE OF IT.

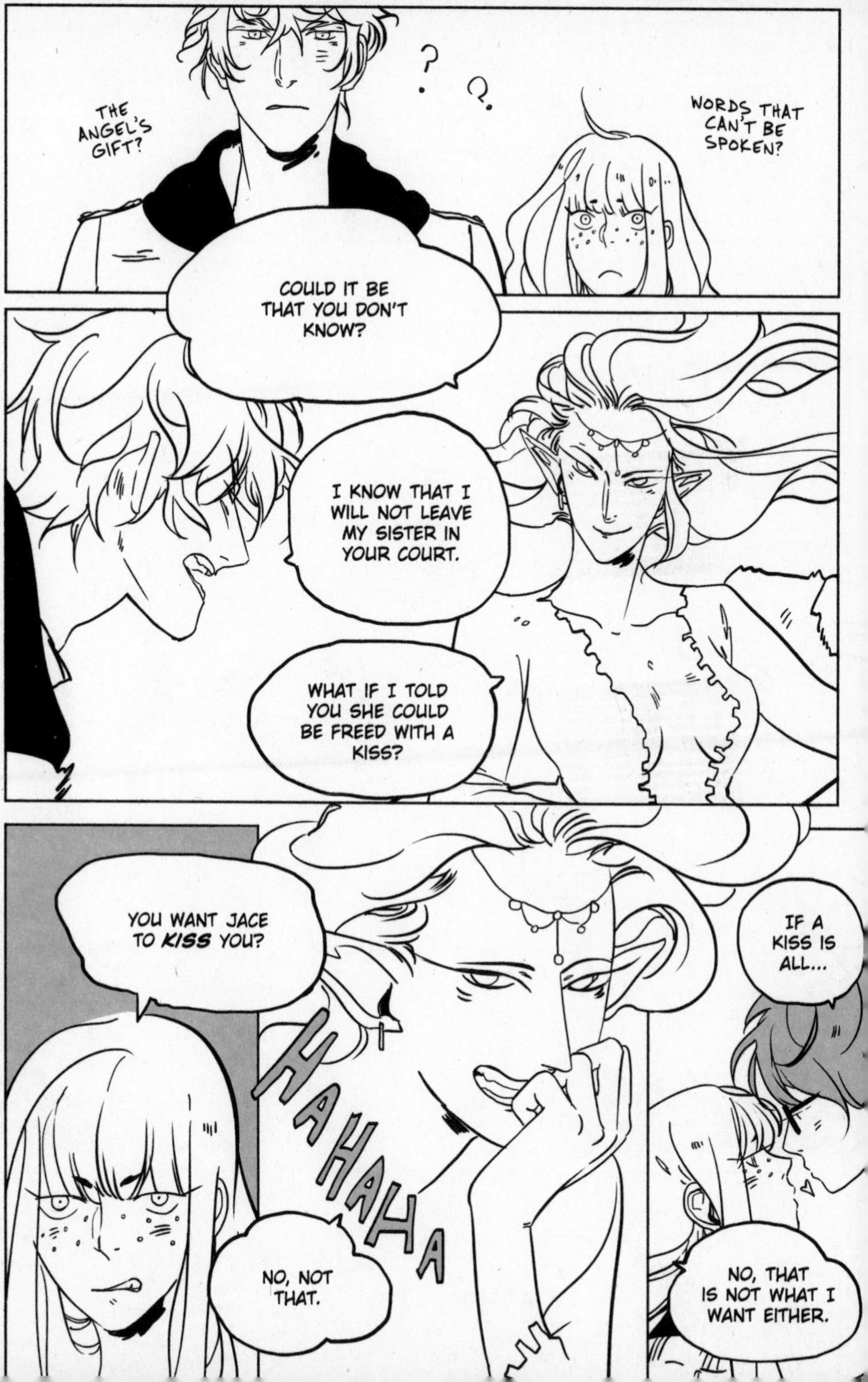
THE ANGEL'S GIFT?
WORDS THAT CAN'T BE SPOKEN?
COULD IT BE THAT YOU DON'T KNOW?
I KNOW THAT I WILL NOT LEAVE MY SISTER IN YOUR COURT.
WHAT IF I TOLD YOU SHE COULD BE FREED WITH A KISS?
YOU WANT JACE TO *KISS* YOU?
NO, NOT THAT.
HAHAHAHA
IF A KISS IS ALL...
NO, THAT IS NOT WHAT I WANT EITHER.

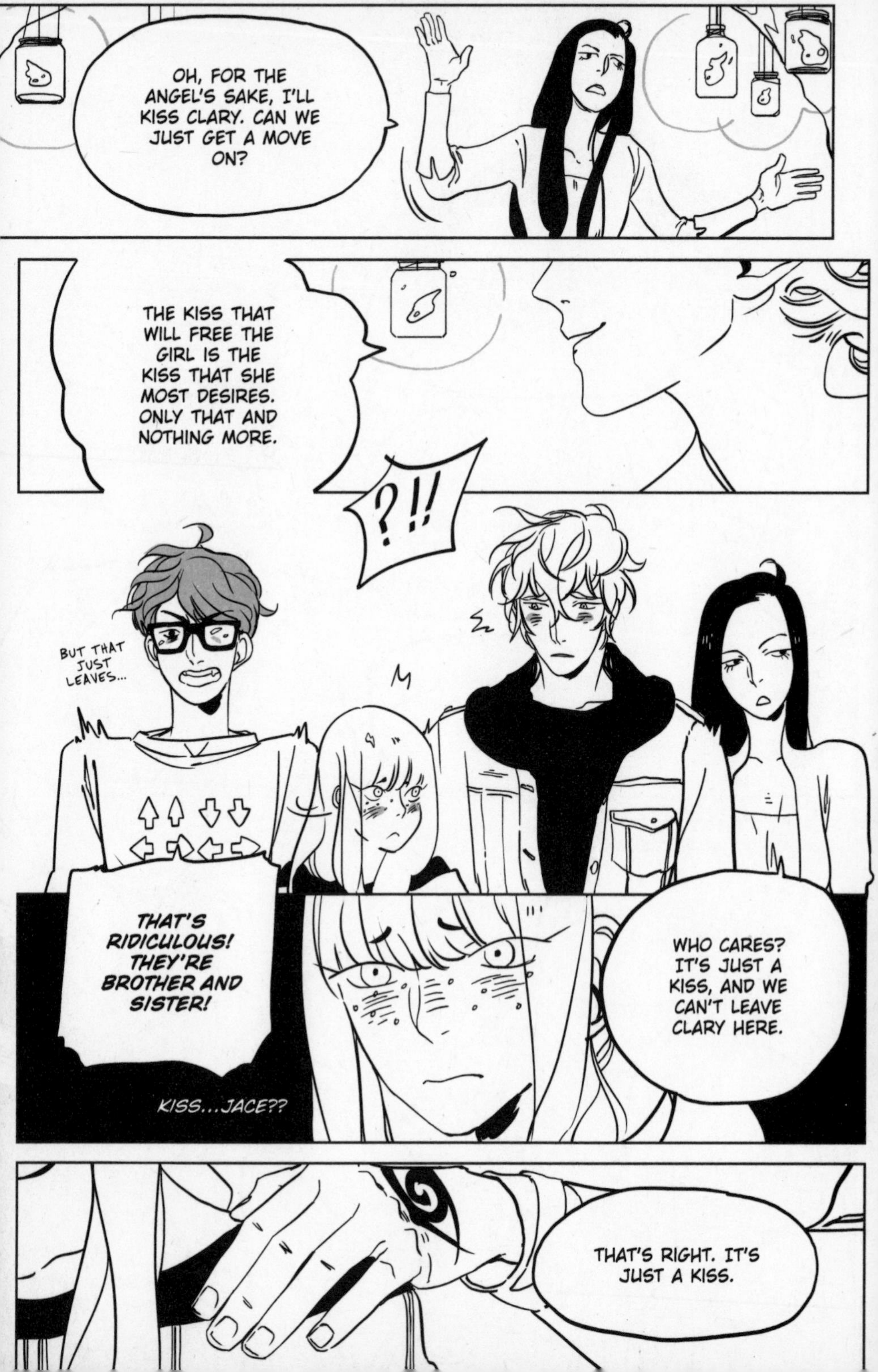
OH, FOR THE ANGEL'S SAKE, I'LL KISS CLARY. CAN WE JUST GET A MOVE ON?
THE KISS THAT WILL FREE THE GIRL IS THE KISS THAT SHE MOST DESIRES. ONLY THAT AND NOTHING MORE.
?!!
BUT THAT JUST LEAVES...
THAT'S RIDICULOUS! THEY'RE BROTHER AND SISTER!
KISS...JACE??
WHO CARES? IT'S JUST A KISS, AND WE CAN'T LEAVE CLARY HERE.
THAT'S RIGHT. IT'S JUST A KISS.

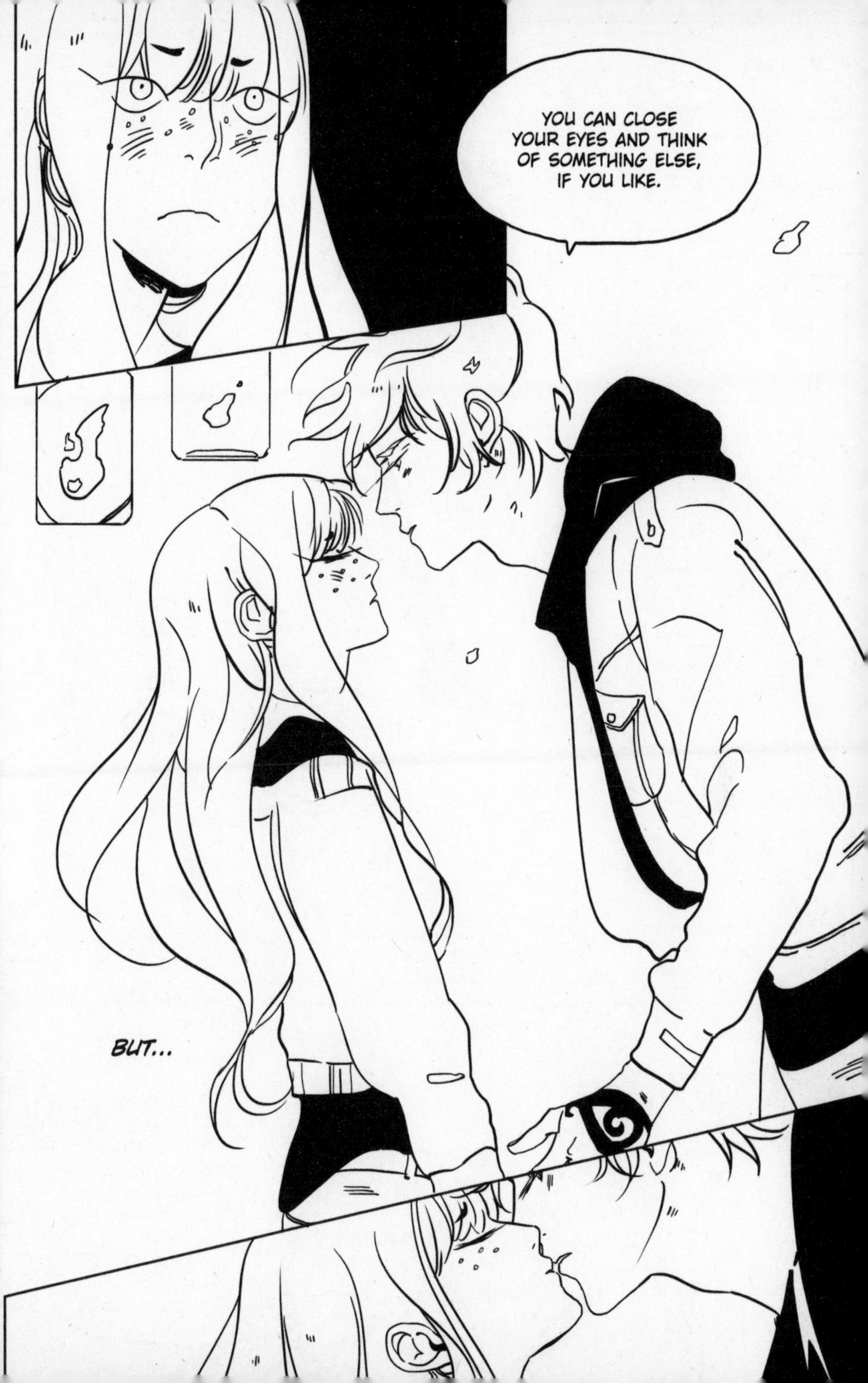
YOU CAN CLOSE YOUR EYES AND THINK OF SOMETHING ELSE, IF YOU LIKE.
BUT...

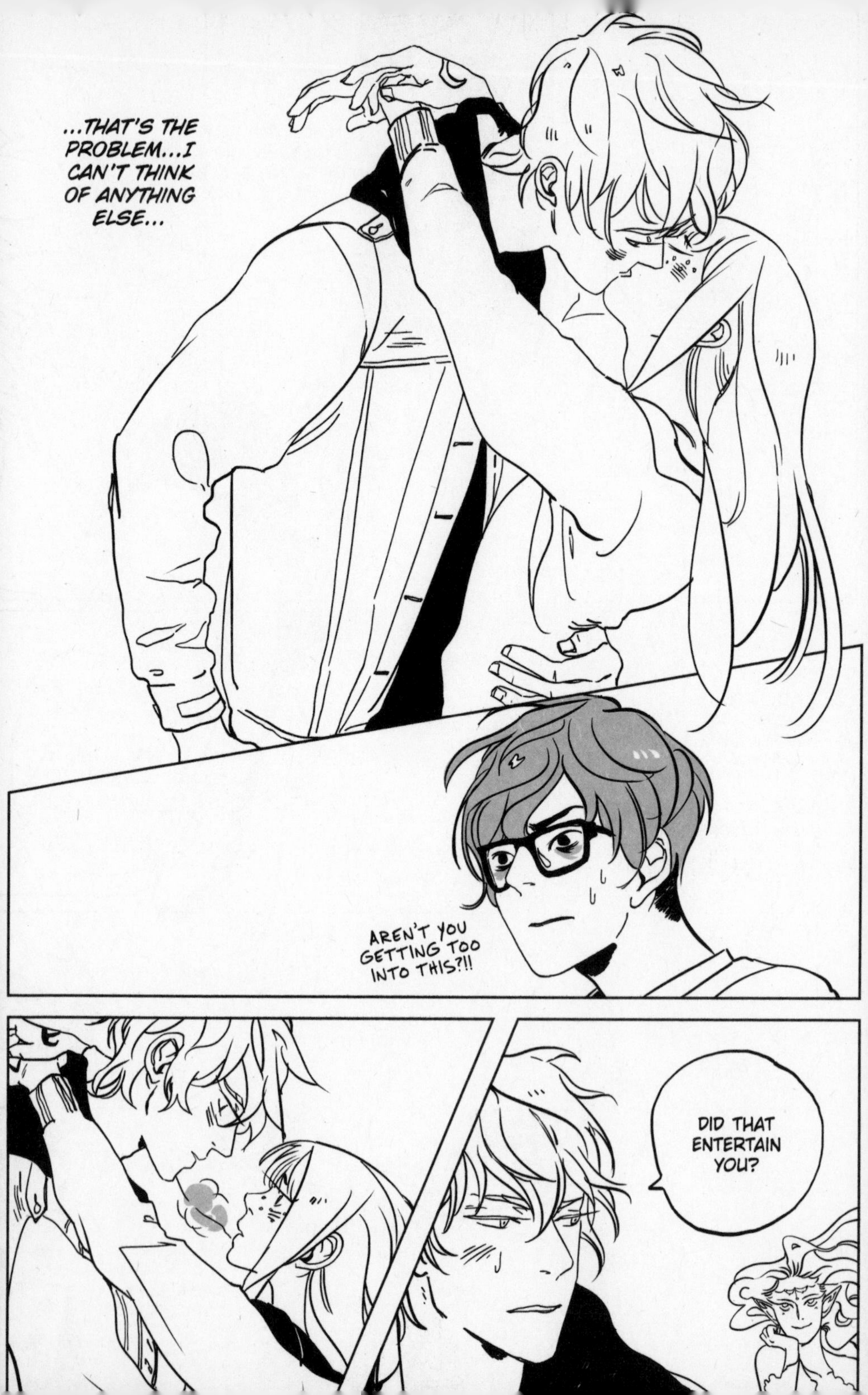
...THAT'S THE PROBLEM...I CAN'T THINK OF ANYTHING ELSE...
AREN'T YOU GETTING TOO INTO THIS?!!
DID THAT ENTERTAIN YOU?

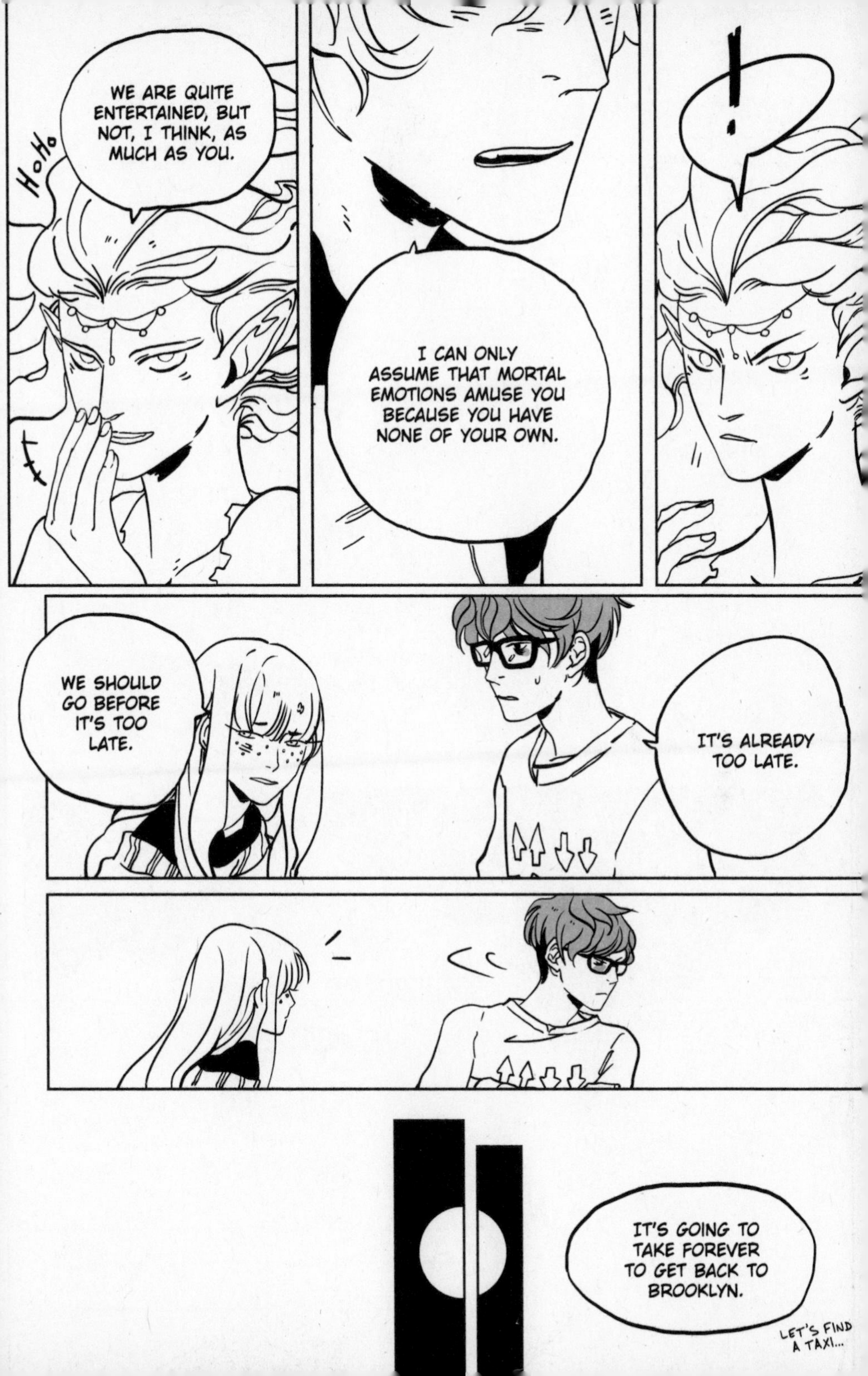
HoHo
WE ARE QUITE ENTERTAINED, BUT NOT, I THINK, AS MUCH AS YOU.
I CAN ONLY ASSUME THAT MORTAL EMOTIONS AMUSE YOU BECAUSE YOU HAVE NONE OF YOUR OWN.
!
WE SHOULD GO BEFORE IT'S TOO LATE.
IT'S ALREADY TOO LATE.
IT'S GOING TO TAKE FOREVER TO GET BACK TO BROOKLYN.
LET'S FIND A TAXI...

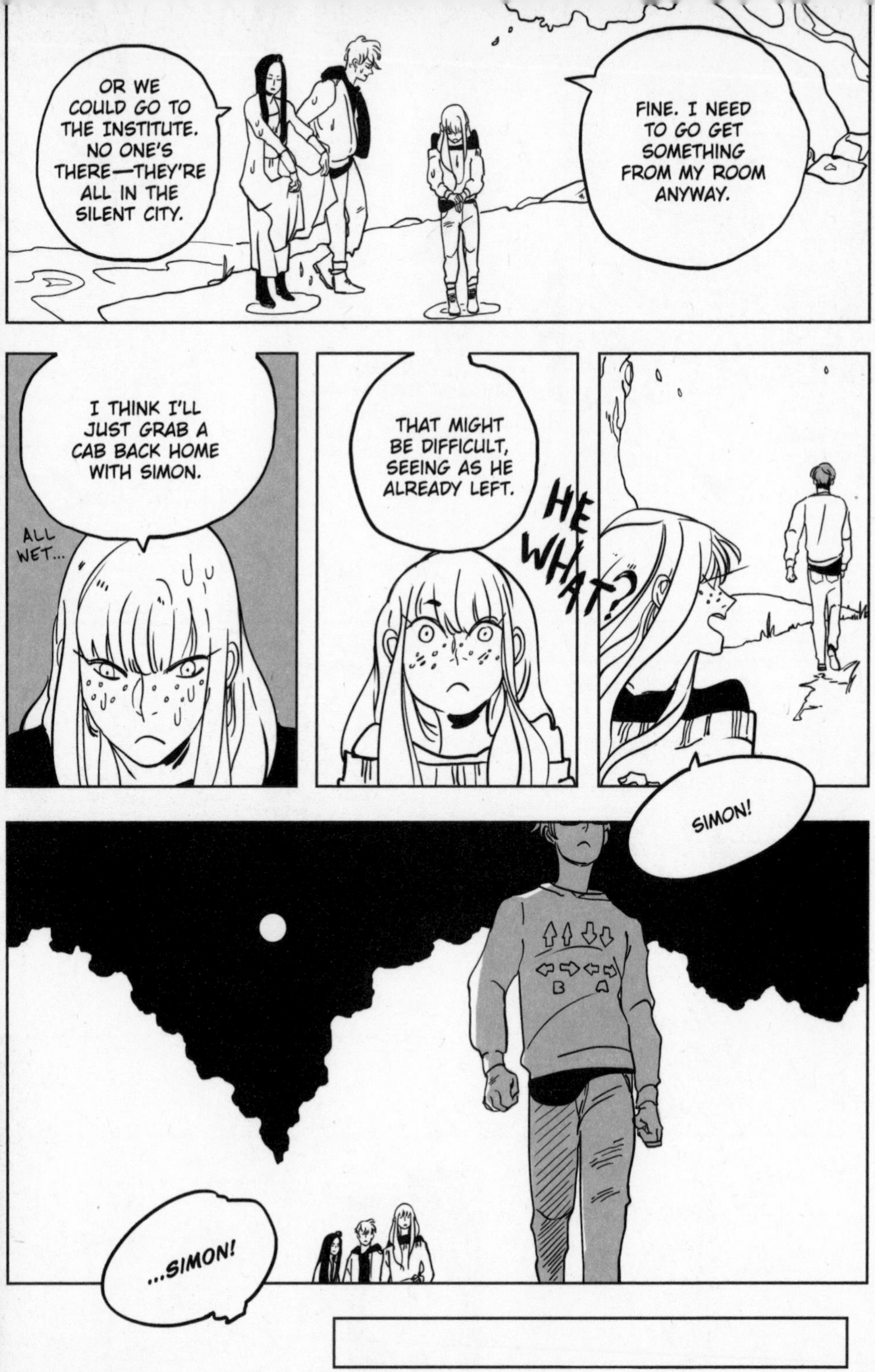
OR WE COULD GO TO THE INSTITUTE. NO ONE'S THERE—THEY'RE ALL IN THE SILENT CITY.
FINE. I NEED TO GO GET SOMETHING FROM MY ROOM ANYWAY.
I THINK I'LL JUST GRAB A CAB BACK HOME WITH SIMON.
ALL WET...
THAT MIGHT BE DIFFICULT, SEEING AS HE ALREADY LEFT.
HE WHAT?
SIMON!
...SIMON!

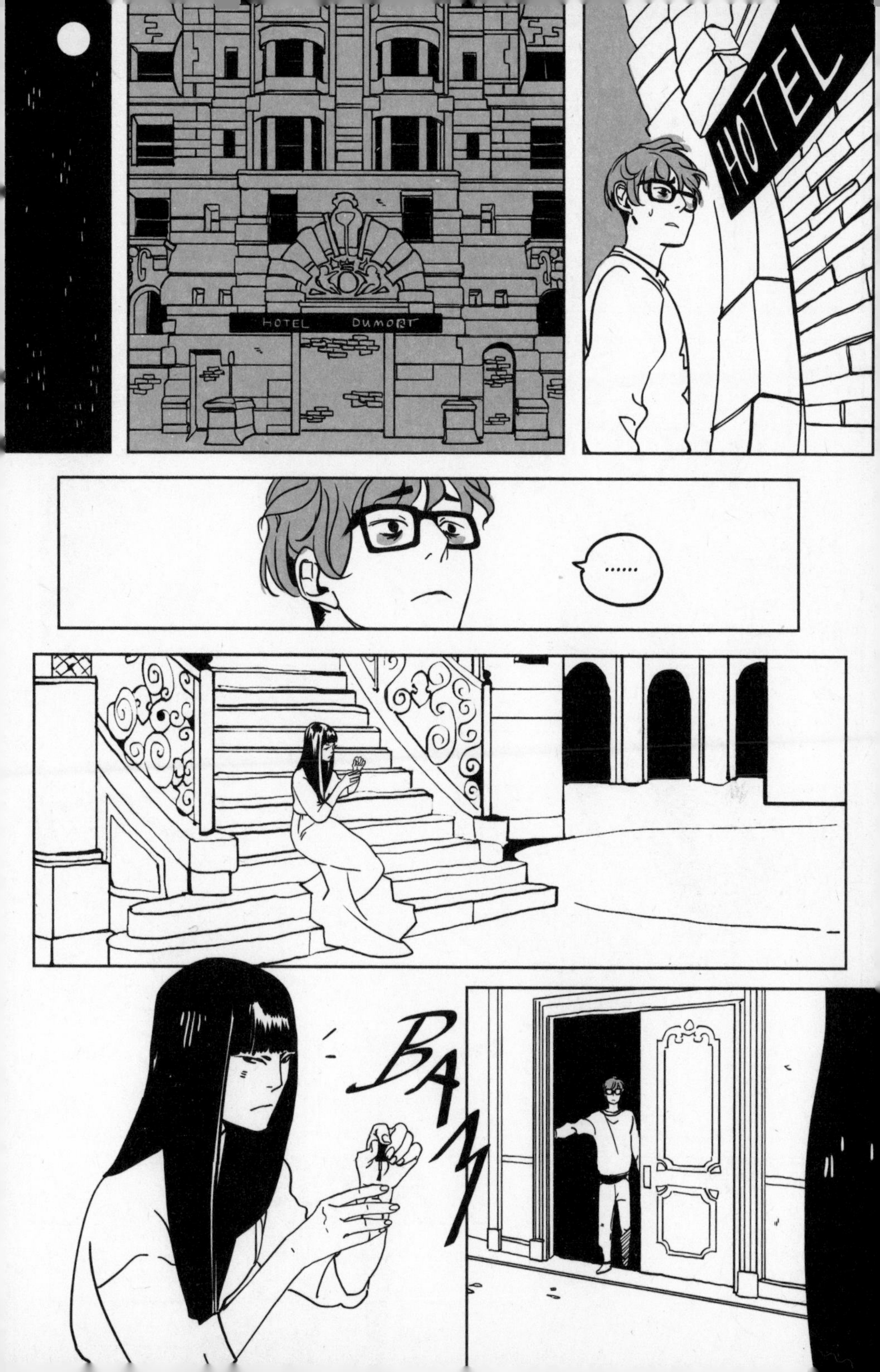
HOTEL DUMORT
HOTEL
......
BAM

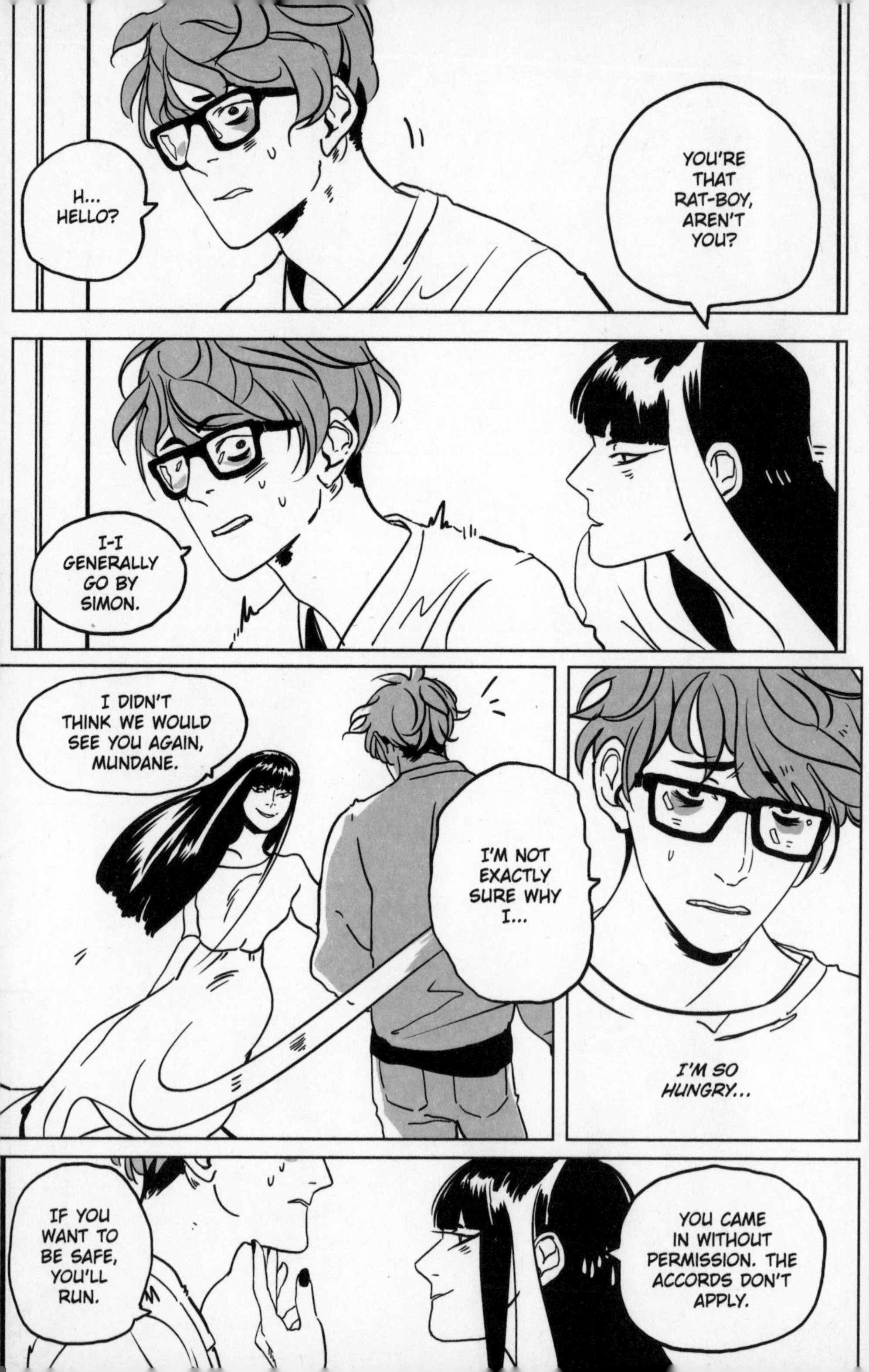
H... HELLO?
YOU'RE THAT RAT-BOY, AREN'T YOU?
I-I GENERALLY GO BY SIMON.
I DIDN'T THINK WE WOULD SEE YOU AGAIN, MUNDANE.
I'M NOT EXACTLY SURE WHY I...
I'M SO HUNGRY...
IF YOU WANT TO BE SAFE, YOU'LL RUN.
YOU CAME IN WITHOUT PERMISSION. THE ACCORDS DON'T APPLY.

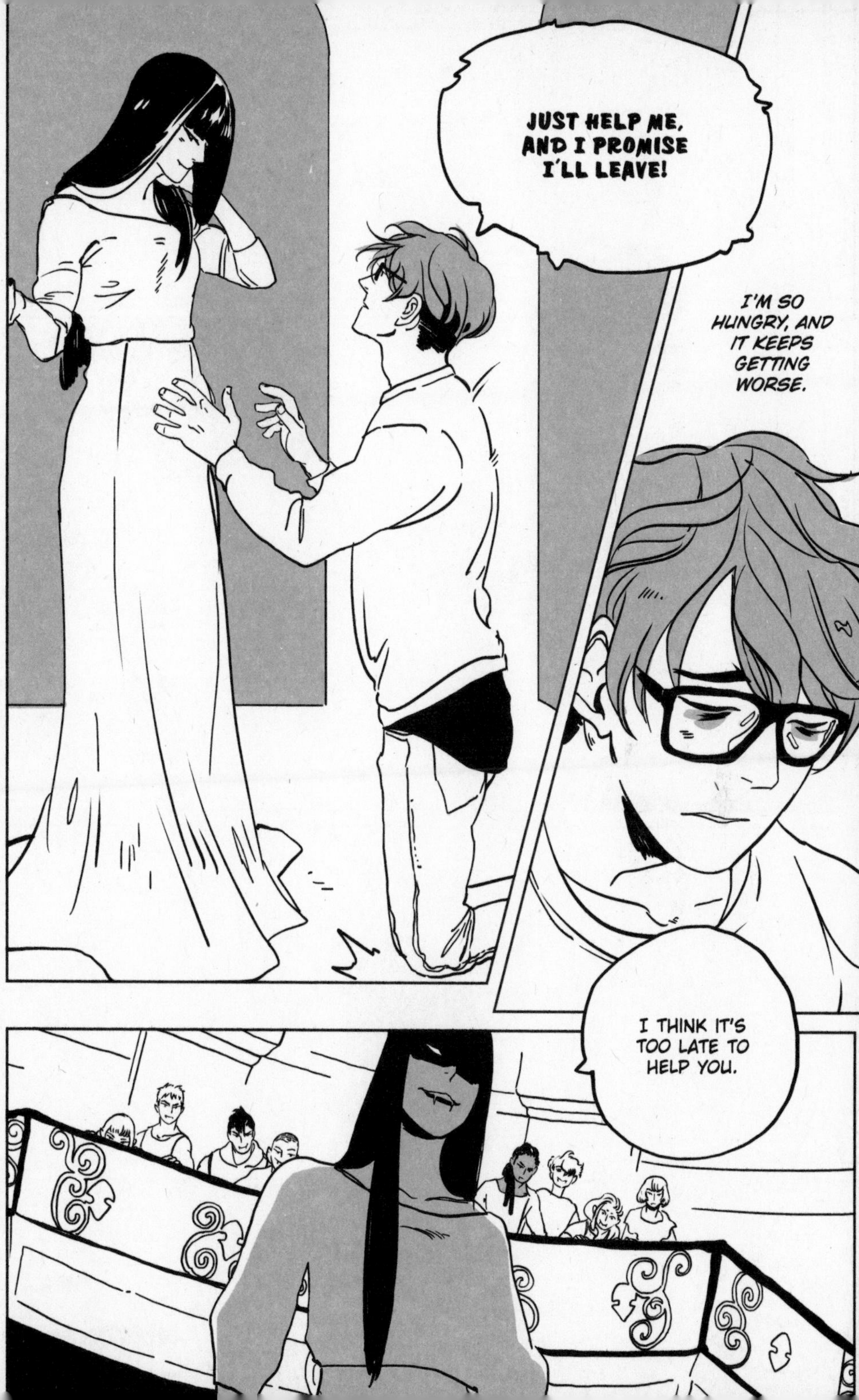
JUST HELP ME, AND I PROMISE I'LL LEAVE!
I'M SO HUNGRY, AND IT KEEPS GETTING WORSE.
I THINK IT'S TOO LATE TO HELP YOU.

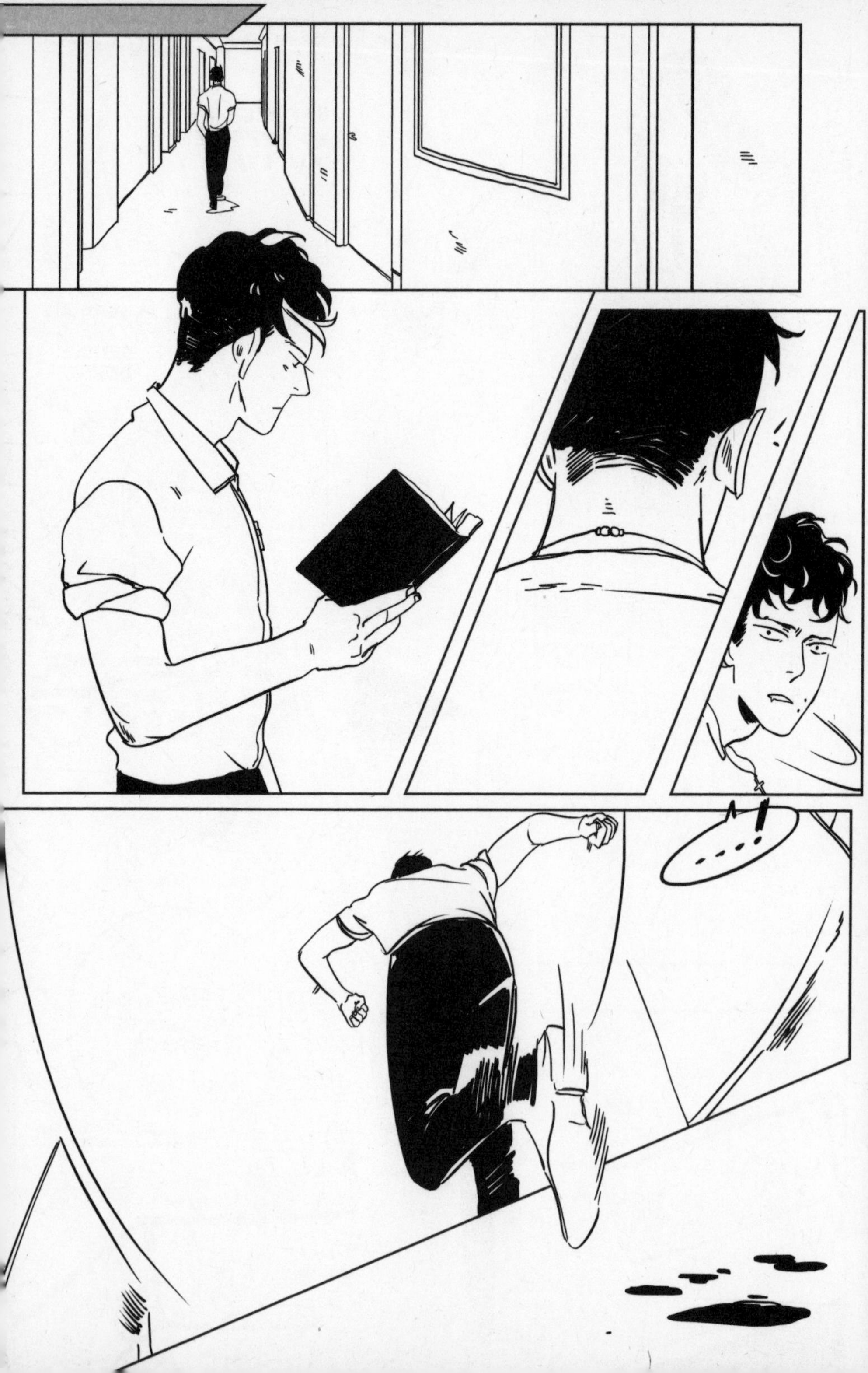
...!

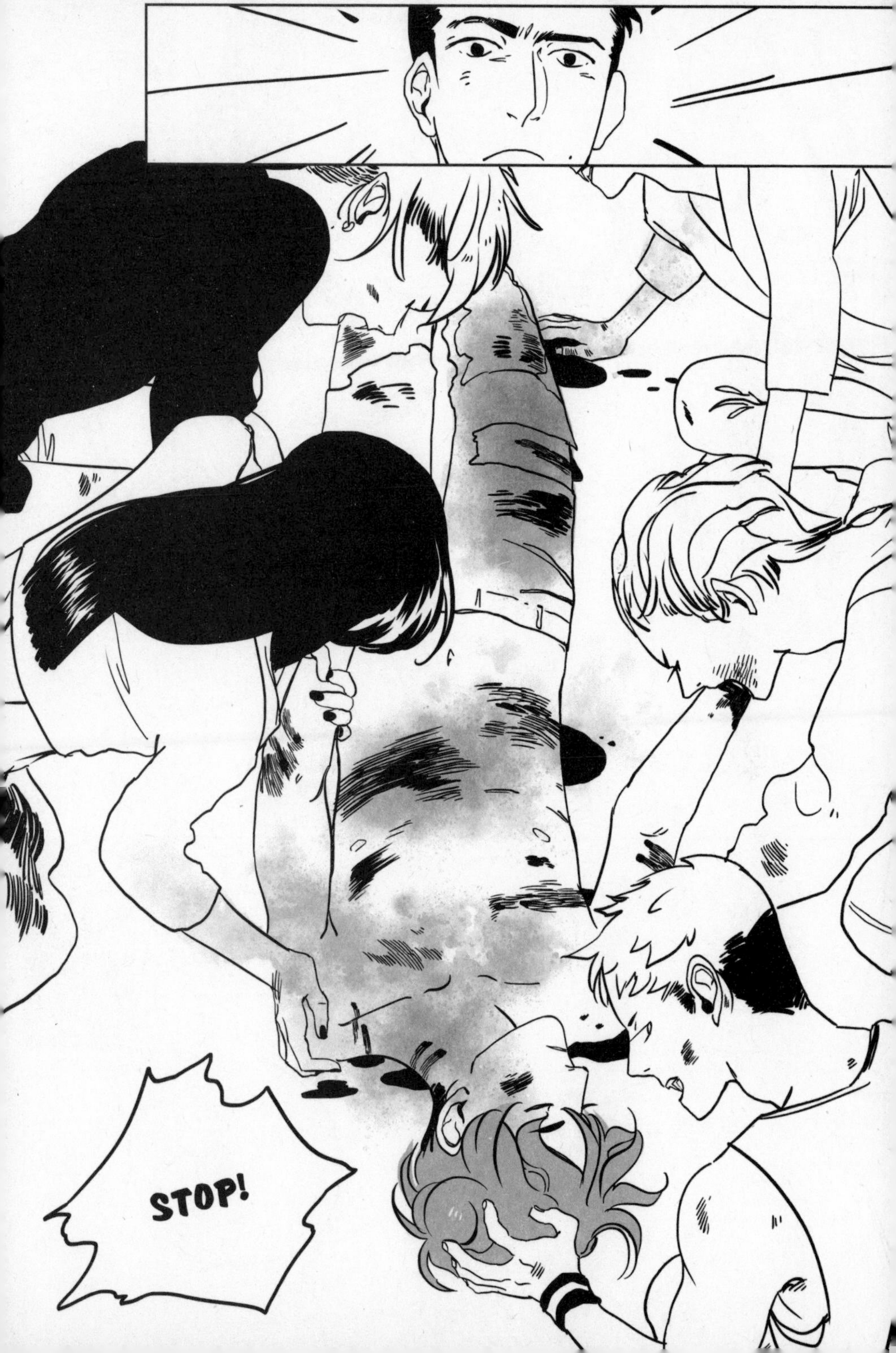
STOP!

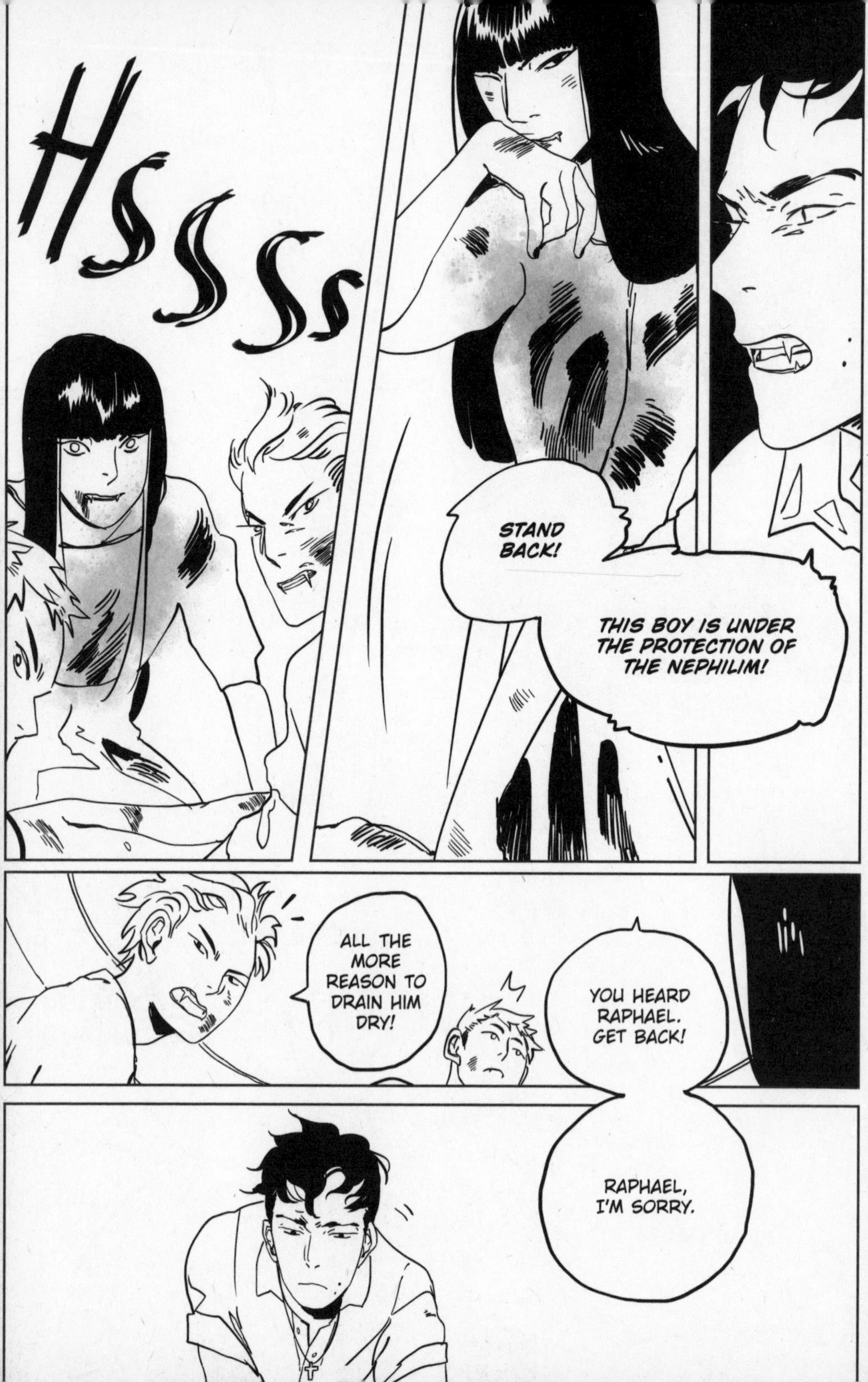
HSSSS
STAND BACK!
THIS BOY IS UNDER THE PROTECTION OF THE NEPHILIM!
ALL THE MORE REASON TO DRAIN HIM DRY!
YOU HEARD RAPHAEL. GET BACK!
RAPHAEL, I'M SORRY.

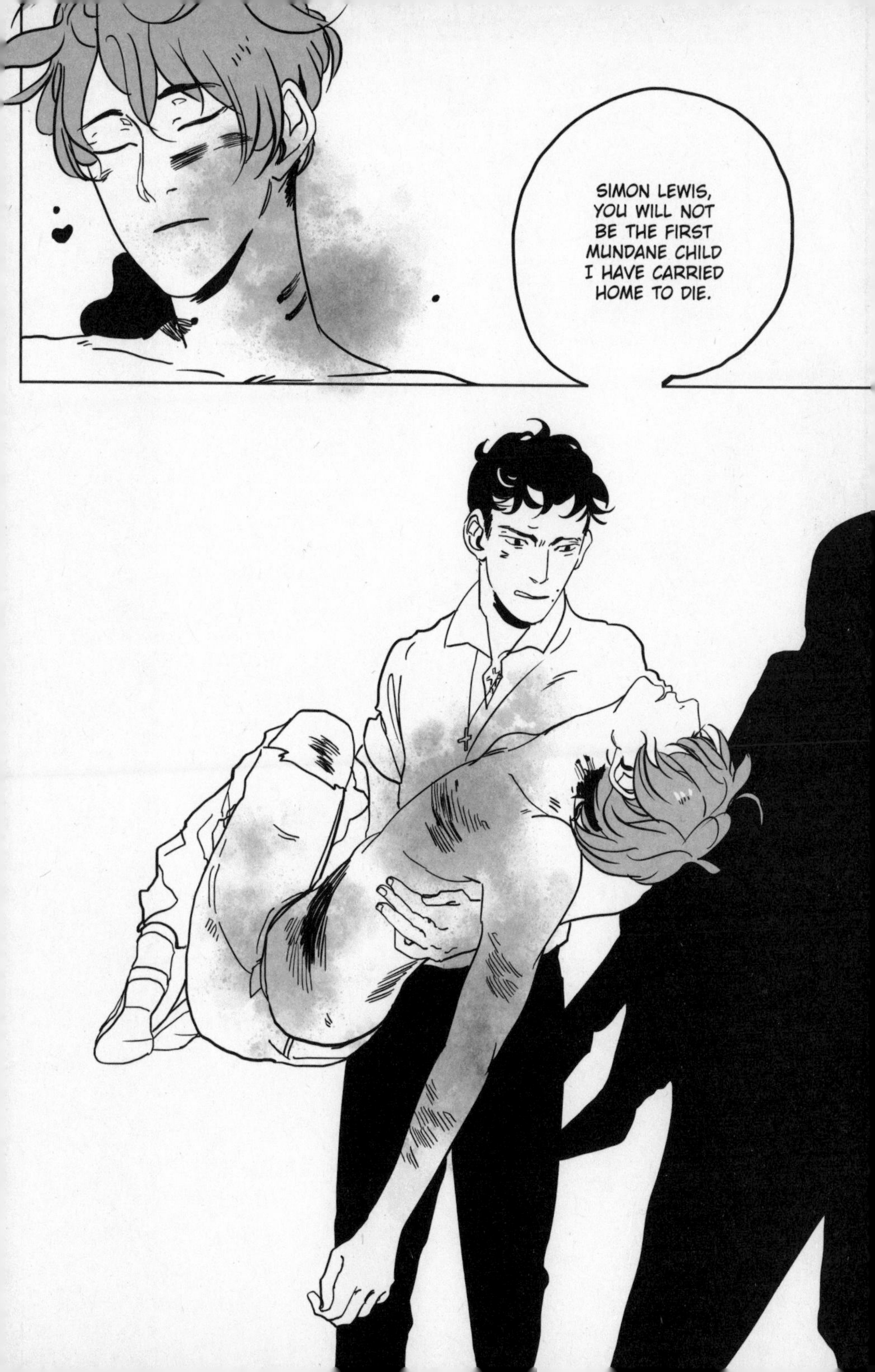
SIMON LEWIS, YOU WILL NOT BE THE FIRST MUNDANE CHILD I HAVE CARRIED HOME TO DIE.

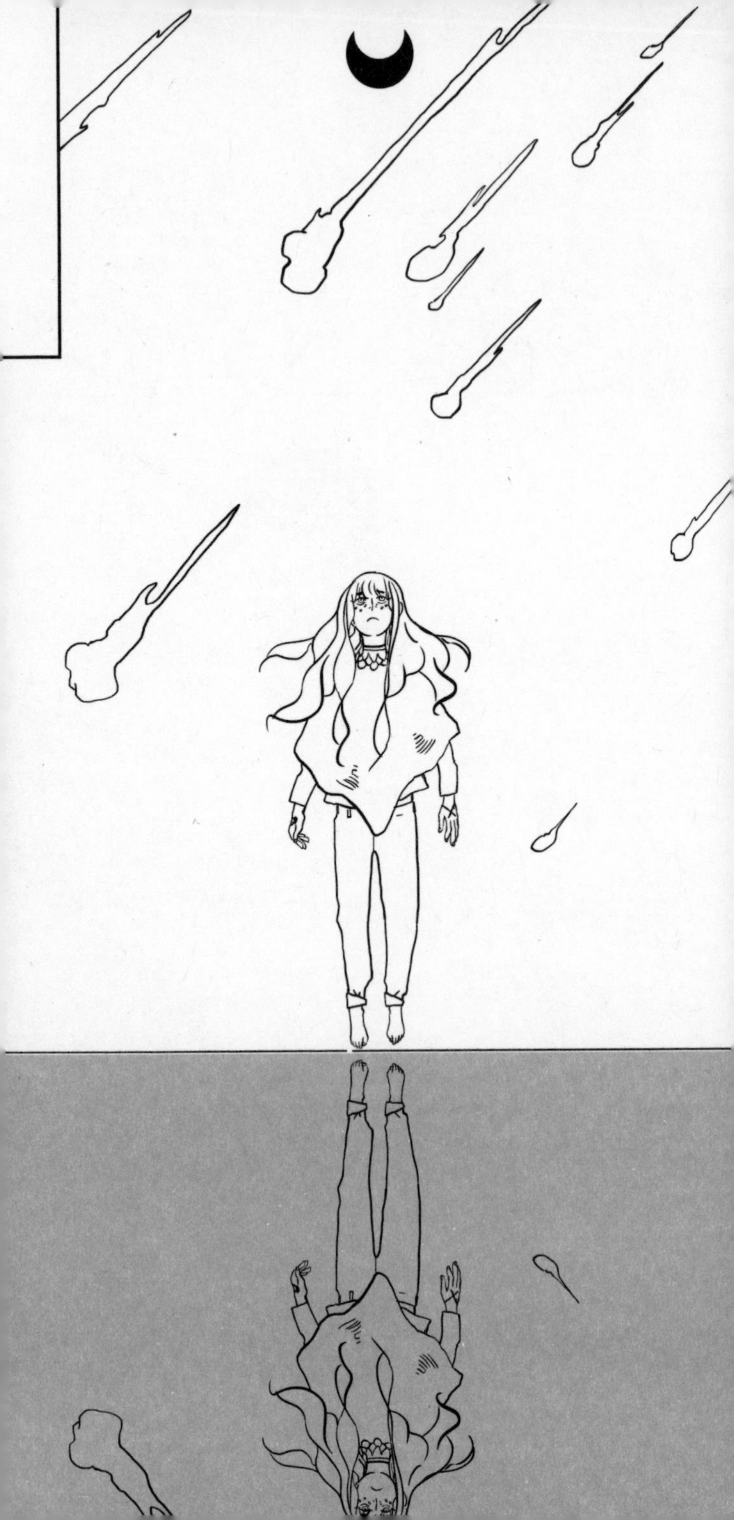

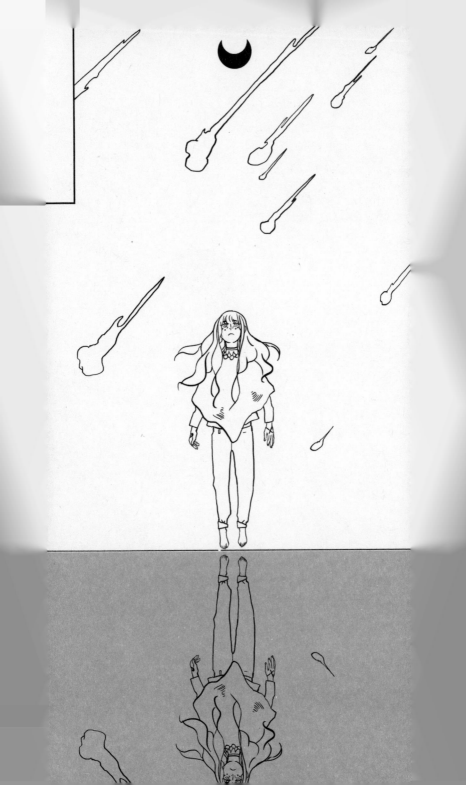

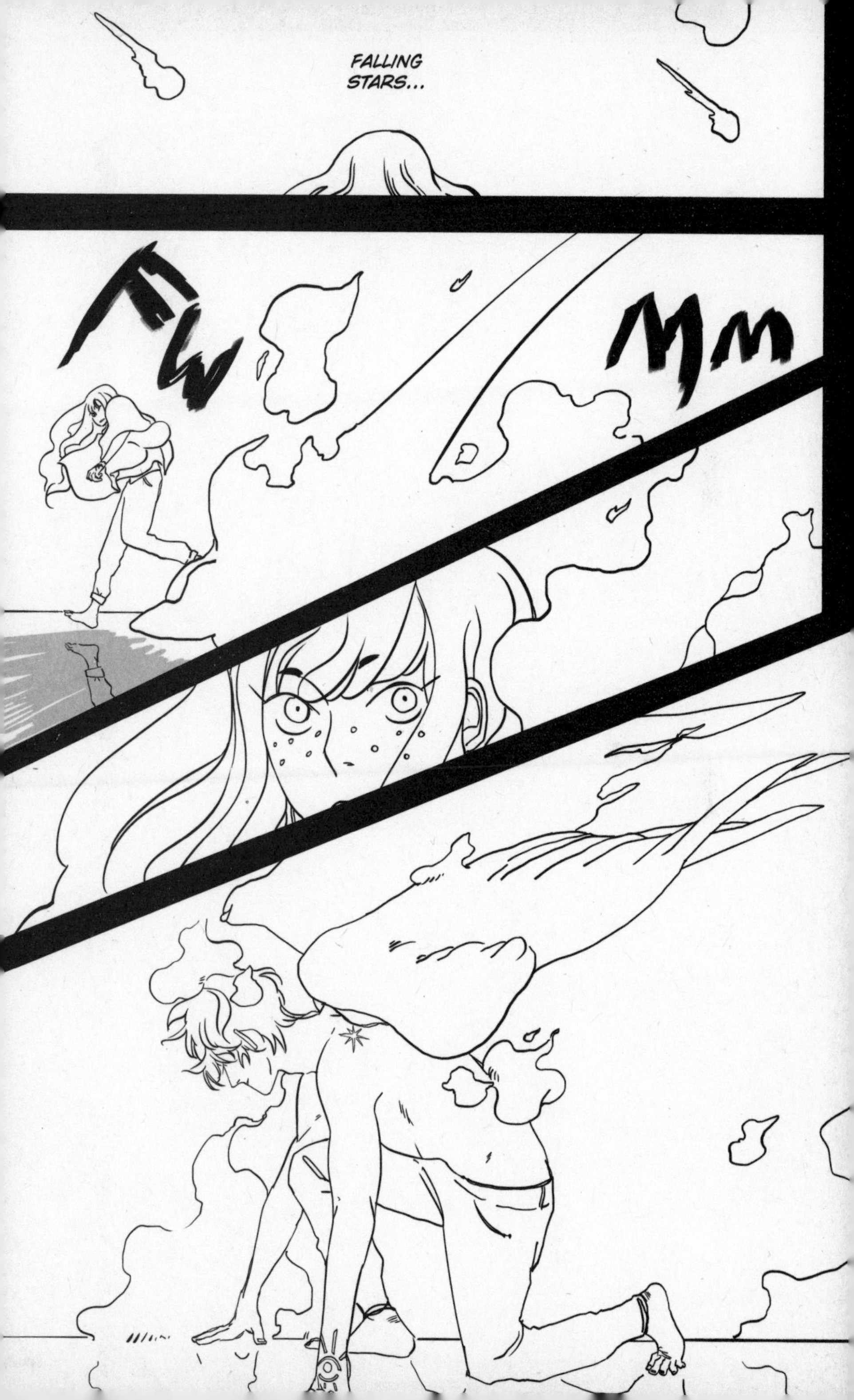
FALLING STARS...
FWMM

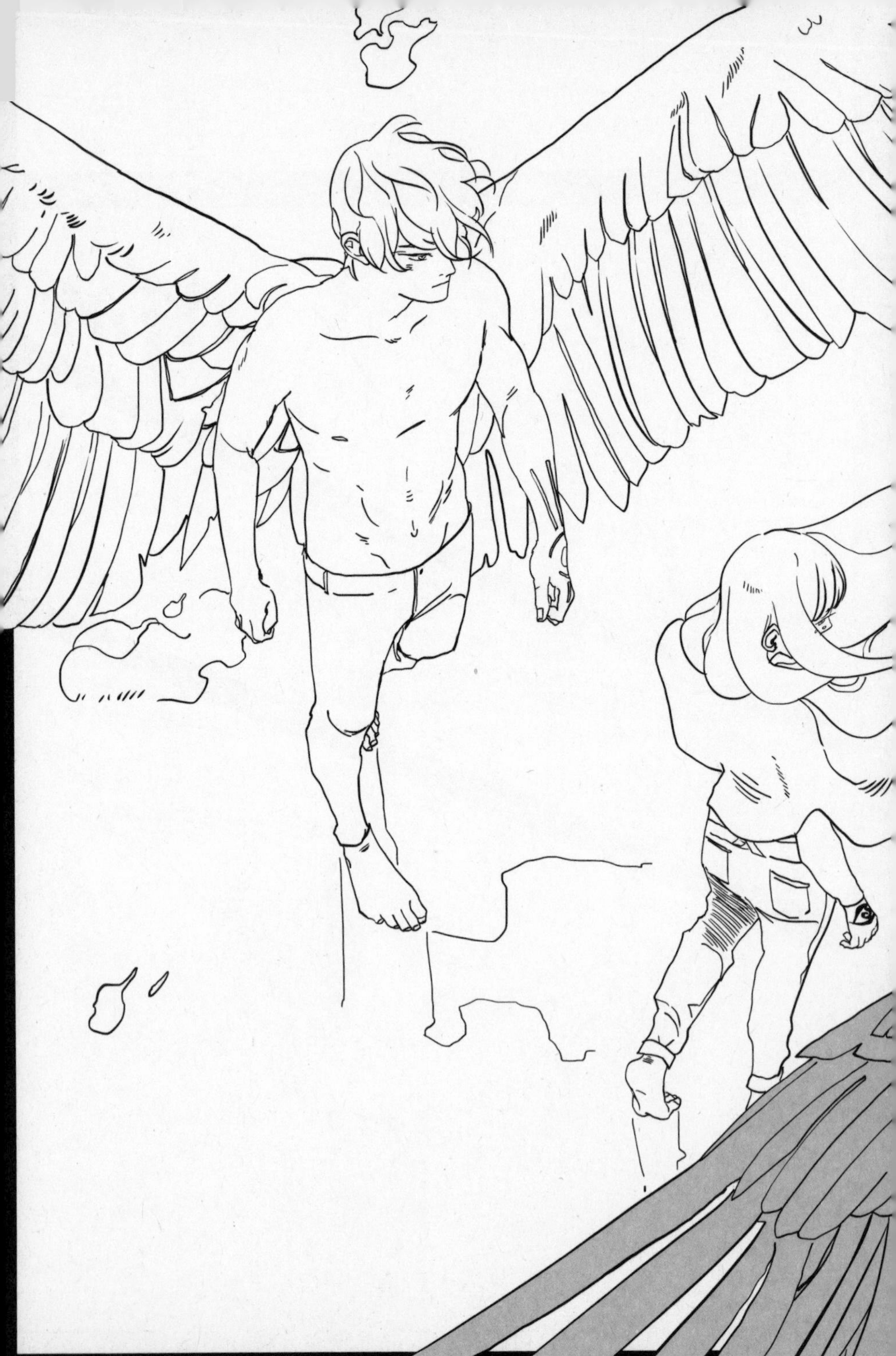

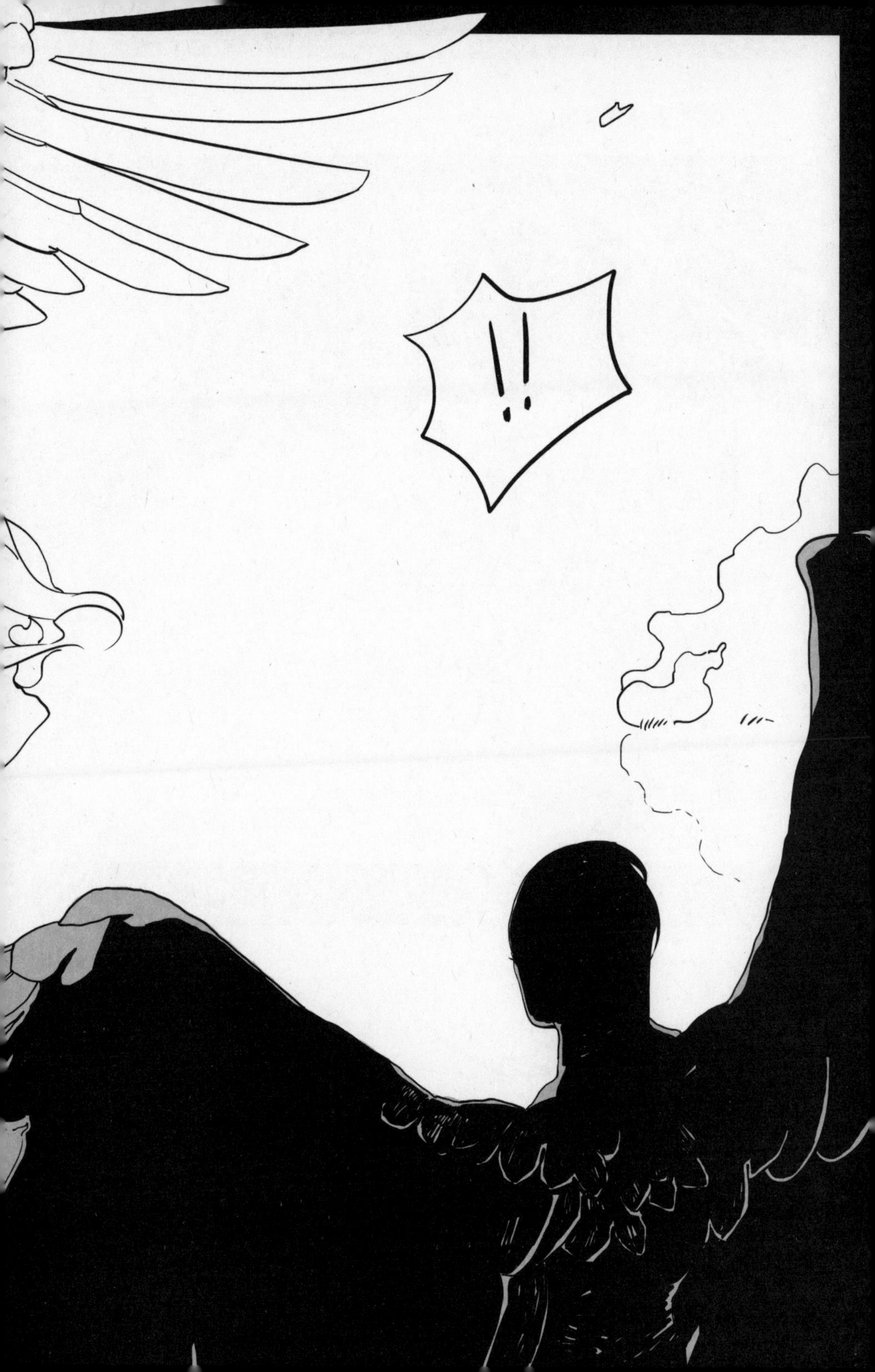
!!

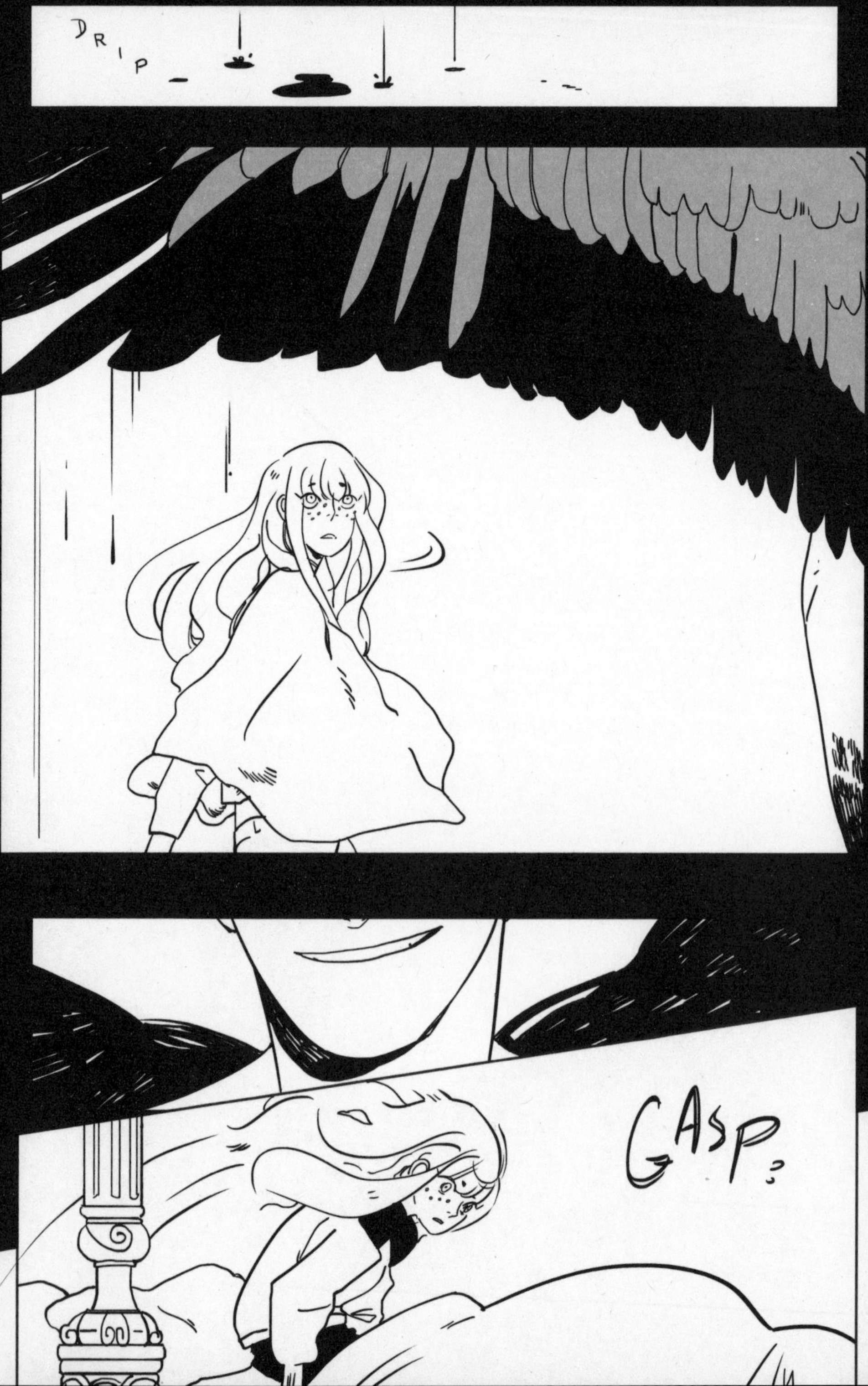
DRIP
GASP

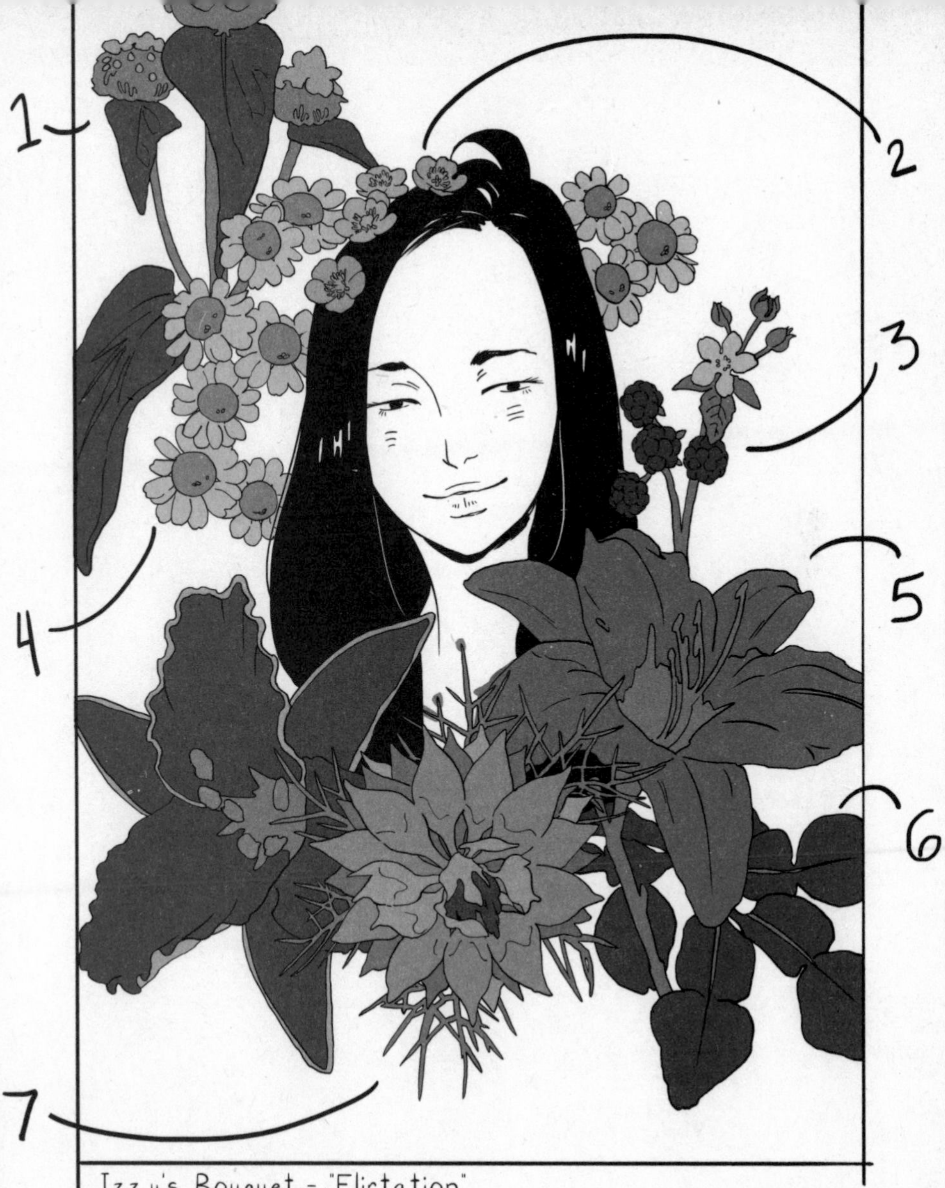
1
2
3
4
5
6
7

Izzy's Bouquet - "Flirtation"

1) Jerusalem Sage - Earthly Delights

2) Buttercup - Rich in Charms

3) Blackberry - Dangerous Pride

4) Feverfew - Flirt

5) Daylily - Coquette

6) Bergamot - Your Wiles are Irresistible

7) Nigella - Kiss Me Twice Before I Die

THE MORTAL INSTRUMENTS

THE GRAPHIC NOVEL

Chapter 17

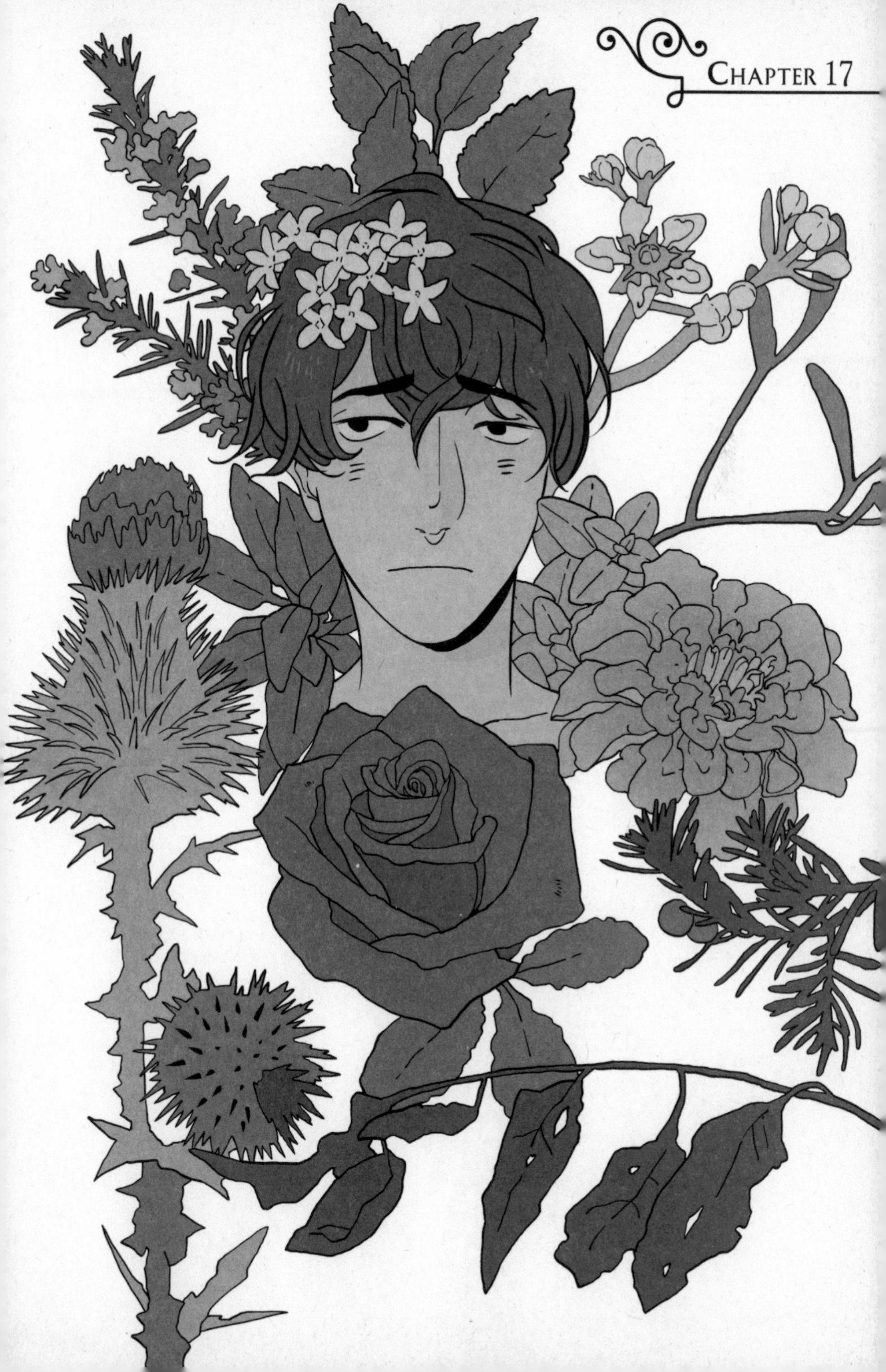

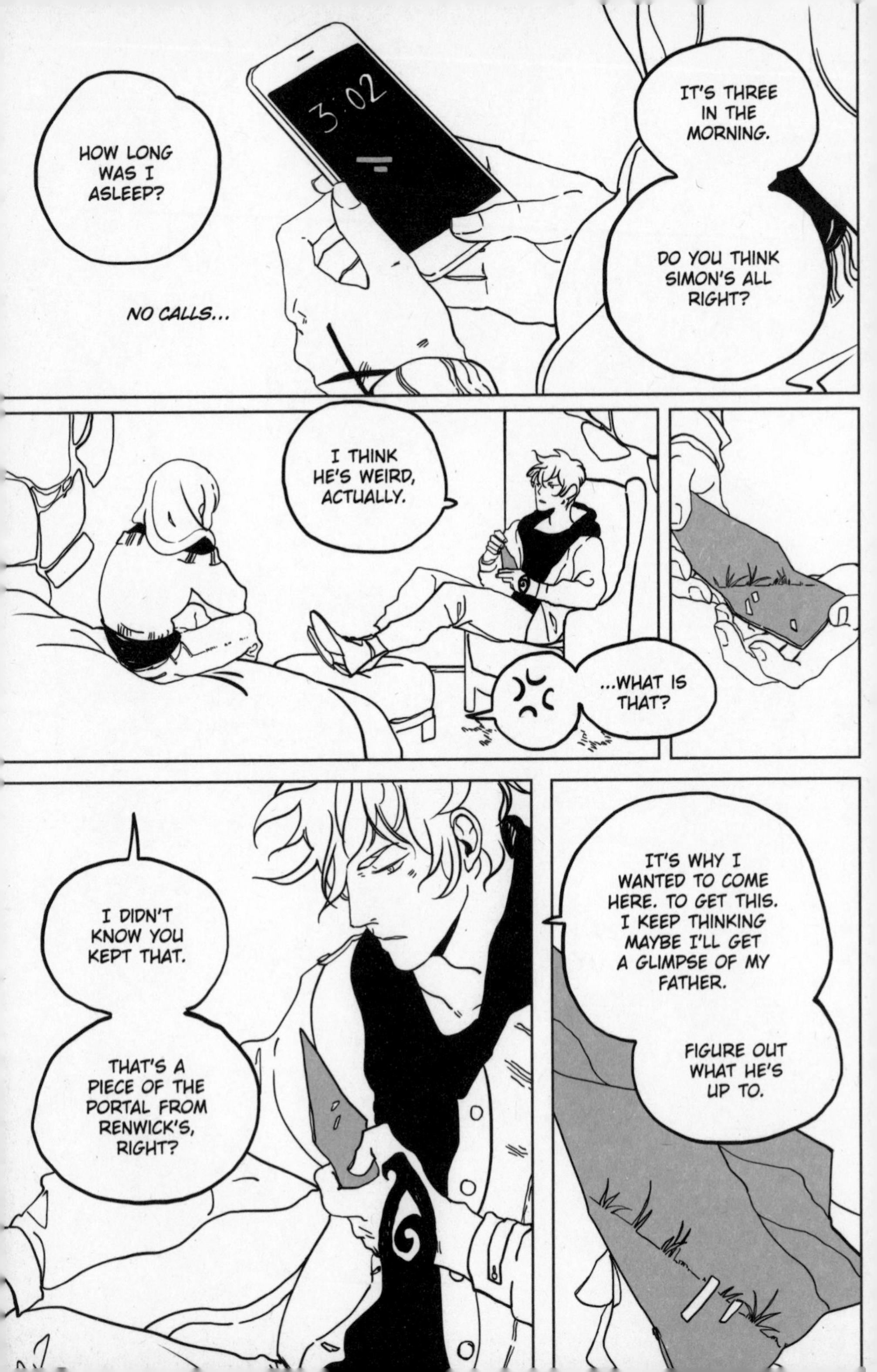
HOW LONG WAS I ASLEEP?
3:02
NO CALLS...
IT'S THREE IN THE MORNING.
DO YOU THINK SIMON'S ALL RIGHT?
I THINK HE'S WEIRD, ACTUALLY.
...WHAT IS THAT?
I DIDN'T KNOW YOU KEPT THAT.
THAT'S A PIECE OF THE PORTAL FROM RENWICK'S, RIGHT?
IT'S WHY I WANTED TO COME HERE. TO GET THIS. I KEEP THINKING MAYBE I'LL GET A GLIMPSE OF MY FATHER.
FIGURE OUT WHAT HE'S UP TO.

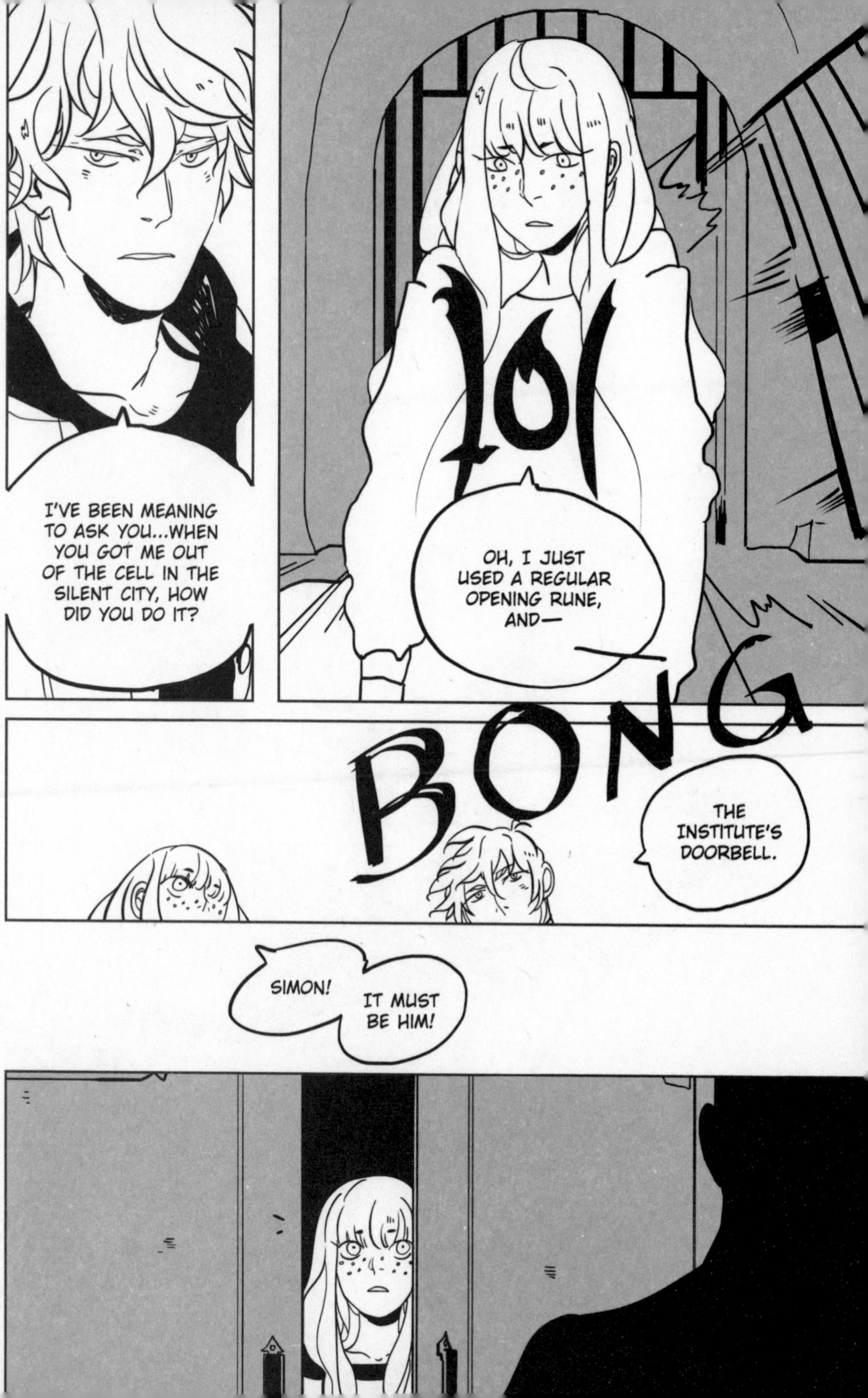
I'VE BEEN MEANING TO ASK YOU...WHEN YOU GOT ME OUT OF THE CELL IN THE SILENT CITY, HOW DID YOU DO IT?
OH, I JUST USED A REGULAR OPENING RUNE, AND—
BONG
THE INSTITUTE'S DOORBELL.
SIMON!
IT MUST BE HIM!

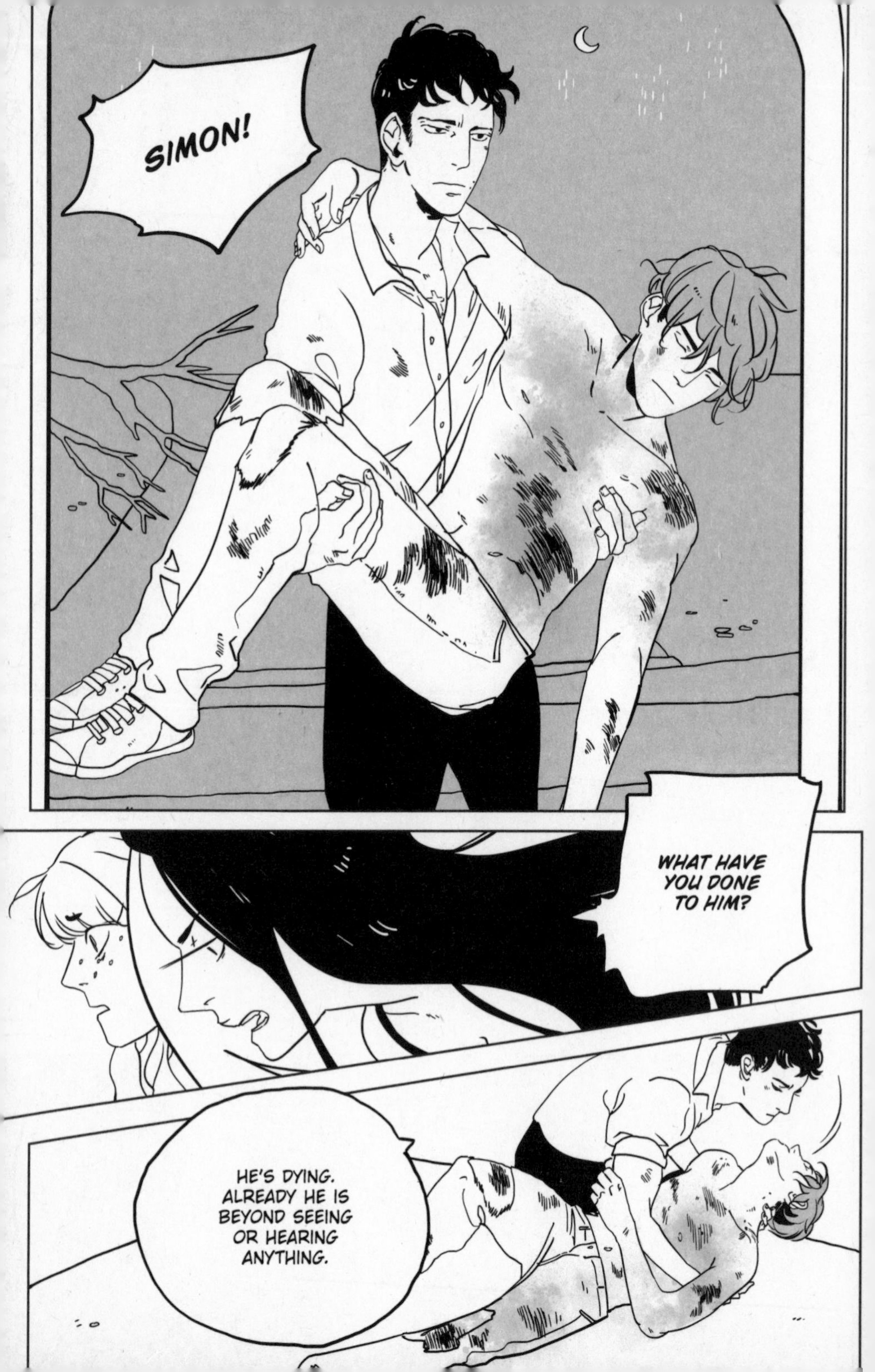
SIMON!
WHAT HAVE YOU DONE TO HIM?
HE'S DYING. ALREADY HE IS BEYOND SEEING OR HEARING ANYTHING.

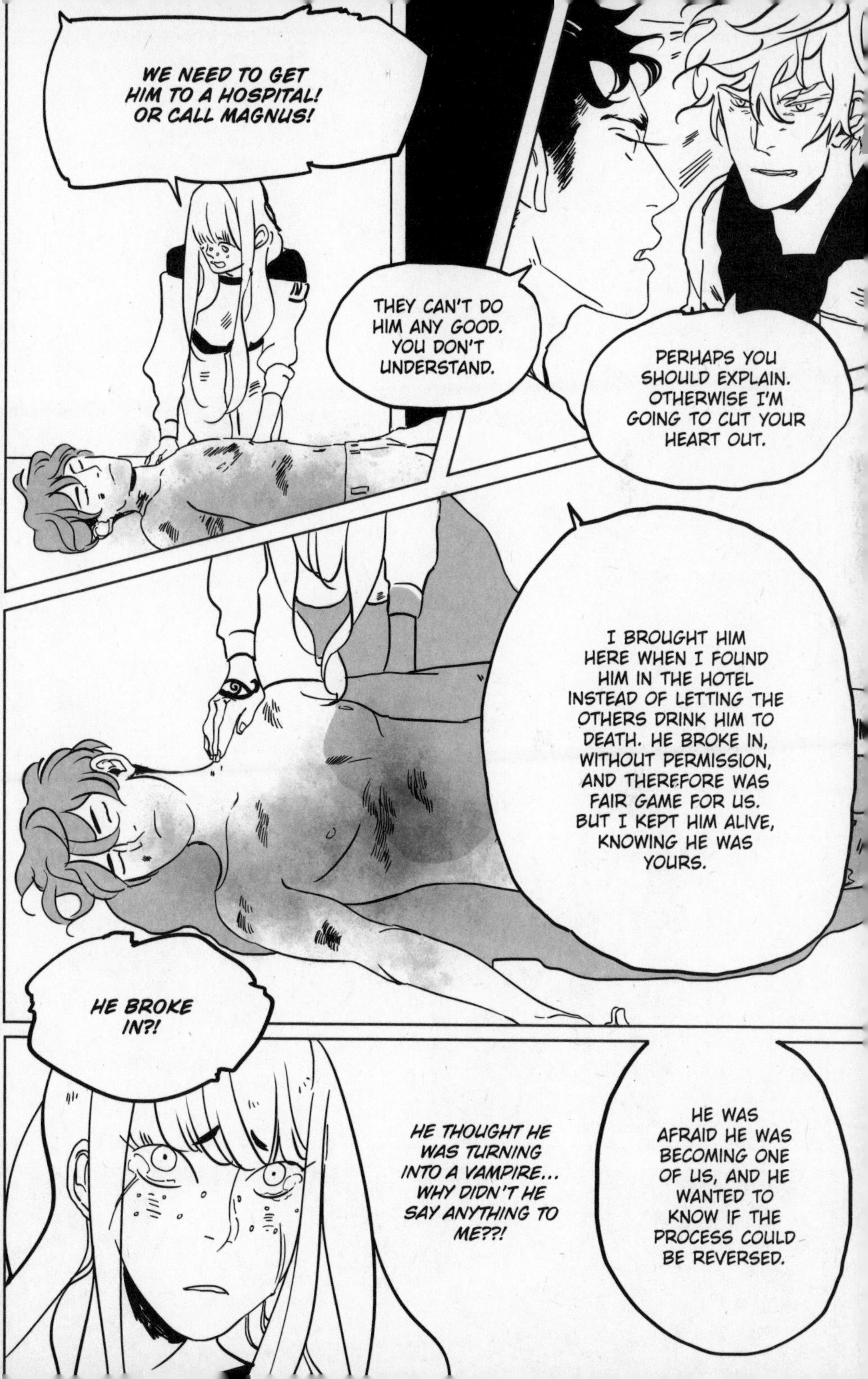
WE NEED TO GET HIM TO A HOSPITAL! OR CALL MAGNUS!
THEY CAN'T DO HIM ANY GOOD. YOU DON'T UNDERSTAND.
PERHAPS YOU SHOULD EXPLAIN. OTHERWISE I'M GOING TO CUT YOUR HEART OUT.
I BROUGHT HIM HERE WHEN I FOUND HIM IN THE HOTEL INSTEAD OF LETTING THE OTHERS DRINK HIM TO DEATH. HE BROKE IN, WITHOUT PERMISSION, AND THEREFORE WAS FAIR GAME FOR US. BUT I KEPT HIM ALIVE, KNOWING HE WAS YOURS.
HE BROKE IN?!
HE THOUGHT HE WAS TURNING INTO A VAMPIRE... WHY DIDN'T HE SAY ANYTHING TO ME??!
HE WAS AFRAID HE WAS BECOMING ONE OF US, AND HE WANTED TO KNOW IF THE PROCESS COULD BE REVERSED.

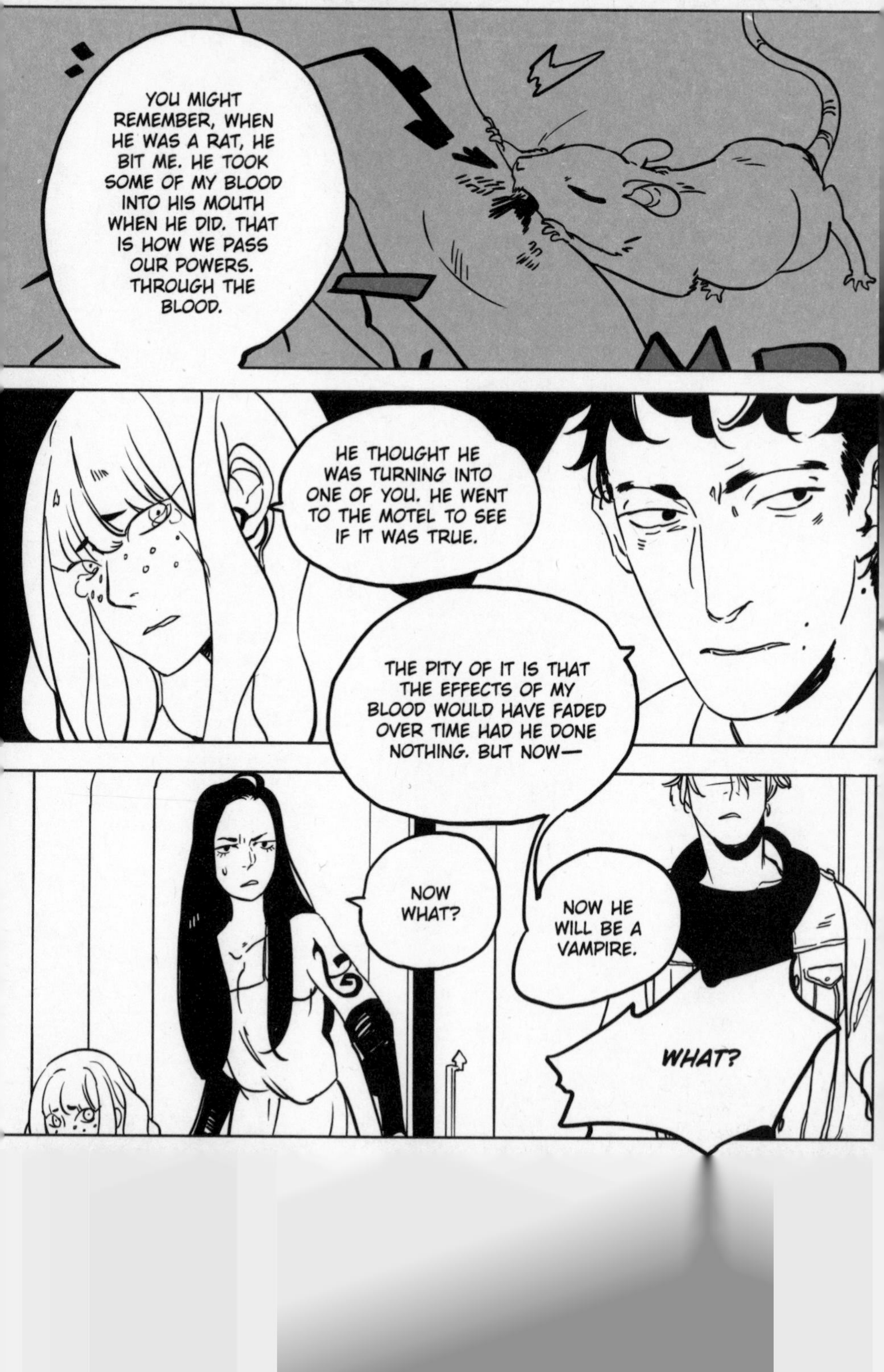
YOU MIGHT REMEMBER, WHEN HE WAS A RAT, HE BIT ME. HE TOOK SOME OF MY BLOOD INTO HIS MOUTH WHEN HE DID. THAT IS HOW WE PASS OUR POWERS. THROUGH THE BLOOD.
HE THOUGHT HE WAS TURNING INTO ONE OF YOU. HE WENT TO THE MOTEL TO SEE IF IT WAS TRUE.
THE PITY OF IT IS THAT THE EFFECTS OF MY BLOOD WOULD HAVE FADED OVER TIME HAD HE DONE NOTHING. BUT NOW—
NOW WHAT?
NOW HE WILL BE A VAMPIRE.
WHAT?

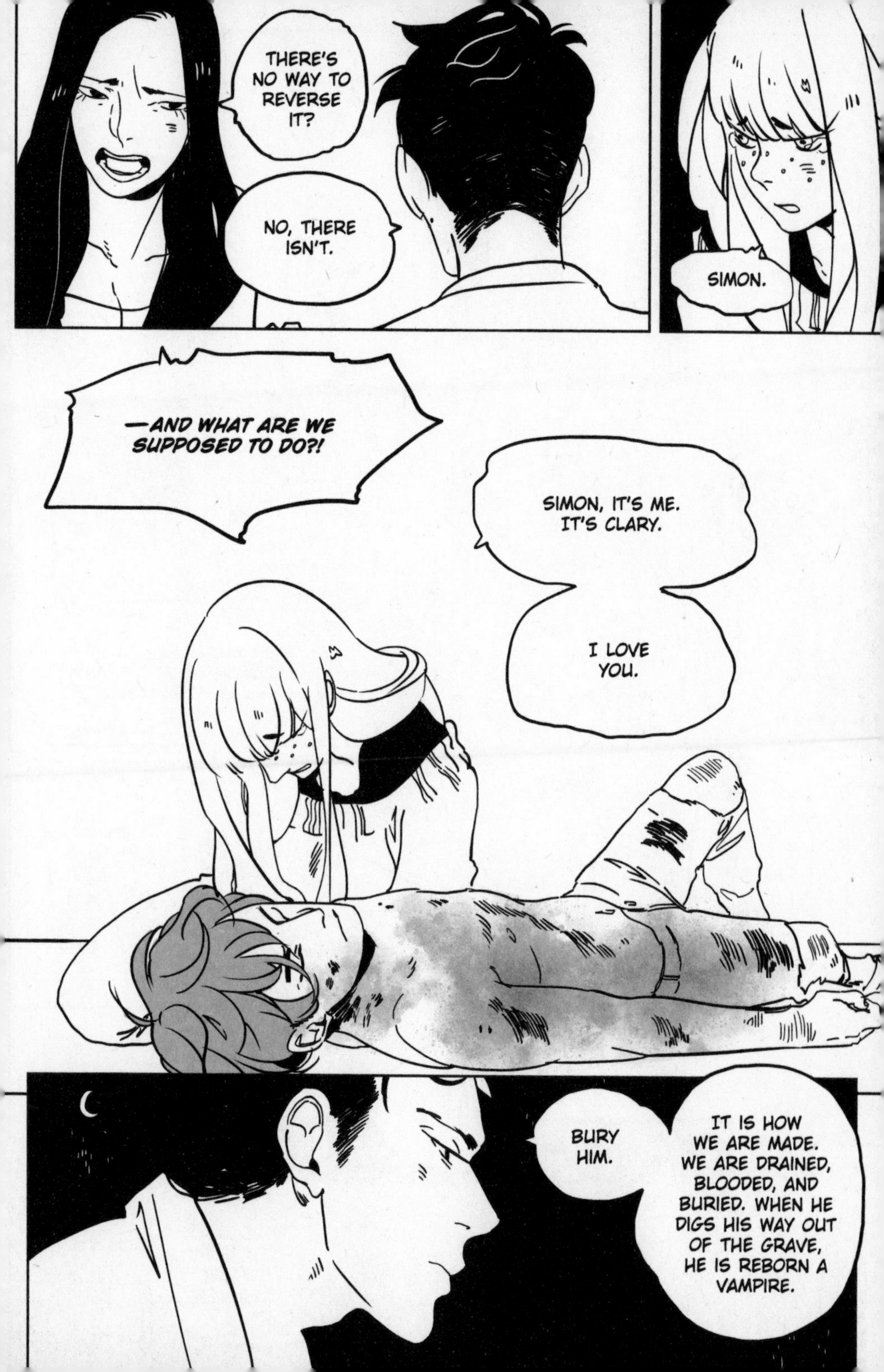
THERE'S NO WAY TO REVERSE IT?
NO, THERE ISN'T.
SIMON.
—AND WHAT ARE WE SUPPOSED TO DO?!
SIMON, IT'S ME. IT'S CLARY.
I LOVE YOU.
BURY HIM.
IT IS HOW WE ARE MADE. WE ARE DRAINED, BLOODED, AND BURIED. WHEN HE DIGS HIS WAY OUT OF THE GRAVE, HE IS REBORN A VAMPIRE.

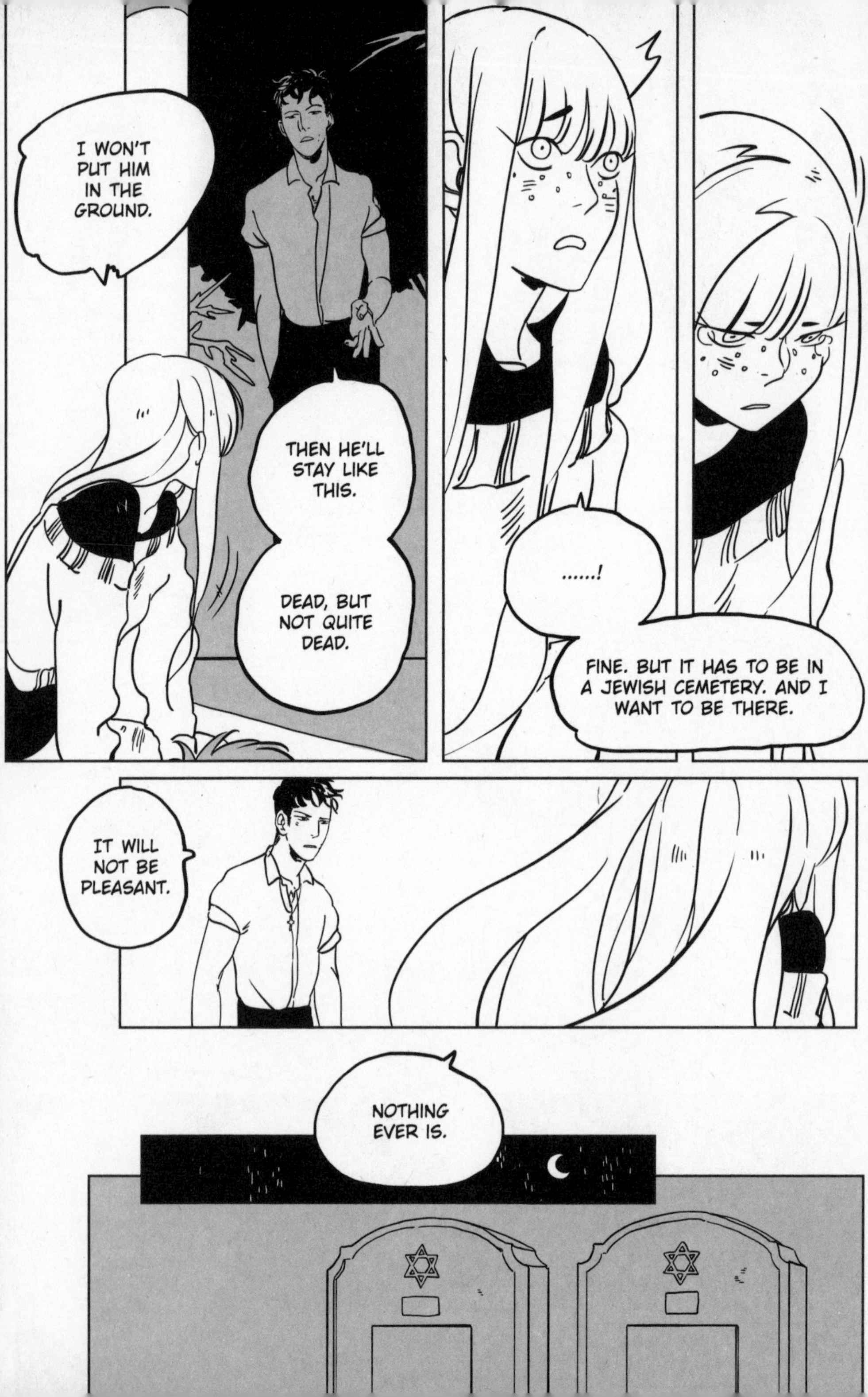
I WON'T PUT HIM IN THE GROUND.
THEN HE'LL STAY LIKE THIS.
DEAD, BUT NOT QUITE DEAD.
......!
FINE. BUT IT HAS TO BE IN A JEWISH CEMETERY. AND I WANT TO BE THERE.
IT WILL NOT BE PLEASANT.
NOTHING EVER IS.

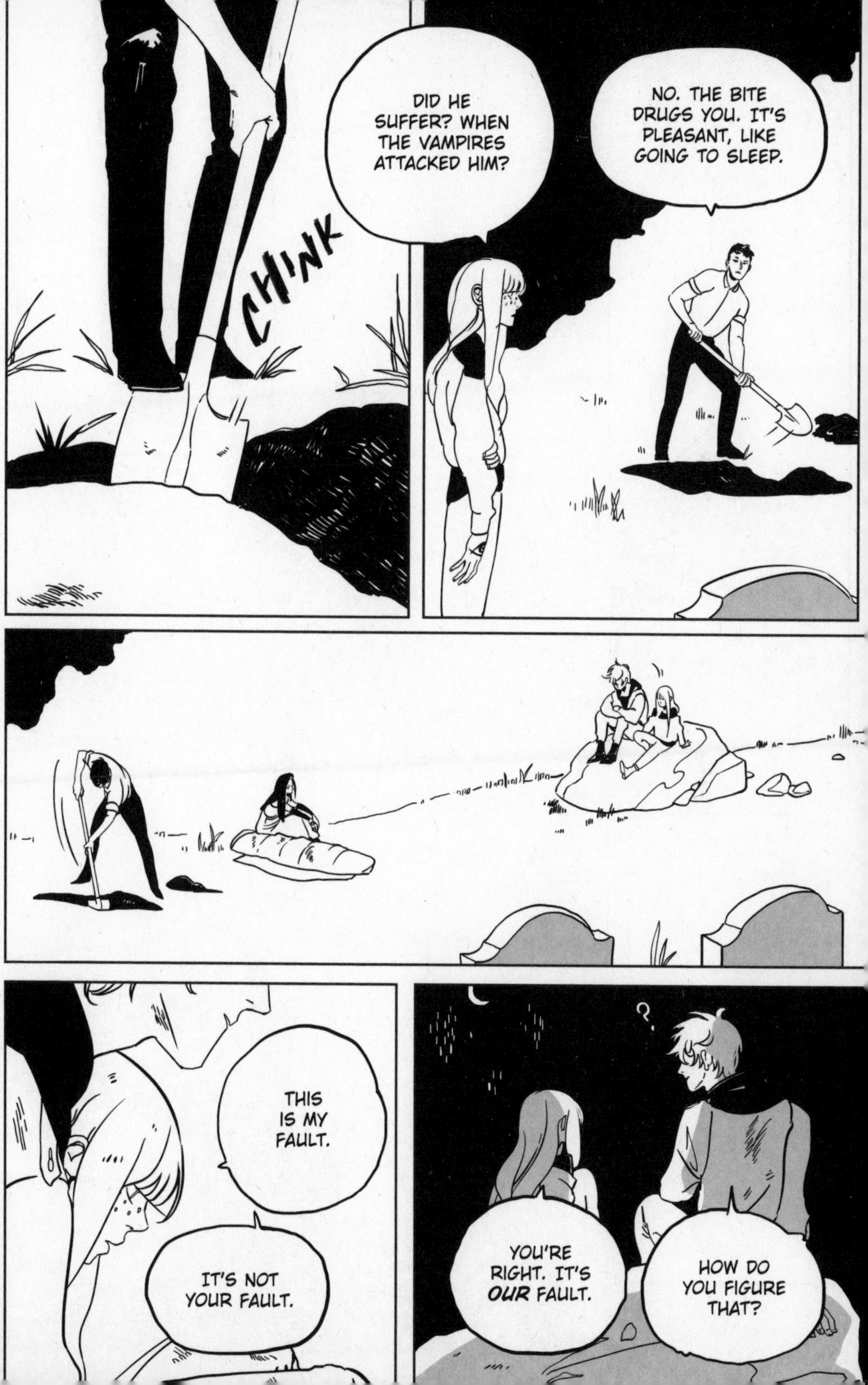
CHINK
DID HE SUFFER? WHEN THE VAMPIRES ATTACKED HIM?
NO. THE BITE DRUGS YOU. IT'S PLEASANT, LIKE GOING TO SLEEP.
THIS IS MY FAULT.
IT'S NOT YOUR FAULT.
YOU'RE RIGHT. IT'S *OUR* FAULT.
HOW DO YOU FIGURE THAT?

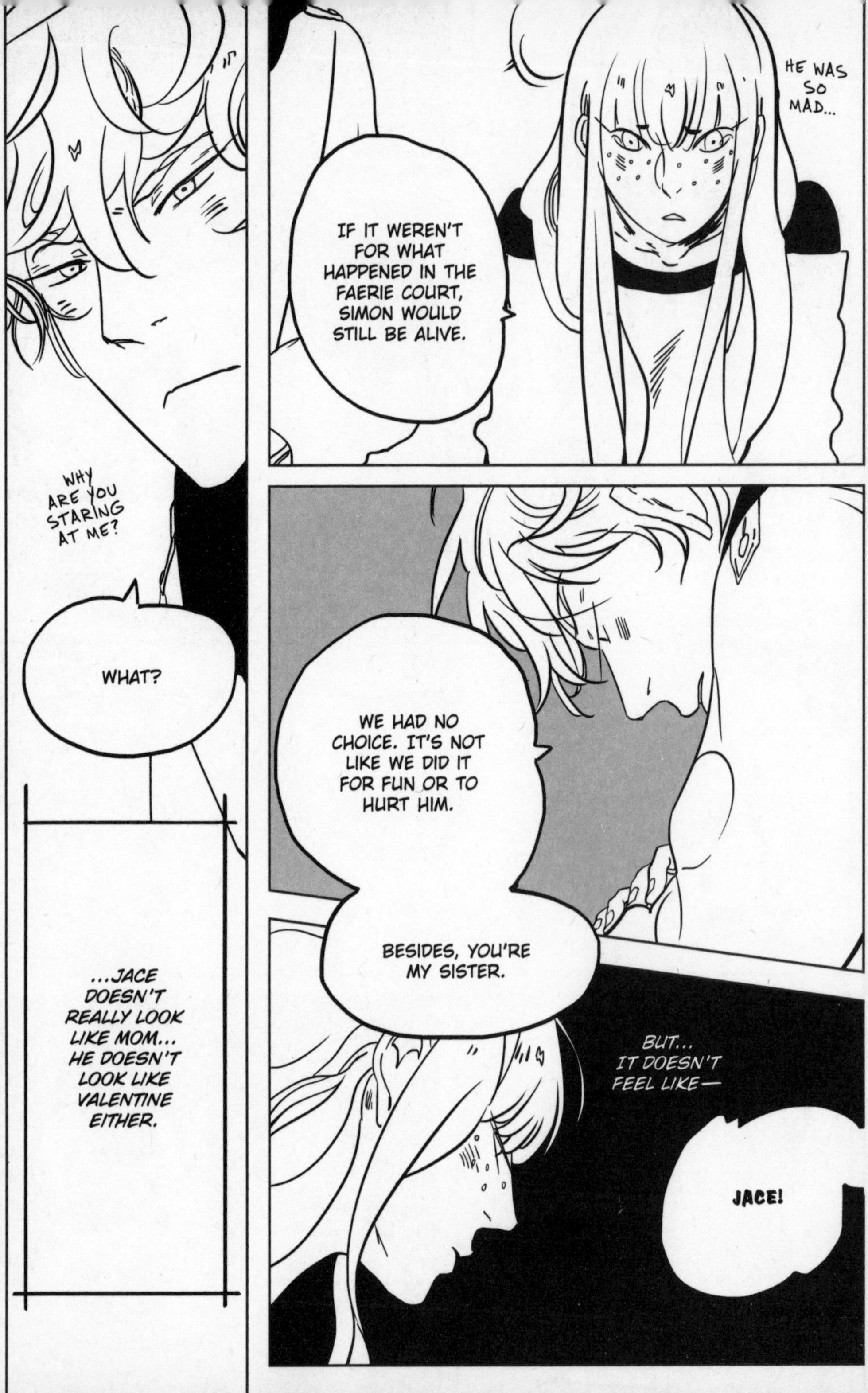
WHY ARE YOU STARING AT ME?
WHAT?
...JACE DOESN'T REALLY LOOK LIKE MOM... HE DOESN'T LOOK LIKE VALENTINE EITHER.
IF IT WEREN'T FOR WHAT HAPPENED IN THE FAERIE COURT, SIMON WOULD STILL BE ALIVE.
HE WAS SO MAD...
WE HAD NO CHOICE. IT'S NOT LIKE WE DID IT FOR FUN OR TO HURT HIM.
BESIDES, YOU'RE MY SISTER.
BUT... IT DOESN'T FEEL LIKE—
JACE!

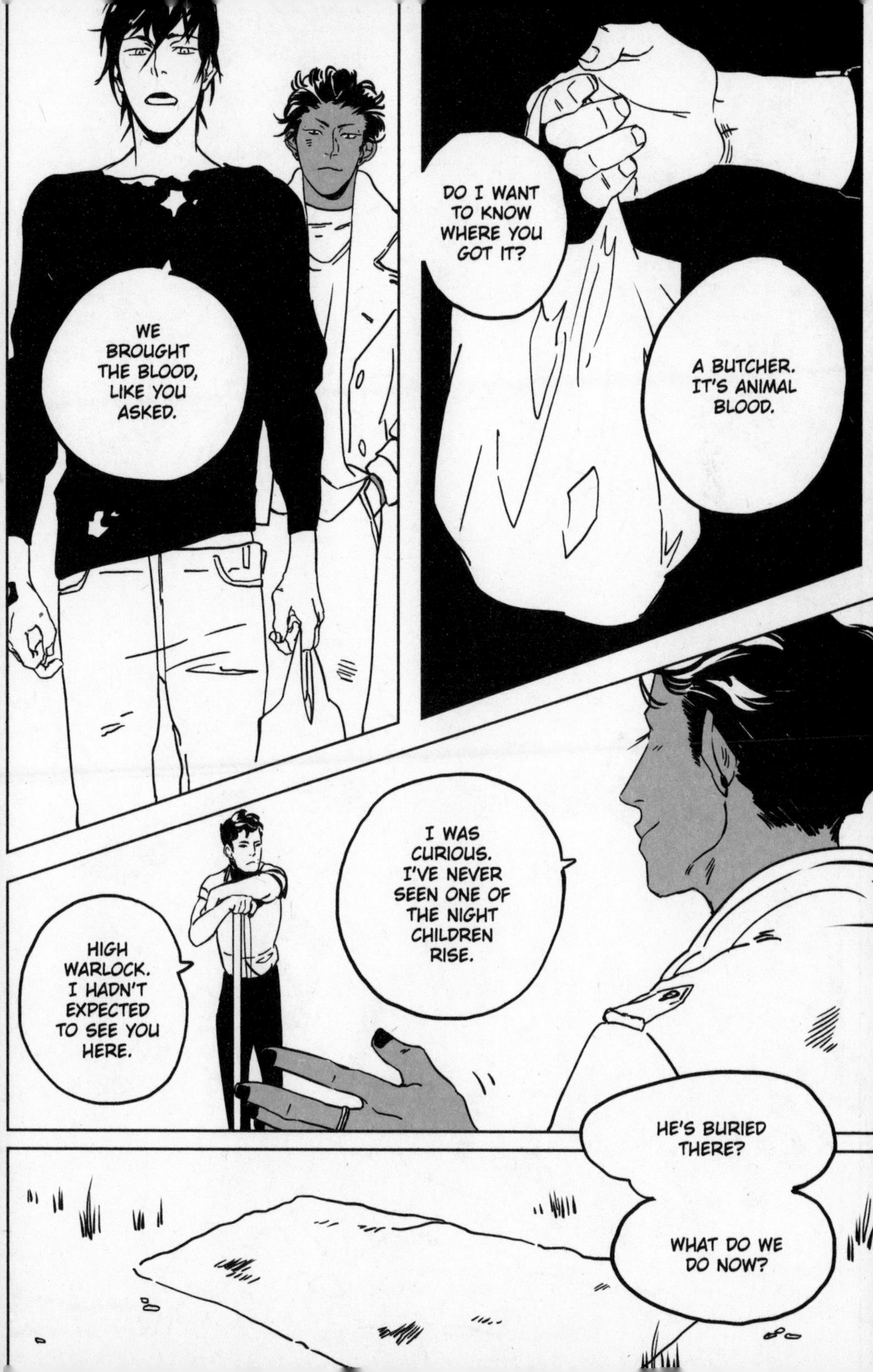
WE BROUGHT THE BLOOD, LIKE YOU ASKED.
DO I WANT TO KNOW WHERE YOU GOT IT?
A BUTCHER. IT'S ANIMAL BLOOD.
HIGH WARLOCK. I HADN'T EXPECTED TO SEE YOU HERE.
I WAS CURIOUS. I'VE NEVER SEEN ONE OF THE NIGHT CHILDREN RISE.
HE'S BURIED THERE?
WHAT DO WE DO NOW?

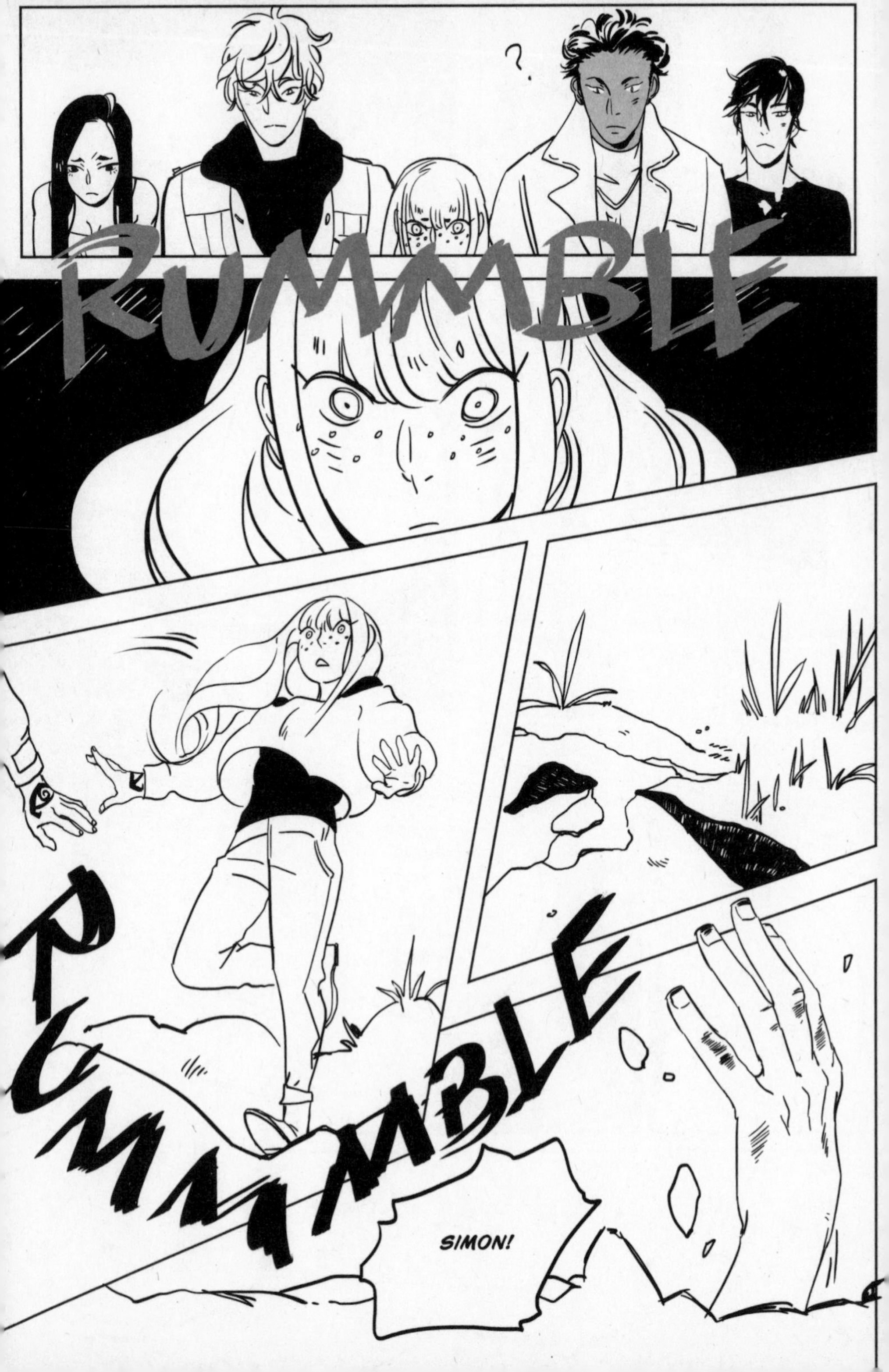
?
RUMMBLE
RUMMBLE
SIMON!

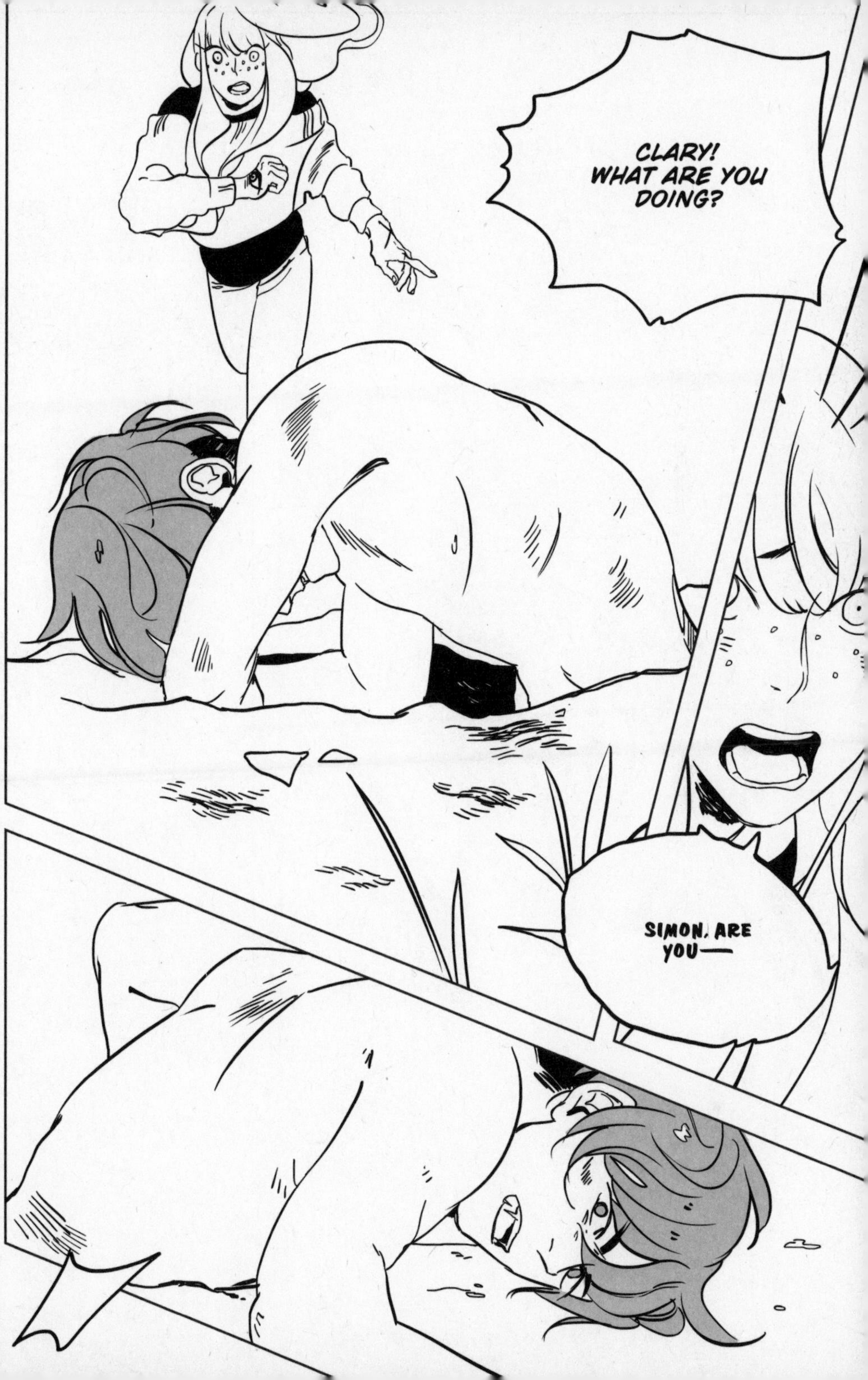
CLARY! WHAT ARE YOU DOING?
SIMON, ARE YOU—

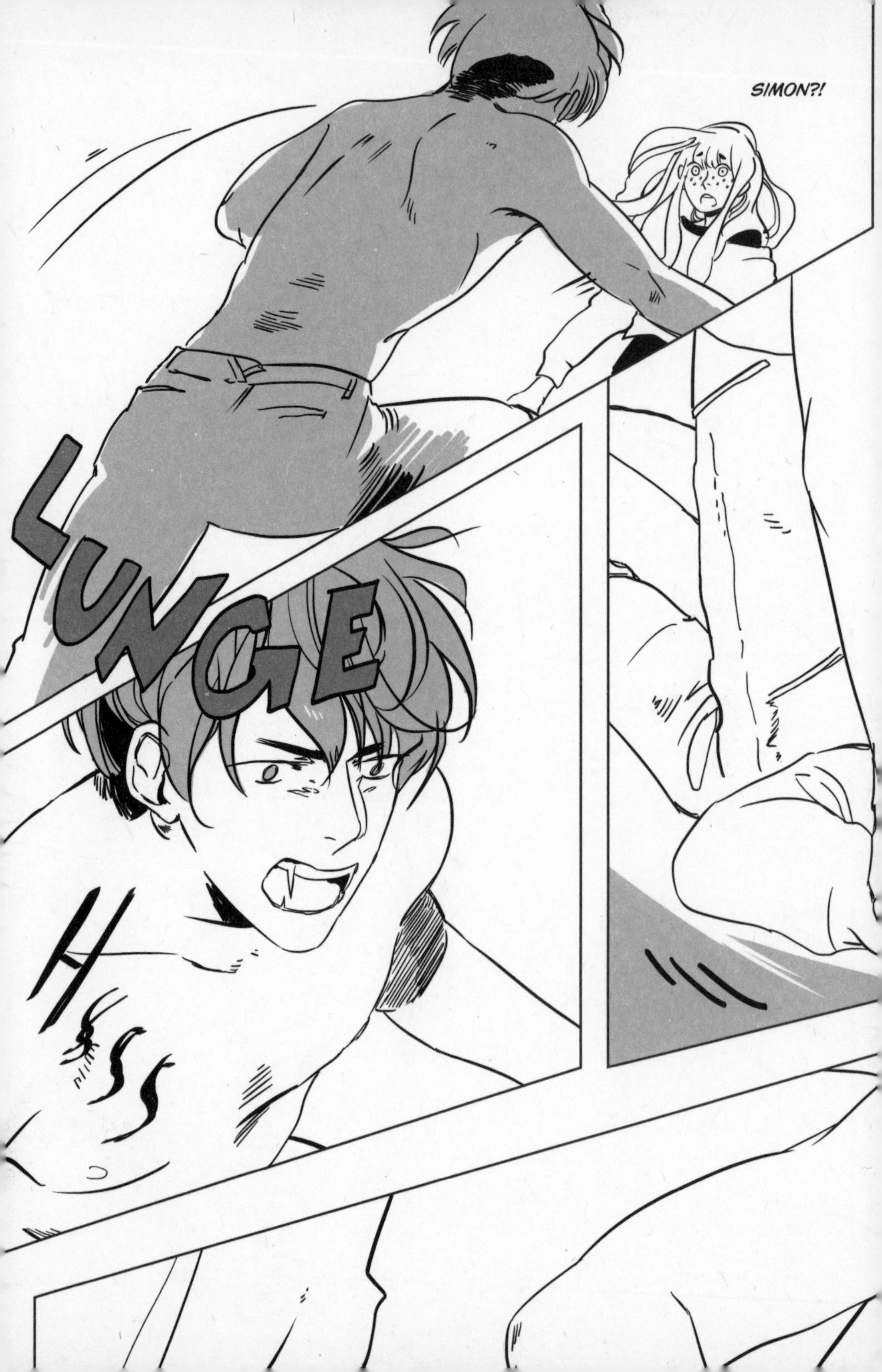
SIMON?!
LUNGE
HISS

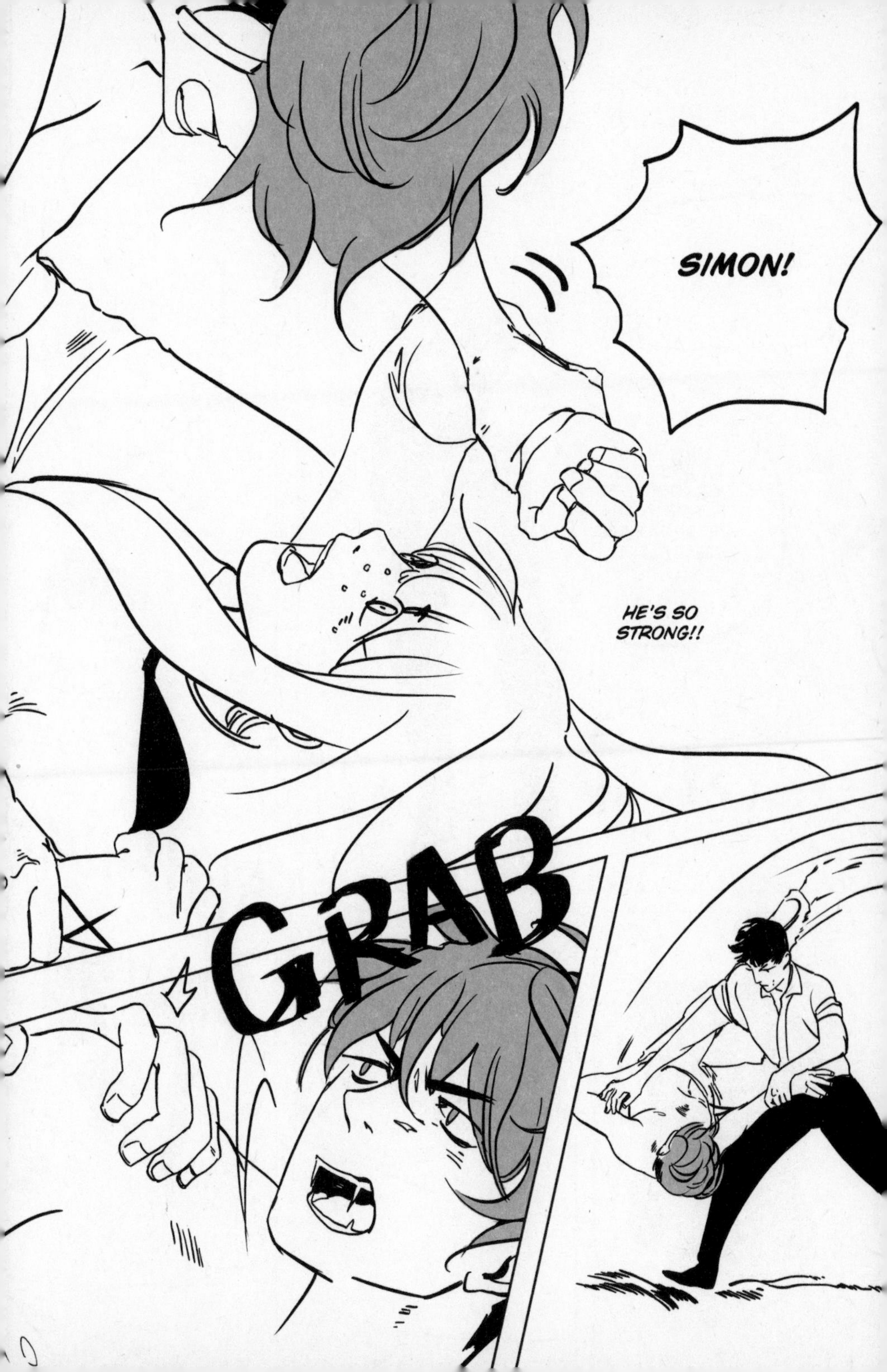
SIMON!
HE'S SO STRONG!!
GRAB

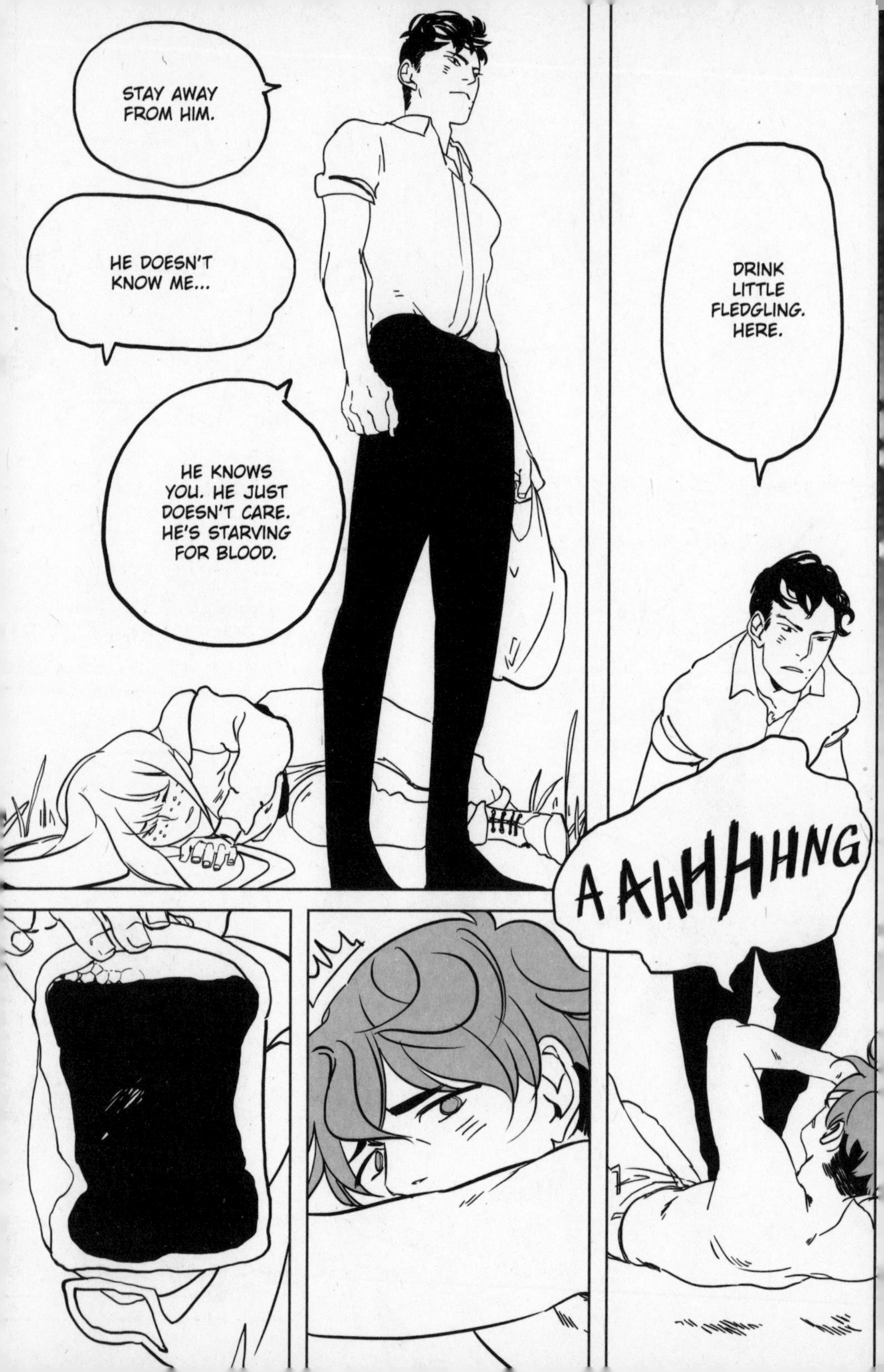
STAY AWAY FROM HIM.
HE DOESN'T KNOW ME...
HE KNOWS YOU. HE JUST DOESN'T CARE. HE'S STARVING FOR BLOOD.
DRINK LITTLE FLEDGLING. HERE.
AAHHHHNG

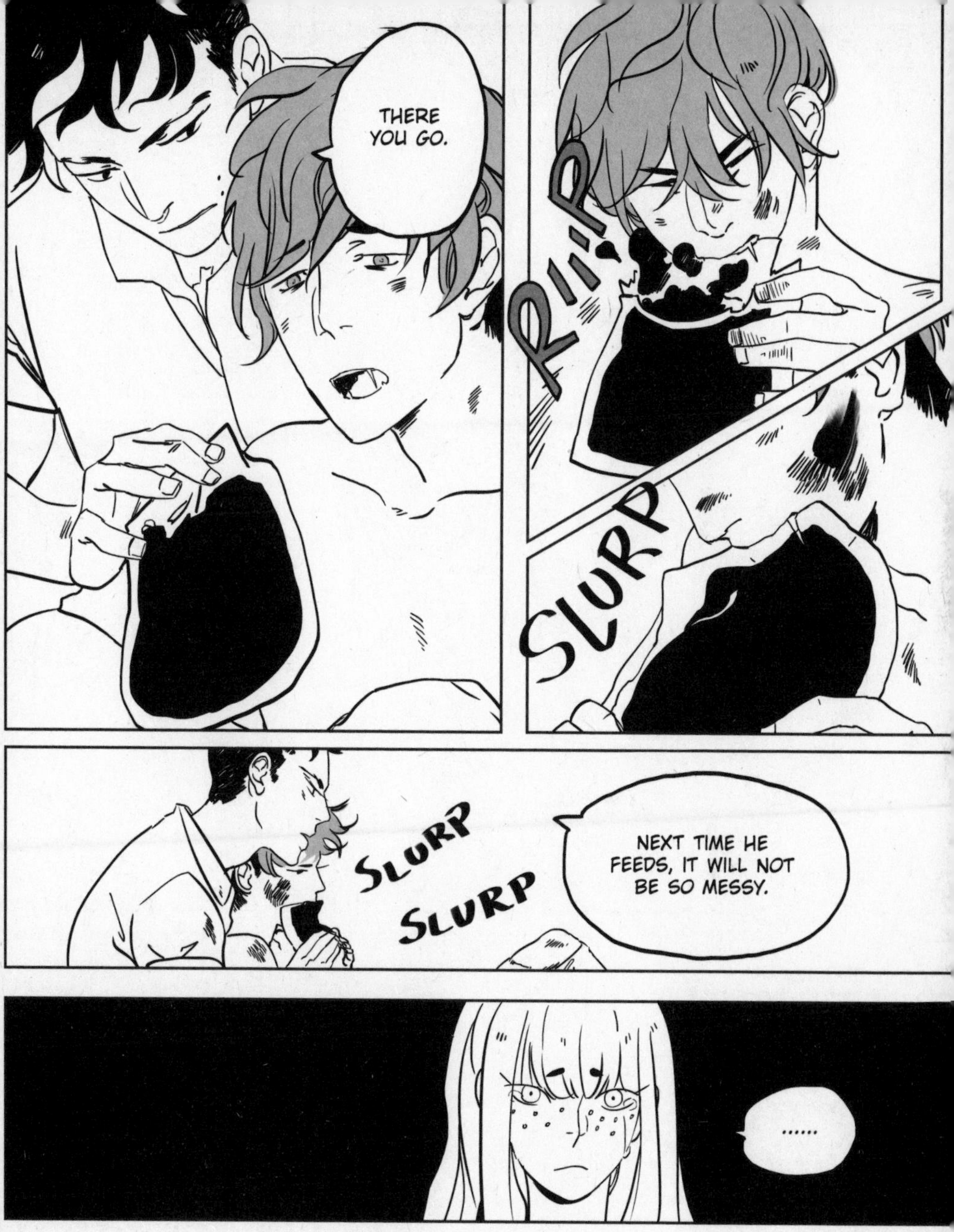
THERE YOU GO.
RIIIP
SLURP
SLURP
SLURP
NEXT TIME HE FEEDS, IT WILL NOT BE SO MESSY.
......

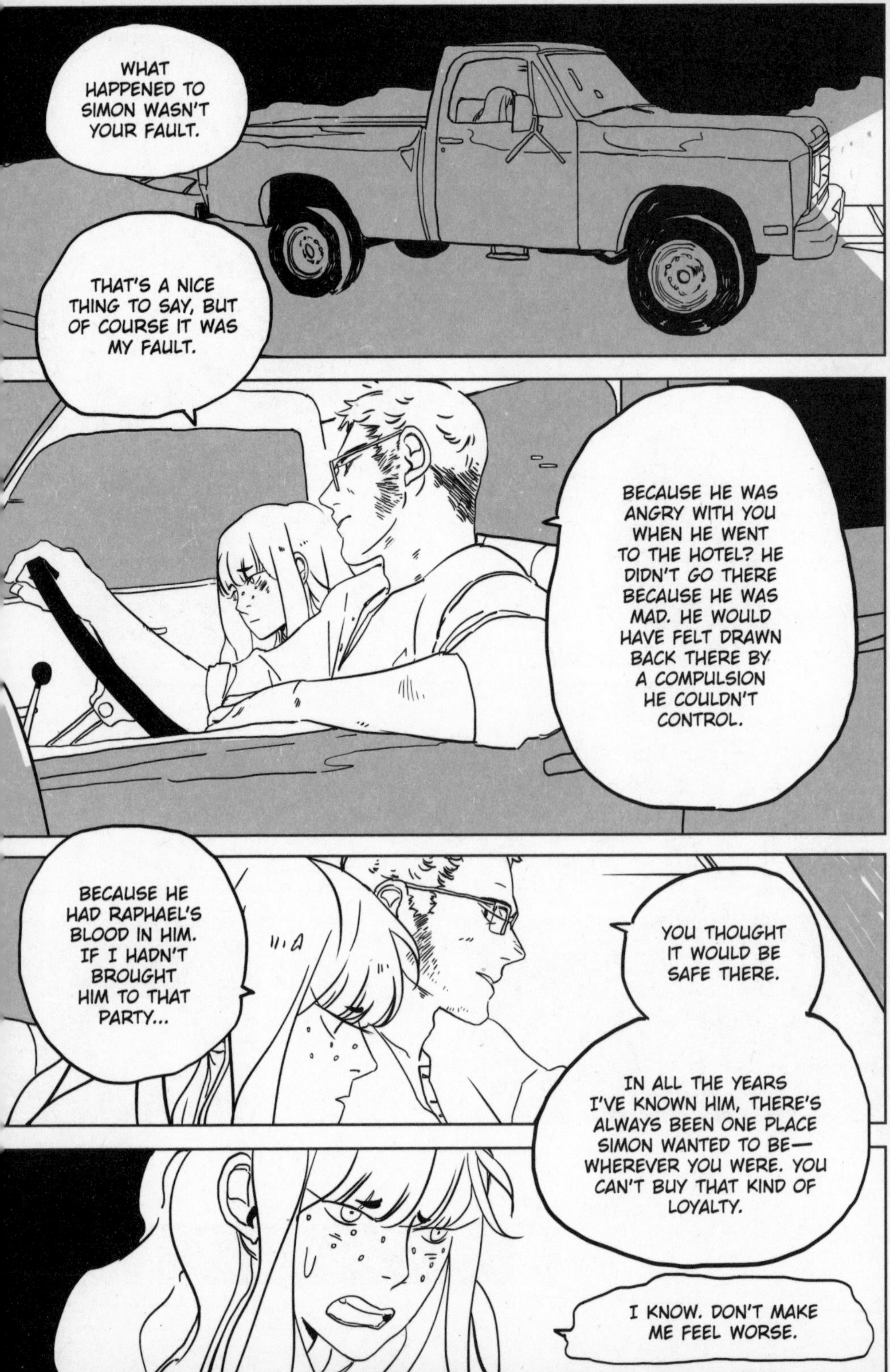
WHAT HAPPENED TO SIMON WASN'T YOUR FAULT.
THAT'S A NICE THING TO SAY, BUT OF COURSE IT WAS MY FAULT.
BECAUSE HE WAS ANGRY WITH YOU WHEN HE WENT TO THE HOTEL? HE DIDN'T GO THERE BECAUSE HE WAS MAD. HE WOULD HAVE FELT DRAWN BACK THERE BY A COMPULSION HE COULDN'T CONTROL.
BECAUSE HE HAD RAPHAEL'S BLOOD IN HIM. IF I HADN'T BROUGHT HIM TO THAT PARTY...
YOU THOUGHT IT WOULD BE SAFE THERE.
IN ALL THE YEARS I'VE KNOWN HIM, THERE'S ALWAYS BEEN ONE PLACE SIMON WANTED TO BE— WHEREVER YOU WERE. YOU CAN'T BUY THAT KIND OF LOYALTY.
I KNOW. DON'T MAKE ME FEEL WORSE.

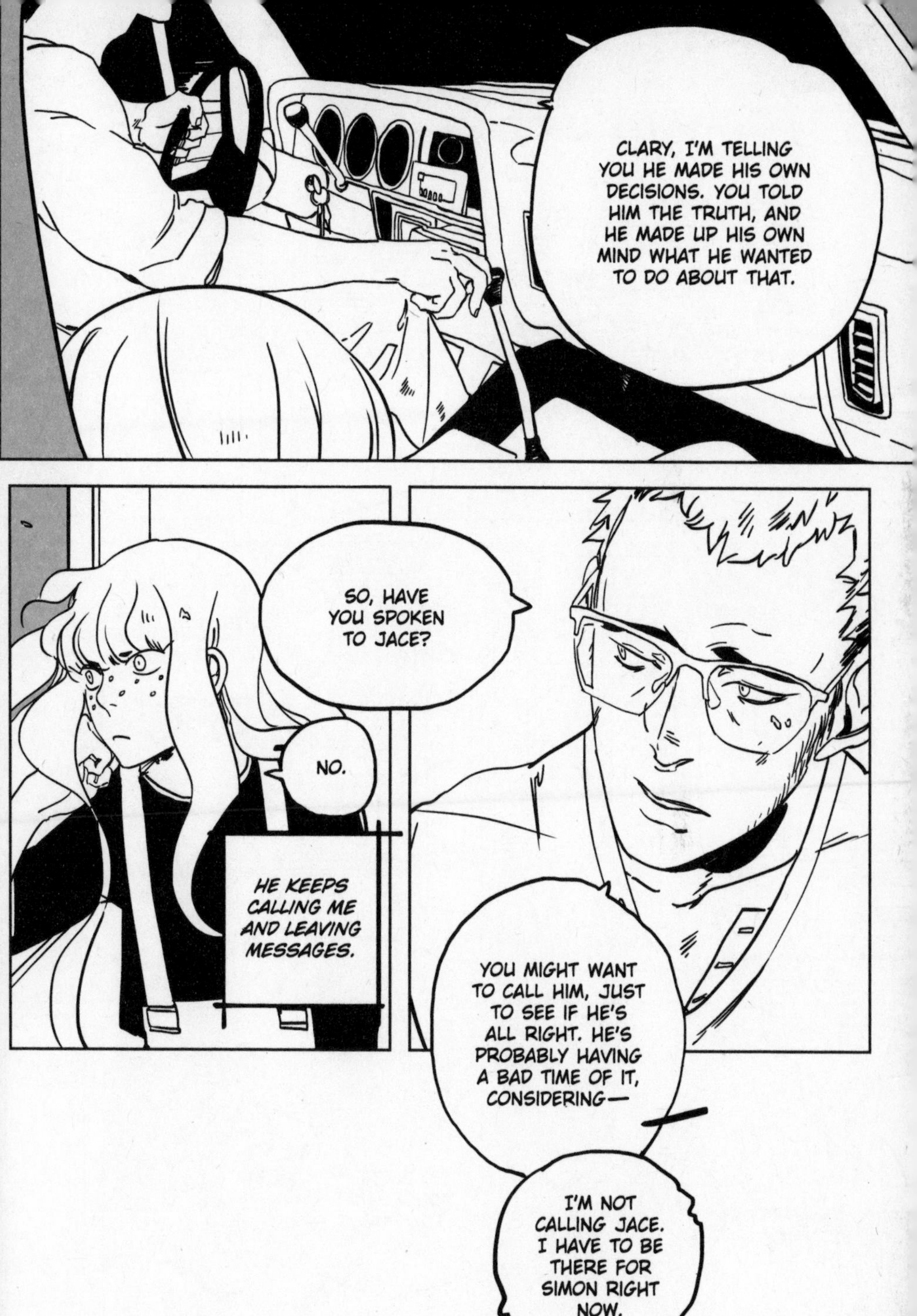
CLARY, I'M TELLING YOU HE MADE HIS OWN DECISIONS. YOU TOLD HIM THE TRUTH, AND HE MADE UP HIS OWN MIND WHAT HE WANTED TO DO ABOUT THAT.
SO, HAVE YOU SPOKEN TO JACE?
NO.
HE KEEPS CALLING ME AND LEAVING MESSAGES.
YOU MIGHT WANT TO CALL HIM, JUST TO SEE IF HE'S ALL RIGHT. HE'S PROBABLY HAVING A BAD TIME OF IT, CONSIDERING—
I'M NOT CALLING JACE. I HAVE TO BE THERE FOR SIMON RIGHT NOW.

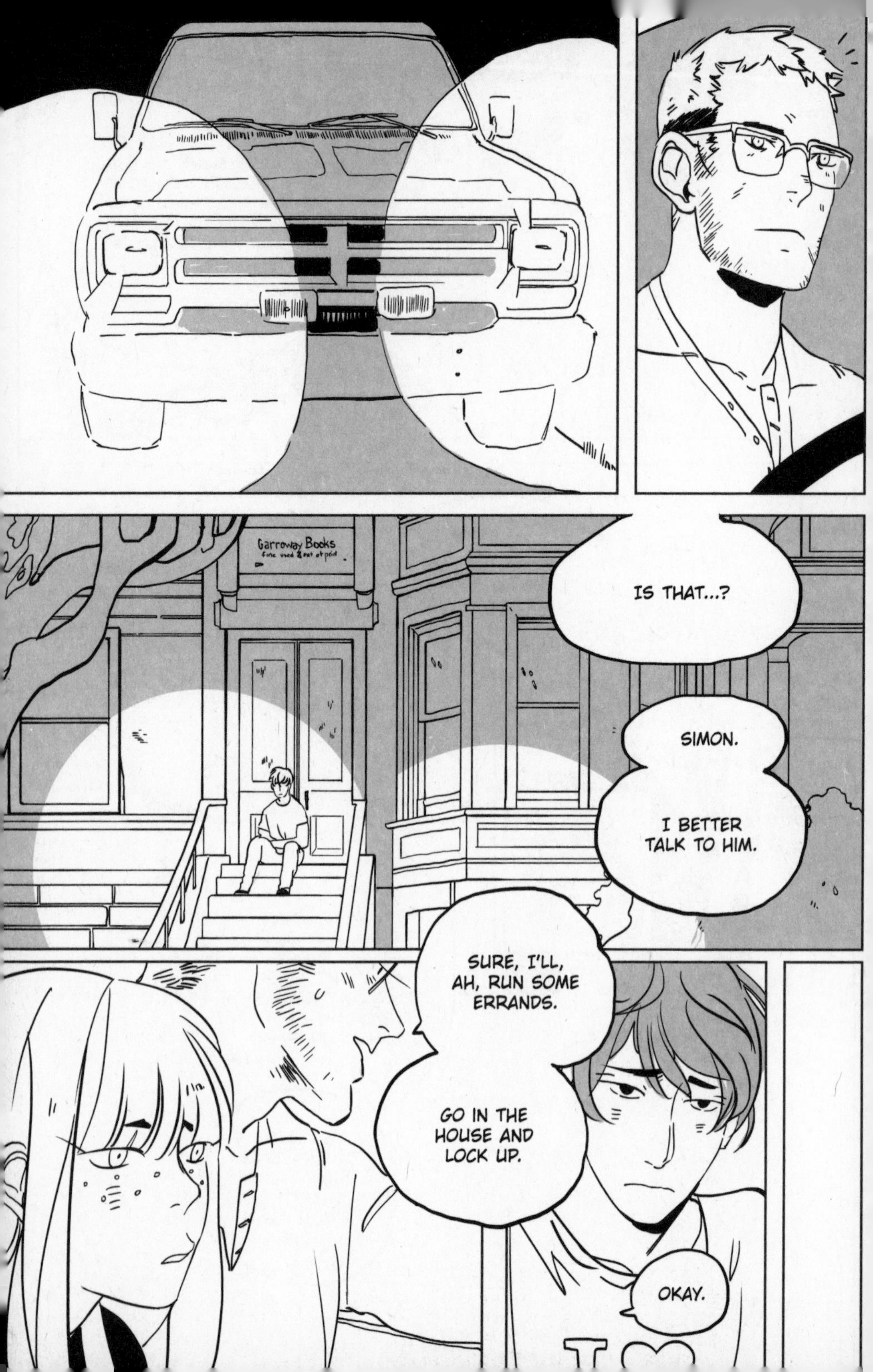
Garroway Books
fine used & out of print
IS THAT...?
SIMON.
I BETTER TALK TO HIM.
SURE, I'LL, AH, RUN SOME ERRANDS.
GO IN THE HOUSE AND LOCK UP.
OKAY.

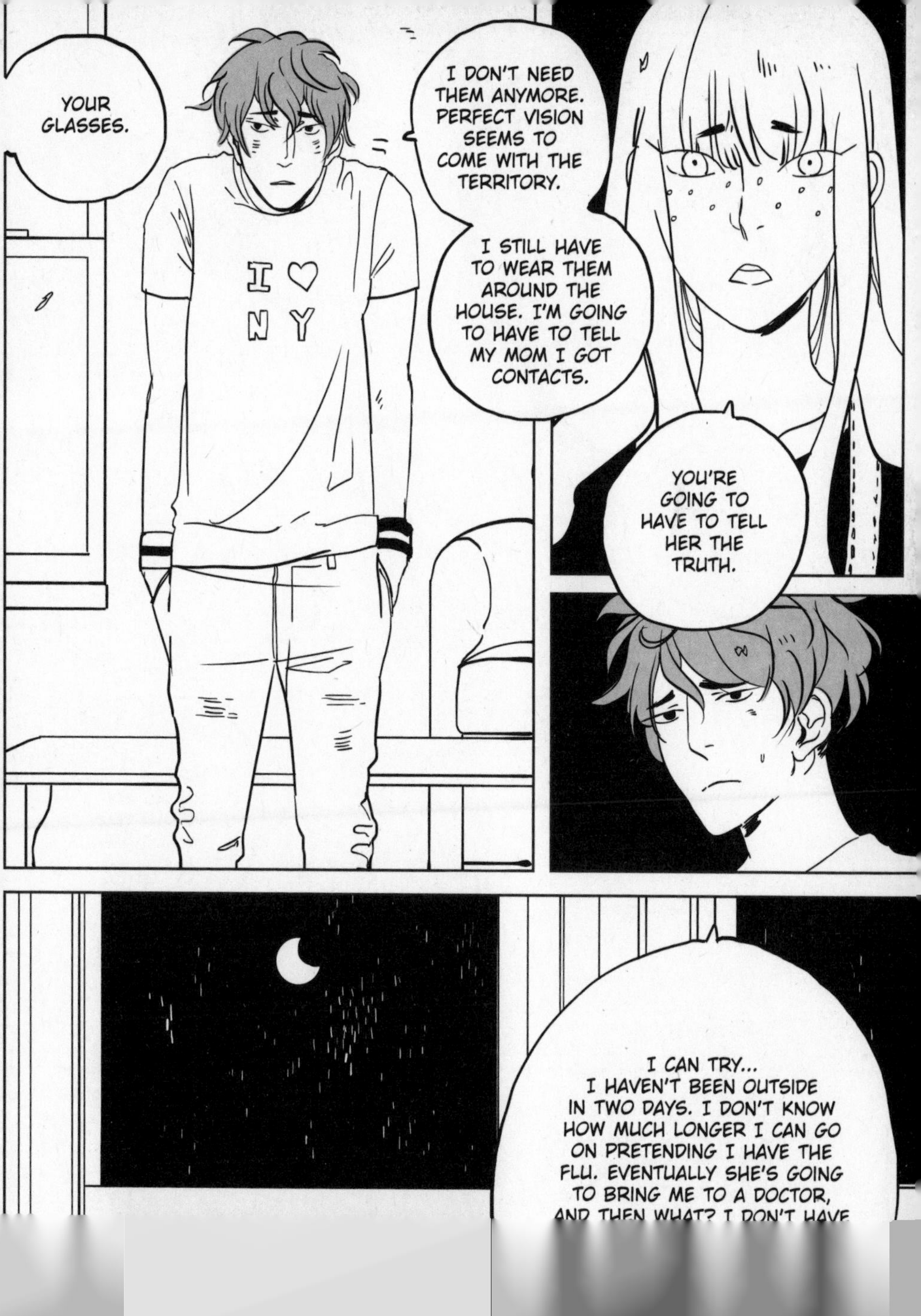
YOUR GLASSES.
I DON'T NEED THEM ANYMORE. PERFECT VISION SEEMS TO COME WITH THE TERRITORY.
I STILL HAVE TO WEAR THEM AROUND THE HOUSE. I'M GOING TO HAVE TO TELL MY MOM I GOT CONTACTS.
YOU'RE GOING TO HAVE TO TELL HER THE TRUTH.
I CAN TRY... I HAVEN'T BEEN OUTSIDE IN TWO DAYS. I DON'T KNOW HOW MUCH LONGER I CAN GO ON PRETENDING I HAVE THE FLU. EVENTUALLY SHE'S GOING TO BRING ME TO A DOCTOR,

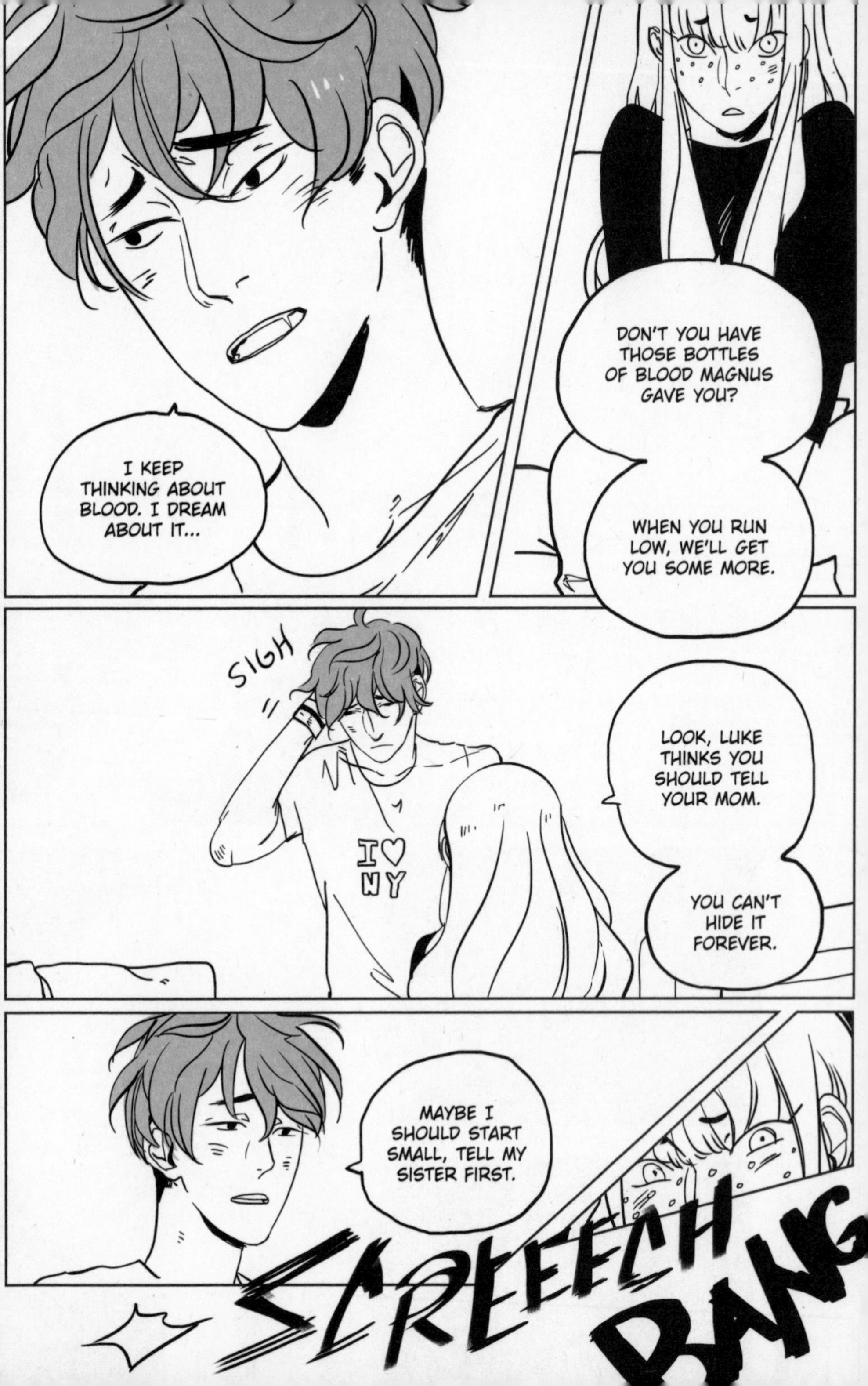
I KEEP THINKING ABOUT BLOOD. I DREAM ABOUT IT...
DON'T YOU HAVE THOSE BOTTLES OF BLOOD MAGNUS GAVE YOU?
WHEN YOU RUN LOW, WE'LL GET YOU SOME MORE.
SIGH
I ♥ NY
LOOK, LUKE THINKS YOU SHOULD TELL YOUR MOM.
YOU CAN'T HIDE IT FOREVER.
MAYBE I SHOULD START SMALL, TELL MY SISTER FIRST.
SCREEECH
BANG

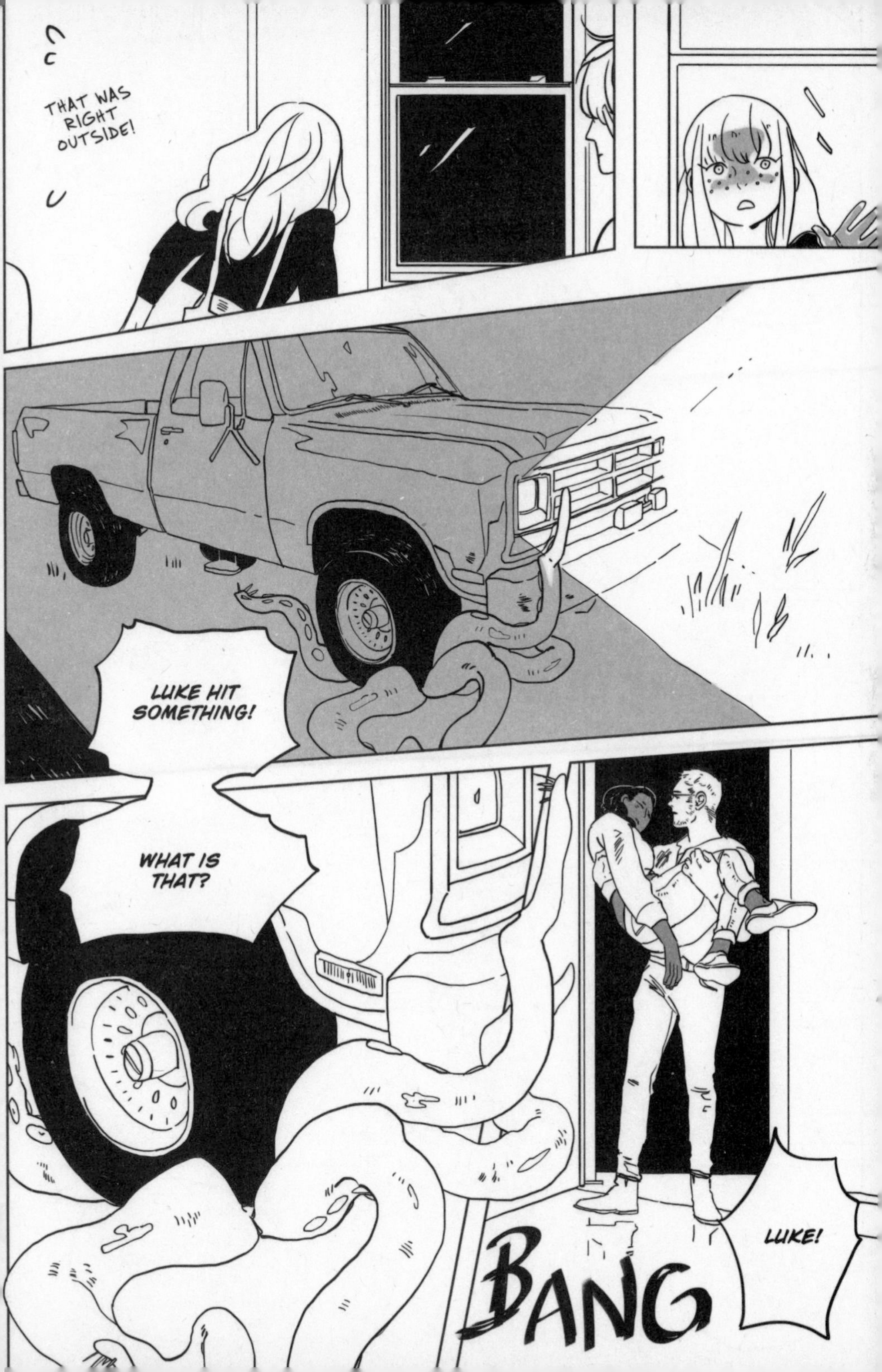
THAT WAS RIGHT OUTSIDE!
LUKE HIT SOMETHING!
WHAT IS THAT?
BANG
LUKE!

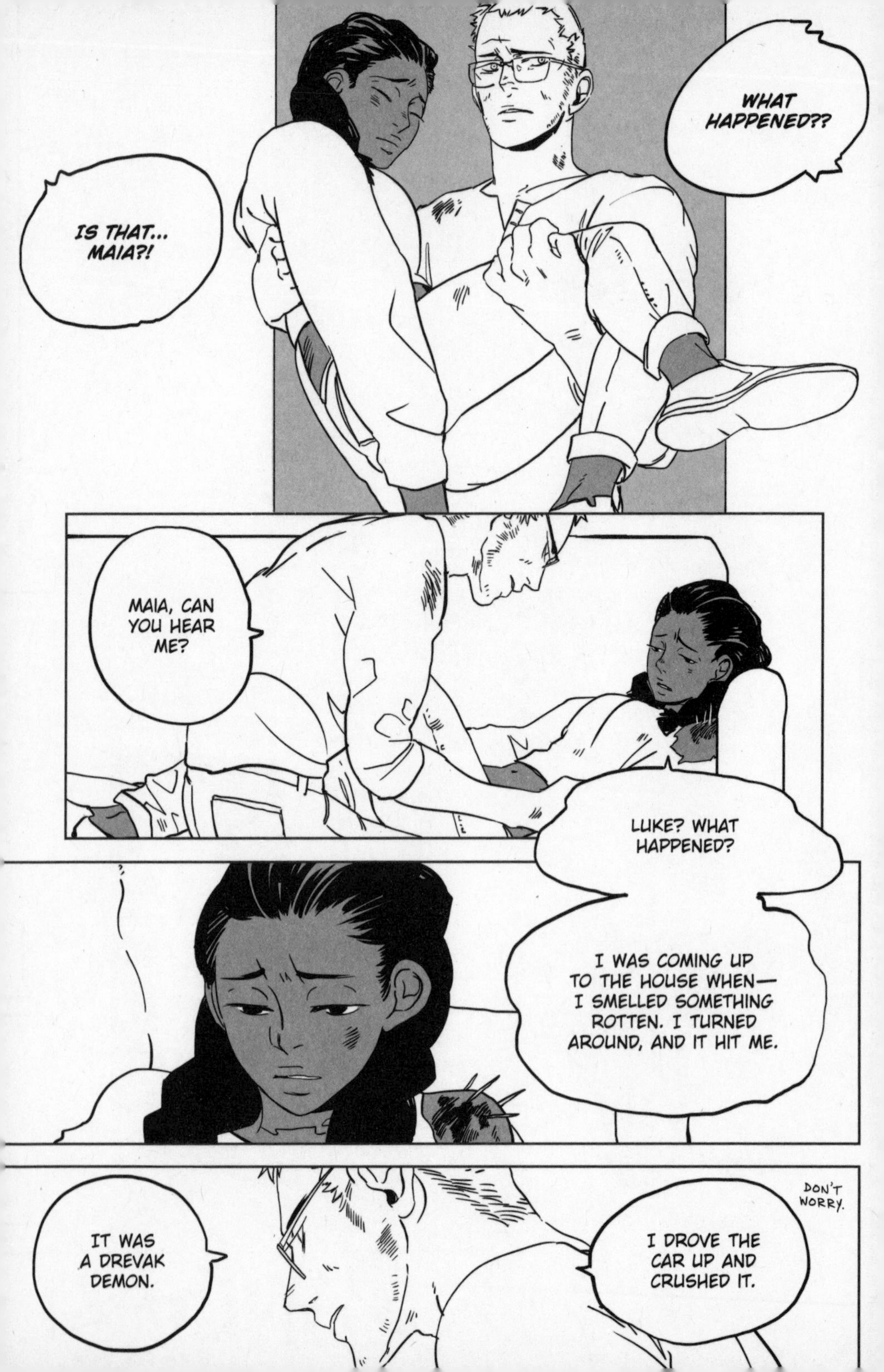
IS THAT... MAIA?!
WHAT HAPPENED??
MAIA, CAN YOU HEAR ME?
LUKE? WHAT HAPPENED?
I WAS COMING UP TO THE HOUSE WHEN— I SMELLED SOMETHING ROTTEN. I TURNED AROUND, AND IT HIT ME.
IT WAS A DREVAK DEMON.
DON'T WORRY.
I DROVE THE CAR UP AND CRUSHED IT.

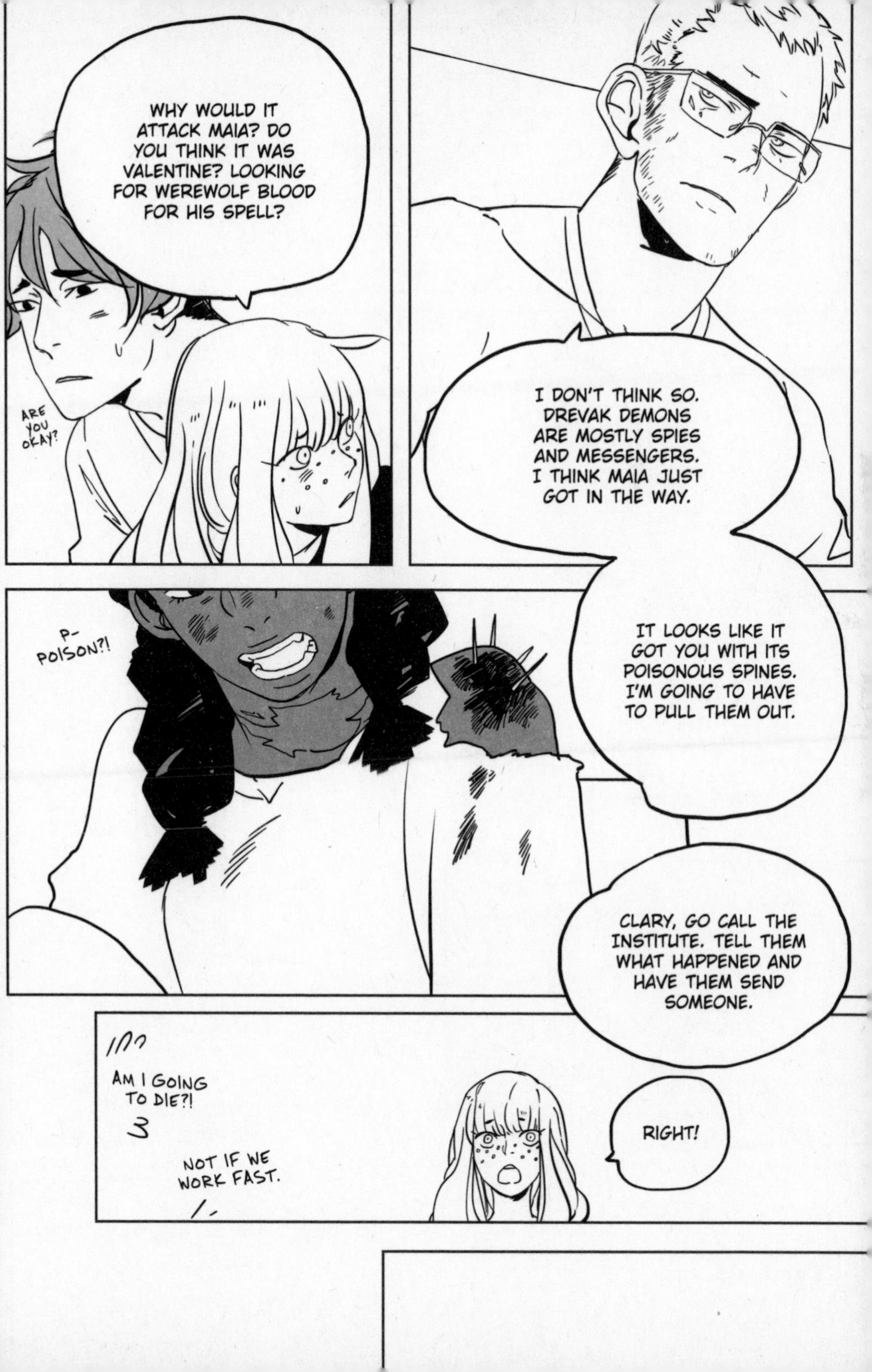
WHY WOULD IT ATTACK MAIA? DO YOU THINK IT WAS VALENTINE? LOOKING FOR WEREWOLF BLOOD FOR HIS SPELL?
ARE YOU OKAY?
I DON'T THINK SO. DREVAK DEMONS ARE MOSTLY SPIES AND MESSENGERS. I THINK MAIA JUST GOT IN THE WAY.
P-POISON?!
IT LOOKS LIKE IT GOT YOU WITH ITS POISONOUS SPINES. I'M GOING TO HAVE TO PULL THEM OUT.
CLARY, GO CALL THE INSTITUTE. TELL THEM WHAT HAPPENED AND HAVE THEM SEND SOMEONE.
AM I GOING TO DIE?!
NOT IF WE WORK FAST.
RIGHT!

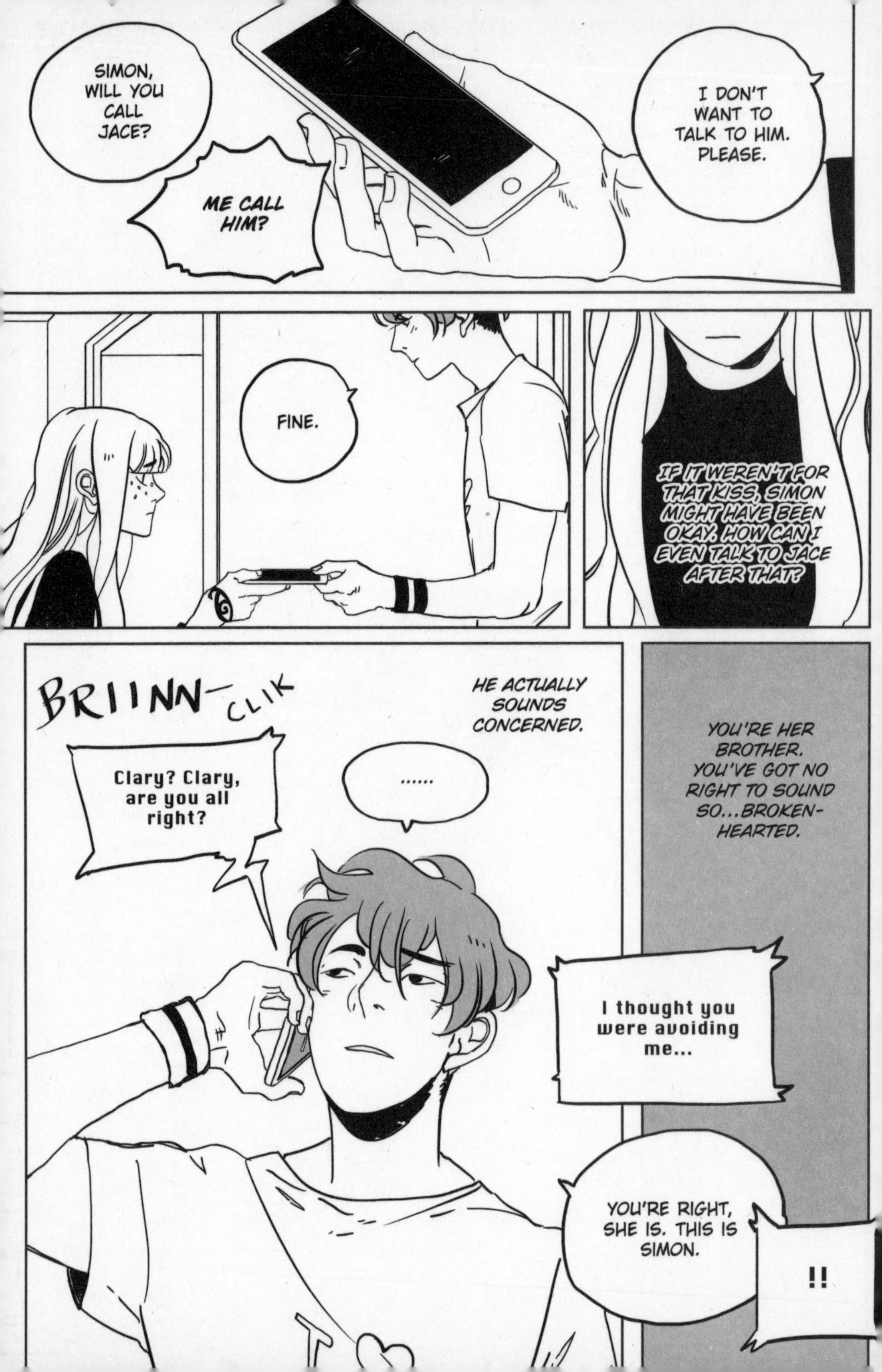
SIMON, WILL YOU CALL JACE?
ME CALL HIM?
I DON'T WANT TO TALK TO HIM. PLEASE.
FINE.
IF IT WEREN'T FOR THAT KISS, SIMON MIGHT HAVE BEEN OKAY. HOW CAN I EVEN TALK TO JACE AFTER THAT?
BRIINN— CLIK
Clary? Clary, are you all right?
......
HE ACTUALLY SOUNDS CONCERNED.
YOU'RE HER BROTHER. YOU'VE GOT NO RIGHT TO SOUND SO...BROKEN-HEARTED.
I thought you were avoiding me...
YOU'RE RIGHT, SHE IS. THIS IS SIMON.
!!

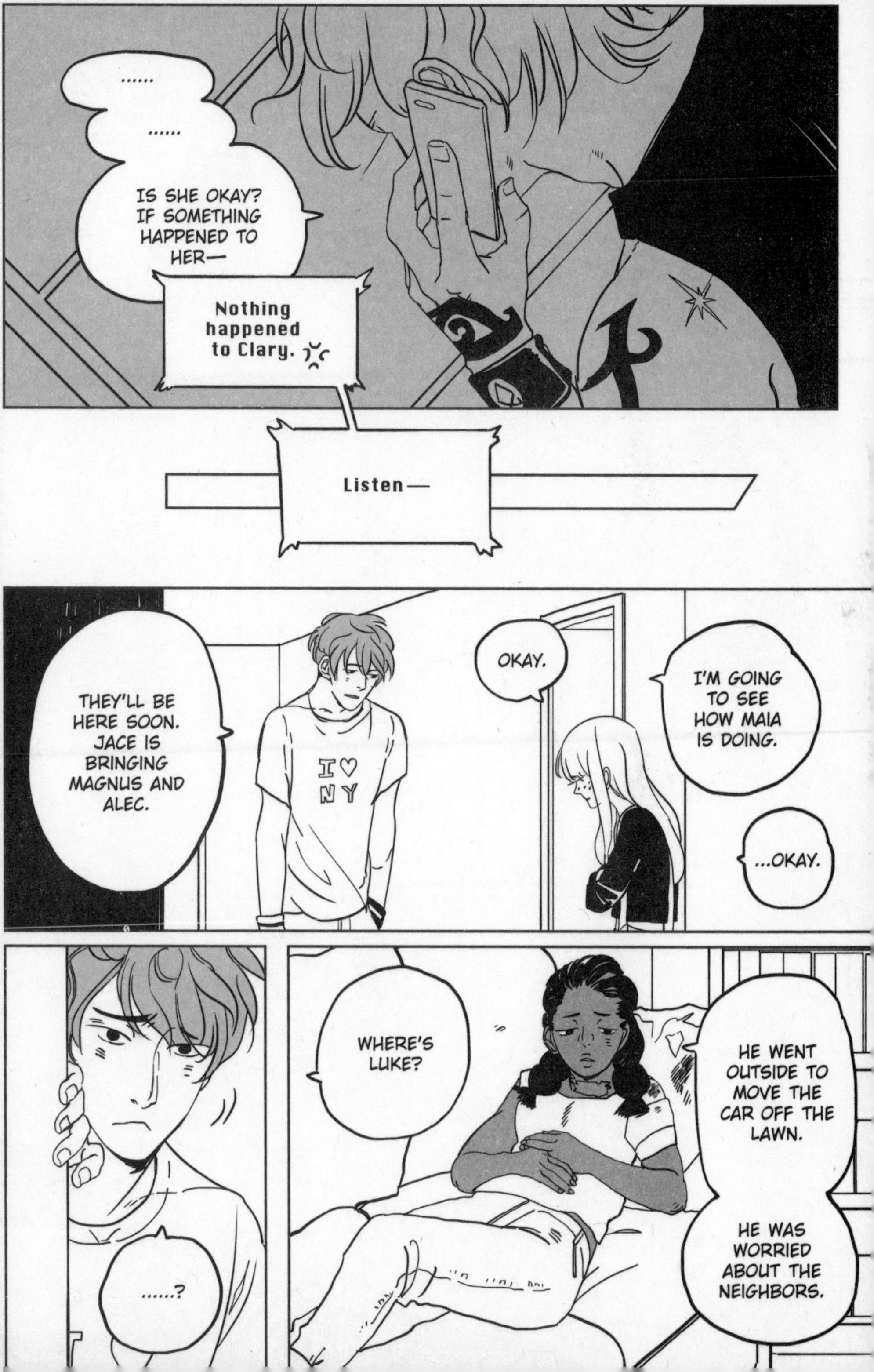
......
......
IS SHE OKAY? IF SOMETHING HAPPENED TO HER—
Nothing happened to Clary.
Listen—
THEY'LL BE HERE SOON. JACE IS BRINGING MAGNUS AND ALEC.
I ♥ NY
OKAY.
I'M GOING TO SEE HOW MAIA IS DOING.
...OKAY.
WHERE'S LUKE?
HE WENT OUTSIDE TO MOVE THE CAR OFF THE LAWN.
HE WAS WORRIED ABOUT THE NEIGHBORS.
......?

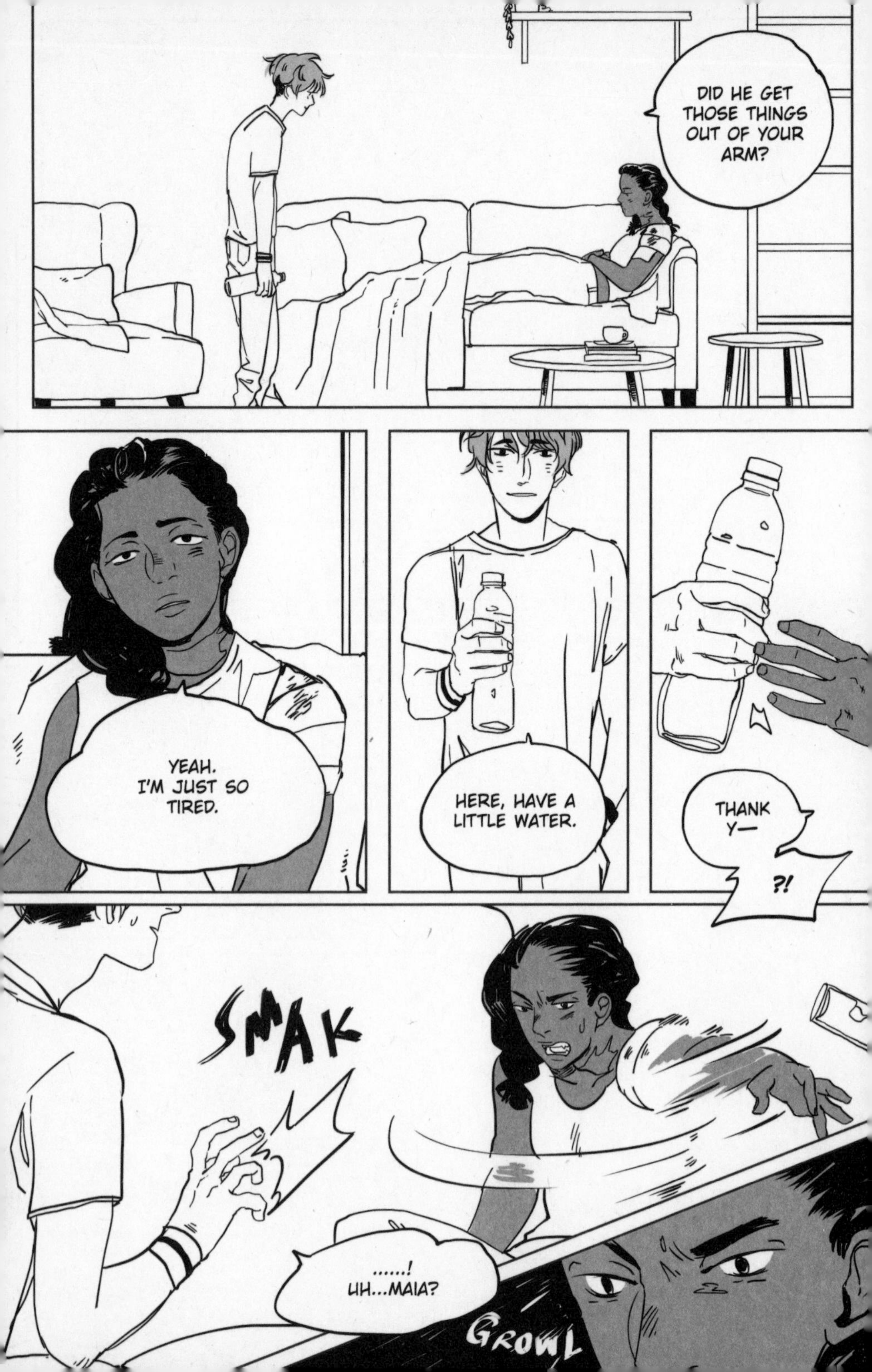
DID HE GET THOSE THINGS OUT OF YOUR ARM?
YEAH. I'M JUST SO TIRED.
HERE, HAVE A LITTLE WATER.
THANK Y—
?!
SMAK
......!
UH...MAIA?
GROWL

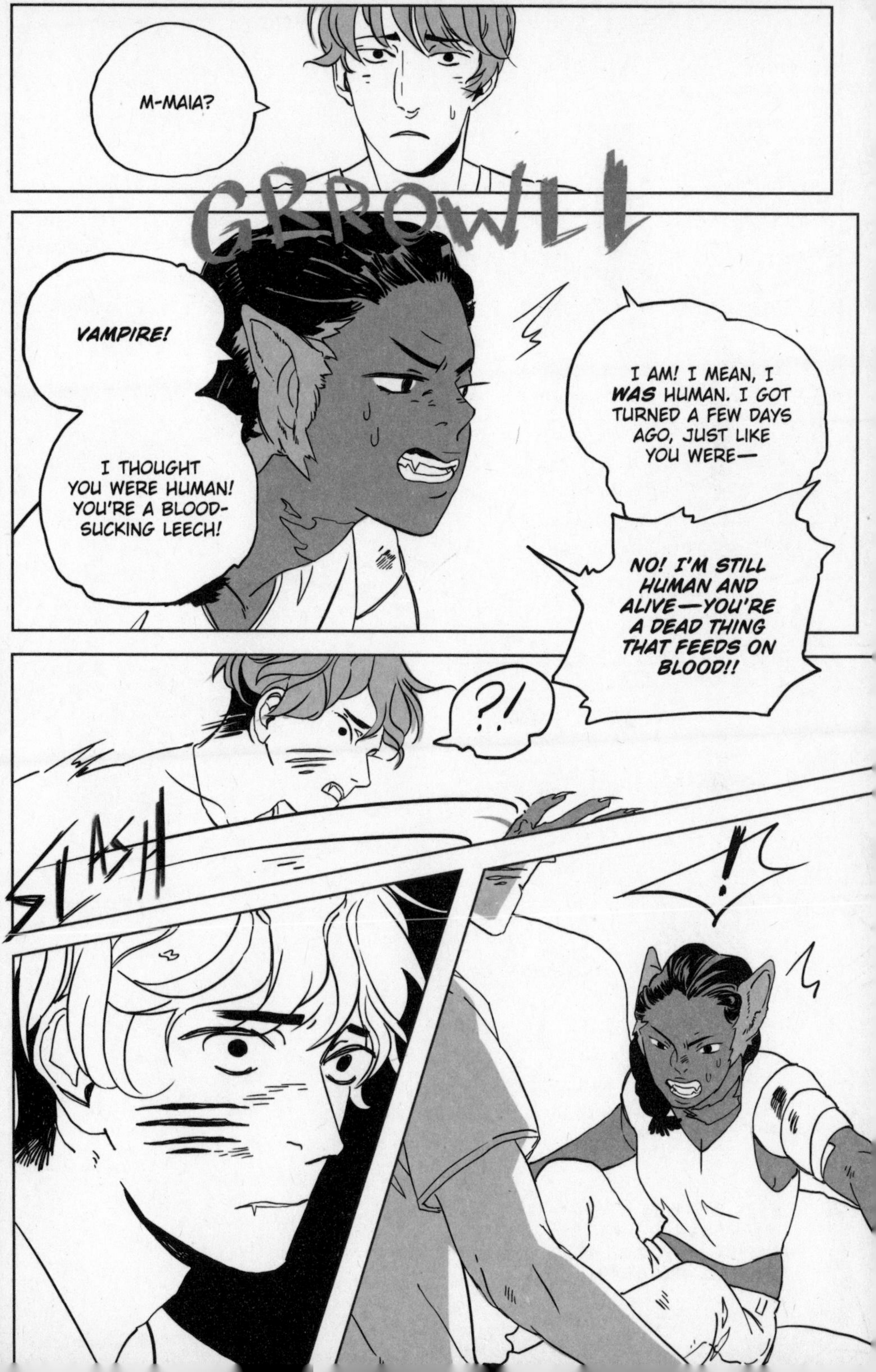
M-MAIA?
GRROWLLL
VAMPIRE!
I THOUGHT YOU WERE HUMAN! YOU'RE A BLOOD-SUCKING LEECH!
I AM! I MEAN, I WAS HUMAN. I GOT TURNED A FEW DAYS AGO, JUST LIKE YOU WERE—
NO! I'M STILL HUMAN AND ALIVE—YOU'RE A DEAD THING THAT FEEDS ON BLOOD!!
?!
SLASH
!

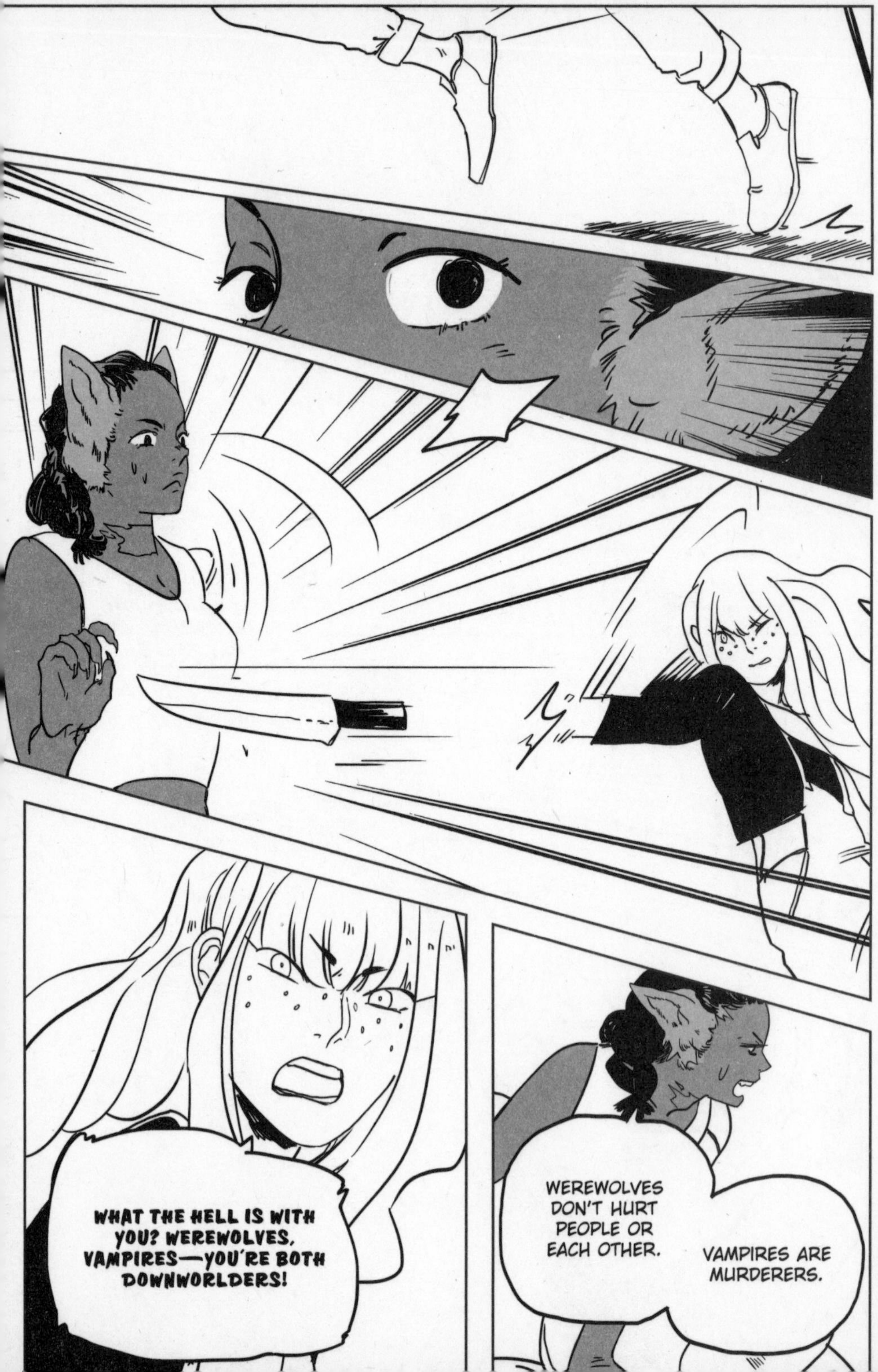
WHAT THE HELL IS WITH YOU? WEREWOLVES, VAMPIRES—YOU'RE BOTH DOWNWORLDERS!
WEREWOLVES DON'T HURT PEOPLE OR EACH OTHER.
VAMPIRES ARE MURDERERS.

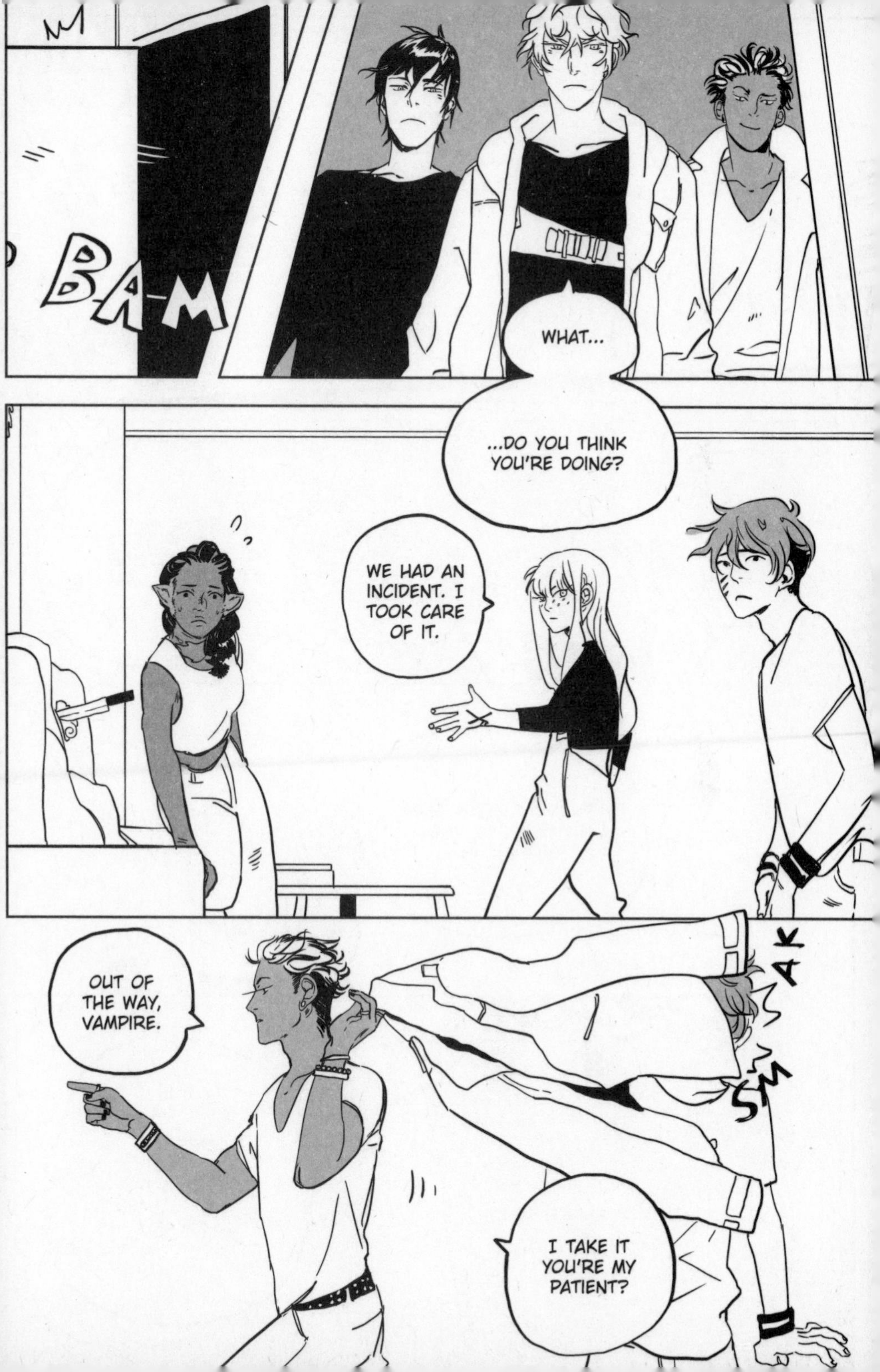
BAM
WHAT...
...DO YOU THINK YOU'RE DOING?
WE HAD AN INCIDENT. I TOOK CARE OF IT.
OUT OF THE WAY, VAMPIRE.
SMAK
I TAKE IT YOU'RE MY PATIENT?

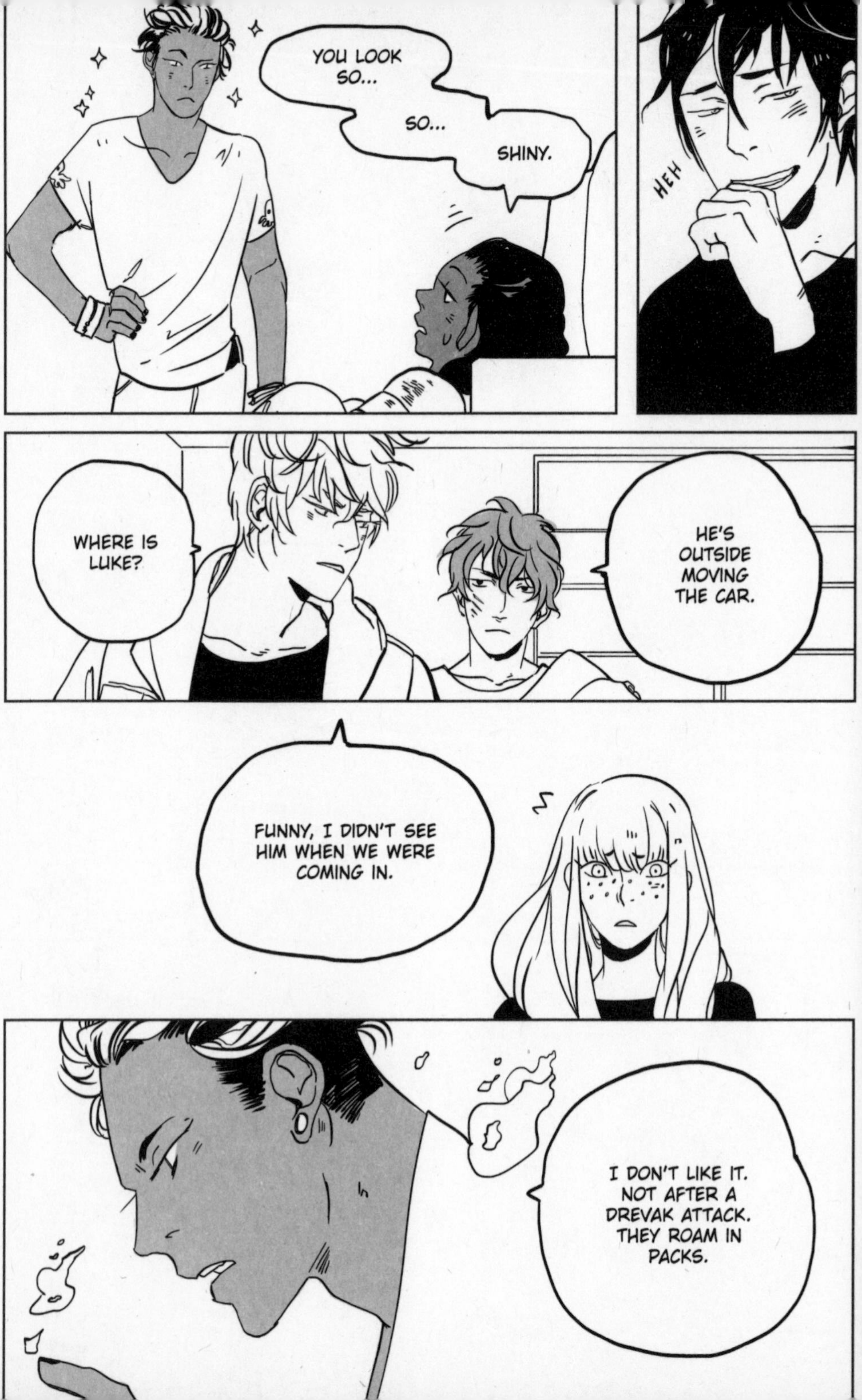
YOU LOOK SO... SO... SHINY.
HEH
WHERE IS LUKE?
HE'S OUTSIDE MOVING THE CAR.
FUNNY, I DIDN'T SEE HIM WHEN WE WERE COMING IN.
I DON'T LIKE IT. NOT AFTER A DREVAK ATTACK. THEY ROAM IN PACKS.

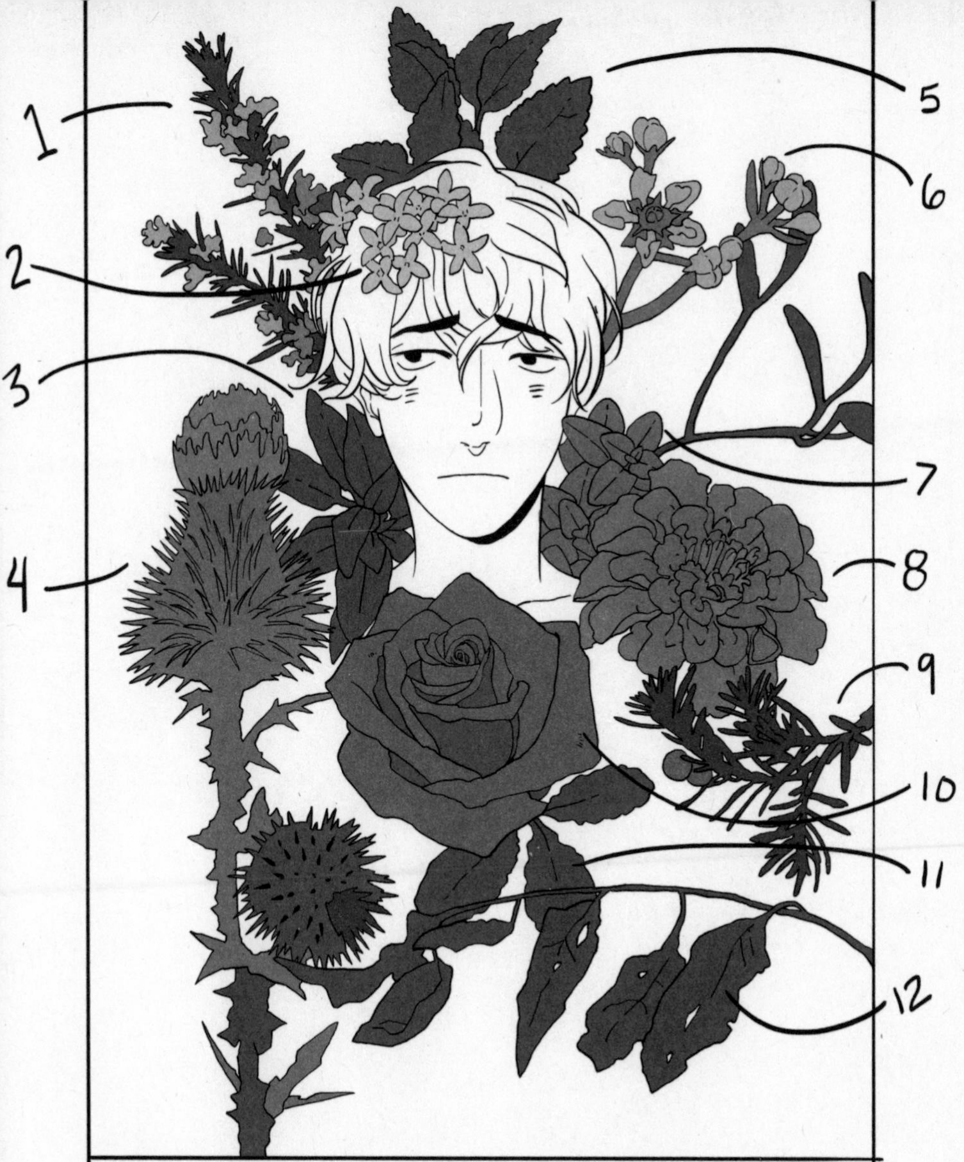
1
2
3
4
5
6
7
8
9
10
11
12

Simon's Bouquet - "Sympathy during a Time of Grief"

1) Rosemary - Remembrance
2) Sweet Woodruff - Eternal Life
3) Sage - Mitigates Grief
4) Thistle - Grief
5) Lemon Balm - Sympathy
6) Rue - Repentance
7) Sweet Marjoram - Comfort
8) Marigold - Grief
9) Yew - Sorrow
10) Rose - Love
11) Primrose Leaf - Sorrow
12) Dead leaves - Sadness

THE MORTAL INSTRUMENTS

THE GRAPHIC NOVEL

Chapter 18

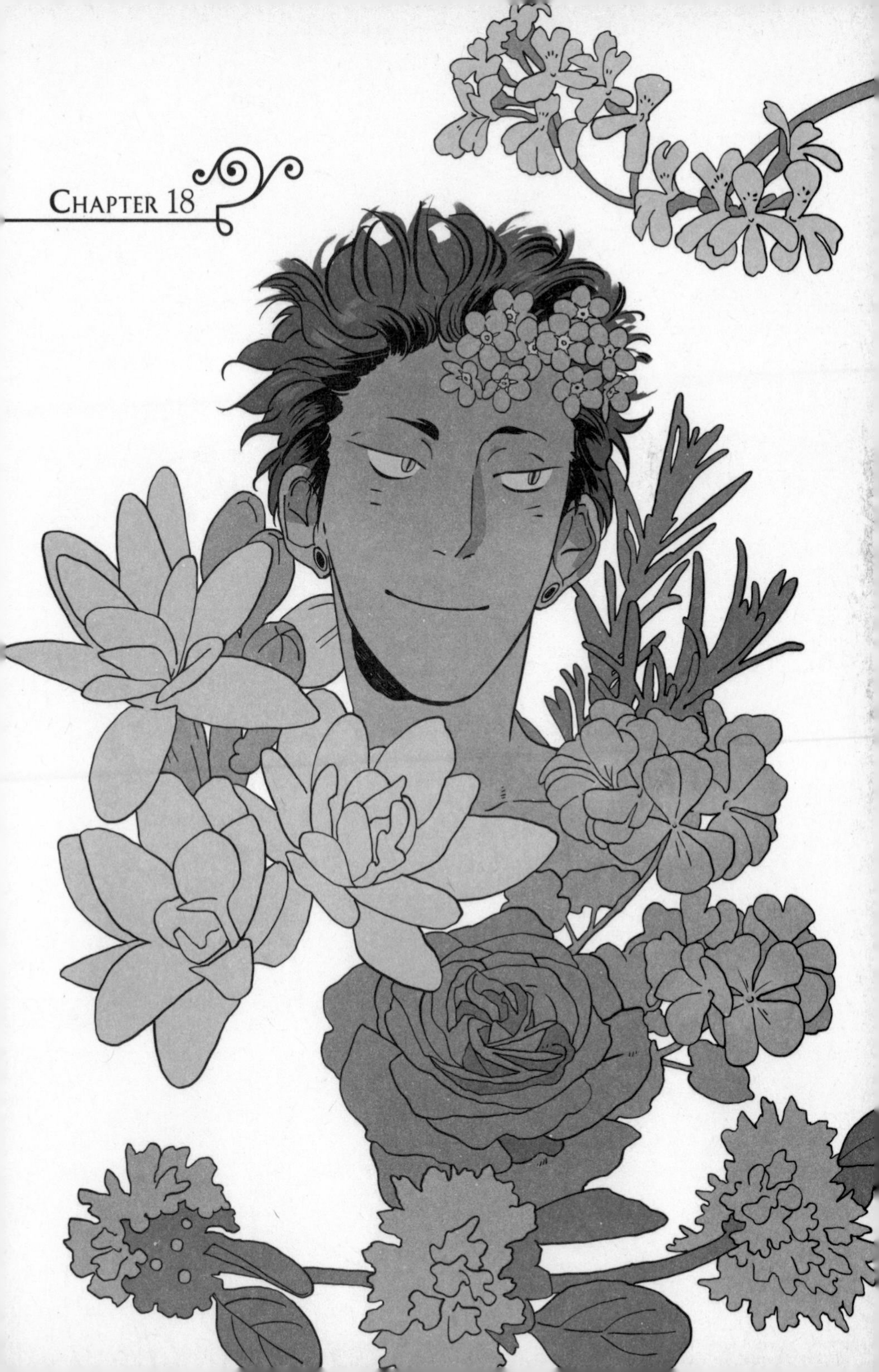

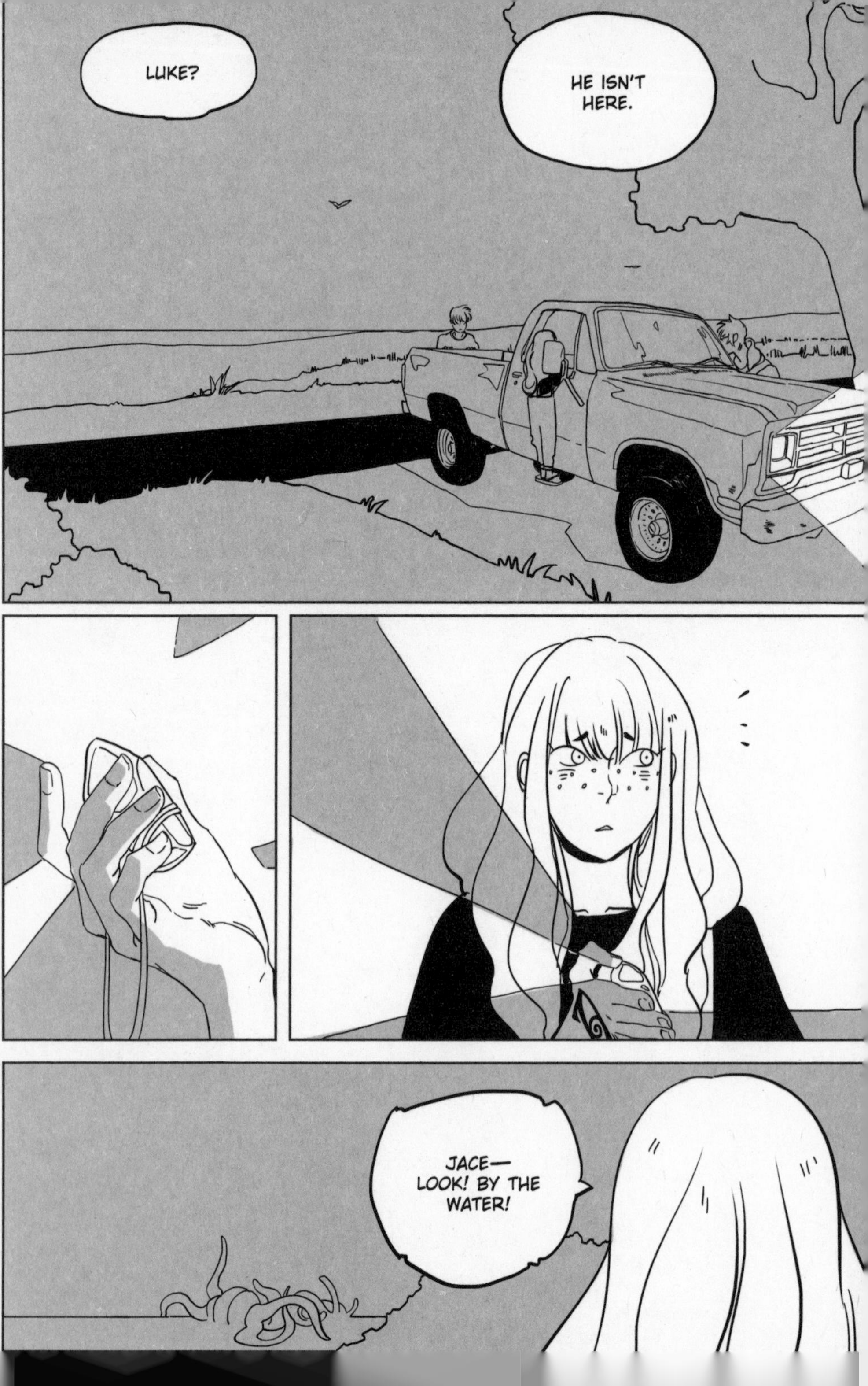
LUKE?
HE ISN'T HERE.
JACE—LOOK! BY THE WATER!

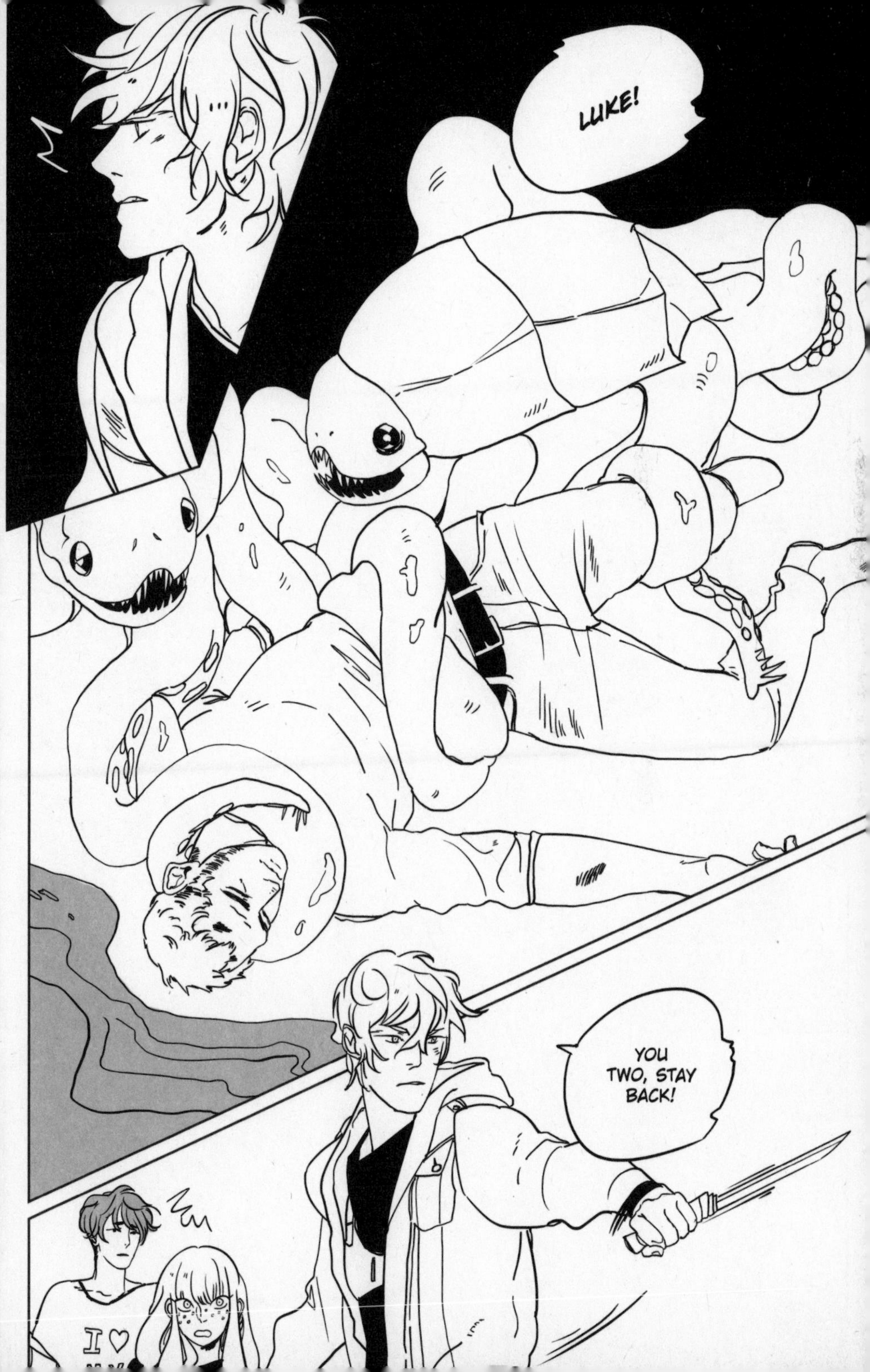
...
LUKE!
YOU TWO, STAY BACK!

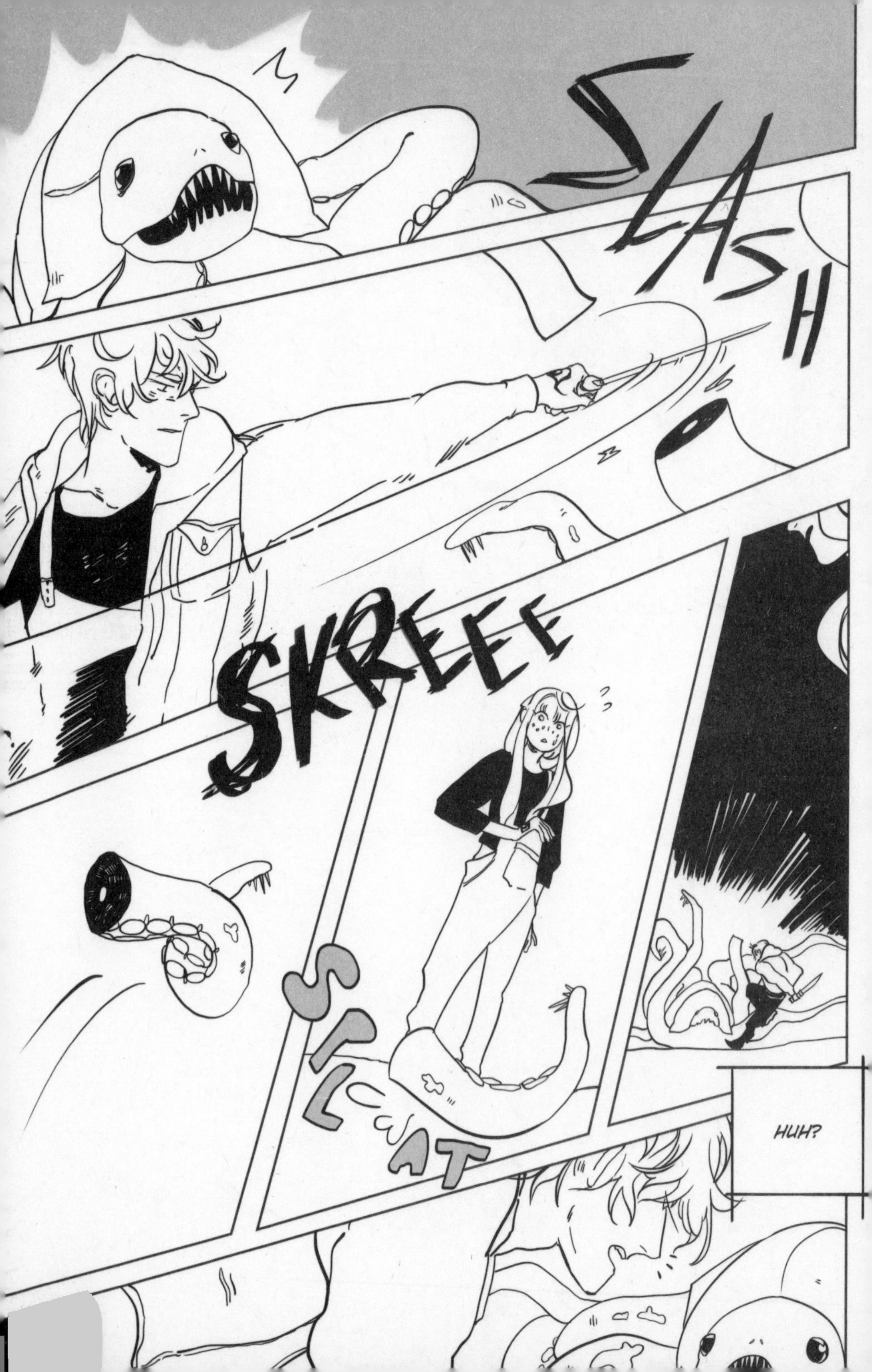
SLASH
SKREEE
SPLAT
HUH?

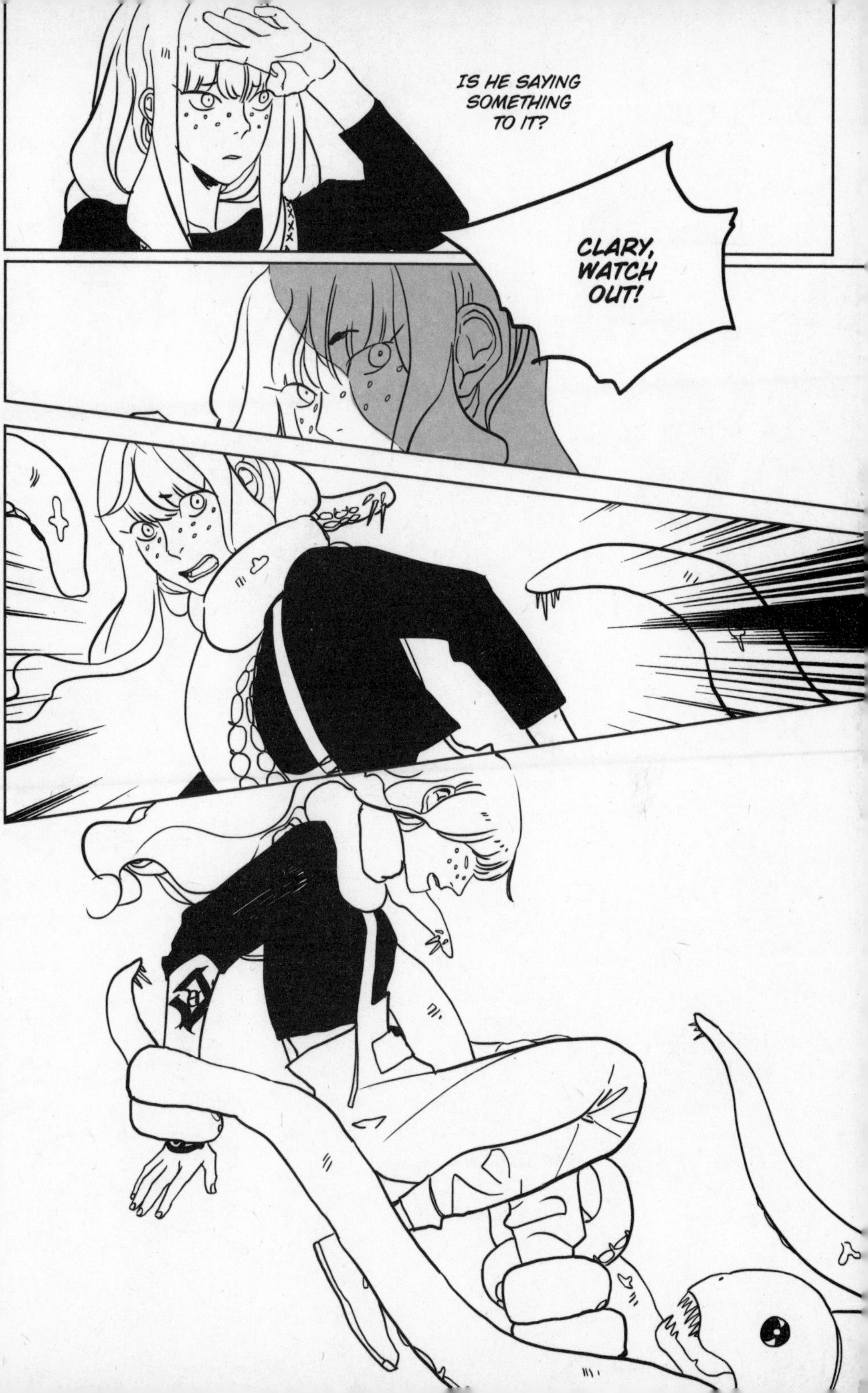
IS HE SAYING SOMETHING TO IT?
CLARY, WATCH OUT!

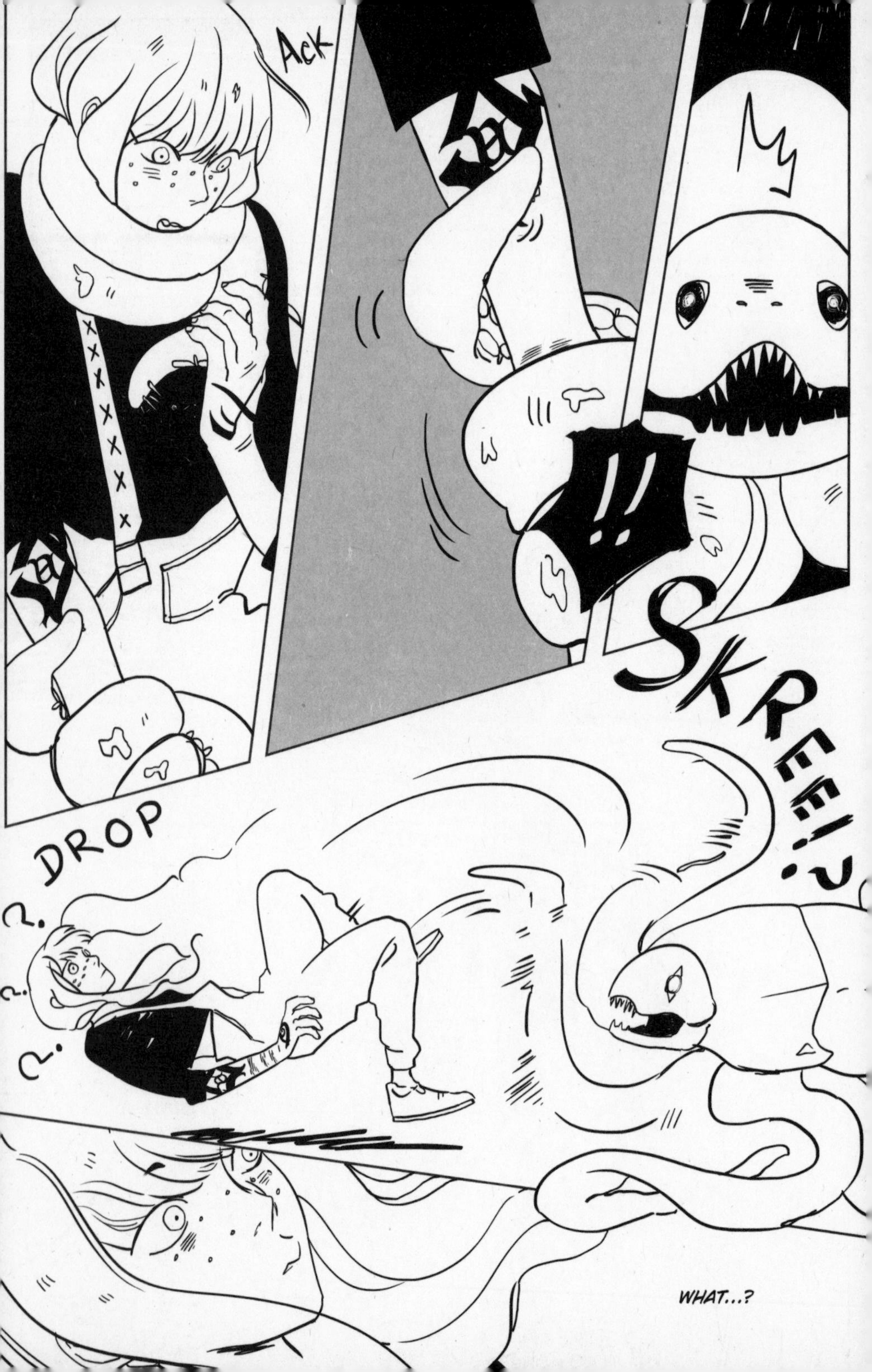

ACK
SKREE!?
DROP
WHAT...?

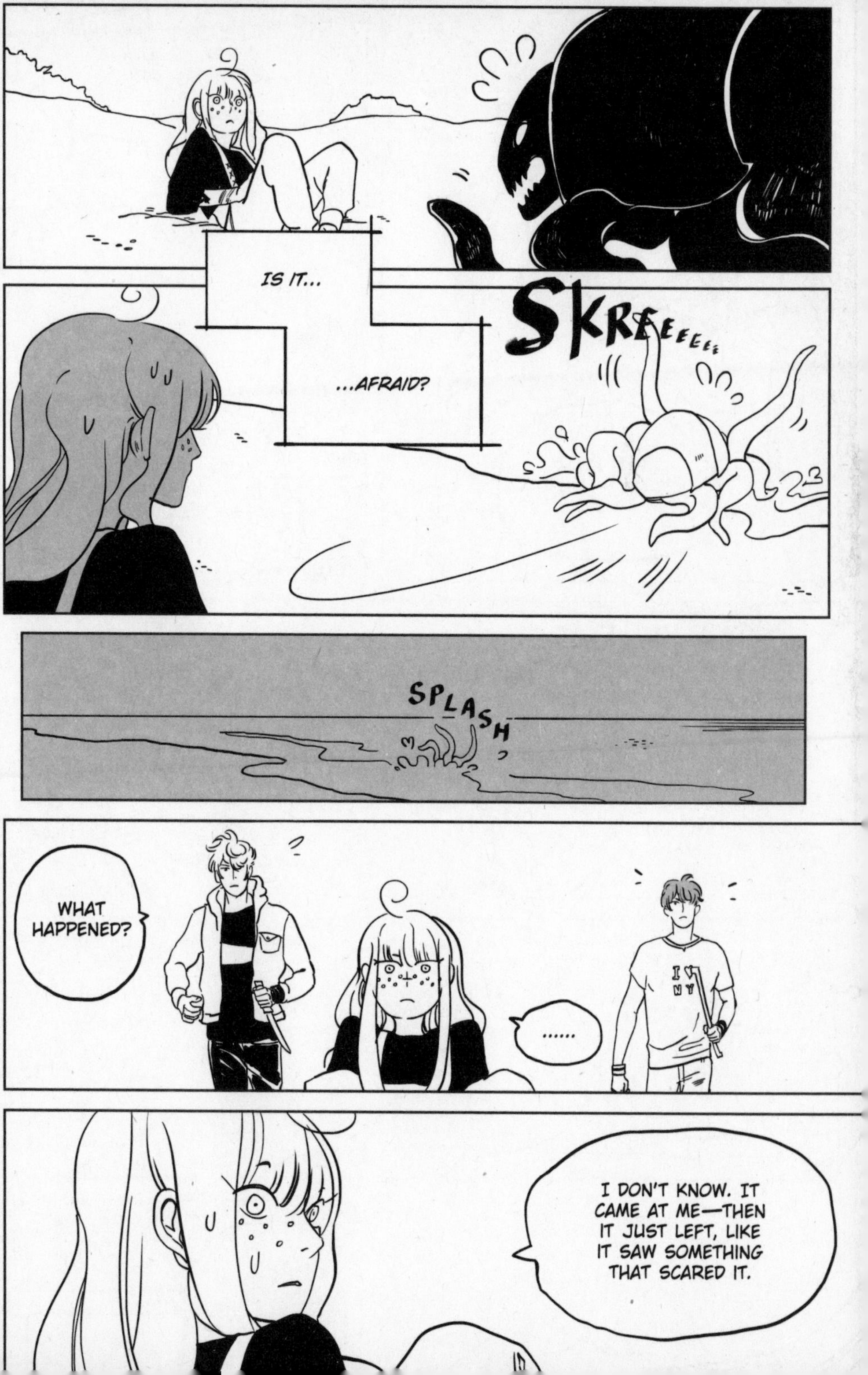
IS IT...
...AFRAID?
SKREEEEEEE
SPLASH
WHAT HAPPENED?
......
I DON'T KNOW. IT CAME AT ME—THEN IT JUST LEFT, LIKE IT SAW SOMETHING THAT SCARED IT.

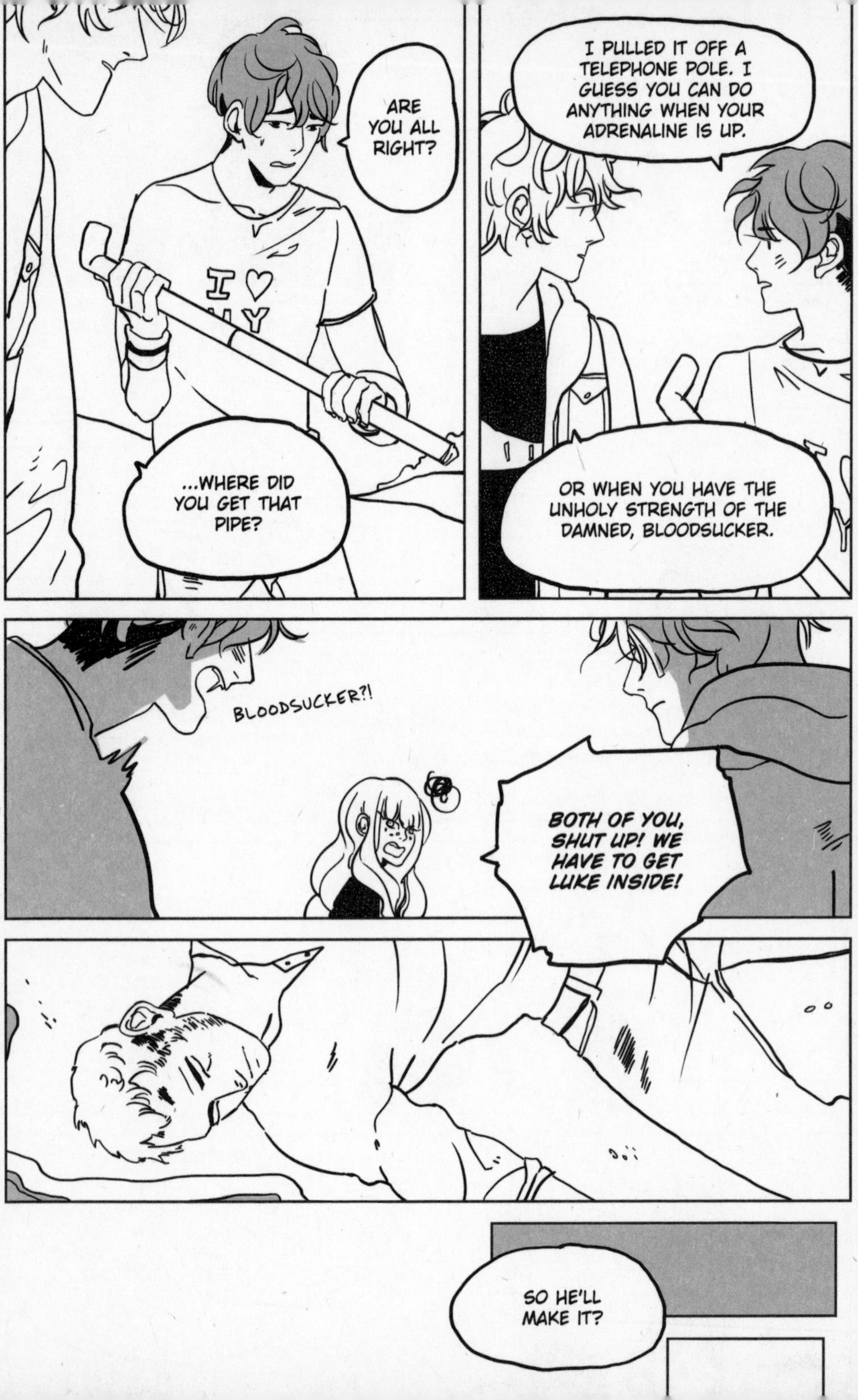
ARE YOU ALL RIGHT?
...WHERE DID YOU GET THAT PIPE?
I PULLED IT OFF A TELEPHONE POLE. I GUESS YOU CAN DO ANYTHING WHEN YOUR ADRENALINE IS UP.
OR WHEN YOU HAVE THE UNHOLY STRENGTH OF THE DAMNED, BLOODSUCKER.
BLOODSUCKER?!
BOTH OF YOU, SHUT UP! WE HAVE TO GET LUKE INSIDE!
SO HE'LL MAKE IT?

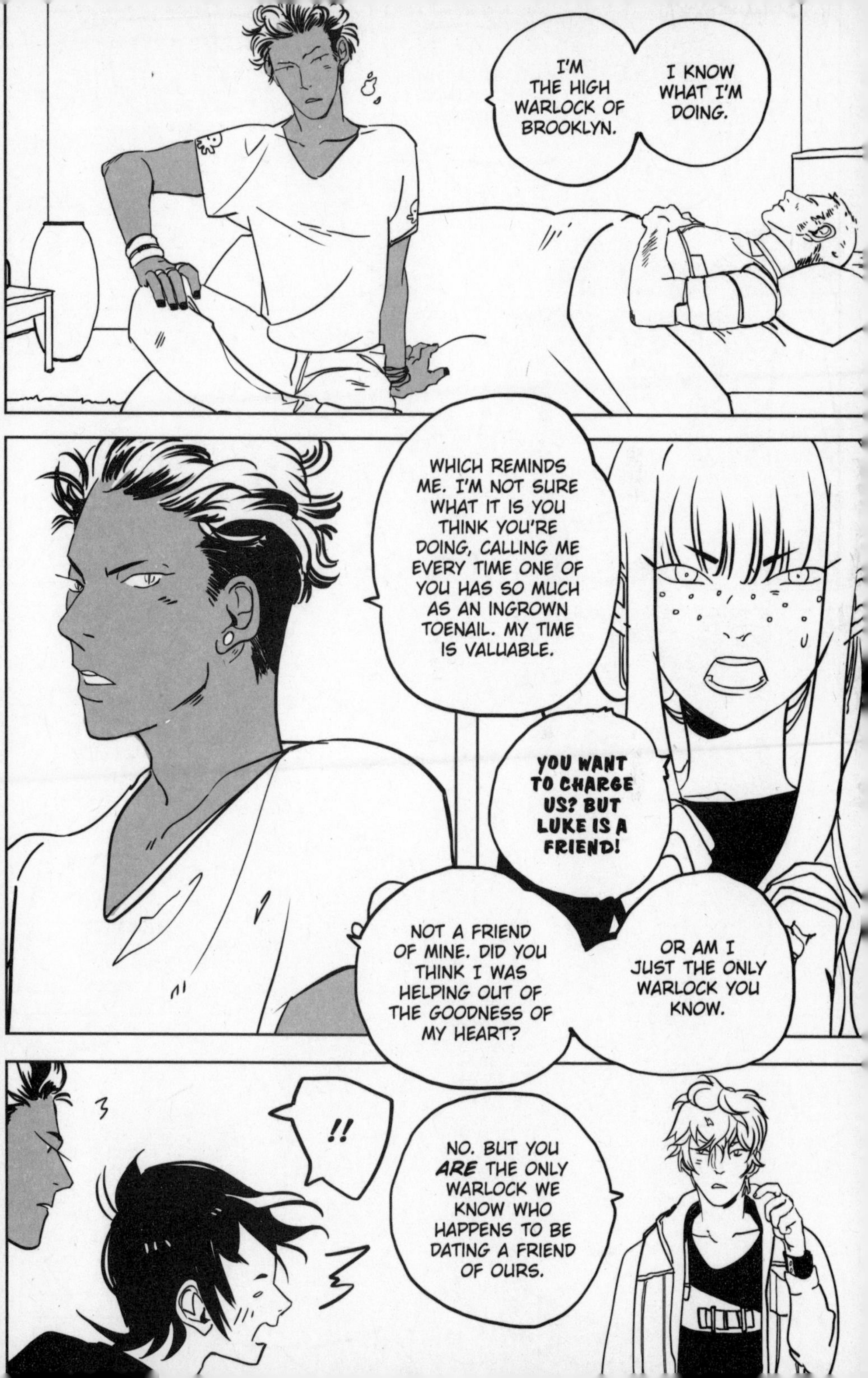
I'M THE HIGH WARLOCK OF BROOKLYN.
I KNOW WHAT I'M DOING.
WHICH REMINDS ME. I'M NOT SURE WHAT IT IS YOU THINK YOU'RE DOING, CALLING ME EVERY TIME ONE OF YOU HAS SO MUCH AS AN INGROWN TOENAIL. MY TIME IS VALUABLE.
YOU WANT TO CHARGE US? BUT LUKE IS A FRIEND!
NOT A FRIEND OF MINE. DID YOU THINK I WAS HELPING OUT OF THE GOODNESS OF MY HEART?
OR AM I JUST THE ONLY WARLOCK YOU KNOW.
!!
NO. BUT YOU ***ARE*** THE ONLY WARLOCK WE KNOW WHO HAPPENS TO BE DATING A FRIEND OF OURS.

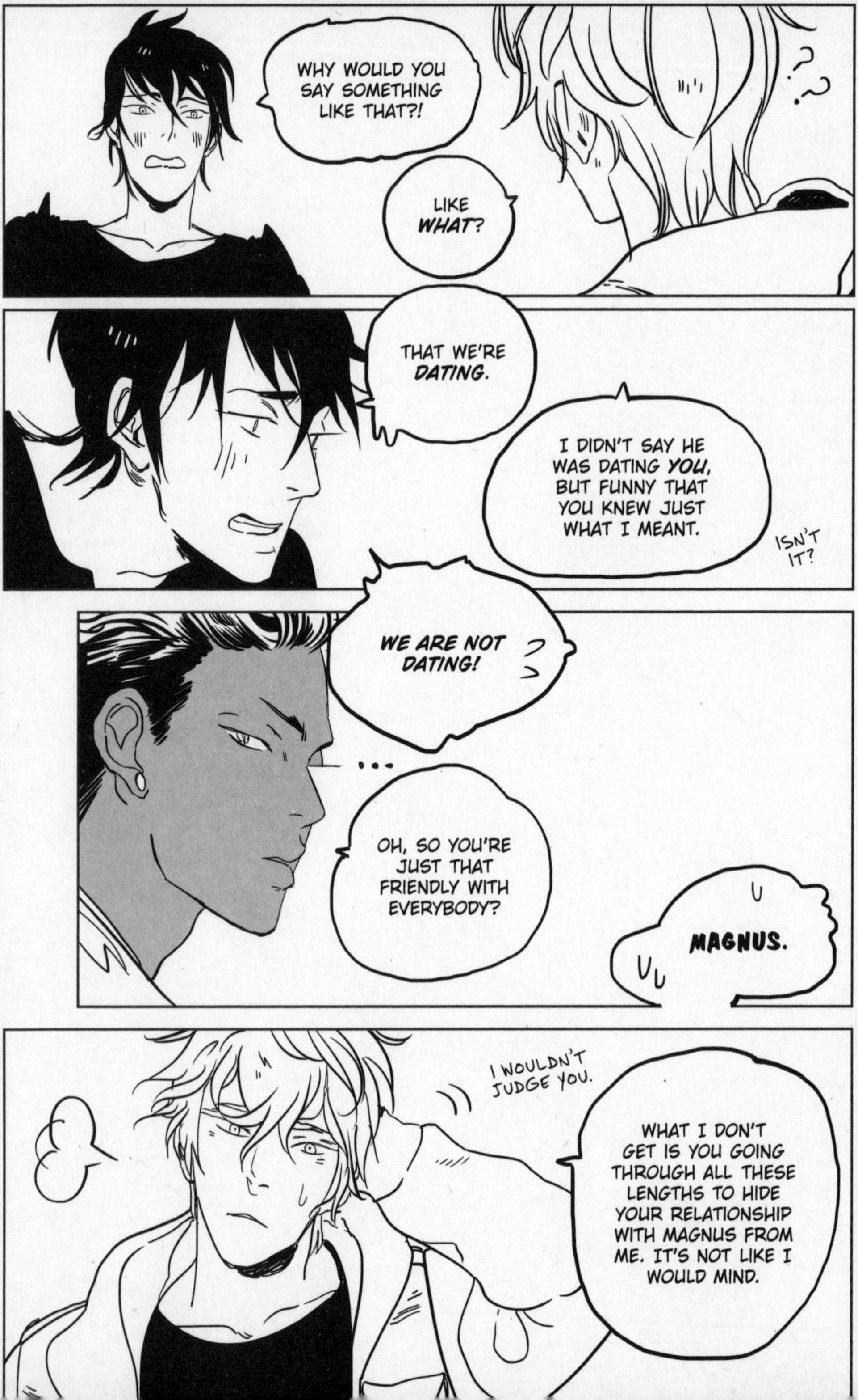
WHY WOULD YOU SAY SOMETHING LIKE THAT?!
LIKE *WHAT*?
THAT WE'RE *DATING*.
I DIDN'T SAY HE WAS DATING *YOU*, BUT FUNNY THAT YOU KNEW JUST WHAT I MEANT.
ISN'T IT?
WE ARE NOT DATING!
...
OH, SO YOU'RE JUST THAT FRIENDLY WITH EVERYBODY?
MAGNUS.
I WOULDN'T JUDGE YOU.
WHAT I DON'T GET IS YOU GOING THROUGH ALL THESE LENGTHS TO HIDE YOUR RELATIONSHIP WITH MAGNUS FROM ME. IT'S NOT LIKE I WOULD MIND.

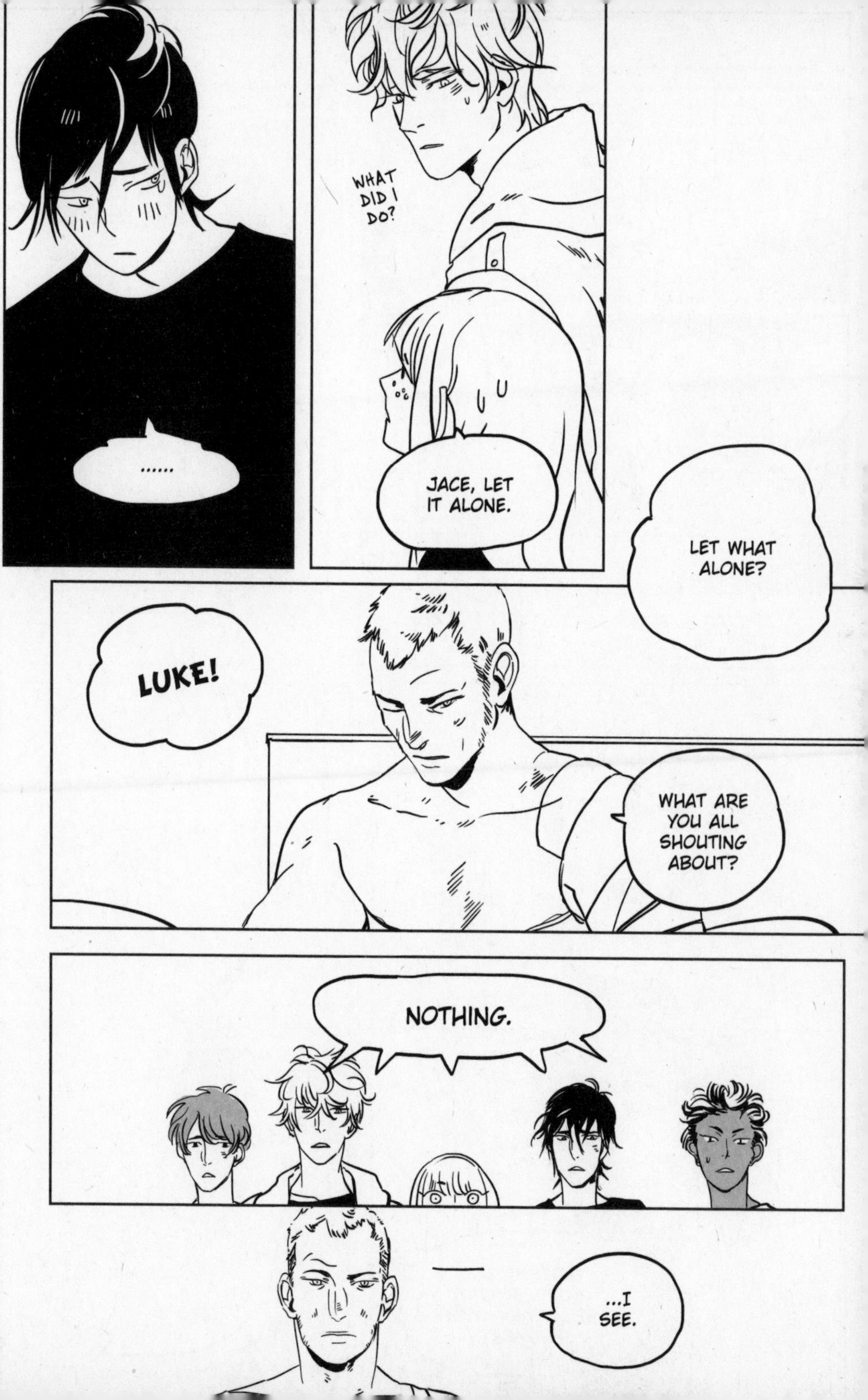
......
WHAT DID I DO?
JACE, LET IT ALONE.
LET WHAT ALONE?
LUKE!
WHAT ARE YOU ALL SHOUTING ABOUT?
NOTHING.
...I SEE.

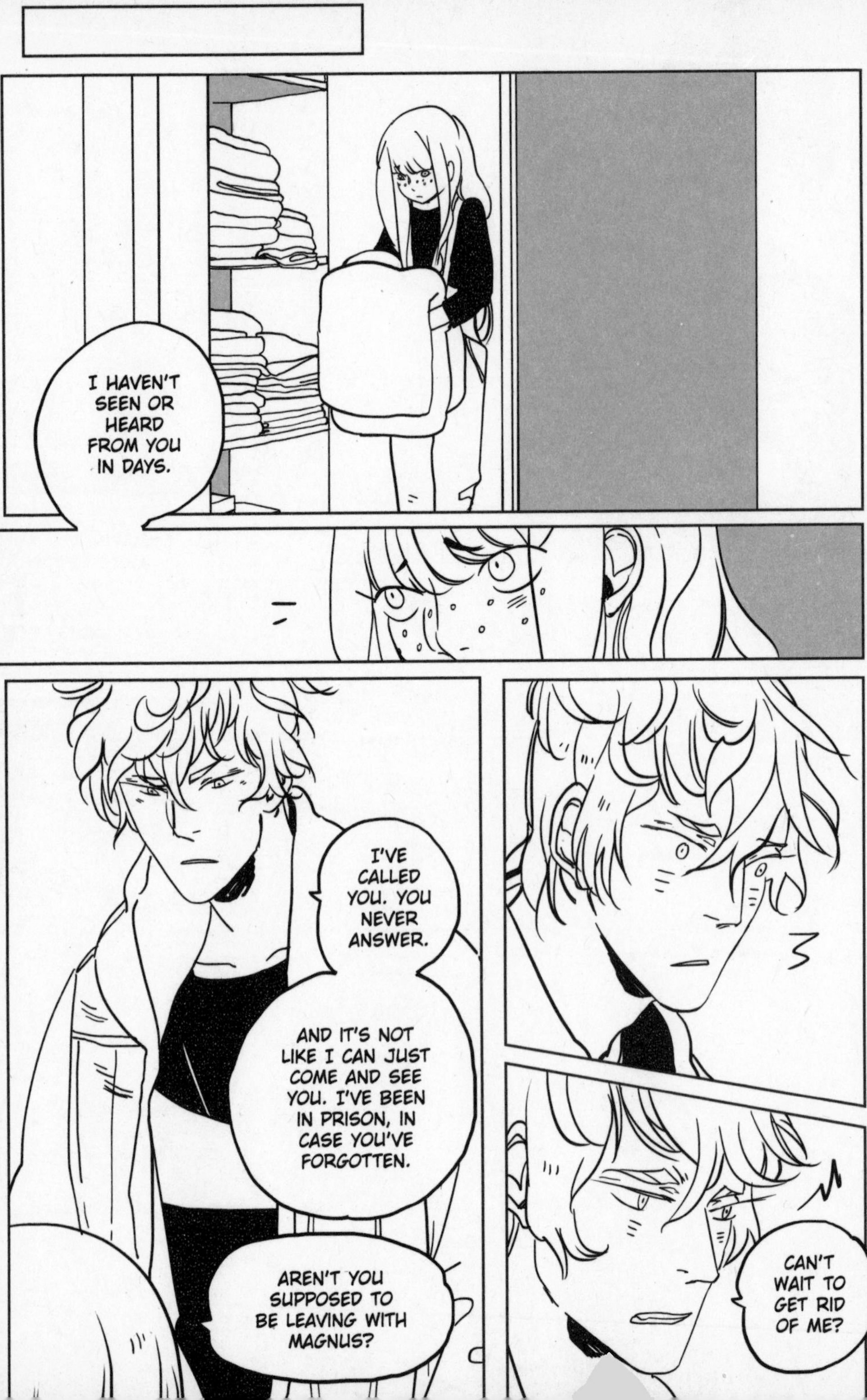
I HAVEN'T SEEN OR HEARD FROM YOU IN DAYS.
I'VE CALLED YOU. YOU NEVER ANSWER.
AND IT'S NOT LIKE I CAN JUST COME AND SEE YOU. I'VE BEEN IN PRISON, IN CASE YOU'VE FORGOTTEN.
AREN'T YOU SUPPOSED TO BE LEAVING WITH MAGNUS?
CAN'T WAIT TO GET RID OF ME?

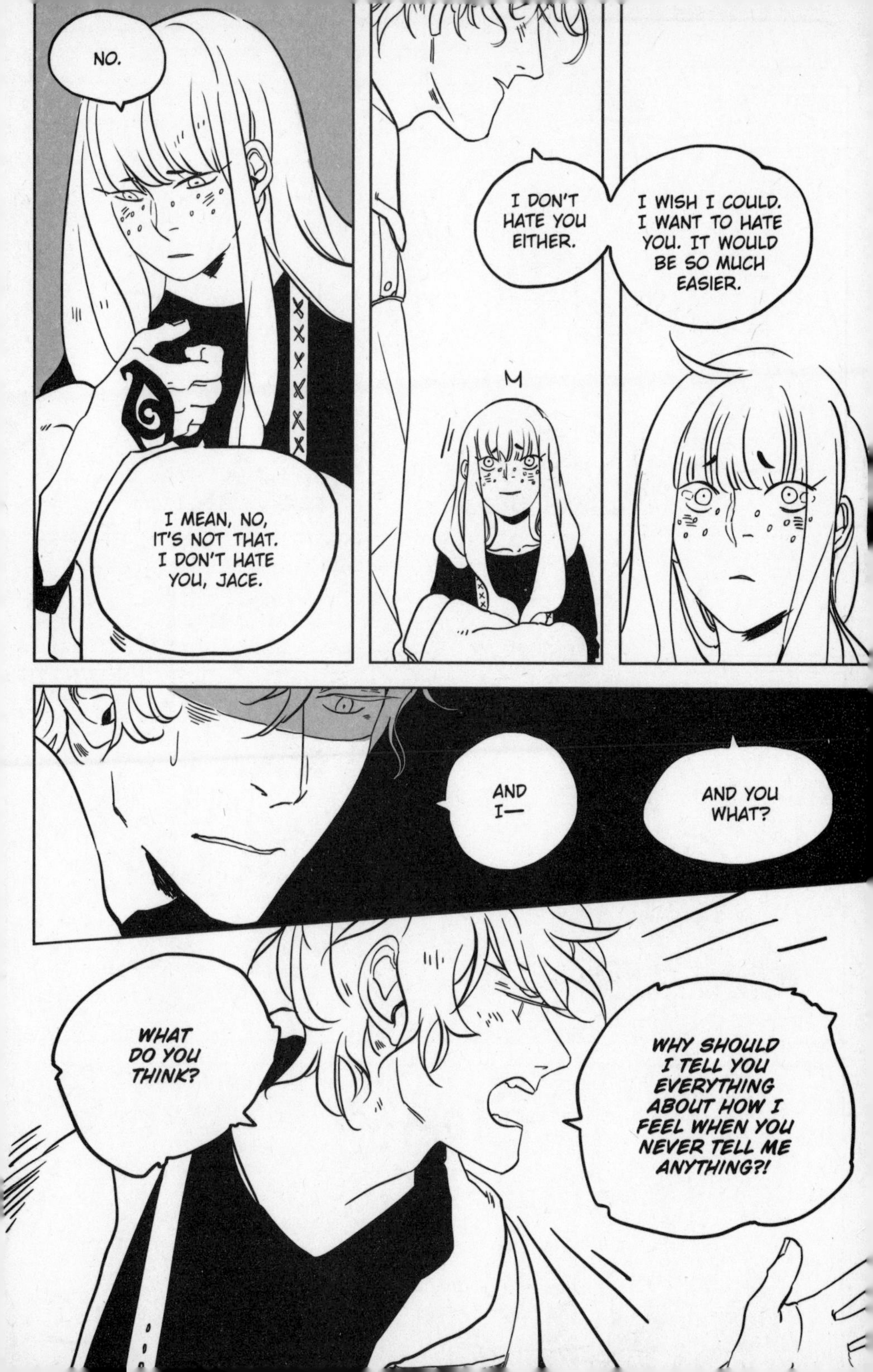
NO.
I MEAN, NO, IT'S NOT THAT. I DON'T HATE YOU, JACE.
I DON'T HATE YOU EITHER.
M
I WISH I COULD. I WANT TO HATE YOU. IT WOULD BE SO MUCH EASIER.
AND I—
AND YOU WHAT?
WHAT DO YOU THINK?
WHY SHOULD I TELL YOU EVERYTHING ABOUT HOW I FEEL WHEN YOU NEVER TELL ME ANYTHING?!

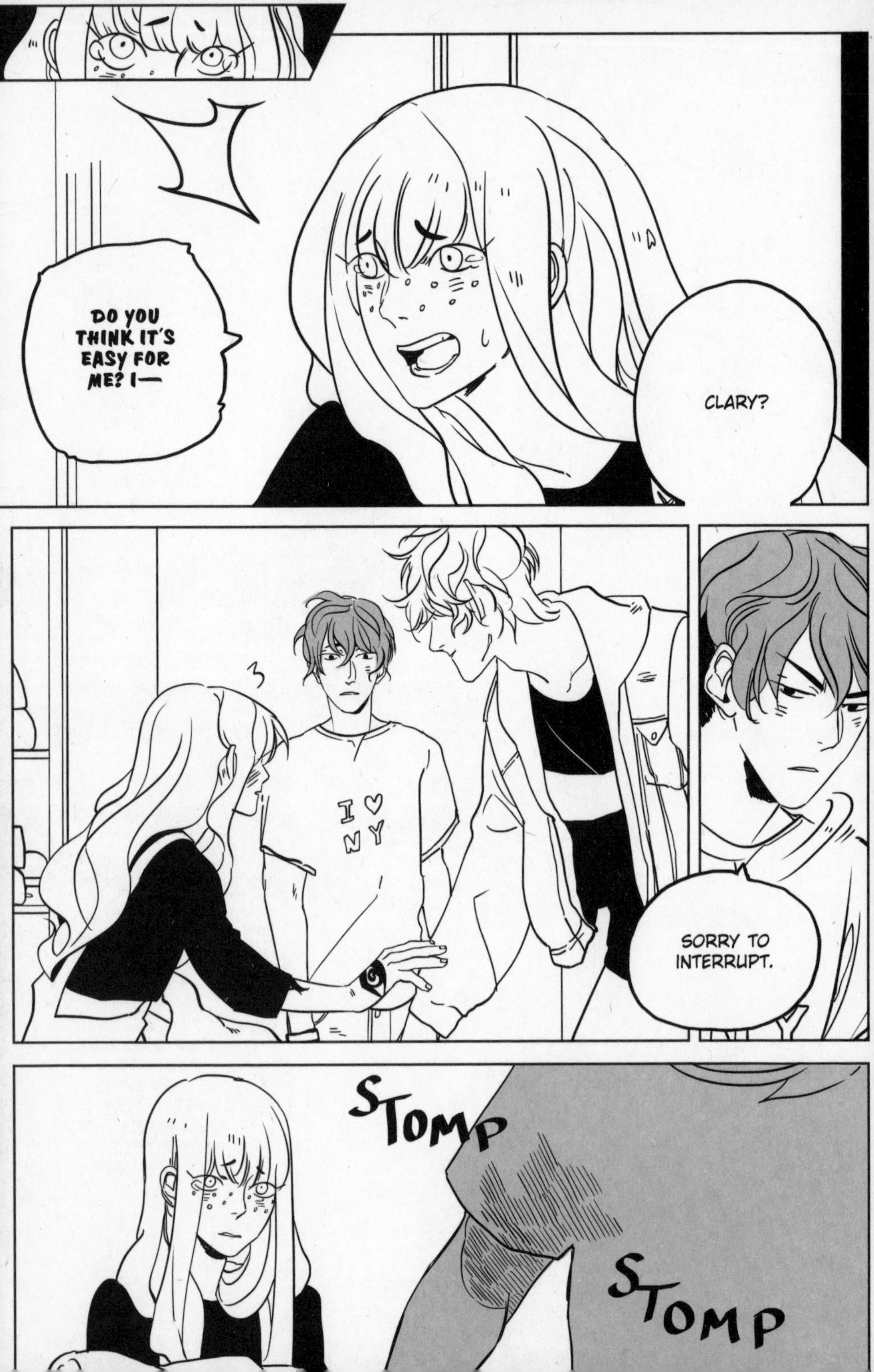
DO YOU THINK IT'S EASY FOR ME? I—
CLARY?
SORRY TO INTERRUPT.
STOMP
STOMP

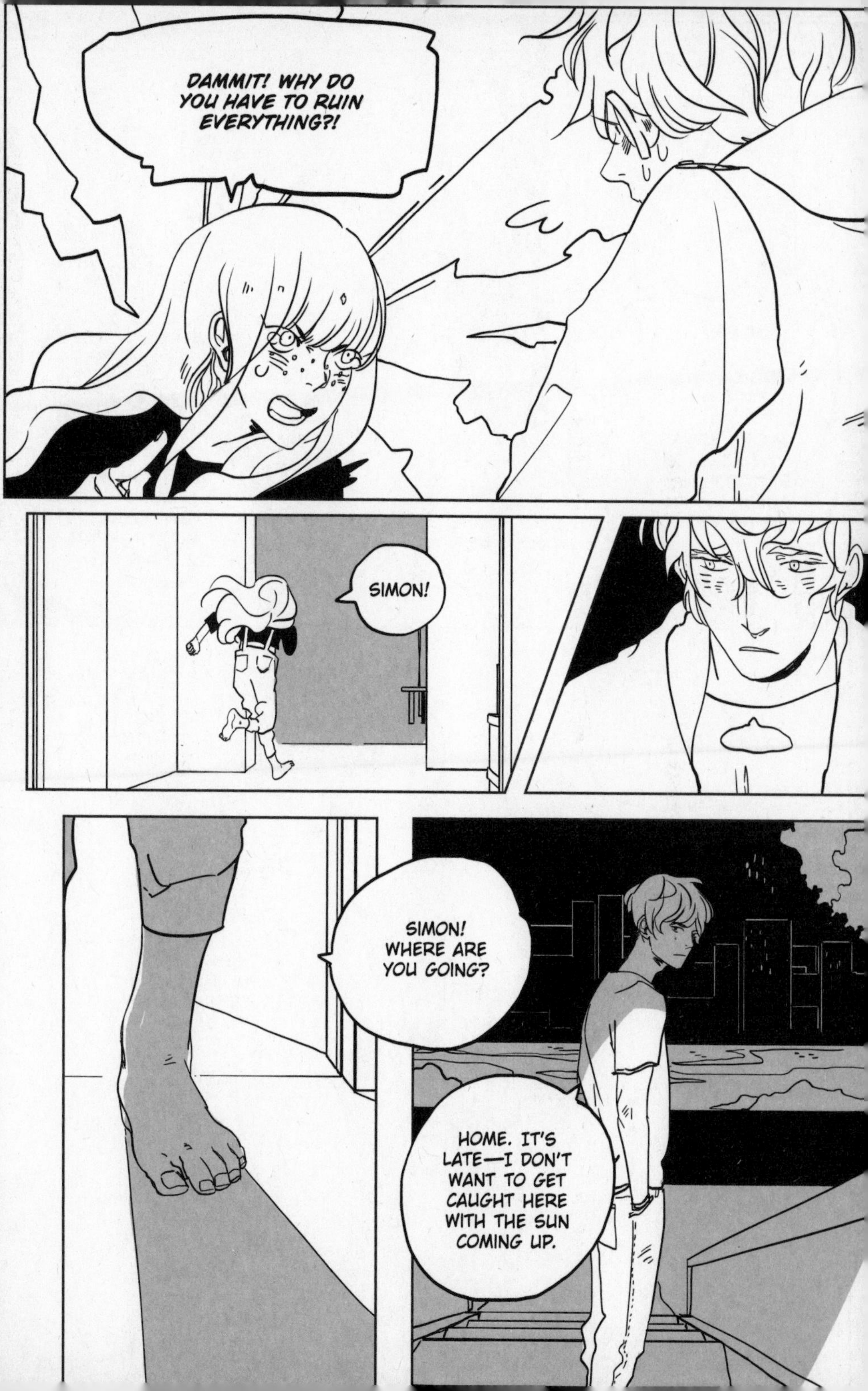
DAMMIT! WHY DO YOU HAVE TO RUIN EVERYTHING?!
SIMON!
SIMON! WHERE ARE YOU GOING?
HOME. IT'S LATE—I DON'T WANT TO GET CAUGHT HERE WITH THE SUN COMING UP.

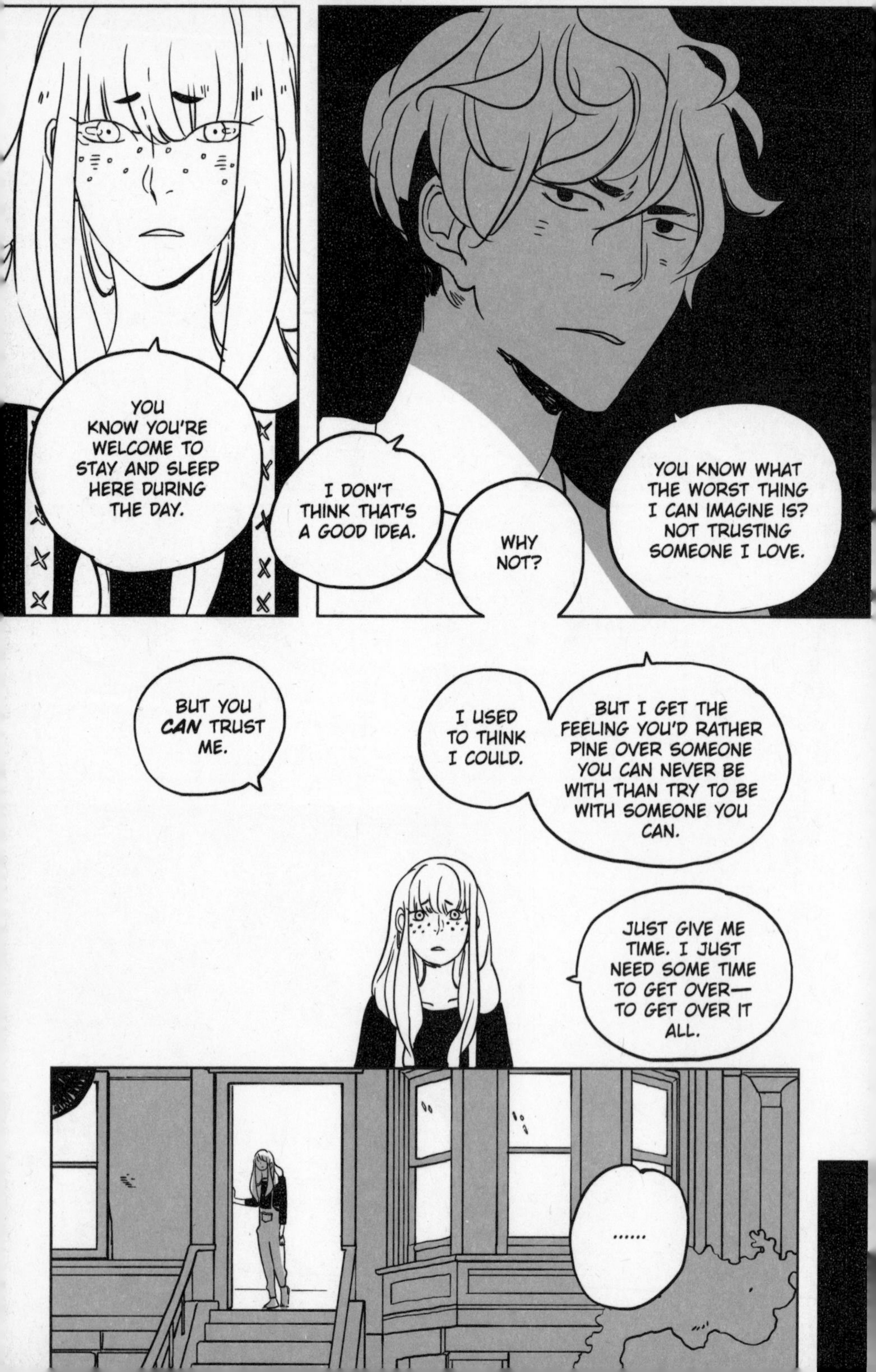
YOU KNOW YOU'RE WELCOME TO STAY AND SLEEP HERE DURING THE DAY.
I DON'T THINK THAT'S A GOOD IDEA.
WHY NOT?
YOU KNOW WHAT THE WORST THING I CAN IMAGINE IS? NOT TRUSTING SOMEONE I LOVE.
BUT YOU *CAN* TRUST ME.
I USED TO THINK I COULD.
BUT I GET THE FEELING YOU'D RATHER PINE OVER SOMEONE YOU CAN NEVER BE WITH THAN TRY TO BE WITH SOMEONE YOU CAN.
JUST GIVE ME TIME. I JUST NEED SOME TIME TO GET OVER— TO GET OVER IT ALL.
......

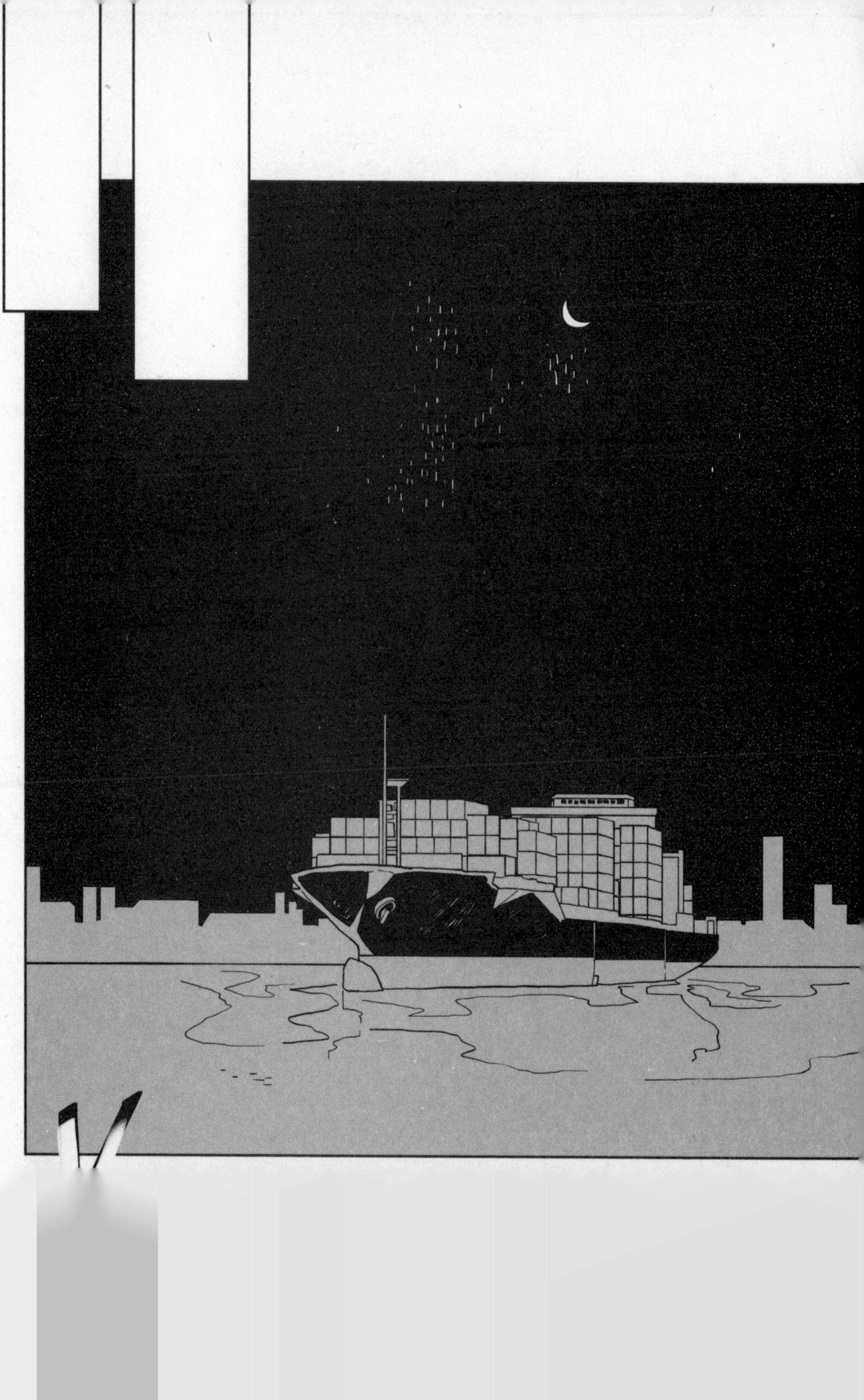

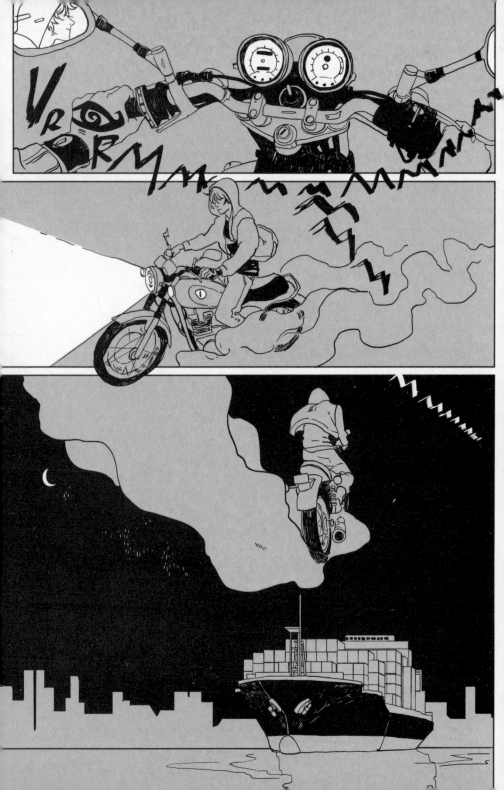

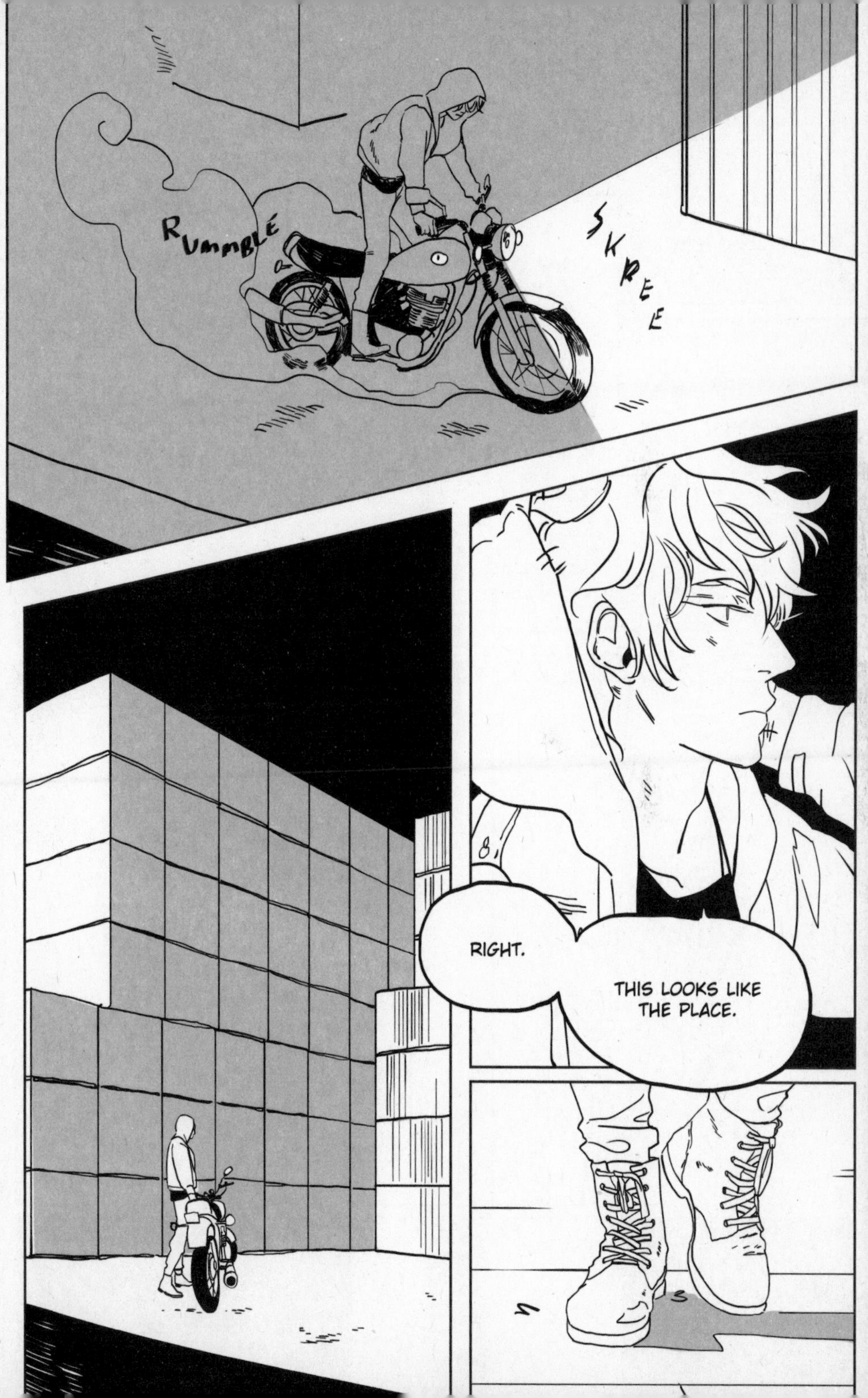
RUMMBLE
SKREE
RIGHT.
THIS LOOKS LIKE THE PLACE.

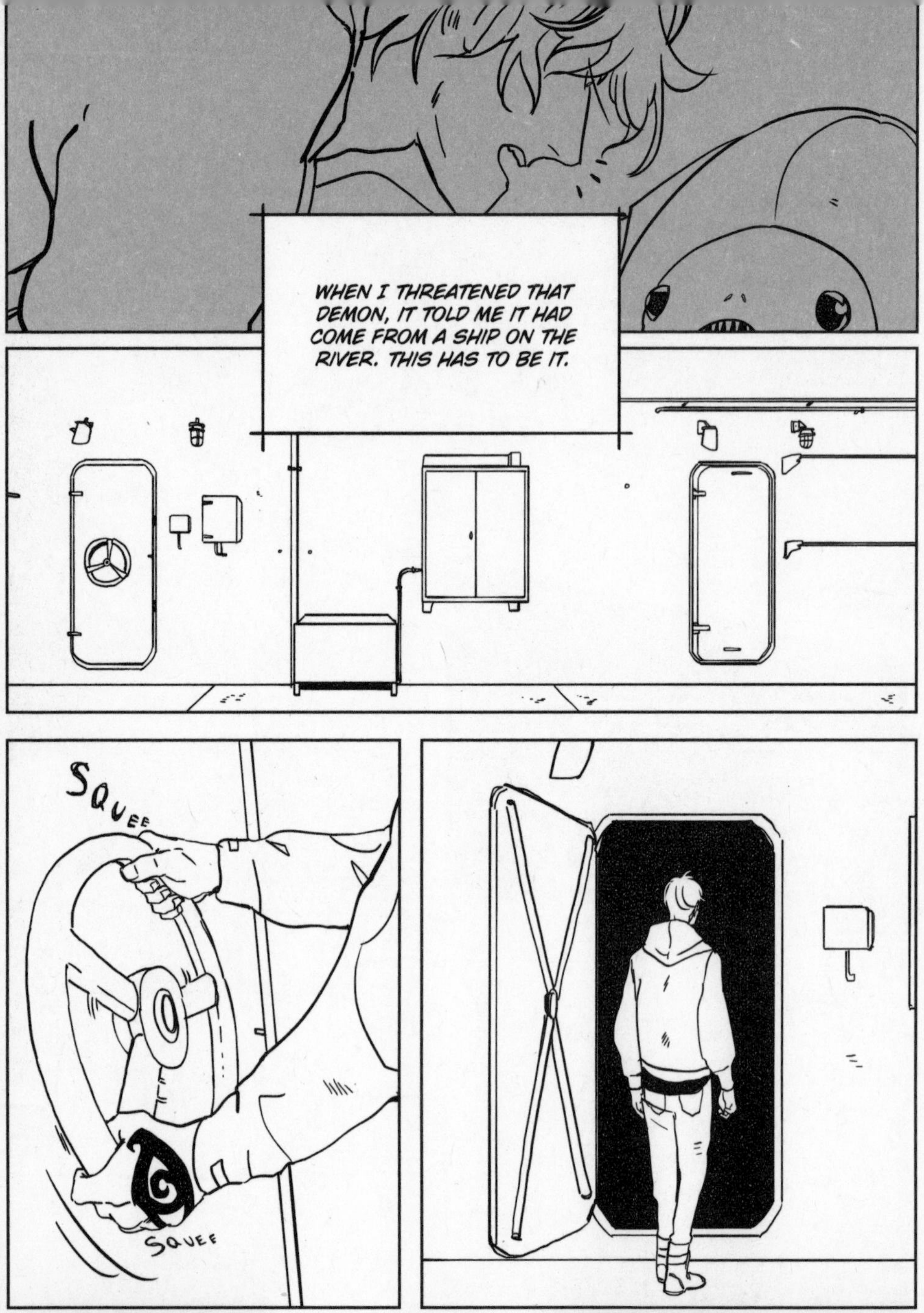
WHEN I THREATENED THAT DEMON, IT TOLD ME IT HAD COME FROM A SHIP ON THE RIVER. THIS HAS TO BE IT.
SQUEE
SQUEE

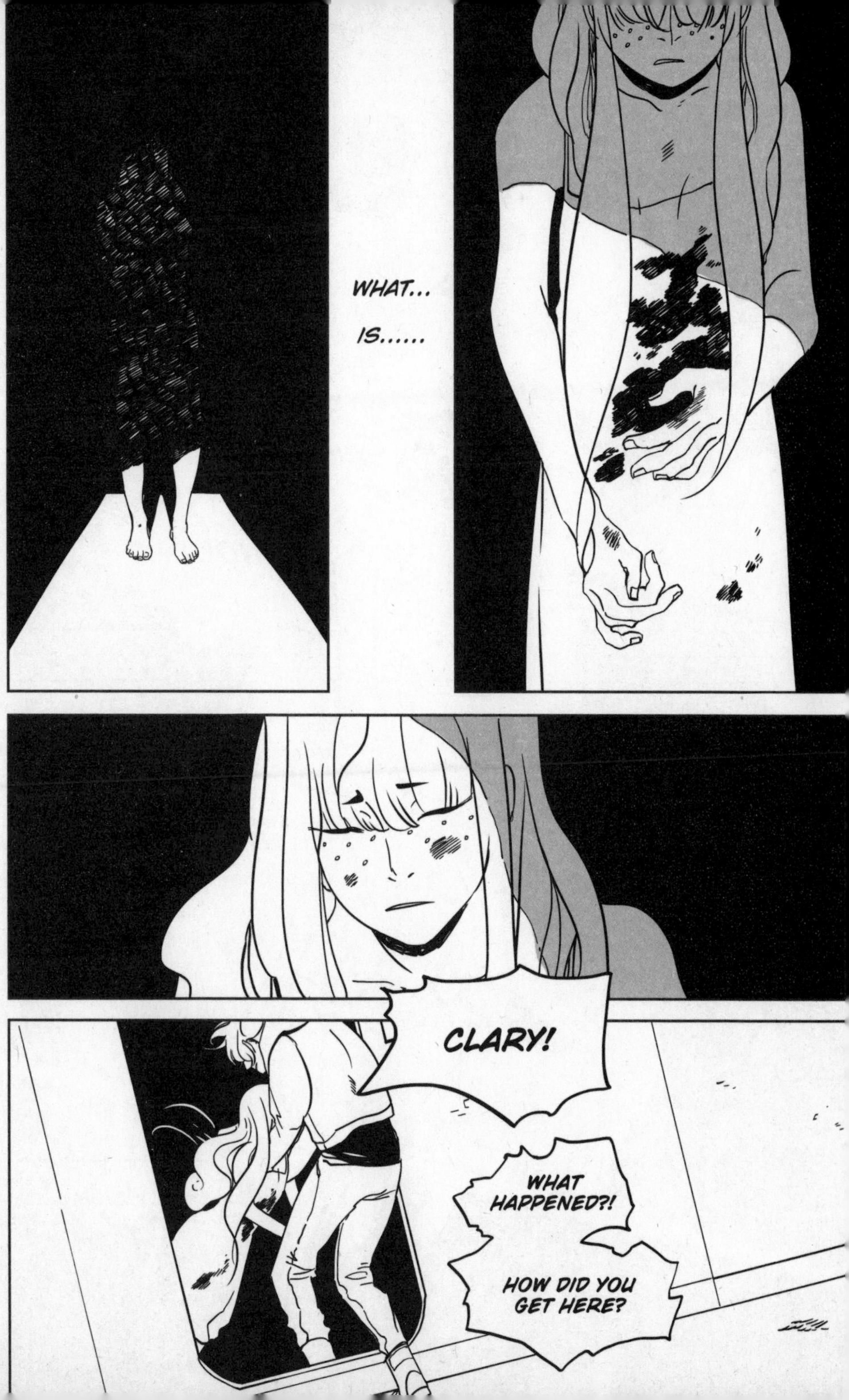
WHAT...
IS......
CLARY!
WHAT HAPPENED?!
HOW DID YOU GET HERE?

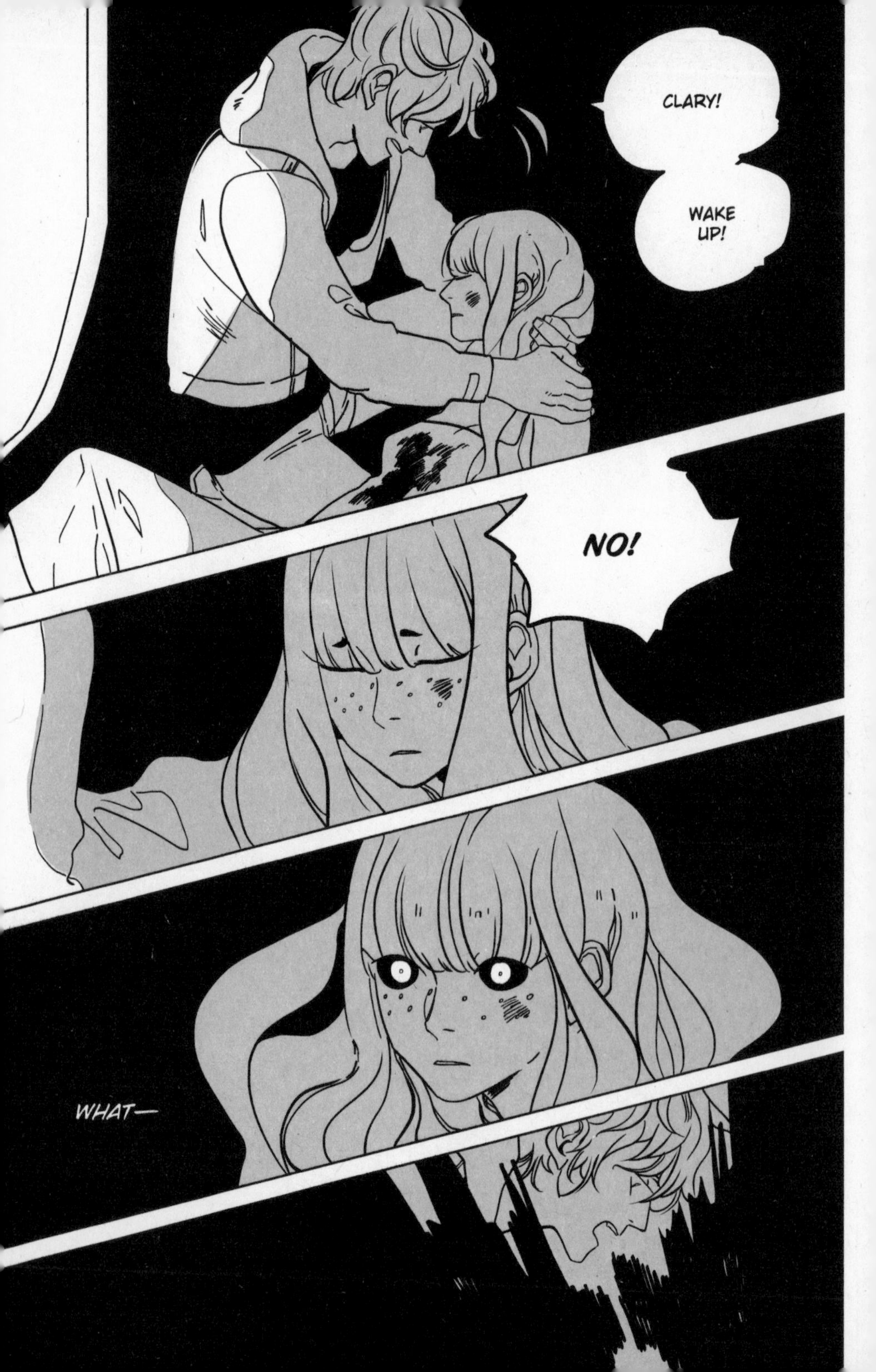
CLARY!
WAKE UP!
NO!
WHAT—

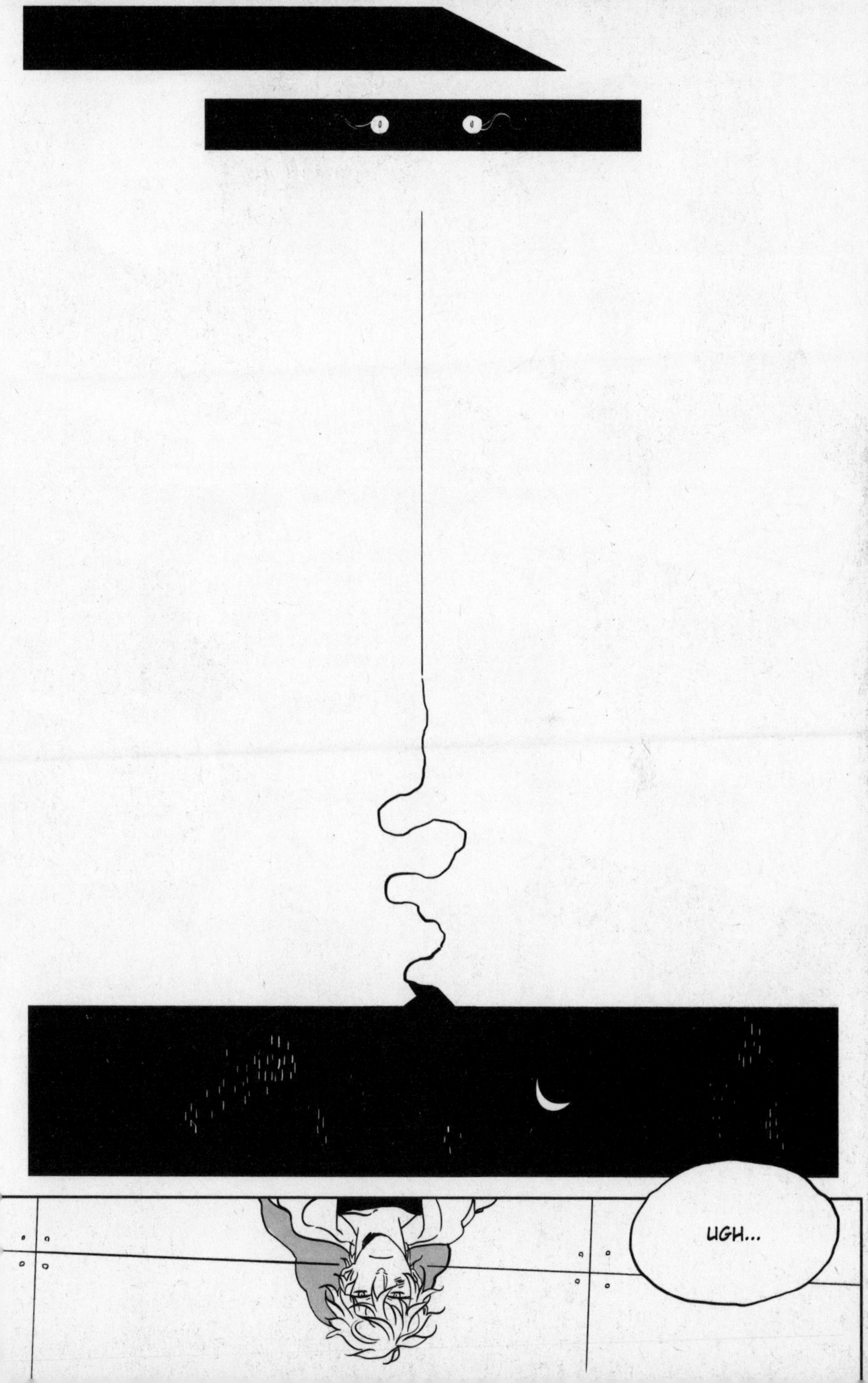
UGH...

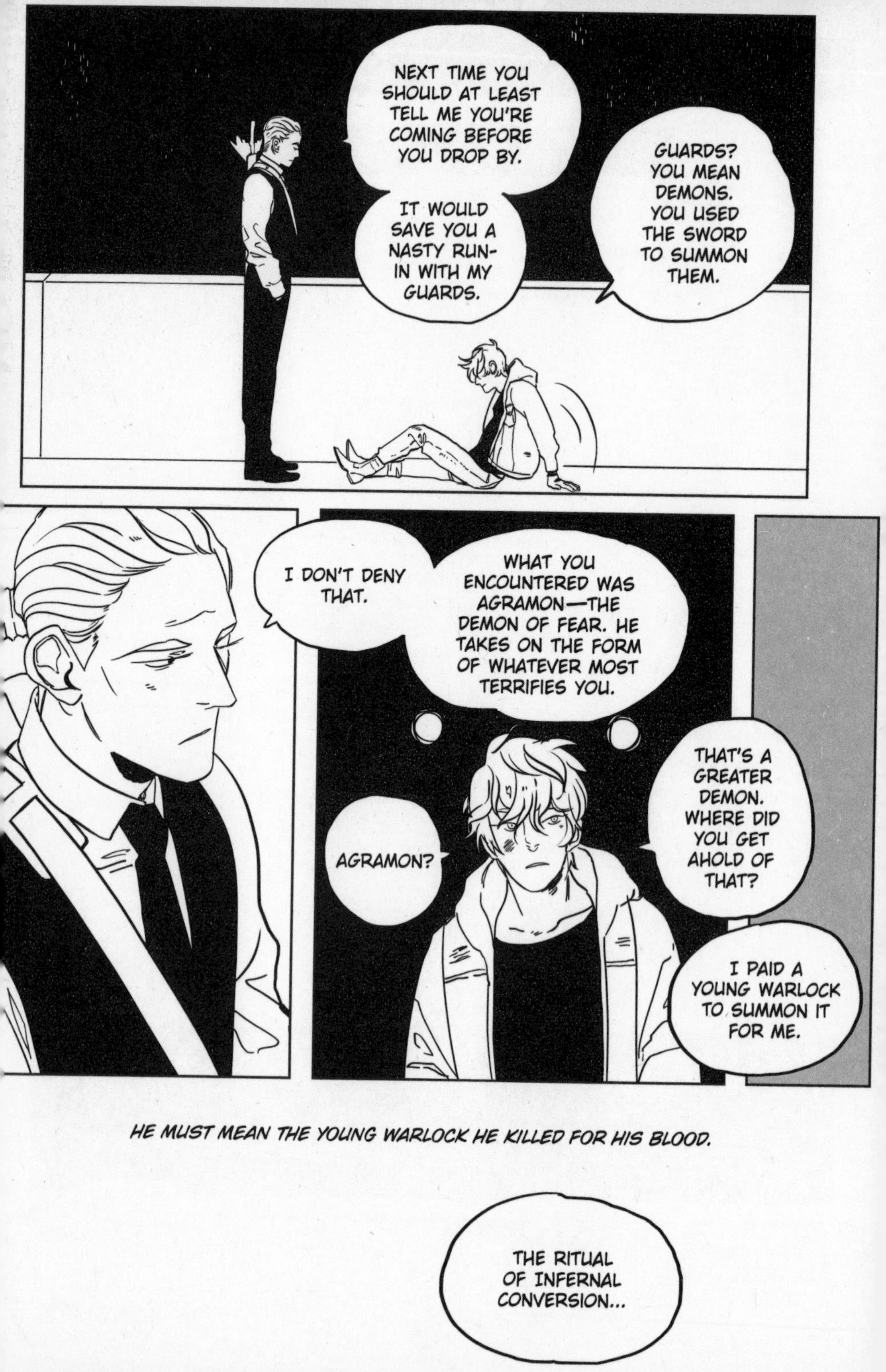
NEXT TIME YOU SHOULD AT LEAST TELL ME YOU'RE COMING BEFORE YOU DROP BY.
IT WOULD SAVE YOU A NASTY RUN-IN WITH MY GUARDS.
GUARDS? YOU MEAN DEMONS. YOU USED THE SWORD TO SUMMON THEM.
I DON'T DENY THAT.
WHAT YOU ENCOUNTERED WAS AGRAMON—THE DEMON OF FEAR. HE TAKES ON THE FORM OF WHATEVER MOST TERRIFIES YOU.
AGRAMON?
THAT'S A GREATER DEMON. WHERE DID YOU GET AHOLD OF THAT?
I PAID A YOUNG WARLOCK TO SUMMON IT FOR ME.
HE MUST MEAN THE YOUNG WARLOCK HE KILLED FOR HIS BLOOD.
THE RITUAL OF INFERNAL CONVERSION...

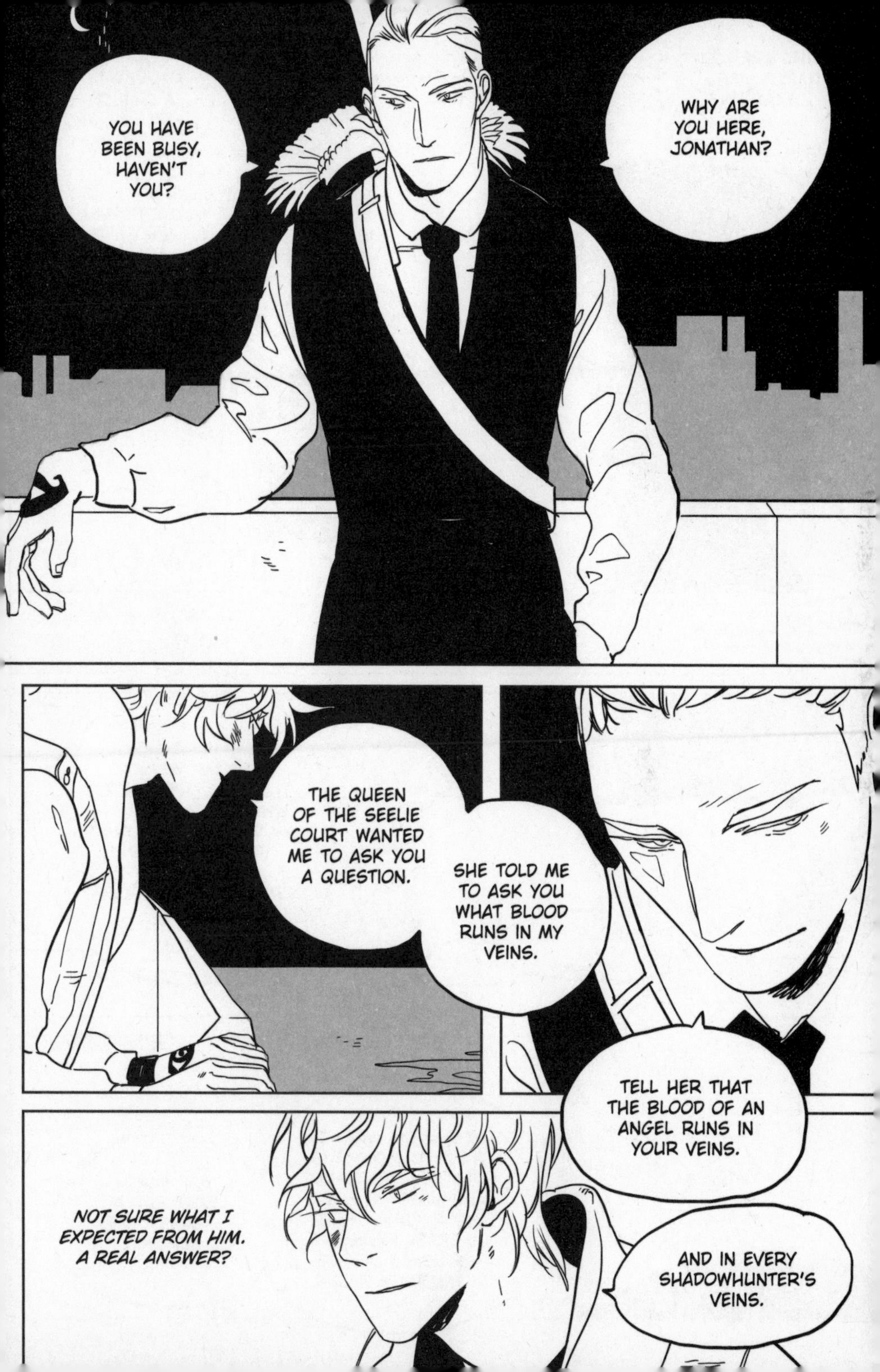

YOU HAVE BEEN BUSY, HAVEN'T YOU?
WHY ARE YOU HERE, JONATHAN?
THE QUEEN OF THE SEELIE COURT WANTED ME TO ASK YOU A QUESTION.
SHE TOLD ME TO ASK YOU WHAT BLOOD RUNS IN MY VEINS.
TELL HER THAT THE BLOOD OF AN ANGEL RUNS IN YOUR VEINS.
NOT SURE WHAT I EXPECTED FROM HIM. A REAL ANSWER?
AND IN EVERY SHADOWHUNTER'S VEINS.

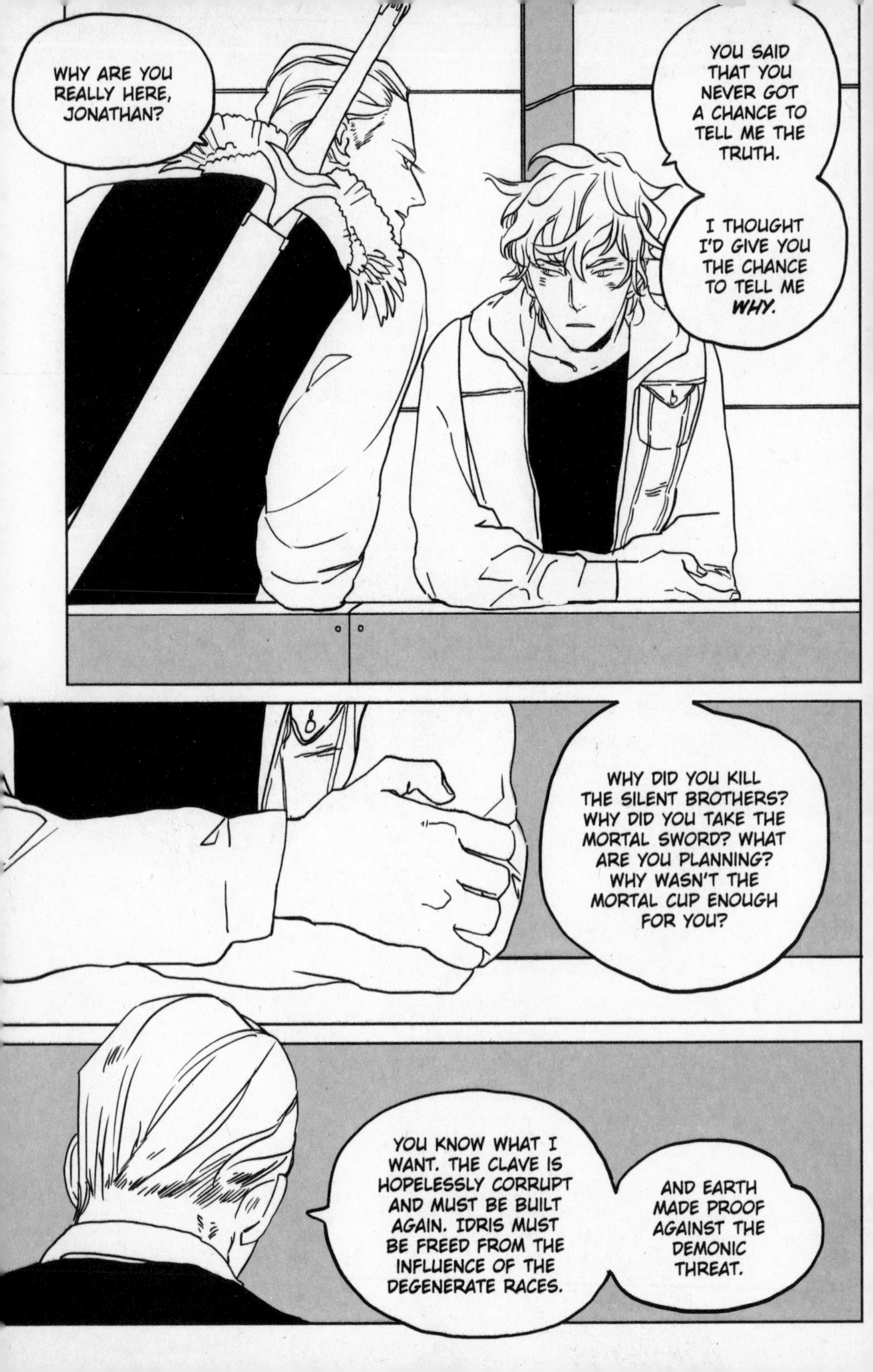
WHY ARE YOU REALLY HERE, JONATHAN?
YOU SAID THAT YOU NEVER GOT A CHANCE TO TELL ME THE TRUTH.
I THOUGHT I'D GIVE YOU THE CHANCE TO TELL ME *WHY.*
WHY DID YOU KILL THE SILENT BROTHERS? WHY DID YOU TAKE THE MORTAL SWORD? WHAT ARE YOU PLANNING? WHY WASN'T THE MORTAL CUP ENOUGH FOR YOU?
YOU KNOW WHAT I WANT. THE CLAVE IS HOPELESSLY CORRUPT AND MUST BE BUILT AGAIN. IDRIS MUST BE FREED FROM THE INFLUENCE OF THE DEGENERATE RACES.
AND EARTH MADE PROOF AGAINST THE DEMONIC THREAT.

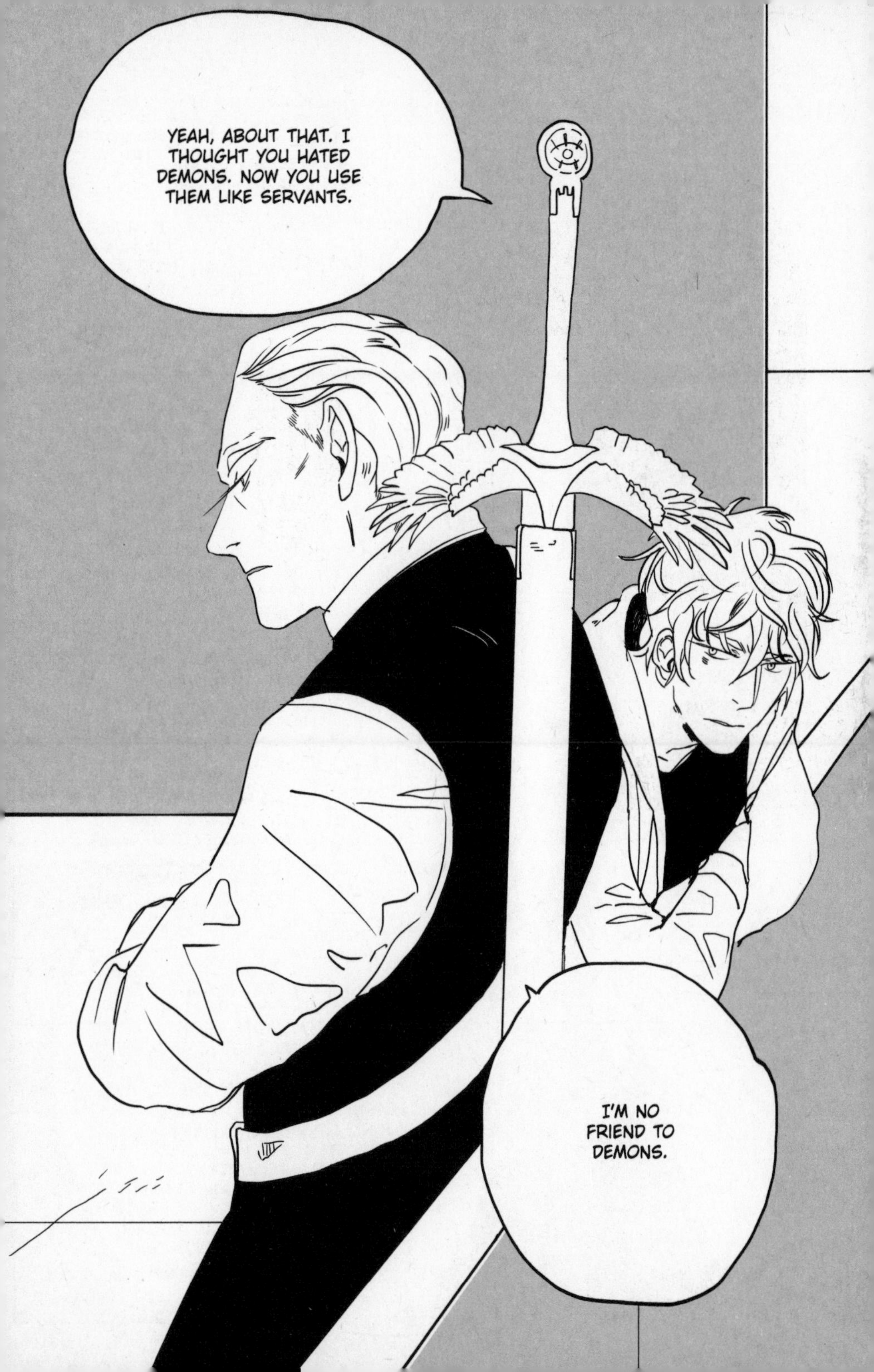
YEAH, ABOUT THAT. I THOUGHT YOU HATED DEMONS. NOW YOU USE THEM LIKE SERVANTS.
I'M NO FRIEND TO DEMONS.

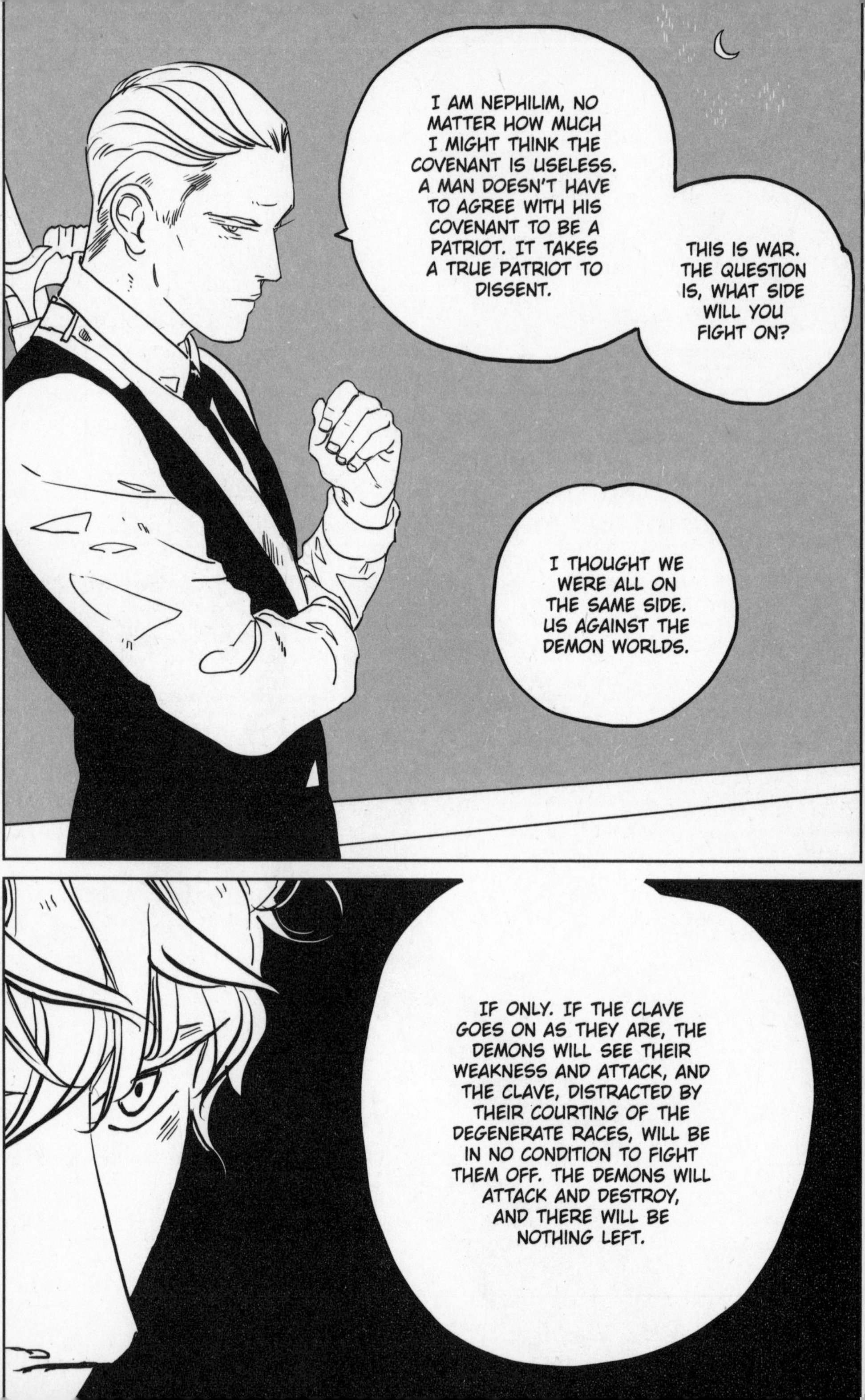
I AM NEPHILIM, NO MATTER HOW MUCH I MIGHT THINK THE COVENANT IS USELESS. A MAN DOESN'T HAVE TO AGREE WITH HIS COVENANT TO BE A PATRIOT. IT TAKES A TRUE PATRIOT TO DISSENT.
THIS IS WAR. THE QUESTION IS, WHAT SIDE WILL YOU FIGHT ON?
I THOUGHT WE WERE ALL ON THE SAME SIDE. US AGAINST THE DEMON WORLDS.
IF ONLY. IF THE CLAVE GOES ON AS THEY ARE, THE DEMONS WILL SEE THEIR WEAKNESS AND ATTACK, AND THE CLAVE, DISTRACTED BY THEIR COURTING OF THE DEGENERATE RACES, WILL BE IN NO CONDITION TO FIGHT THEM OFF. THE DEMONS WILL ATTACK AND DESTROY, AND THERE WILL BE NOTHING LEFT.

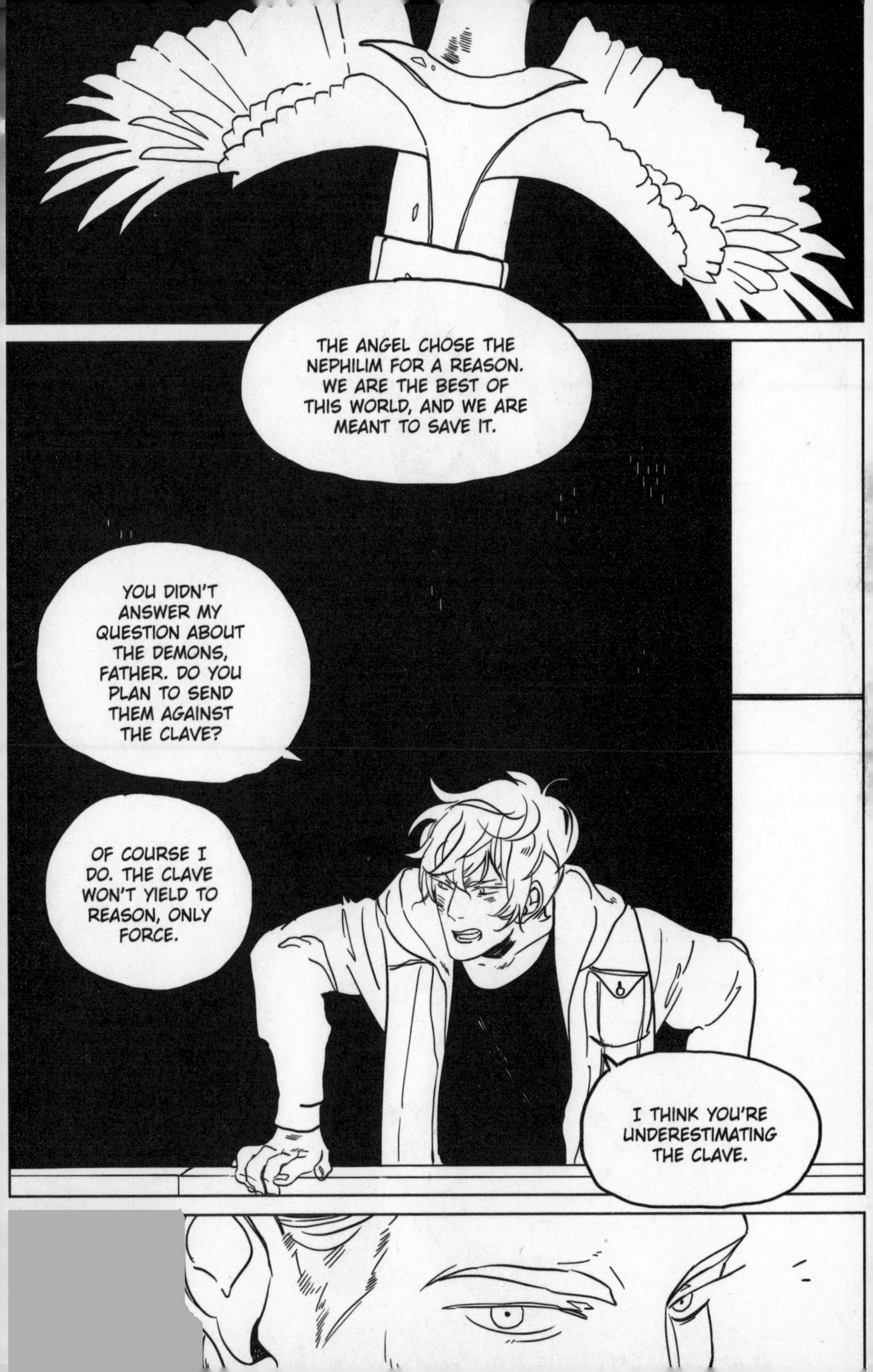
THE ANGEL CHOSE THE NEPHILIM FOR A REASON. WE ARE THE BEST OF THIS WORLD, AND WE ARE MEANT TO SAVE IT.
YOU DIDN'T ANSWER MY QUESTION ABOUT THE DEMONS, FATHER. DO YOU PLAN TO SEND THEM AGAINST THE CLAVE?
OF COURSE I DO. THE CLAVE WON'T YIELD TO REASON, ONLY FORCE.
I THINK YOU'RE UNDERESTIMATING THE CLAVE.

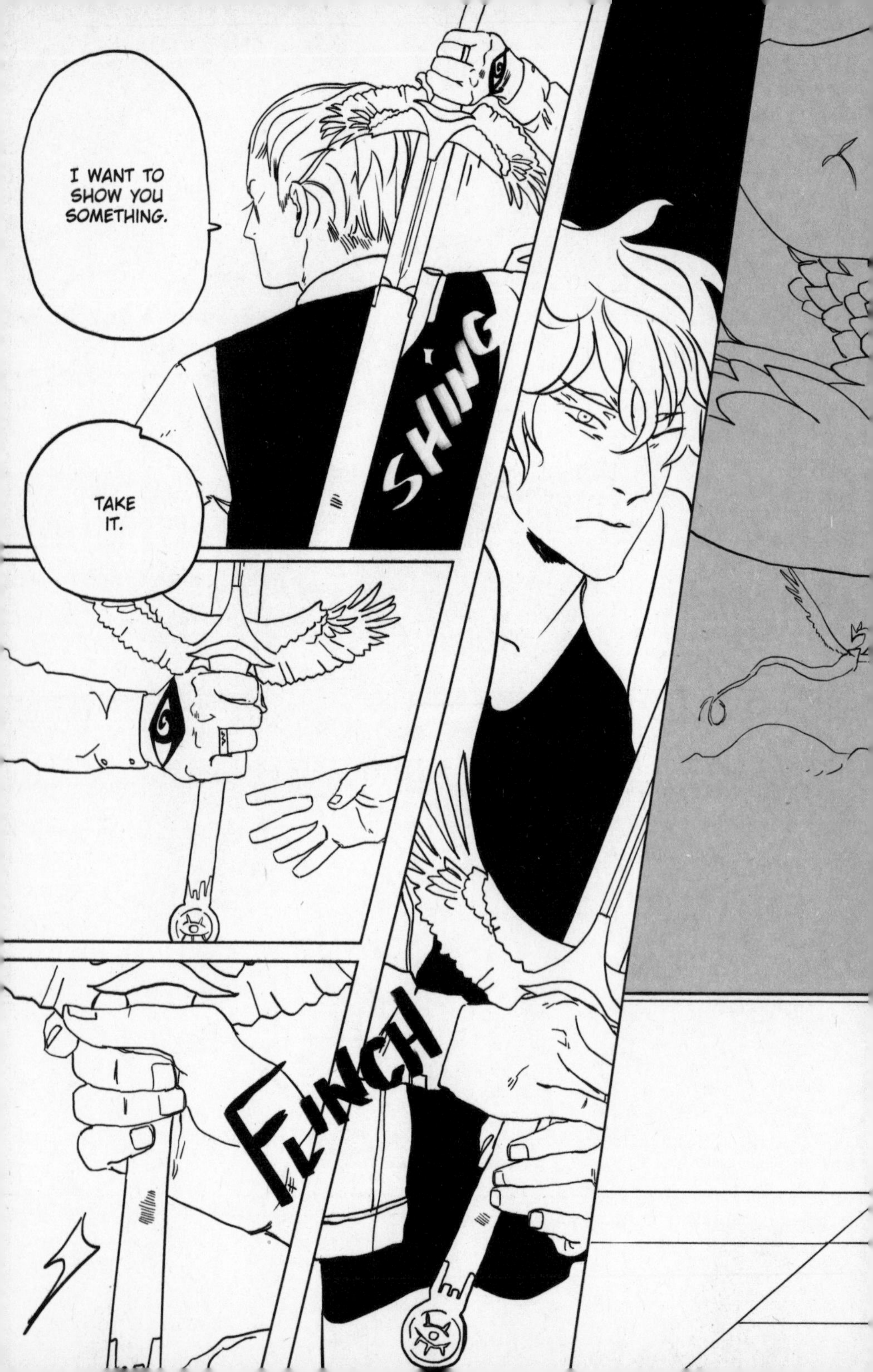
I WANT TO SHOW YOU SOMETHING.
SHING
TAKE IT.
FLINCH

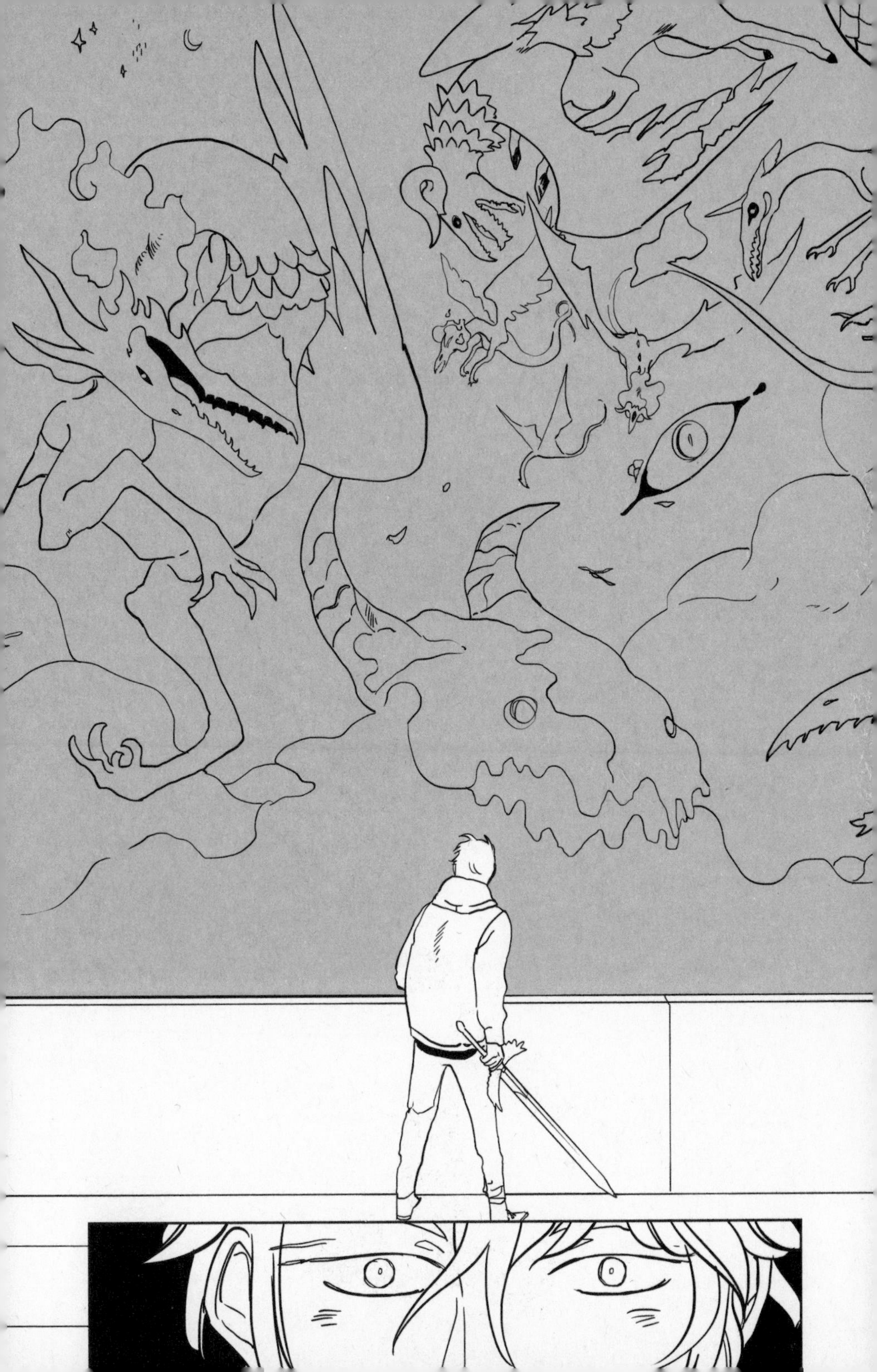

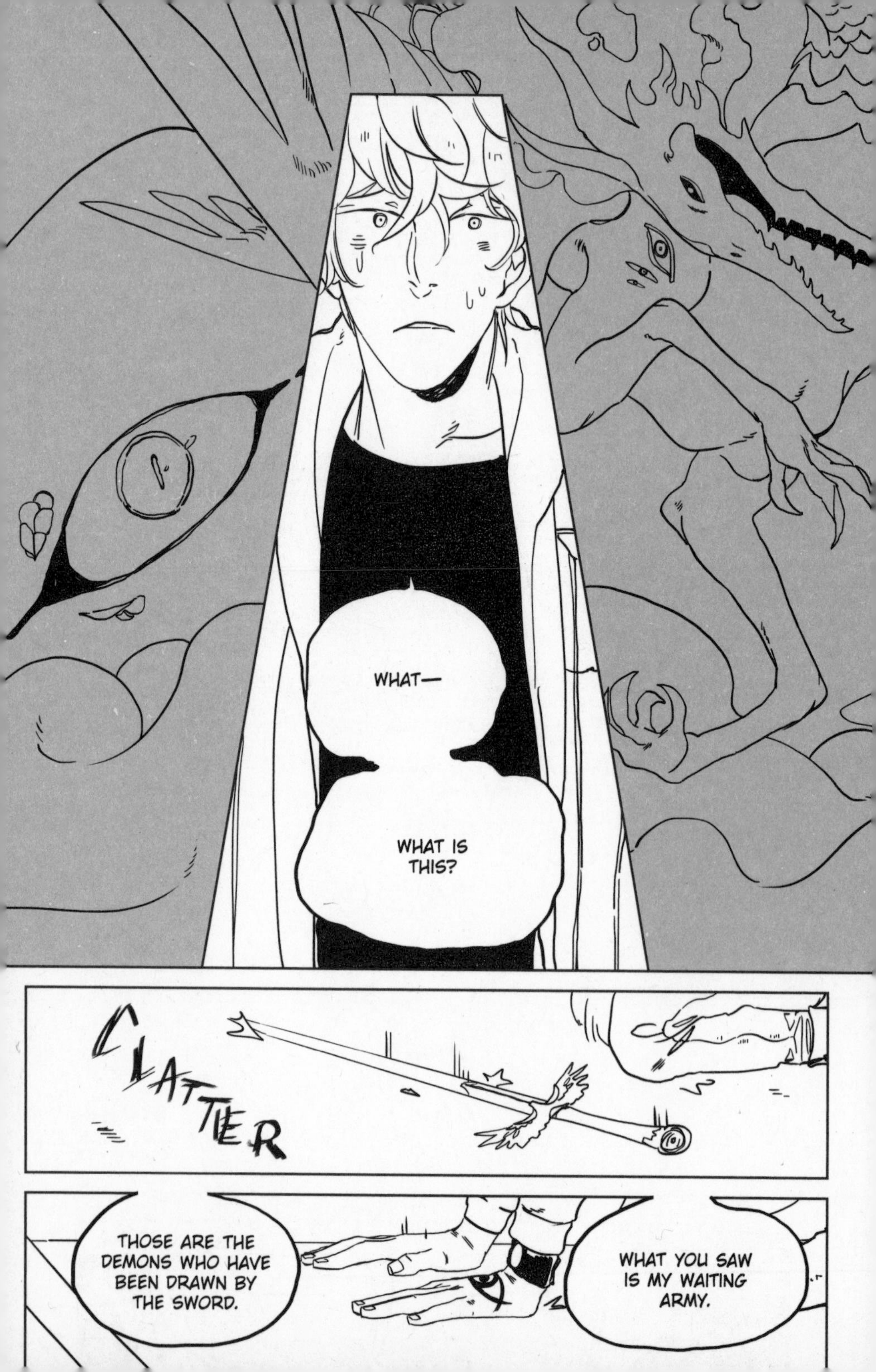
WHAT—
WHAT IS THIS?
CLATTER
THOSE ARE THE DEMONS WHO HAVE BEEN DRAWN BY THE SWORD.
WHAT YOU SAW IS MY WAITING ARMY.

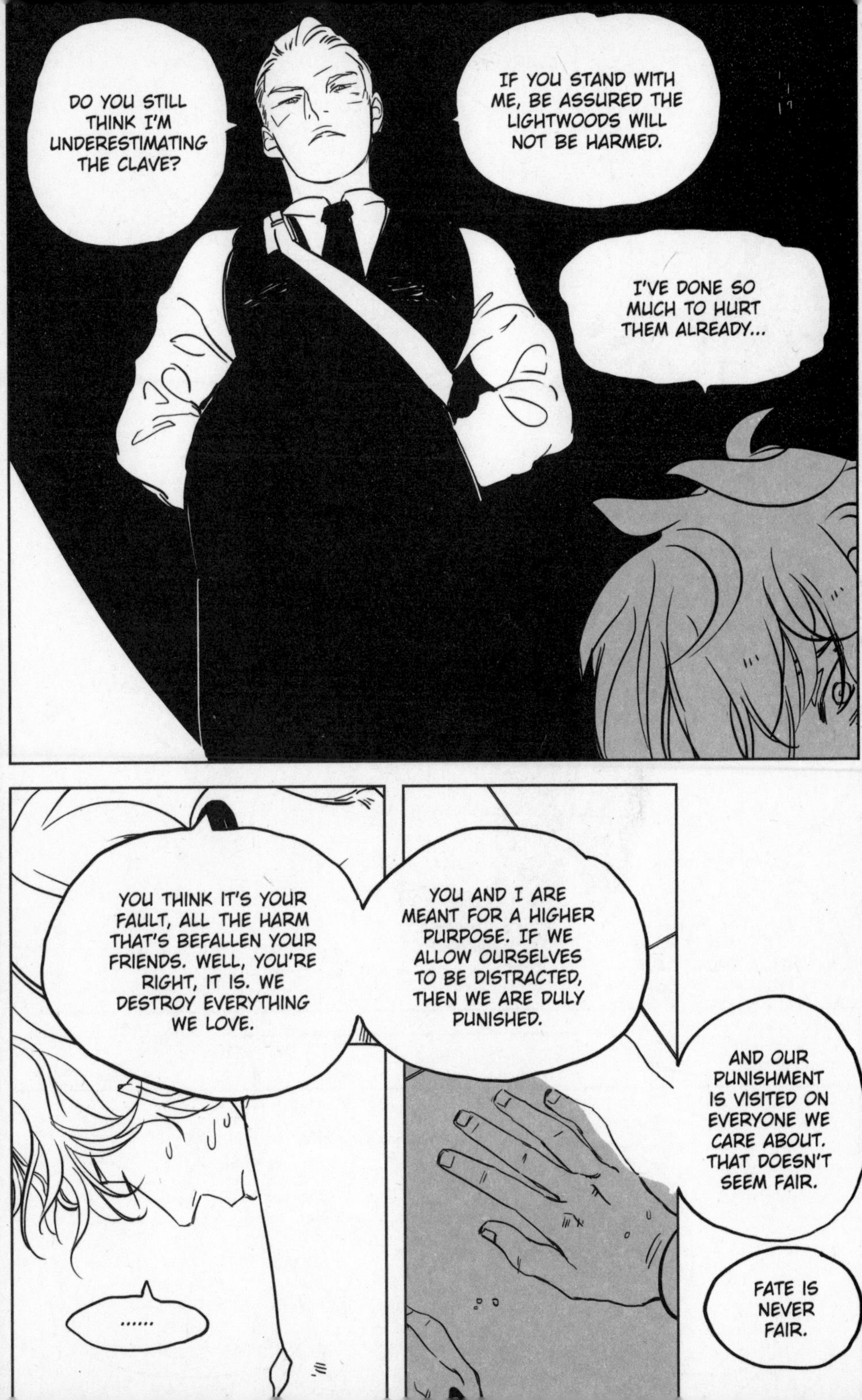
DO YOU STILL THINK I'M UNDERESTIMATING THE CLAVE?
IF YOU STAND WITH ME, BE ASSURED THE LIGHTWOODS WILL NOT BE HARMED.
I'VE DONE SO MUCH TO HURT THEM ALREADY...
YOU THINK IT'S YOUR FAULT, ALL THE HARM THAT'S BEFALLEN YOUR FRIENDS. WELL, YOU'RE RIGHT, IT IS. WE DESTROY EVERYTHING WE LOVE.
......
YOU AND I ARE MEANT FOR A HIGHER PURPOSE. IF WE ALLOW OURSELVES TO BE DISTRACTED, THEN WE ARE DULY PUNISHED.
AND OUR PUNISHMENT IS VISITED ON EVERYONE WE CARE ABOUT. THAT DOESN'T SEEM FAIR.
FATE IS NEVER FAIR.

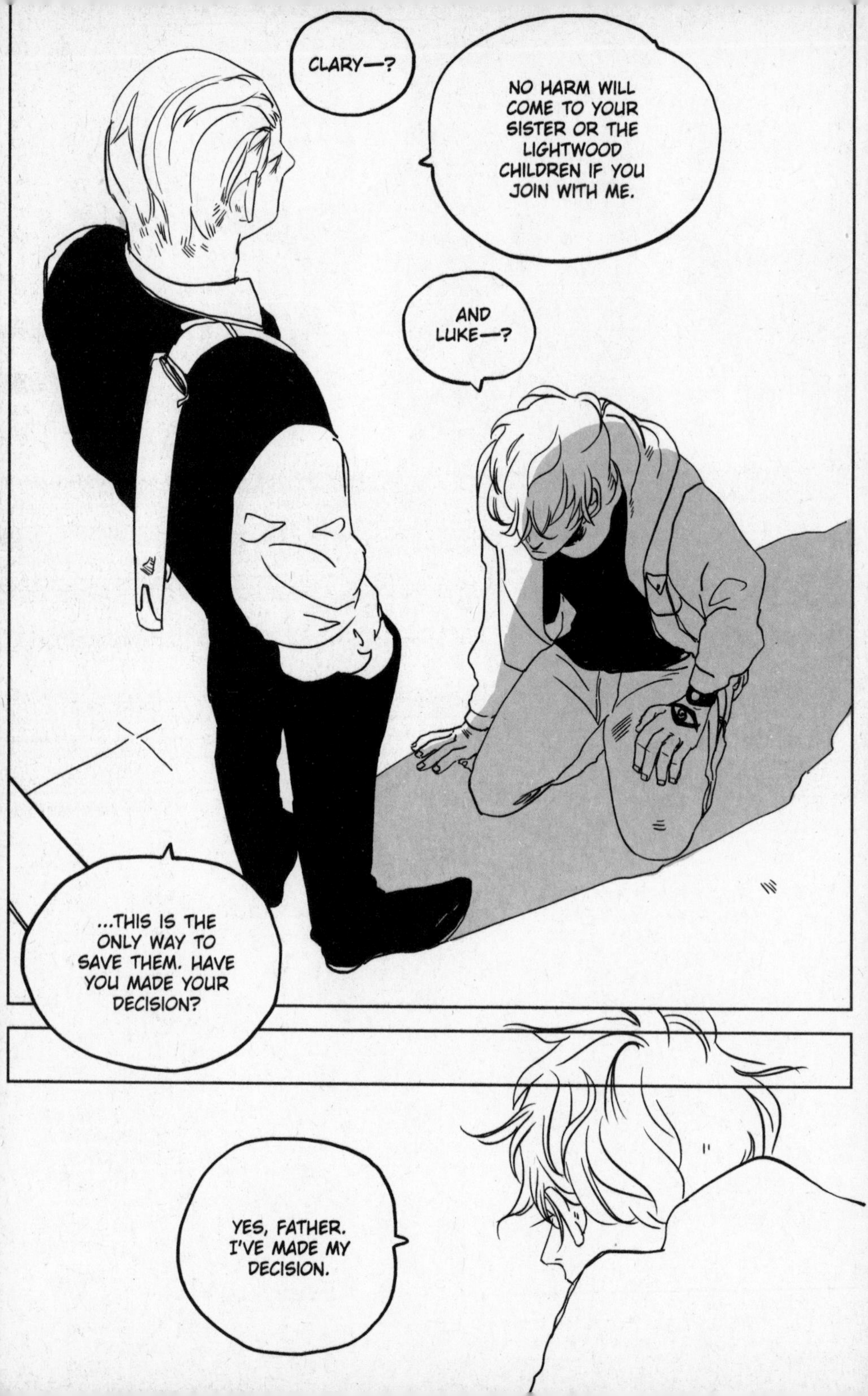
CLARY—?
NO HARM WILL COME TO YOUR SISTER OR THE LIGHTWOOD CHILDREN IF YOU JOIN WITH ME.
AND LUKE—?
...THIS IS THE ONLY WAY TO SAVE THEM. HAVE YOU MADE YOUR DECISION?
YES, FATHER. I'VE MADE MY DECISION.

To be continued in the fourth volume of

THE MORTAL INSTRUMENTS
THE GRAPHIC NOVEL

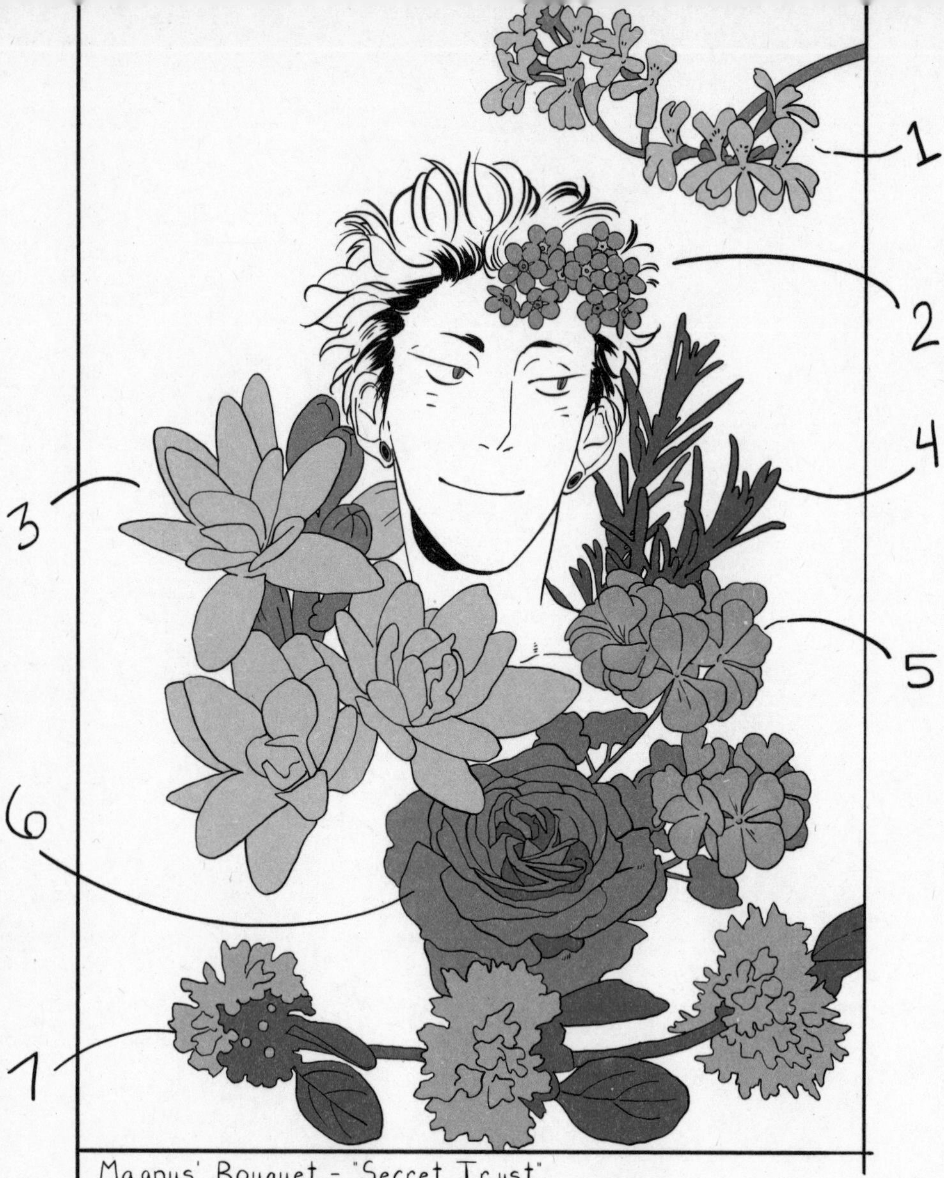
1
2
3
4
5
6
7

Magnus' Bouquet - "Secret Tryst"

1) Nutmeg Geranium - An Unexpected Meeting

2) Forget Me Not - True Love

3) Tuberose - Dangerous Love

4) Rosemary - Remembrance

5) Rose Geranium - Preference

6) Red Rose - Passion $ Love

7) Pennyroyal - Flee